COMPARATIVE PHYSICAL EDUCATION AND SPORT VOLUME 3

COMPARATIVE PHYSICAL EDUCATION AND SPORT VOLUME 3

Edited by
March L. Krotee, PhD
Eloise M. Jaeger, PhD
University of Minnesota

Human Kinetics Publishers, Inc.
Champaign, Illinois

Library of Congress Cataloging-in-Publication Data

International Seminar on Comparative Physical
  Education and Sport (3rd : 1982 : University
  of Minnesota)
  Comparative physical education and sport, volume 3.

  "Proceedings of the Third International Seminar on
Comparative Physical Education and Sport held July 21-
24, 1982, at the University of Minnesota, Minneapolis,
Minnesota"—T.p. verso.
  Includes bibliographies.
  1. International Seminar on Comparative Physical
Education and Sport (3rd : 1982 : University of
Minnesota) 2. Physical education and training—
Study and teaching—Congresses. I. Krotee, March L.
II. Title.
GV205.I625 1982   613.7'1   84-14367
ISBN 0-87322-047-1

Proceedings of the Third International Seminar on Comparative Physical
Education and Sport held July 21-24, 1982 at the University of Minnesota,
Minneapolis, Minnesota

Senior Editor: Gwen Steigelman, PhD
Production Director: Ernie Noa
Assistant Production Director: Lezli Harris
Copy Editor: Barbara Harrison
Typesetters: Sandra Meier and Angela Snyder
Text Layout: Denise Mueller
Text and Cover Design: Julie Szamocki
Printed By: Braun-Brumfield, Inc.

ISBN: 0-87322-047-1
Copyright © 1986 by Human Kinetics Publishers, Inc.

Printed in the United States of America

10 9 8 7 6 5 4 3 2 1

Human Kinetics Publishers, Inc.
Box 5076, Champaign, IL 61820

Contents

Foreword

By now it is a well-known fact that the interest in comparative physical education and sport has mushroomed within the past decade or two. The Third International Seminar on Comparative Physical Education and Sport held on the University of Minnesota campus in Minneapolis, July 21 to 24, 1982, reflects this growing interest. A new seminar attendance record was set with 86 participants representing some 22 countries in attendance. However, the International Society on Comparative Physical Education and Sport (ISCPES) will continue to be dedicated to the seminar format to ensure the quality of the presentations, contagious enthusiasm, and continuous interaction among delegates that makes the seminar atmosphere hard to match. The Minnesota seminar was one of the finest in this regard!

ISCPES is a relatively new organization, founded in 1978 at the First International Seminar held at Wingate Institute, Israel. Two years later, the Second International Seminar was held at Dalhousie University in Halifax, Nova Scotia, Canada.

The main purpose of the 1982 seminar was to exchange ideas about comparative physical education and sport research and teaching. Thirty-eight presentations were given, headed by two keynote speakers: Donald W. Anthony, Director of the Center for International Sports Exchange, United Kingdom (whose presentation appears in these proceedings), and Per-Olaf Åstrand, Karolinska Institute, Stockholm, Sweden. There was a great breadth of presentations offered depending upon scholarly background, nationality, and professional interest, including the interfacing with some of our colleagues in international and development education. An art display in Nolte Center provided us with further evidence that the ISCPES has many friends in related areas who can share information and add to our profession.

The seminar was sponsored by the School of Physical Education, Recreation, and School Health Education, the College of Education, and the Office of International Programs in cooperation with the Department of Conferences, Continuing Education, and Extension of the University of Minnesota. For the generous support of Human Kinetics Publishers, Inc. in publishing these proceedings, and for the professional support of the editors, March L. Krotee and Eloise M. Jaeger, ISCPES is very grateful.

Appreciation also is extended to March L. Krotee, University of Minnesota, who directed the seminar with the assistance of the ISCPES Scientific Committee and Steering Committee. The ISCPES Executive Board served in an advisory capacity; John C. Pooley, Dalhousie University,

Canada; Svein Stensaasen, University of Oslo, Norway; Uriel Simri, Wingate Institute, Israel; and C. Lynn Vendien, University of Massachusetts, United States, are to be recognized in this regard.

It is hoped these excellent proceedings will stimulate further interest in the study, research, and teaching of comparative physical education and sport. Perhaps reading the proceedings of this Third Seminar may even inspire some people to make a commitment to join ISCPES and plan to make the world a smaller and better habitat. Congratulations for a job well done to all involved in the Third Seminar.

C. Lynn Vendien
President, ISCPES

Preface

As with any seminar of this magnitude, it is impossible to capture all the elements that are thought to comprise a legitimate body of knowledge. As arduously as one may plan, the temporal framework is too short, and the scope and depth of the domain of comparative and international physical education and sport are too infinite. Realizing this dilemma, the International Society on Comparative Physical Education and Sport, in cooperation with the School of Physical Education, Recreation, and School Health Education, the College of Education, and the Office of International Programs of the University of Minnesota, brought together some of the most qualified and dynamic leaders in the field of comparative and international physical education and sport.

As editors of these proceedings, we have attempted not to alter any meaning or significant portion of the selected research papers when preparing and sequencing them for the final manuscript. We must apologize and take responsibility if we have fallen short in this regard.

We would also be remiss if we did not acknowledge the gracious assistance of Lynn Vendien of the University of Massachusetts, Amherst; Uriel Simri of Wingate Institute, Israel; John Pooley of Dalhousie University, Canada; and Bruce Bennett of Ohio State University in the undertaking of this significant academic endeavor. Sincere appreciation must also be directed to Lauri Graven of the Department of Conferences at the University of Minnesota, Joan Campbell of Bemidji State University, Bassem Kablaoui of the University of Minnesota, Harry Krampf of the University of Minnesota, Duluth, and Yu-Kwong Yuen, Hong Kong University, who did so much to attend to the details that significantly contributed to the success of the seminar. Also to be recognized and congratulated are the 86 seminar participants, representing 22 nations, who cooperated fully in every phase of the seminar and without whom the seminar would have never been fully realized.

March L. Krotee
Eloise M. Jaeger

Acknowledgments

Each manuscript selected for presentation and publication in these proceedings underwent a rigorous review process. The International Society on Comparative Physical Education and Sport (ISCPES) wishes to extend its appreciation to the following members who served on the 1982 ISCPES Scientific Committee: Robert H. Beck, Regents Professor, University of Minnesota; Bruce L. Bennett, The Ohio State University; John J. Cogan, University of Minnesota; and March L. Krotee, University of Minnesota.

Opening Address

For a number of years, I have been deeply interested and involved in the international dimensions of education, for the importance of a global perspective on education has always loomed large for me. Everything we do is so obviously linked to people who live in different places and cultures. So strong are these links that our very destinies as Americans will ultimately be the same as those of Ghanans, Britons, and Australians. Years ago, Barbara Ward graphically described our situation: "All of us are passengers on Spaceship Earth, bound together, sharing a common fate."

Like most other observers, I have been disappointed at our continued inability to orient our schools, our curricula, and, hence, our minds to the realities of life on this spaceship. To be fair, there is a very logical reason for our lack of accomplishment in global education. Our attempts to understand our world suffer from a time lag, which greatly inhibits knowing the age in which we live. It's clear that *nations* existed long before the term *nationalism* was invented. The word *revolution* was probably not used in the 1790s to describe life in France. The concept of *internationalism* came into use long after people had begun to develop an international outlook on things.

This conceptual time lag provides a reason but not an excuse for continuing to de-emphasize international education. The rapidity of communication, the tremendous increase in world trade, the fragile character of our "spaceship," and the destructive power of current weapon systems make it imperative that we try to shorten the time lag in our own understanding as much as we can.

And that is why I am very pleased that my college, the College of Education at the University of Minnesota, was the host institution for the Third International Seminar on Comparative Physical Education and Sport. Also, I am very pleased that the Society has chosen to publish proceedings of this meeting as a permanent record documenting what went on here. The written comments left by participants at this conference illustrate that issues in physical education and sport are as international as any other issues. While the international literature in all scholarly areas has grown in recent years, there is still immense need for works which start and continue the important dialogues among people in all fields from different cultures. This book, in and of itself, will not solve anything but will provide yet another opportunity for people to acquire new perspectives, new information, and new attitudes about people and places worldwide. And that is what international education is all about.

William E. Gardner, Dean
College of Education
University of Minnesota

The History of the International Society on Comparative Physical Education and Sport: Background, Status, and Future

C. Lynn Vendien
University of Massachusetts

In the past 3 decades, there has been a growing interest in comparative physical education and sport in our country and throughout the world. Pioneer courses in teaching comparative physical education began as early as 1948 at Springfield College with A.A. (Ted) Kidess. In the 1950s and early 1960s, a few other courses were introduced, but there was little available literature in this area of study and research except for news reports on international sport competitions and proceedings from international congresses. Most of the promotion and motivation for increasing research and study in the area of comparative physical education and sport came from dedicated leaders active in international associations.

In an effort to gain more information about motivation and methodology for teaching comparative courses and to assist teachers in a relatively new field of study, four surveys were conducted:

1. Comparative education (Vendien, 1969)
   - 30 nationally recognized scholars in comparative education
   - 21 responded
2. Comparative health, physical education, recreation, and sport (Miller, 1970)
   - 31 individuals offering courses in comparative health, physical education, recreation, and sport
   - 21 responded
3. Comparative sport and physical education (Vendien, 1975)
   - 30 national and international scholars teaching comparative sport and physical education
   - 29 responded
4. Comparative international sport and physical education (Vendien & Nixon, 1977)
   - 300 international and national scholars assumed to be teaching comparative sport and physical education
   - 190 responded

The first survey by Vendien in 1969 involved 30 nationally recognized scholars in the long established field of comparative education who gathered information on methodology of teaching comparative education courses. The second survey by Miller in 1970 included 31 national scholars regarding teaching courses in comparative health, physical education, and recreation. The third survey by Vendien in 1975 included 30 national and international scholars regarding teaching courses in comparative sport and physical education. The fourth survey by Vendien and Nixon in 1977 included 300 national and international scholars regarding teaching comparative sport and physical education courses and the need for an international comparative organizational structure. Of the 190 responses to the questionnaire, 128 expressed a strong interest in such an organization. Detailed information from these surveys can be found in the Proceedings from the First International Seminar on Physical Education and Sport, held at Wingate Institute, Israel, December, 1978.

In the early pioneer years, the need for a textbook was obvious. The first book was introduced by Pierre Seurin in 1961, *L'Education Physique dans le Monde*, covering 42 countries. The second was done in 1968, *The World Today in Health, Physical Education, and Recreation*, by C. Lynn Vendien and John E. Nixon. This text covered 26 countries. Another text completed in 1975, *Comparative Physical Education and Sport* by Bruce L. Bennett, Maxwell L. Howell, and Uriel Simri, covered 35 countries. Many well-known recent books include a section on international physical education and sport. The collection of monographs, *Sport and Physical Education Around the World*, edited by William Johnson, was updated and placed in book form in 1980; 1982 to 1983 will see a second edition of the Bennett, Howell, and Simri book and a new text, *Sport and Physical Education in Today's World*, by Vendien and Nixon. Still, admittedly, we are just beginning to skim the surface of an exciting and limitless field of study.

Organizations Contributing to Comparative Literature, Research, and Study

Today many organizations contribute to comparative literature, research, and study in the area of comparative physical education and sport. A few are listed:

FIEP	International Federation of Physical Education
HISPA	International Association for History of Sport and Physical Education
IAPESGW	International Association of Physical Education and Sport for Girls and Women
ICHPER	International Council for Health, Physical Education and Recreation
ICSPE	International Council on Sport and Physical Education

IRC of AAHPERD   International Relations Council of the American Alliance for Health, Physical Education, Recreation, and Dance

ISCPES   International Society on Comparative Physical Education and Sport

UNESCO   United Nations Educational, Scientific and Cultural Organization

Since the early 1960s, on the national level in the United States, the IRC (International Relations Council) of the AAHPERD (American Alliance of Health, Physical Education, Recreation, and Dance) has been devoting at least three or four sessions to the topic of comparative/international sport and physical education at the national convention each year. In the late 1960s, ICHPER made an outstanding contribution to the area of comparative physical education and sport when the ICHPER Worldwide Questionnaire Reports were produced, including the following parts:

* Part 1—Physical Education and Games
* Part II—Teacher Training for Physical Education
* Part III—The Status of Teachers of Physical Education

In 1975, at the Congress in Rotterdam, ICHPER again led the way by offering several specialty group sessions, one of which was comparative sport and physical education. In 1977 at the Congress in Mexico City, in 1979 at the Congress in Kiel, and in 1981 at the Congress in Manila, the specialty comparative sessions continued to be offered with increasing interest. Discussion time was provided in the sessions at Rotterdam and Mexico City to examine the need for a comparative organization. This organization, ISCPES, was founded in 1978, so at ICHPER Kiel in 1979 and ICHPER Manila in 1981, the benefits of the organization were evident.

First International Seminar on Comparative Physical Education and Sport

Finally, the long-overdue dream of an international conference came true the Christmas week of 1978. The First International Seminar on Comparative Physical Education and Sport met at the Wingate Institute in Israel, under the direction of Uriel Simri. It was a group of some 60 delegates, dedicated leaders from around the world. The quality of the participants, the packed program of excellent presentations, the feelings of caring and belonging to a closely knit group, along with a very special social-cultural program made this First Seminar on Comparative Physical Education and Sport an outstanding success—one never to be forgotten.

The often discussed need for an international organization on comparative physical education and sport continued throughout the seminar. On

December 29, 1978, interested delegates met and the International Committee on Comparative Physical Education and Sport (ICCPES) was officially formed and a Steering Committee elected. Members included C. Lynn Vendien, chairperson, USA; Uriel Simri, secretary-treasurer, Israel; John C. Pooley, Canada; and Svein Stensaasen, Norway. The Steering Committee was asked to explore possibilities and make recommendations for

- affiliation with another organization,
- administrative functions,
- membership categories,
- constitution and by-laws, and
- plans for a second international seminar.

The suggested purpose of the newly formed ICCPES was

- to strengthen and promote specialized areas of comparative physical education and sport;
- to encourage development of programs of study;
- to help exchange research and information;
- to support and cooperate with local, national, and international organizations with similar goals;
- to organize meetings, bringing together people of the world working in comparative physical education and sport; and
- to issue appropriate publications (fall, winter, spring).

ICCPES memberships were composed of

- founding members—all those who attended the First International Seminar on Comparative Physical Education and Sport, and
- charter members—all those who joined before the Second International Seminar.

Second International Seminar on Comparative Physical Education and Sport

The Second International Seminar on Comparative Physical Education and Sport was held in September, 1980, at Dalhousie University in Halifax, Nova Scotia, Canada, under the direction of John C. Pooley. Some 50 delegates representing 13 countries met for a very full, rich and challenging period, once again contributing to the development of a relatively new area of study, comparative physical education and sport.

Actions taken were

- changing the name of ICCPES to ISCPES,
- changing the name of the Steering Committee to the Executive Committee,

- adopting a constitution that was drafted prior to the seminar (ISCPES Publications, no. 5, 1980), and
- establishing membership categories as active, supportive, institutional, student, and honorary.

Third and Fourth International Seminars on Comparative Physical Education and Sport

In July 1982, some 86 delegates representing 22 countries and, for the first time, all continents gathered on the campus of the University of Minnesota under the direction of March L. Krotee for the Third International Seminar on Comparative Physical Education and Sport to continue discussion on this topic. A record number of papers and presentations focusing on pure research, methodology, and topical versus descriptive approaches to comparative or even international sport and physical education was presented.

Plans are underway for the Fourth International Seminar to be held in the Federal Republic of Germany under the leadership of Herbert Haag. A continued surge in interest and professionalism is anticipated.

Need for a Future Program of Action

There is a need to continue moving ahead in a program of action. We need to reexamine our purposes, aims and objectives, membership goals, and benefits. We need to share ideas, materials, research, and even course outlines to help establish new comparative courses of study both on the graduate and undergraduate levels. More active membership involvement will help promote and develop better understanding internationally along with growth and strength of the organization.

References

ICCPES (1978, December 29, 30). Minutes of organizational meetings. *First International Seminar on Comparative Physical Education and Sport*, Wingate Institute, Israel.

ICCPES (1979, 1980). *Newsletter* (Nos. 1, 2, 3, 4). International Committee on Comparative Physical Education and Sport, Wingate, Israel.

ICHPER (1975, August 18-22). *Proceedings of the 18th World Congress of the International Council on Health, Physical Education, and Recreation*, Rotterdam, The Netherlands.

ICHPER (1977, August 9-12). *Proceedings of the 20th World Congress of the International Council on Health, Physical Education, and Recreation*, Mexico City, Mexico.

ICHPER (1979, July 23-27). *Proceedings of the 22nd World Congress of the International Council on Health, Physical Education, and Recreation*, Kiel, Germany.

ISCPES (1978). *Proceedings of the First International Seminar on Comparative Physical Education and Sport*, Wingate, Israel.

ISCPES (1980). *Proceedings of the Second International Seminar on Comparative Physical Education and Sport*, Dalhousie University, Halifax, Nova Scotia.

ISCPES (1980, 1981, 1982). *Comparative physical education and sport* (Nos. 5, 6, 7, 8, 9). Wingate: Israel.

The Role of Comparative and International Physical Education and Sport in Modern Society

March L. Krotee
University of Minnesota

In today's modern society it is clear that the survival of humankind will require cooperative solutions to the myriad of challenging problems that face an ever more complex and interdependent world. Our educational institutions and professions, specifically physical education, health, recreation, and sport, whose operational philosophies, processes, and practices were conceived and nurtured in a preglobal era, now face perhaps the greatest challenge in their short history: the challenge of educating the young about the world—about other nations' and cultures' beliefs, feelings, aspirations, and actions. They face the ultimate challenge of educating the young to the interrelatedness and interaction of humankind rather than simply identifying uniqueness or differences in an artificial, isolated, self-contained, and self-serving fashion.

The concept of global education or educating for world understanding, including "global fairness," sets a significant conceptual stage that affects our profession and, therefore, the role of comparative and international physical education and sport. The concepts of a shrinking earth and the interrelatedness of humankind are not new, having been prominently integrated in the United Nations Educational, Scientific, and Cultural Organization's (UNESCO) International Charter of Physical Education and Sport developed in Paris, France, November 21, 1978. The Charter supports the notion that geographical or geopolitical regions or peoples are no longer nor can they be envisaged as isolated from the rest of the world.

We must face this educational reality and responsibility and begin to cultivate a sensitivity to the need to gain a greater knowledge and understanding regarding all phases of this dynamic interrelatedness. Rapidly dispersing beliefs, values, and social thoughts, delicately intertwined with distributive demographic factors (i.e., population, health, wealth, and life expectancy), and the world's capability of advanced technology and instantaneous communication point to the urgency for greater global understanding and cooperation. At no time in the brief history of humankind has this urgency been intensified to the level that now exists.

> Many great civilizations in history have collapsed at the very height of their achievement because they were unable to analyze their basic problems, to change direction and to adjust to the new situations which faced them by concerting their wisdom and strength. Today the civilization which is facing such a challenge is not just one small part of mankind—it is mankind as a whole. (Kurt Waldheim)

Our profession, through organizations such as the International Society for Comparative Physical Education and Sport (ISCPES), must lead the way to develop sound and meaningful conceptual frameworks from which to launch the message that we intend to meet the teaching (including curricular strategy), research, and service challenge of the 21st century! We intend to deal with the challenge of attacking and impacting on global issues that transcend national boundaries, such problems and issues as peace, hunger, disease, energy, human rights, economy, environmental and ecological harmony that are integral to developing a healthy and productive quality of life.[1] These problems and issues can be influenced by our profession, which, concomitantly, is transnational in nature and scope and provides us with an unmatched educational vehicle to develop not only the full potential of the individual but the enhancement of the quality of life for all.

The Current Status and Pathway for the Profession

There is little doubt that those of us concerned and actively involved in the profession of comparative and international education have a difficult task ahead. Reports from organizations such as the Modern Language Association (1980) and the Council on Learning's "Education and the World View Project" assessed our nation's (United States) second language capability and knowledge of world affairs as scandalous, incompetent, and dangerously inadequate. Data revealing that (a) only 15% of our high school students study a second language, (b) only 8% of our colleges and universities require a language for admission, (c) college seniors could answer only 50% of the Global Understanding Survey, and (d) at most, 5% of our future teachers take courses related to other peoples or cultures reflect the educational ethnocentrism and analytic "big-nation-syndrome" blinder that must be modified through the educational process. As if the above fundamental cognitive, attitudinal, personal, and communicative obstacles are not in themselves a formidable challenge, our profession must also contend with the explosion of knowledge and the unparalleled international access to the sporting and physical education process. The above, tempered with such sporting and physical education process dysfunctions as the socialization of women, equalization of opportunity to participate, abuse of youth, and cheating and violence, easily outline that we are our most formidable enemy.

Placed within the proper global context, the pathway for the profession is clearly marked and is conceptualized in UNESCO's 1974 recommendations concerning education.

Education shall be directed to the full development of the human personality and to the strengthening of respect for human rights and fundamental freedoms. It shall promote understanding, tolerance and friendship among all nations, racial or religious groups, and shall further the activities of the United Nations for the maintenance of peace. (Article 26, UNESCO, Universal Declaration of Human Rights, 1974)

In order to enable every individual to actively promote international solidarity and cooperation, UNESCO has forged guiding principles of educational policy that call for

- an international dimension and a global perspective in education at all levels and in all its forms,
- understanding and respect for all peoples, their cultures, civilizations, values, and ways of life, including domestic ethnic cultures and cultures of other nations,
- an awareness of the increasing global interdependence between peoples and nations,
- the development of abilities to communicate with others,
- an awareness not only of the rights, but also of the duties, incumbent upon individuals, social groups, and nations towards each other,
- understanding of the necessity for international solidarity and cooperation, and
- readiness on the part of the individual to participate in solving the problems of his community, his country, and the world at large.

Clearly, the guiding principles of UNESCO lay a conceptual framework from which our profession must adopt and modify its own aims and objectives in order to meet the challenge of the future. This framework is best stated by Lord Noel-Baker, British Olympic medalist (1920) and Nobel Peace Prize recipient (1959): "After a lifetime in world affairs, I have found sport to be the most rich, the most noble. In a nuclear age, sport is man's best hope" (Anthony, 1980).

The Role of the Comparative and International Educator

The role of the profession is to elucidate the need to place the development of physical education and sport on a transnational level in each of the three functional dimensions of academic commitment, that of teaching, research, and service. In the academic domains, a massive reeducation of our institutions' administrations, faculties, and staffs must be undertaken to ensure wholesome philosophical support for internationalizing physical education and sport. This will open our institutions' minds and hearts to the realization that curricula must be revised, developed, and internationalized. Language acquisition, student visitation and exchange, international community speakers' bureaus, and internationally based experimental laboratories must be encouraged. Computerization (storage and retrieval), media presentations, and community awareness

Play	Leisure pursuit & games	Recreational sports	Club sports	Physical education within schools	University sports	Olympic & amateur sport	Professional & performing sport & dance

‑‑‑‑|‑‑‑‑‑|‑‑‑‑‑‑‑|‑‑‑‑‑|‑‑‑‑‑|‑‑‑‑‑‑|‑‑‑‑‑|‑‑‑‑‑→

Figure 1 Physical education sport continuum of formality. Adapted from "The Role of Psychological Study in Physical Activities and Sport" by M.L. Krotee, I.H. Chian, and J.F. Alexander, 1980, *Asian Journal of Physical Education*, 3, p. 83.

projects based on cognitive and affective relationships spanning the entire physical education and sport continuum (see Figure 1) must be placed into action.

We must also assist in increasing the level of support for scholarly exchange and international scholarship consortiums, as well as the development of standardized research tools, protocols, and data banks necessary for effective comparative and international scholarly pursuit. Support for international seminars bringing together scholars and teachers from throughout the world to share and exchange research ideas is still another means of sensitizing the academic community to the needs of the global age.

This action must be couched, however, keeping in mind the total well-being and needs of the student as appropriately recognized by UNESCO's 1978 International Charter concerning physical education and sport.

> Taking into account the diversity of the forms of training and education existing in the world, but noting that, notwithstanding the differences between national sport structures, it is clearly evident that physical education and sport are not confined to the physical well-being and health, but also contribute to the full and well-balanced human being.

As teachers we must initiate an earlier intervention technique involving more creative curricular materials focusing on international experience in an effort to build solid human relations, shape favorable attitudes, and communicate current knowledge concerning other peoples and cultures and our interrelatedness. This application of teaching strategy should continue through the educational process, focusing on specific knowledge and skills to understand cultural differences in all realms of human endeavor. Continuing education, inservice and preservice education programs for teachers, and curricula-related projects for state-wide programs of international inoculation should all be integral segments of fostering cultural self-awareness and improving both the students' and teachers' capacities to respond to the demands of the rapidly expanding sociosphere. These applications will not only serve our young but will also serve to reeducate both the community and our growing international student body (an estimated 326,299 enrolled in United States colleges and universities) as to the skills and expectations of a new and interrelated society.

Our profession must, therefore, focus upon the future, which will find a daily inhabitant increase of 200,000 per day and 73 million per year; a future, which will find our life space and personal environment delicately balanced on a fine scale of interdependence, where understanding, relating, and interaction will be crucial. It is our role as educators to begin to paint a clearer picture of the world through physical education and sport, so that the full potential of humankind may be realized.

Note

1. The list is certainly not exhaustive in nature as such factors as medical care, law, justice, science, and technology also represent salient transcendental dimensions of the sociosphere.

References

Anderson, L. (1968, November). An examination of structures and objectives of international education. *Social Education*, p. xxxii.

Anthony, D. (1980). *A strategy for British sport*. London: C. Hurst and Company.

Becker, J.M. (1979). *Schooling for a global age*. New York: McGraw-Hill.

Becker, J.M., & Porter, M.J. (1966, January). What is education for international understanding? *Social Education*.

Jaspers, J.M.F., et al. (1966). On the development of national attitudes. *European Journal of Social Psychology*, 1, 360-370.

King, D.C. (1971). *International education for spaceship earth*. Washington, DC: Foreign Policy Association.

Krotee, M.L. (1979). A cross-cultural analysis of the pervasiveness of sport and physical activity. *The Physical Educator*, 36, 149-153.

Krotee, M.L. (1979). *The dimensions of sport sociology*. West Point, NY: Leisure Press.

Krotee, M.L. (1979). The rise and demise of sport: A reflection of Uruguayan society. *The Annals of the American Academy of Political and Social Science*, 445, 141-154.

Krotee, M.L. (1980). The cross cultural dimensions of sport psychology. *Journal of Physical Education and Recreation*, 51(9), 48-49.

Krotee, M.L. (1981). The saliency of the study of international and comparative physical education and sport. *Comparative Physical Education and Sport*, 8, 23-27.

Krotee, M.L. (1982). The physical activity program: Past and future. *Journal of Physical Education and Recreation*, 53, 52-55.

Krotee, M.L., & Bart, W.M. (1978). An ethological view of sport. *Journal of Sport Behavior*, 3, 100-104.

Krotee, M.L., & Hatfield, F.C. (1979). *The theory and practice of physical activity*. Dubuque, IA: Kendall/Hunt.

Krotee, M.L., & Schwick, L.C. (1979). The impact of sporting forces on South African apartheid. *The Journal of Sport and Social Issues, 3*, 33-42.

Lambert, W. (1972). *Language, psychology and culture*. Stanford, CA: Stanford University Press.

Moore, W.E. (Ed.). (1967). Global sociology: The world as a singular system. *Order and change: Essays in comparative sociology*. New York: John Wiley and Sons.

Moyer, J.E. (1970). *Bases for world understanding*. Washington, DC: National Education Association.

Pearson, L.B. (1969, February 15). Beyond the nation state. *Saturday Review*.

Torney, J.V. (1977). The international attitudes and knowledge of adolescents in nine countries. *International Journal of Political Education, 1*, 3-20.

Ward, B. (1966). *Spaceship earth*. New York: Columbia University Press.

Conceptualizing Physical Education Across Cultures: International Development Education and Intercultural Education Perspectives

R. Michael Paige
University of Minnesota

> Sport as a socio-cultural phenomenon must be studied in its contextual setting. How the sport is performed, under what circumstances, and who performs and who observes it are all of prime importance in understanding the meaning of sport. (Hart, 1972, p. ix)

There is little doubt that physical education and sport play an integral part in the societal structure of most nations and cultures. The purpose of this paper is to discuss the fields that I represent, international development education and intercultural education, including theory, research, and practice, which I believe have considerable value in helping us frame our guiding research questions and in providing us with some appropriate conceptual schemas for examining sport-related phenomena. In the brief remarks which follow, I will attempt to articulate the potential contributions of my fields to your inquiries. Moreover, I will place these in a conceptually practical context by suggesting the types of research questions that these fields provoke.

Let me begin by identifying these two areas of inquiry. International development education is a field that has come into its own in the past 20 years. It is an offspring of comparative education, and its scholars have focused their attentions on the relationships between formal and nonformal education, on the one hand, and national development issues (e.g., political development, sociocultural change, economic development, nation-state formation), on the other. Development educators have drawn creatively from the various social and behavioral sciences to explore education and development phenomena. It is, indeed, an interdisciplinary science, within which new theories are constantly emerging and being subjected to empirical tests. International development educators have examined development on a continuum ranging from individual, personality development to macro-level, social-structural development.

Intercultural education is a distinctly different, yet equally intriguing, field. Its foci have been intercultural communication and intercultural relations across a wide variety of social settings. Intercultural educators have sought to examine the effects of cultural variables and cultural differences on interpersonal communication, interpersonal relations, and cultural learning. Intercultural education is also an interdisciplinary science whose scholars have drawn on the fields of psychology, anthropology, social psychology, and sociology for theoretical and conceptual guidance. One of the field's strongest concerns has been with educational activities and their effects in settings comprised of culturally different participants. International sport and physical education events would lend themselves to these types of inquiries.

Having provided a brief introduction to these fields, let me now turn to each of them separately and examine their prospective contributions to analyses of physical education and sport in the international and intercultural contexts.

International Development Education Perspectives

International development education has long been a field interested in teaching and learning processes as these relate to individual and societal growth, change, and development. Scholars have sought to explicate the determinants of learning as well as the nature of learning. They have generated (a) alternative theories of development; (b) alternative theories relating education to development; (c) concepts pertaining to international educational relations, neocolonialism and educational imperialism, dependence and development; (d) theories about the social environment for learning and its effects on learning; and (e) theories about schooling as a socialization process. Applied to comparative physical education and sport, the field would pose a variety of interesting questions.

- What is the role of physical education in the school in terms of individual development?
- What is the relationship between a nation's view of physical education in the school and national development (e.g., national integration, national stability)?
- What is the relationship between a nation's participation in international sports events and its current political ideology?
- In what ways do international sports events influence the participants in terms of their exposure to alternative forms of development and views of development?
- What are the social environmental factors associated with physical education, and how do these relate to individual development and societal development?
- What are the dominant socialization messages associated with physical education, and to what degree are these varying within and across cultures?
- What are the major relationships between physical education and sport in a society and its level of political, sociocultural, economic, and moral development?

- In what ways does a nation's investment in physical education and sport relate to its broader development efforts?
- What are the development consequences of the degree of equitability in distributing physical education and sport facilities across schools and communities?
- Comparatively speaking, what are the various rationales and justifications for national level investments in physical education and sport? In what ways are these seen as development-related investments?
- What are the political development, economic growth or change, and sociocultural change implications of efforts to develop the sport sector within the nation and efforts to participate in international events?

The fundamental question posed by the international development educator is: What is the relationship between physical education and sport and national or international development? If we take the political implications of international sport by way of example, we could easily present competing theories on the political functions of such events. Some might effectively argue that international competitions allow nations to demonstrate, via success in the competition, the benefits of the political systems under which the nations' athletes emerge. Others might theoretically discount this political agenda and argue, instead, that such events promote international dialogue and harmony, better understanding among nations, and international peace.

All of these questions remain to be explored in much greater detail than they have been to date, and all are relevant not only to academicians, but also to practitioners. Theoreticians would urge us not to assume that physical education and sport would have benign development consequences under all circumstances; rather, they would urge us to subject our development-related assumptions to more critical conceptual and empirical scrutiny. I would submit to you that investment and participation in physical education and sport, both at the national and international levels, have significant associations with development as defined at the personal growth and societal change levels. As we begin to more carefully examine who determines physical education policy, who participates, and, more importantly, who succeeds or fails, we can begin to understand how physical education and sport affect development. As Hart (1972) reminds us, "It is important for people in the center of studying, performing and producing sport to be also in the middle of the reformulation of understandings of it" (p. xi). The field of international development education can assist us in this endeavor.

Intercultural Education Perspectives

Physical education and sport activities frequently bring individuals together from quite significantly different cultural, national, religious, political, and socioeconomic backgrounds. The intercultural educator is interested in communication and relations within these multicultural sport gatherings and provides us with conceptual tools to analyze these cross-cultural communication/relations phenomena. The basic communication paradigm currently in vogue suggests that communication within or across cultures is an interactive process, which becomes more complicated as a function of differences among the participants and in the social environments. How one approaches and interprets the meaning of sport may very well be culturally conditioned. How one interacts with other participants may also be a function of cultural background factors. How the sports event itself establishes the social environment for its actors is a matter of great concern to the intercultural education specialist.

Intercultural educators would raise, then, the following questions:

- In what ways do the social environments of international sports events inhibit or promote effective communication across cultures?
- How do the cultural variables associated with sport (e.g., values and norms regarding competition and cooperation) affect the communication among the participants in the event?
- To what degree does the competition inherent in the event create a particular type of social climate? Is there an "international culture of sport"?
- How do the feelings of the participants regarding success and failure in international sports events relate to intercultural relations and communication?
- Under what conditions can international sports events promote positive intercultural communication and attitudes toward culturally different others?
- What are the relative significances of cultural variables and situational (e.g., social environment) variables in determining the level and quality of intercultural communication and relations in international sports events?
- Within cultures, how do values and beliefs regarding physical education and sport influence personality development in terms of such traits as tolerance toward others, authoritarianism, prejudice, and openness?
- Within nations, is performance in sports associated with ethnicity, race, economic class, and so forth? What are the implications for intercultural communication?
- Can the new, third world nations promote national integration of diverse peoples via the application of physical education and sport to communication across cultures?
- Do physical education and sport activities require forms of behavior that promote better communication among the participants?

The intercultural educator is fundamentally concerned with communication and relations among culturally diverse individuals who are brought together under certain institutional arrangements. A physical education class, an international competition, a national Sports Day, a school exercise program, and a club sports event are all examples of events that might bring together in one place and at one time culturally different individuals. Whether those individuals learn to cooperate or not, communicate effectively or not, or relate harmoniously or not may well be a function of the meanings attached to the activities themselves. Theoretically speaking, a highly competitive event may create a social environment for the participants within which communication is inhibited and relationships are strained. It would behoove the physical education and sport practitioner to carefully examine the nature of the activities and their potential effects on the participants' communication and relationships.

The intercultural communication paradigm assists us by examining such factors as personality characteristics, situational variables, communication behavior (verbal and nonverbal), perceptions, cognition across cultures, needs and expectations, and the affective, that is, socioemotional, domain. The research task ahead would be to explore how these variables interact with each other in the physical education and sport context to produce more satisfactory communication and relations among individuals and groups.

In summary, intercultural education focuses our attention upon the reciprocal influence that physical education and sport and intercultural communication and relations have on each other. To the degree that in some physical education and sport settings we wish to facilitate communication across cultures and promote more positive intercultural relations, we should be assisted in our endeavors by reviewing the theories, concepts, and research findings of this field.

Integrating These Perspectives: Toward a New Research Agenda

By way of concluding, let me submit that the perspectives and questions raised by these two fields are not mutually exclusive. It is possible to see some intriguing integration as applied to physical education and sport. One of the most potentially fascinating lines of inquiry would be to examine the social environment of physical education and sport in terms of its influence on intercultural communication within or across nations and, subsequently, the effects of such communication and relationship patterns on national and international development. Many have argued that culturally diverse nation-states must struggle against primordial influences (e.g., attachments to kin, community, and tribe) in order to achieve national integration (Geertz, 1963). New communication patterns must emerge if nations are to become viable and stable. New forms of cooperation must replace ancient antagonisms for nation-states to develop. Multiculturalism, the ability to function effectively in and accept diverse cultural orientations, must replace monoculturalism if interdependence is to come to mean international cooperation among nations.

Physical education and sport at both the national and international levels may have a very important role to play, therefore, in promoting multiculturalism and, hence, in encouraging national and international development. By looking toward the contributions of international development education and intercultural education in terms of their theoretical formulations, concepts, research methods, and research findings, we may eventually discover the conditions under which physical education and sport can more effectively fulfill such a role.

References

Geertz, C. (1963). *Old societies and new states: The quest for modernity in Asia and Africa*. New York: Free Press.

Hart, M.M. (Ed.). (1972). *Sport in the socio-cultural process*. Dubuque, IA: William C. Brown.

Comparative Physical Education and Sport: A Discipline?

Barry Devine
California State University, Northridge

As physical education has developed in its own right, attention has gradually turned toward the comparative aspect of study. While the purely academic viewpoint might suggest that comparative study is justified solely on the basis of intellectual curiosity, obviously many question the relevance and importance of comparative studies.

Whether comparative studies are directed toward physical education and sport in one country (culture) or between countries (cultures), does this type of academic endeavor constitute a discipline or just another field of study? Although it has not been a long time since this question was addressed for physical education, it is fair to proceed with an acknowledgment that it is considered a discipline in its own right at this time.

The following general criteria might suitably be applied in establishing whether an academic discipline exists:

- A body of knowledge exists.
- A general theory or conceptual structure is involved.
- A methodology is evident.
- A specialized vocabulary is generated.
- A generally accepted basic literature exists.
- A process is identifiable and directs the study to a large extent.

The application of these criteria can appropriately establish the level of development towards a discipline that the comparative study of physical education and sport has achieved.

Comparative physical education and sport has historically received only modest attention from members of the physical education profession. In the process of physical education's developing in its own right, attention has gradually and increasingly turned toward the comparative aspect of study. This growth has been accelerated by changes in history such as increased communication, improved transportation, and increased affluence, and perhaps reflects an increase in concern for our fellow man.

While there may be considerable disagreement among members of the physical education profession, comparative physical education and sport may generally be defined as follows:

> A comparative analysis of dominant characteristics and developments in physical education and sport in two or more societies, cultures, countries, or areas for purposes of investigating their similarities and differences. It involves the study of contemporary educational and sport programs in terms of their philosophical foundation; their historical, geographical, economical, political, educational, and cultural background; their aims, problems, and solutions; and their implications for other countries. (Bennett, Howell, & Simri, 1975, p. 3)

Comparative physical education and sport is, then, by definition, cross disciplinary in nature. The affiliation might be with political geography, dealing with political and social institutions from the world perspective, or it might be with political science, dealing with comparative government and international relations.

In describing the major branches of study in comparative education, Bereday (1964, p. xi) includes (a) the survey of education in one country (society, culture), that is, the area study; and (b) merging materials from more than one country (society, culture), that is, the simultaneous comparison. It is important to note, as Noah and Eckstein (1969, p. 112) point out, that the mere presence or absence of foreign country characteristics (society or culture) of data does not guarantee the existence of a comparative method. The key to this transformation of thought lies in the attempt inherent in the social sciences to explain and predict, rather than merely to identify and describe.

Why is Comparative Study Important?

A discussion of whether or not comparative physical education and sport is a discipline undoubtedly leads one to question the importance and relevance of comparative studies. The purist may answer this question by indicating that intellectual curiosity is enough reason to undertake comparative study, that is, knowledge for knowledge sake.

Mallinson (1957, p. 10) has stated that

> To become familiar with what is being done in some other countries than their own, and why it is done, is a necessary part of the training of all serious students of educational issues. . . . Only in that way will they be properly fitted to study and understand their own systems and to plan intelligently for the future which . . . is going to be one where we are thrown into ever closer contact with other peoples and other cultures.

Physical education in the United States has an unusually eclectic character, as any exposure to its history will reveal. Likewise, the origins of sport in this country were clearly linked to other countries, and this association with other countries continues through international sport contests. The problems, then, of physical education and sport in different countries are often similar, and the principles that guide their solution may be identified and compared. Analytical study of these factors and the comparison of attempted solutions of resultant problems are basic to comparative physical education and sport.

The process of studying physical education and sport in other countries is not just a means of understanding other people, but is also a means of knowing our own system better. As Bereday reports (1964, p. 6), "It is self-knowledge born of the awareness of others that is the finest lesson." This practice of dealing with two or more cultures at the same time permits us to deduct lessons for our system from the achievements and the mistakes of other systems and to appraise issues from a global rather than an ethnocentric perspective. This, in turn, permits us to be always aware of the views of other nations and will, it is hoped, lead to a relaxation in national pride so that events and voices from abroad can count in the continuous appraisal and examination of our own system of physical education and sport.

Because of the role played by the United States in offering aid for the improvement of physical education and sport to other countries, it is imperative that we understand the systems in these countries. Programs through the Peace Corps, the Agency for International Development, the State Department, and many private institutions necessitate this awareness. Through the greater sensitivity resulting from thorough analysis by dispassionate study without ethnocentric interference, a real contribution can be made toward international understanding.

What is a Discipline?

Perhaps further debate about whether physical education itself is a discipline is passé. Certainly those of us in the profession consider it a discipline, and many institutions have proceeded to change the names of their departments to reflect the body of knowledge that identifies our pursuit as a discipline. Although this position may be clear and conclusive in the minds of professional physical educators, there is some question as to the breadth of its acceptance among members of other more traditional disciplines, and such acceptance by other related disciplines would appear to be one criterion of a discipline.

What then are the criteria that determine the status of an academic field of study as a discipline? The very concept of a discipline is one of the most overworked and ill-defined terms utilized in the academic world, according to Dressel and Mayhew (1974, p. 11). This lack of consistency for assessing the status of an academic endeavor can prove frustrating to the academic wishing to measure the significance of his or her work. The following criteria are typically applied to a field of study to establish whether it ranks as a discipline.

- A body of knowledge exists that has a reasonably logical taxonomy; in this way scholars can tell, at least quantitatively, where gaps exist in accepted knowledge. This body of knowledge relates to vital issues and is aimed at the achievement of stated objectives.
- The discipline involves some generally accepted body of theory, a unique conceptual structure. Included are techniques for theory testing and revision.
- An accepted body of consistently applied techniques of analysis or methodology is essential. This methodology is stylized in more precise disciplines such as mathematics, physics, chemistry, and experimental psychology. These methods lead to ways of learning and knowing the domain of the discipline.
- A discipline relies on accurate language, so a specialized vocabulary is usually generated. The comparative nature of this subject necessitates the use of extremely accurate language in communication within its ranks and to those outside its confines.
- A generally accepted basic literature outlines the parameters of a discipline, thereby helping to define the importance of issues in one field as contrasted to another. A discipline is generally characterized by a substantial history and is linked to and recognized by other disciplines.
- A discipline is recognized as a process, and it is perhaps this sense of sequence which is the key criterion. This process is what enables scholars to predict where they will look next in enlarging the body of knowledge.

As scholarly fields mature and gain acceptance, they acquire certain characteristics that symbolize their status as disciplines. Scholarly associations emerge, which are restricted to those with some competence in the field; and journals appear, which use peer judgments to screen materials for competent scholarship. Eventually the development of a recognized sequence of experiences for the preparation of scholars and researchers in the discipline emerges.

Is Comparative Physical Education and Sport a Discipline?

When comparative physical education and sport is compared to the criteria listed above, the results are inconsistent—on some criteria the subject measures up much better than on others. Certainly school physical education programs and the multitude of sport programs in the world provide a clear subject matter. The field has a specific methodological concern that is shared with other comparative disciplines, such as comparative government, education, economics, political systems, and anthropological cross-cultural studies; that concern is for the development of valid methods for comparison.

The theory or conceptual structure upon which comparative physical education and sport is based appears to be emerging rapidly. While originally closely allied to other parts of physical education, scholars are currently developing a conceptual structure more specifically for the comparative point of view. The accuracy of descriptive and definitive language for comparative purposes leaves something to be desired, as any scholar will recognize. Because this deficit is so significant in the comparative process, its development must be considered critical to further growth.

The literature on comparative physical education and sport is rapidly defining the limits of its study. The extensive gathering of bibliographical information by Myrtis Herndon (1972a, b) is a milestone in the definition of comparative physical education and sport by its literature. In the critical criterion of being recognized as a process, comparative physical education and sport is an infant. A sense of sequence or process is emerging, but the process is neither well-defined nor apparent to the outsider. While the other trappings of a discipline are emerging (associations, journals, and professional recognition), the subject is as yet low on maturity and high on potential. Realistically, it is unlikely that the classification of comparative physical education and sport as a discipline would be without dispute at this time. There are many who still maintain that physical education, itself, has not yet attained the status of a discipline, and, thus, would never recognize the comparative component differently.

Franklin Henry has defined physical education as a discipline in no uncertain terms (1964). By recognizing physical education as a recent academic discipline, the consideration of comparative physical education and sport is simplified. An examination of the criteria above makes it clear that full status as a discipline is not warranted at this time. There does, however, appear to be evidence that comparative physical education and sport is fulfilling more of the criteria than before; hence, use of the term *emerging* is appropriate. At some time in the future, by reference to the criteria, it might no longer be necessary to use emerging as a descriptive term.

The discipline of physical education is made up of several subdisciplines. One such subdiscipline includes study from the comparative viewpoint, and, like any cross-disciplinary field of study, it is difficult to delimit segmentally. As the new discipline of physical education matures, its students can expect to give more attention to the subject content of the emerging subdiscipline of comparative physical education and sport.

References

Bennett, B.L., Howell, M.L., & Simri, U. (1975). *Comparative physical education and sport*. Philadelphia: Lea & Febiger.

Bereday, G.Z.F. (1964). *Comparative method in education*. New York: Holt, Rinehart, & Winston.

Dressel, P.L., & Mayhew, L.B. (1974). *Higher education as a field of study*. San Francisco: Jossey-Bass.

Eckstein, M.A., & Noah, H.J. (1969). *Scientific investigations in comparative education*. Toronto: Macmillan.

Heath, K.G. (1958, October). Is comparative education a discipline? *Comparative Education Review*, **2**(2).

Henry, F. (1964, September). Physical education: An academic discipline. *JOHPER*, pp. 32-33, 69.

Herndon, M.E. (1972a). *Comparative physical education and international sport: I. A bibliographic guide.* Washington, DC: International Relations Council of the American Association for Health, Physical Education, and Recreation.

Herndon, M.E. (1972b). *Comparative physical education and international sport: II. A bibliographic guide.* Washington, DC: International Relations Council of the American Association for Health, Physical Education, and Recreation.

Kobayashi, T. (1971). *Survey on current trends in comparative education and sport.* Hamburg: UNESCO Institute of Education.

Mallinson, V. (1957). *An introduction to the study of comparative education.* New York: Macmillan.

Miller, B.W. (1975, March). *Comparative physical education and sport—A discipline?* Paper delivered to the International Relations Council at the annual convention of American Alliance for Health, Physical Education, and Recreation, Atlantic City, NJ.

Noah, H.J., & Eckstein, M.A. (1969). *Toward a science of comparative education.* New York: Macmillan.

Marshaling the Social Sciences and Humanities to Assess the Intercultural Significance of Physical Education and Sport

Earle F. Zeigler
University of Western Ontario

The inauguration of the International Society on Comparative Physical Education and Sport quite obviously marked the beginning of a new era within the profession. The writer, as a person who left the United States temporarily in 1949 to teach and coach in Canada, had the feeling that he was going to a foreign country. Thus, efforts were made to identify himself immediately with what was called the Foreign Relations Committee of the former College Physical Education Association and the International Relations Council promoted so ably by Dorothy Ainsworth within the American Association for Health, Physical Education, and Recreation (as it was formerly known).

If it were not for these early and continuing experiences and a return to Canada in 1971, it is quite possible that the writer would be presently numbered among that vast majority of physical educators and coaches in the United States who feel that "if anything worthwhile is going to happen, it will be here" and that "it had better be made available in the English language if I am to be expected to pay attention to it." This may sound like harsh, unfair criticism, but it is my considered opinion that far too much of this attitude still prevails.

For reasons such as this, it is important that this international society was inaugurated at the 1978 conference in Israel; that the second conference was held in Canada; and that this third seminar is being held in Minneapolis within the United States. Great significance should be attached to this development for a number of different reasons. For example, it is through efforts such as this that we in this profession may be able to assist civilization to move a bit faster toward what Glasser (1972) has identified as "civilized identity society," in which the concern of humans will again focus on such concepts as self-identity, self-expression, and cooperation. Postulating that so-called "primitive-identity" societies ended in a great many areas several thousand years ago when populations increased sharply and some countries found it necessary to take essential resources from neighboring societies, he argues that a "civilized survival" situation ensued. Now for the continuation of life on this planet as we know it, it is possible for mankind to enter a phase of civilized identity society (Glasser, 1972). Obviously a society such as the ISCPES can make a contribution in this direction.

Further support for this possible contribution comes from the findings of Kaplan (1961), who found certain "recurring elements in the various world philosophies" based on his analysis of the situation. Despite the "hot and cold" wars of the present, he theorizes that there are indeed four recurring themes of rationality, activism, humanism, and preoccupation with values present in the leading world philosophies. In his opinion, organizations such as this offer greater hope to people from various countries as they plan for the future.

Three Fundamental Concepts

For reasons such as the above, the writer, more than a decade ago, recommended the necessity of establishing the fundamental importance of three concepts in the years immediately ahead—the concepts of communication, diversity, and cooperation (Zeigler, 1975).

First, the concept of communication has now become vitally important because a "fourth revolution" is occurring within this area. The world has moved from the invention of speech, to writing, to mechanical reproduction of the printed word, and now to relay stations in space creating a blanketing communications network that will make possible a type of international personal relationship hitherto undreamed of by men and women (Asimov, 1970). This development has fantastic implications for the profession of physical education and sport, making it mandatory that we view this aspect of our task in a new light. Basically, however, the world must win this race; that is, this vastly improved means of communication must be employed to foster international goodwill and cooperation rather than as a means to help the superpowers blow us all up more effectively!

Second, the concept of diversity—the state or fact of being different, unlike, or diverse—must be fostered as well. We are a diverse lot, so to speak, and we must come to understand this diversity ever so much better than we do at present. It is at this point that the struggle between the world's leading ideologies comes into focus. Communists argue that mankind must pass through four stages: from agrarianism to capitalism, and from there to socialism and eventual ideal communism. Having already reached the third stage, we can observe that they have completely stifled the concept of diversity in their culture. Can we indeed have a world where significant diversity is permitted? Must we have a type of Skinner's (1971) *operant conditioning* involving behavior modification so that people's actions are regulated more stringently than ever before because of overpopulation and many other deterrents? This is the major issue that must be addressed in the years immediately ahead, and we can only hope that this problem can be worked out peacefully.

Third, the concept of cooperation must be paramount, along with the two mentioned above, in our planning for the future. Cooperation implies working together for a common purpose or benefit. As the world grows smaller, so to speak, we simply must pay ever so much more attention to international relations. This will be vital within society generally, as well as in the field of education. Consequently, it is most important for us in the field of physical education and sport as we develop new plans and extend the horizons for cooperation in the various aspects of our field among individuals, groups, and societies on earth and in space.

"Third Wave" World

As we approach this new world, this world of the 21st century, we must ask ourselves what this Third Wave world is going to mean to us in the field of physical education and sport. We are people who are interested in human motor performance in sport, dance, play, and exercise within our own countries, our own continents, our own hemispheres, and on a worldwide basis. We are not looking at this topic only from the standpoint of comparative *education*, but even more broadly in the sense that our profession has a responsibility to serve people of *all* ages and cultures on a womb-to-tomb basis, including preschool, school, college, university, and all ages of adult life from the 20s up through the 80s or later. Human motor performance of a correct and desirable nature is, therefore, being regarded as a lifelong process. Our role is to so guide general education that all people will truly comprehend the need for healthful and enjoyable physical activity to promote (a) circulo-respiratory efficiency, (b) joint flexibility, (c) adequate muscular strength, and (d) the development and maintenance of correct and functional segmental alignment of bodily parts to foster health, functional efficiency, and aesthetic movement.

Our problem, then, is to devise a step-by-step approach for the description, interpretation, comparison, and evaluation of prevailing patterns of human movement in sport, dance, play, and exercise from a cross-cultural standpoint. As matters stand now, many travelers' tales have been told; but, very little educational borrowing has been carried out in our field, for example, in a culture that tends to think the best answers to problems are found right here at home in North America. A number of other countries have been more cosmopolitan in this regard, and their relative progress is significant. A certain amount of international educational cooperation has occurred, but language barriers, economic shortages, new types of nationalism, and other barriers have hampered development. For example, many have come to North America to learn, but very few of us have the desire, much less the language capability or the funds to go elsewhere to learn.

Thus, Stages 4 and 5 of Noah and Eckstein's (1969) analysis of the development of comparative education must be designated as possibly being in the future for us in physical education and sport. At the moment, we have not "identified the forces and factors shaping national educational systems," nor have we entered "the stage of social science explanation, that uses the empirical quantitative methods of economics, political science, and sociology to clarify relationships between education and society."

Concluding Statement

The essence of these comments at this point is, therefore, that the next step for those committed to both a subdisciplinary and subprofessional

Table 1 Sport and Developmental Physical Activity

Areas of scholarly study and research	Subdisciplinary aspects	Subprofessional aspects
1. Background, meaning, and significance	History Philosophy International and comparative study	International Professional ethics
2. Functional effects of physical activity	Exercise physiology Anthropometry and body composition	Fitness and health appraisal Exercise therapy
3. Sociocultural and behavioral aspects	Sociology Psychology (individual and social) Anthropology Political science Geography Economics	Application of theory to practice
4. Motor learning and development	Psychomotor learning Physical growth and motor development	Application of theory to practice
5. Mechanical and muscular analysis of motor skills	Biomechanics Neuroskeletal musculature	Application of theory to practice
6. Management theory and practice	Theory about the management function	Application of theory to practice
7. Program development (theory and practice)	Theory about program development[a]	Application of theory to practice
8. Evaluation and measurement	Theory about the measurement function	Application of theory to practice

[a]General education; professional preparation; intramural sports and physical recreation; intercollegiate athletics; programs for the handicapped, including curriculum and instructional methodology.

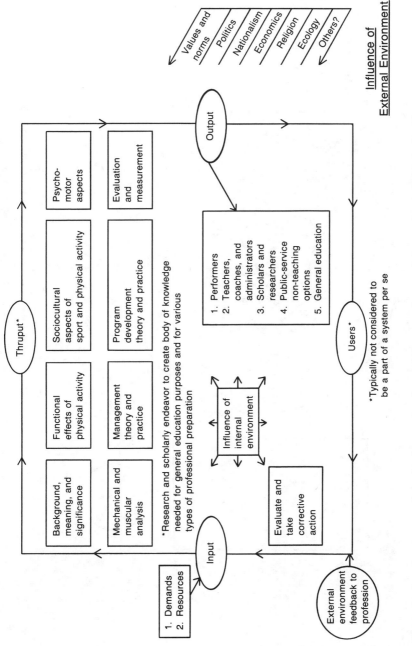

Figure 1 A systems approach to development and use of theory and research in sport and physical education.

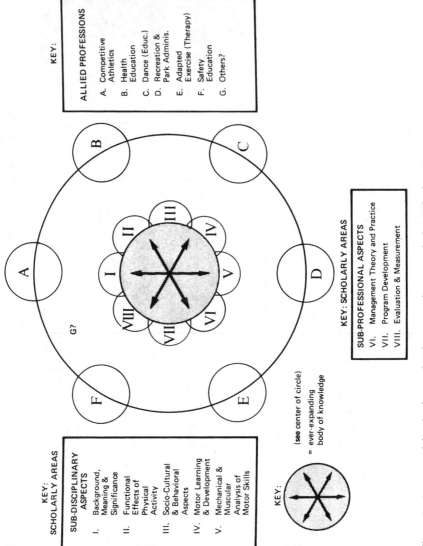

Figure 2   A proposal for the future development of sport and physical education.

approach to what some have called international and comparative physical education and sport should be the development of an international plan or strategy for a worldwide analysis of our area of concern. What we need is a step-by-step approach for the description, interpretation, comparison, and evaluation of prevailing patterns of human movement in sport, dance, play, and exercise—an analysis that is carried out from a cross-cultural standpoint.

We need to work for agreement on a presently acceptable taxonomy that describes, as accurately as possible, the subdisciplinary and sub-professional components of the profession (Table 1). From this point, the next step would logically be an effort to develop a mechanism whereby people in this field around the world would have available for their professional endeavor a series of ordered generalizations explaining the status of our body of knowledge (Figures 2 and 3). Only in this way will we know where we stand, where we should be heading, and where we should be planning cooperative scholarly endeavors to solve our mutual problems. Assuredly, this is the path that must be followed. Those interested in international and comparative physical education and sport must marshal the social science and humanities scholars within the field to assess the intercultural significance of physical education and sport. In this way, it may be possible for the profession to reach its potential on a worldwide basis.

References

Asimov, I. (1970, October 24). The fourth revolution. *Saturday Review*, pp. 17-20.

Glasser, W. (1972). *The identity society*. New York: Harper and Row.

Kaplan, A. (1961). *The new world of philosophy* (pp. 7-10). Boston: Houghton Mifflin.

Noah, H.J., & Eckstein, M.A. (1969). *Toward a science of comparative education*. New York: Macmillan.

Skinner, B.F. (1971). *Beyond freedom and dignity*. New York: Alfred A. Knopf.

Zeigler, E.F. (1975). *Personalizing physical education and sport philosophy*. Champaign, IL: Stipes.

Comparative Sport Pedagogy— Comparative Education: A Basic Intrarelationship Within Educational Sciences

Herbert Haag
Christian-Albrechts-Universität Kiel
Institut für Sport und Sportwissenschaften

The comparative research approach is a very basic research paradigm and is also valid for sport science research. It may be used in all three fundamental concepts of research methodology: namely, the historical, the descriptive, and the experimental approach. It also may be used in regard to different theory fields of sport science and the research done in these areas.

Sport pedagogy is one of the theory fields to which this research approach might be applied. Within sport sciences, according to a certain model, seven theory fields can be distinguished: sport medicine, sport biomechanics, sport psychology, sport pedagogy, sport sociology, sport history, and sport philosophy.

A basic hypothesis is that intra- and interrelationships are necessary for the understanding and constant development of sport sciences as an academic field. Intrarelationships are, for example, the relationships of sport medicine to medicine, of sport pedagogy to pedagogy (education), and so forth. These are the relationships of a theory field of sport sciences to the respective mother or related science. Interrelationships are, for example, sport pedagogy to sport history, to sport philosophy, and so forth; they are important for the so-called interdisciplinary approach. Within this analysis an attempt will be made to describe and explain the basic intrarelationship of comparative sport pedagogy to comparative education. This intrarelationship has to be seen on the basis of the one between sport pedagogy and education. The comparative research dimension, however, is a very basic one, which can be linked to the intrarelationship dimension. Therefore, it will be necessary to concentrate in this analysis on three major aspects.

- Analysis of the concept of educational sciences
- Discussion of the concept of sport pedagogy
- Description of the comparative research dimension

On the basis of these major aspects, an attempt will be made to adequately cover the given topic, which is of fundamental importance for the status and self-understanding of pedagogy, in specific, and sport sciences in general, especially under the comparative dimension of generating further knowledge on the phenomenon of sport.

Model of Sport Science—Intra- and Interrelationships

First, it seems necessary to explain the status and self-understanding of sport science, because this is the larger framework for the discussion of the given topic. There are certain criteria that are valid for evaluating the status of sport science and are already leading to a so-called meta-theory of sport science, which is explained in terms of a 7-theory-field-model. Intra- and interrelationships are two important relationship directions in adequately describing this model of sport science.

Criteria for Evaluating the Status of Sport Science

Two sets of criteria, internal and external, can be distinguished in order to either describe the nature of sport science or to judge its development status, which can be characterized by several theses (Haag, 1976, pp. 56-62).

- The originating of sport science is connected with the increasing importance of science in present life. Sport science is an example of a *social phenomenon of major importance* becoming the nucleus of scientific endeavor (Baitsch, Grupe, & Lotz, 1972; Simri, 1974).
- Sport science is a so-called, theme-oriented science; and as a young scientific field closely connected with several mother or related sciences, it requires an *interdiscipline* between different scientific approaches (Krotee, 1979; Singer et al., 1972).
- The basic content dimension of sport science is *movement* as one basic behavior dimension of human beings realized during work, daily necessities, and free time.
- This basic movement dimension, which is realized in a wide variety of forms from play to work, is a phenomenon with *international character*. Therefore, sport science is a scientific field with strong international communication and exchange.
- Newly developed scientific fields require a balanced approach between *basic and applied research*, because the latter can only be developed on the former.
- Originating sciences, like sport science, must observe the general scientific discussion very closely, because the *process of theory building* has only started and is still a long way from an acknowledged and well-developed scientific field.

There are also a number of formal criteria that can serve to describe the development status of sport science.

- The number of *sport science journals* has increased to a great extent nationally and internationally. This includes journals for the whole field of sport science (e.g., *Canadian Journal of Applied Sport Science*), for certain theory fields of sport science (e.g., *International Journal of Physical Education*), and for certain themes or problems (e.g., *Leistungssport*).
- There are presently available about 30 *sport science book series* in the German language dealing with various aspects of theory and practice in sport.
- National and international *congresses* are increasing to a great extent. Congress reports are becoming a valuable resource for the latest developments in sport science.
- More and more institutions of higher learning have introduced study curricula leading to *master's and doctor's degrees*. Full professorships were introduced as a necessary precondition for the development of a scientific field.
- Within institutions of higher learning, *departments or colleges for sport science* have received the same organizational recognition as other scientific fields.
- The changing of *terminology* from theory of physical education to sport science can be observed worldwide, especially within the German speaking countries. Terms like physical education, gymnology, kinetics, kinanthropology, motology, or theory of physical culture are, therefore, describing more and more specific aspects of sport science.

Meta-Theory of Sport Science

A meta-theory of sport science as a scientific field would deal mainly with two major subjects: its content description and its research methodology. Both aspects are discussed on the basis of a certain perception of sport science, its task, responsibility perception of scientific truth, and so forth.

For *content description* a multidimensional approach will be used including three dimensions. This model has been developed by the author only recently (Haag, 1978).

- The organization-oriented approach has four fields of application (Grupe, 1971): (a) physical education, school sport, and sport for youth; (b) recreational sport, sport for everybody, and sport for all; (c) performance and competitive sport; and (d) top level athletics.
- The problem-oriented approach is based on themes that are characteristic for the social phenomenon of sport. The content description is becoming relatively concrete and is dealing with topics like movement, health, recreation, coaching, play, competition, and so forth.

- The theory-field-oriented approach deals with applied scientific fields that have to be seen in close relationship to long-developed scientific disciplines, and it will be discussed later in more detail.

For the *research methodology* a model developed by the author may be used (Haag, 1982), which is valid for both theoretical-hermeneutic and empirical-analytical research. The model is characterized by five steps.

1. Scientific theory is important as a starting point, because it reflects the aims, objectives, and necessity of doing research, and the precondition and the consequences of science. Two major aspects should be distinguished in order to really understand this aspect; namely, "modes of gaining knowledge" and "scientific-political justification for science."
2. Basic research methods are distinguished, according to a model by Fox (1969), into historical, descriptive (status quo), and experimental research.
3. Research designs need to be differentiated, because the three basic research methods have to be seen on a continuum allowing many variations of these basic research paradigms.
4. Techniques of data collection are important in order to collect the relevant data by techniques like content analysis, questioning, observing, testing, and so forth.
5. Techniques of data analysis are necessary in order to analyze the collected data in the light of the stated hypothesis by numerical and/or nonnumerical techniques, which are both applied within sport science.

7-Theory-Field-Model

As indicated earlier, it is also possible to distinguish a certain number of theory fields that are derived from already established scientific fields. These theory fields have an applied character and are not clearly limited to a certain number. However, the so-called 7-theory-field-model, developed by the author within the department of sport pedagogy at Kiel University, seems to provide a good rationale for the perception of sport science. The seven theory fields are divided into three groups (Haag, 1979).

- Anatomical-physiological-mechanical foundations: sport medicine/sport biomechanics
- Foundations of social and behavioral sciences: sport psychology/sport pedagogy/sport sociology
- Historical-philosophical foundations: sport history/sport philosophy

With the help of this model the existing relationships within the science can be understood clearly.

Intrarelationship/Interrelationship

This distinction of relationships was proposed by Heckhausen at the 10th anniversary of the working group for sport psychology (ASP) of the Federal Republic of Germany. Because the scientific field has become very complex and diversified, it is more and more necessary to also see relationships besides the strong tendency for separation and specialization.

Intrarelationship is the relationship of a theory field of sport science to the respective "mother" or related science. These are, in most cases, long established scientific fields. The theory fields of sport science can be seen as applied aspects of the related science. The relationship of sport pedagogy to the science of education is an example, which would also very closely imply the topic of this analysis, namely, the comparative aspect. This relationship is necessary in order to engage in high-quality scientific thinking and research results on a broad scale.

Interrelationship indicates that the seven theory fields need a close connection to each other, especially within the three subgroups of the 7-theory-field-model. Overspecialization can become very dangerous for the world of science, and there is a necessity to see this dimension of relationships.

Analysis of the Concept of Educational Sciences

The concept of educational sciences will be analyzed in four possible steps. First, some remarks have to be made to a necessary meta-theory. Then the status of educational sciences will be briefly characterized, and finally, the content and research dimension will be analyzed.

Meta-Theory

The development and status of education as a scientific field have been quite different in various countries. Within this analysis it is impossible to deal with this variety; the following remarks in relation to its development in the Federal Republic of Germany may serve as an example to explain this issue.

In the past there was often a certain confusion between education as a scientific field (Erziehungswissenschaft) and as a practical field (Erziehungslehre) (Brezinka, 1972). There was also a distinction between "hermeneutic pedagogy" and "empirical education science." These strong alternatives, however, are disappearing; there can be observed, according to Wehle (1973), a scientific consolidation in three directions.

- Establishment of education as a science in clear distinction from the neighboring disciplines of psychology and sociology.
- Development of a study curriculum of education science as opposed to practical teaching.

- Interpretation of education as one social and behavioral science with hermeneutic and empirical research concepts.

Within this modern framework of educational science, sport pedagogy can be seen in line with religion, literature, music, art, and language education as describing one aspect of human culture and its educational relevance. It is important to note that for all those subfields of education, a dialectic relationship of theoretical/scientific and practical/applied aspects has to be seen.

Status of Educational Sciences

Since 1945 there has been a change in terminology from Pädagogik to Erziehungswissenschaft. This new status of the field is characterized by several different aspects.

- The new term should indicate a scientific consolidation and a clearer distinction from psychology and sociology.
- The study of Erziehungswissenschaft should have scientific character and not be just a master course in how to teach.
- The new term indicates a change in the scientific perception of the field from a dualistic pedagogy (normative-individual) to a humanities-oriented field to a part of social science.
- A process of differentiation is going on in regard to different theoretical concepts.

In general, one can see that the status of educational sciences has been improved since 1945 to a great extent.

Content Dimension

The content dimension of education sciences can best be explained by a model that was developed by the author and uses five distinguishing criteria.

- Systematic: general, historical, comparative
- Part aspects: social, work, professional education
- Ages: pedagogy, ondragogy, geragogy
- Neighboring disciplines: educational psychology, educational sociology, educational philosophy
- Cultural areas: religious, literature, music, art, language, sport education

Interestingly enough, there is available one proposal of Röhrs for defining major aspects of education sciences, including the aspect of physical education. He divides the content into the following aspects: social education, special education, economics education, school education, sport pedagogy, history of education, comparative education, and didactics/methodics. Even if this approach does not seem to be very systematical, it is interesting that sport pedagogy is contained within this content model.

Research Dimension

The research dimension within educational sciences has to be very broad due to the many questions on themes that are of relevance for the field. Bockelmann (1970) has distinguished three dimensions in order to categorize theory building in education sciences.

- Hermeneutic-speculative types of theories
- Descriptive-phenomenological types of theories
- Empirical positivistic types of theories

Because theories are the outcome of research, an indication of the research dimension can be derived from this model.

Another approach with similar results has been taken by Fox (1969) and is characterized by the distinction of time and intent in selecting research methods. In a varied form this approach to identifying the research dimension can be seen in Figure 1. Thus, this model also proves the variety of research dimensions that are valid for educational sciences.

Analysis of the Concept of Sport Pedagogy

The concept of sport pedagogy has to be analyzed in a similar way to the educational sciences, because there is a very clear relationship between the theory field of sport pedagogy and educational sciences as related sciences. First, some meta-theoretical ideas will be developed as a basis

Time / Intent	Past / Historical	Present / Survey	Future / Experiment
Description	Simple Historical	Simple survey Case study	Single group experiment
Comparison	Parallel Historical	Multiple group survey	Multiple group experiment

Figure 1 Model for selecting research methods.

for the description of the status of sport pedagogy, at least on a selected basis. From there, it is possible to describe the content and research dimension.

Meta-Theory

There have been a number of writings regarding the aspects of a meta-theory of sport pedagogy. Meinberg (1981) referred to four different variations that can be perceived as a basis for meta-theoretical thinking in regard to this subject.

* Anthropological sport pedagogy
* Communicative sport pedagogy
* Scientific sport pedagogy
* System-theoretical sport pedagogy

Status of Sport Pedagogy

The inclusion of sport pedagogy within educational science has taken place only recently in the Federal Republic of Germany. Röhrs started this development in 1969 by including sport pedagogy in his fundamental work *Allgemeine Erziehungswissenschaft* along with issues like history of education, school education, and comparative education. Since that time, more and more researchers in education recognize sport pedagogy as one applied scientific subfield of education (Menze, 1976; Röhrs, 1972).

In order to develop a concept of sport pedagogy as a part of sport science, it is especially important to understand the genesis of sport pedagogy from the theory of physical education (Haag, 1978). Mester (1973) has described these relationships very clearly.

* In the 1950s, the ideas of reform-pedagogy were adapted into the theory of physical education.
* In the 1960s, there was a change from the educational aspects of physical education to sport pedagogy as it relates to society.
* In the 1970s, sport science originated with one part or theory field called sport pedagogy (Lotz, 1975).

A number of models and theoretical frameworks have been developed for describing the content dimension of sport pedagogy as a part of sport science (Grupe, 1969; Meusel, 1976; Schmitz, 1973, 1978, 1979; Widmer, 1977). Within this analysis it is not possible to deal with various models and theoretical frameworks of this kind; however, the content dimension of sport pedagogy as seen within sport science (physical education) in the United States should be mentioned briefly, because it is an interesting counterpoint to the perception of sport pedagogy as a theory field of sport science within the German discussion (Haag, 1978; NCPEAM, 1968; NCPEAM/NAPECW, 1967).

According to the present status of the discussion of scientific theory in the United States, one can assume that there is not yet a visible theory field of sport pedagogy that is a component of sport science. Physical education (Henry, 1964), however, is the nucleus, the process and the reality on which different scientific theoretical fields should concentrate their work; it is not seen as an independent scientific theoretical field. In the *Big-Ten Body of Knowledge Project in Physical Education*, the following content concept has been developed for the American theory of physical education: physiology of exercise organization theory, sociology of sport and physical education, biomechanics movement theory, sport psychology, history, philosophy, and comparative physical education and sport (Haag, 1972).

Another example is a publication with the title *Physical Education: An Interdisciplinary Approach* (Singer et al., 1972), in which physical education is seen as a focal point for different scientific and sport science endeavors. In this publication, the results of the theoretical fields of sport science, namely, physiology, physics, psychology, sociology, anthropology, and philosophy are used to build the interdisciplinary scientific framework for the investigation of the process of physical education.

It can be summarized that sport pedagogy in the United States is not yet seen as a scientific theoretical field of sport science; instead, physical education serves as the focal point for the different scientific and sport scientific endeavors. This fact is astonishing, because education in general has found a broad and empirical scientific foundation, especially in the United States. The aspect of physical education or sport pedagogy, however, is not viewed as a theoretical field with its own scientific existence, as is the case in German speaking countries.

Content Dimension

There are many models available to describe the content of sport pedagogy (Beyer & Röthig, 1976), including one developed by the author and his colleagues in the department of sport pedagogy at the Institute of Sport and Sport Sciences of the University of Kiel. In this model the content of sport pedagogy is perceived as the "questions and problems which are related to teaching and learning processes in and through movement, realized in different forms of the social reality of sport including the conscious dealing with this reality" (Haag, 1976).

One basis of this model is the so-called "Berlin didactic model," which tries to explain instructional processes with six factors: anthropological conditions (teacher/pupil), sociocultural conditions, aims and objectives, content, methods, and media. This model can also be applied for teaching and learning processes that go beyond instruction in school and that indicate the broader connotation of sport.

In order to avoid certain static aspects of this factor model, a process model is also used indicating certain actions that should be performed when dealing with teaching and learning processes; such actions include analyzing, planning, realizing, and evaluating. The combination of the factor model and the process model results in the model for content description of sport pedagogy.

- Analyzing of prerequisites and preconditions of teaching-learning processes in sport (institutional and noninstitutional framework/teacher teaching of sport/children, pupils, adults, and learning of sport).
- Planning of teaching and learning processes in sport (preconditions as variables for planning/aims and objectives/contents).
- Realizing of teaching-learning processes in sport (organization, methods, media).
- Evaluating of teaching and learning processes in sport (assessing of learning results, judging of learning results, changing of determining factors of teaching and learning processes).

According to this model, sport pedagogy deals with teaching and learning aspects in sport, occurring within and outside of educational institutions as related to the different phases of human life; it deals with the possibilities and limitations of education through sport. This relates to a broad scale of factors that are important for teaching and learning processes in sport.

Research Dimension

The research tradition in education in the Federal Republic of Germany until recently has been predominantly hermeneutic-theoretical. This is also true for research in physical education or sport pedagogy (Willimczik, 1968). Only since about 1970 have empirical-analytical research designs been applied more frequently. The first research program for the field of sport science in the Federal Republic of Germany was initiated in 1969 by the Central Committee for Research in Sport, and recent research programs were formulated by the Federal Institute of Sport Science (BISp) in Cologne in 1972 and 1976; this institute also gives money for well-justified research requests and awards research grants.

The most precise retrospective view can be given by mentioning the fields of concentration for research in sport pedagogy as outlined in the 1976 program of the BISp (Kirsch, 1978).

Theory and Methods of Sport Instruction
- Multidimensional evaluation methods of sport instruction, as well as evaluation instruments and tests within instructional research.
- Development of methods for counseling about talent and for the determining of talent by the physical education teacher, including measures of talent support.
- Behavior and behavior change of the teacher; conditions of physical education teacher training, and their consequences for sport instruction.

- Plans for extended study for physical education teachers.
- Optimization of the usage of media within sport instruction.
- Evaluation of situations and influencing factors in sport instruction (learning surroundings).

Theory of Sport Curriculum
- Movement games for infant and preschool children.
- Empirical foundation of basic qualifications for sport instruction.
- Evaluation instruments for curricula and their parts, especially in primary schools and grades 5 to 10 (Sekundarstufe 1).
- Models and concepts for sport in grades 11 to 13 (Sekundarstufe II), especially the field of concentration called sport.
- Interaction and communication analysis of the action field sport under aspects of sport pedagogy.

Theory and Organization of Specific Aspects of Sport
- Investigations of the educational planning of coaching in sport clubs and sport associations.
- Comparative investigations of the concept, content, and effectiveness of fitness programs.
- Development of model concepts of sport for older people.
- Didactic models of therapy and rehabilitation within sport for the mentally and physically handicapped and in other areas of social work.
- Plans for sport for all.

Description of the Comparative Research Dimension

After the analysis of educational sciences and sport pedagogy as an applied field of these sciences, the so-called intrarelationship can be explained for the comparative research dimension.

Criteria of Comparative Research in Educational Sciences

Among the many researchers who are dealing with comparative education, the concept of Bereday (1964) is discussed quite often. He distinguishes two major simultaneous procedural steps, namely, juxtaposition and comparison. Juxtaposition means defining the statement or theme, systematically collecting the relevant data from two or more countries, and stating the hypothesis for the comparative analysis. The comparison distinguishes between balanced comparison (comparison of similar data in different countries) and illustrative comparison (comparison of educational practices to illustrate comparative points without generalization). This proposal for the general educational dimension can also be applied for sport pedagogy.

Model for Comparative Research in Sport Pedagogy

The comparative research in sport pedagogy can be viewed on the basis of the above described criteria in two dimensions.

- Horizontal: comparison in different social settings (states) at a certain time.
- Vertical: comparison in different time sections in regard to the same questions.

Of course, there is also the possibility of combining both horizontal and vertical, which results in a very complex research design, implying more countries and different time sections.

Perspectives of Comparative Research in Sport Pedagogy

There are several reasons why the comparative research approach is especially applied within the theory field of sport pedagogy.

- Comparative education is a well-developed part of educational science. Journals (e.g., *Comparative Education Review, Comparative Education*), organizations (e.g., Comparative and International Education Society), and centers (e.g., Comparative Education Center of the University of Chicago) prove this fact. It is, therefore, possible for comparative physical education to look for guidance and help (Bereday, 1964; Hans, 1951; Kandel, 1933; Noah & Eckstein, 1969).
- Physical education, the process of teaching and learning in the field of sport (physical activity), lends itself to cross-cultural comparison, because it is one of the fundamental themes of sport science.
- In all states and societies, physical education is, in one way or another, part of the educational setting. Therefore, it is quite obvious that the comparative research approach could be applied adequately.

Despite these opportunities for real comparative research, reports of investigations are rather limited. Exceptions include the analyses by Bennett, Howell, and Simri (1975), in which they compared a number of countries with regard to 16 sport-specific topics.

As there are many publications that collect and analyze sport-specific aspects according to countries, this could be a basis for real comparative studies. The best examples of reports of this kind are the publications by Hunt (*Games and Sport the World Around*) (1964), Vendien and Nixon (*The World Today in Health, Physical Education and Recreation*) (1968, 1981), and Johnson (*Sport and Physical Education Around the World*) (1980).

Two terms other than comparative physical education and foreign physical education must be distinguished (Nixon, 1970).

- *International physical education*, meaning cross-national relations and cooperation, as well as exchange of information and personnel (Haag, 1978; Johnson, 1980; Lowe, Kanin, & Strenk, 1978).
- *Developmental physical education*, meaning the dynamics and interactions of variables, especially related to developing countries (United States Delegation, 1976).

The clear distinction of foreign, international, and developmental physical education from comparative physical education contributes to a better understanding of the real meaning of comparative physical education. Very often, research is labeled as comparative without meeting the criteria for this research approach. This can be observed in spite of the fact that many scholars have dealt with aspects of research strategies and methods that should be employed in true comparative research as applied to physical education and sport (Anthony, 1966; Broom, 1971; Connell, 1959; Howell, Howell, & Toohey, 1979; ICCPES, 1979; Morrison, 1971).

It should also be stressed that the scope of research possibilities in comparative physical education is very broad, especially from a methodological point of view. It reaches from empirical methods (Foshay, 1963, 1964) to the philosophical approach (Lauwerys, 1959). In this connection it can be pointed out that all too often comparative education or physical education is linked very closely to just the theoretical-hermeneutic research approach, which is too limited, because the whole range of possible research methods and designs can be applied within the comparative research approach (Howell, 1971). This again implies the great opportunity for this kind of research to be promoted much more in the future.

References

Anthony, D.W. (1966). Physical education as an aspect of comparative education. *Gymnasion*, 3, 2, 3-6.

Baitsch, H., Grupe, O., & Lotz, F. (Eds.). (1972). *Sport im blickpunkt der wissenschaften*. Berlin, Heidelberg, New York: Springer.

Bennett, B.L., Howell, M.L., & Simri, U. (1975). *Comparative physical education and sport*. Philadelphia: Lea and Febiger.

Bereday, L. (1964). *Comparative method in education*. New York: Holt, Rinehart and Winston.

Beyer, E., & Röthig, P. (1976). *Beiträge zur gegenstandsbestimmung der sportpädagogik*. Schorndorf: Hofmann.

Bockelmann, H. (1970). Pädagogik, erziehung, erziehungswissenschaft. *HbpädGr Bd. II* (pp. 178-267). München: Kösel.

Brezinka, W. (1972). *Von der pädagogik zur erziehungswissenschaft*. Weinheim: Beltz.

Broom, E.F. (1971). An approach to comparative research. *Bibliographies and techniques*. Champaign, IL: Stipes.

Connell, W.F. (1959). The methodology of research in comparative education. In School of Education, New York University (Ed.), *Research in comparative education*. New York: New York University School of Education.

Fox, D.J. (1969). *The research process in education*. New York: Holt, Rinehart and Winston.

Grupe, O. (1969). *Grundlagen der sportpädagogik*. München: Barth.

Grupe, O. (1971). Einleitung in die sportwissenschaft. *Sportwissenschaft*, 1, 1, 3-9.

Haag, H. (1972). Sportpädagogik in den Vereinigten staaten. In H. Baitsch et al. (Eds.), *Sport im blickpunkt der wissenschaften* (pp. 173-180). Berlin, Heidelberg, New York: Springer.

Haag, H. (1976). Die bedeutung der sportinformatik für die sportwissenschaft. In J. Recla et al. (Eds.), *Kreative sportinformatic* (pp. 56-63). Schorndorf: Hofmann.

Haag, H. (1976). Inhaltsdimension der sportpädagogik. In H. Andrecs & S. Redl (Eds.), *Forschen-lehren-handeln* (pp. 22-33). Wien: Österr. Bundesverlag.

Haag, H. (1978). *Sport pedagogy. Content and methodology*. Baltimore, MD: University Park Press.

Haag, H. (1978). International dimensions of sport education and sport science. In B. Lowe, D.B. Kanin, & A. Strenk (Eds.), *Sport and international relations* (pp. 562-571, Bibliographie 587-613). Champaign, IL: Stipes.

Haag, H. (1979). Development and structure of a theoretical framework for sport science (sportwissenschaft). *Quest*, **31**, 1, 25-35.

Haag, H. (1982). Research methodology in sport science. Implication for the comparative research approach. In J. Pooley & C.A. Pooley (Eds.), *ISCPES-Halifax 1980* (pp. 89-110). Halifax: Dalhousie University.

Hans, N. (1951). *Comparative education*. London: Routledge and Kegan.

Henry, F.M. (1964). Physical education: An academic discipline. *Journal of Health, Physical Education, and Recreation, 7*, 32-33.

Howell, R., Howell, M.L., & Toohey, D.M. (Eds.). (1979). *Methodology in comparative physical education and sport*. Champaign, IL: Stipes.

Hunt, S.E. (1964). *Games and sport around the world*. New York: Ronald Press.

Johnson, W. (Ed.). (1980). *Sport and physical education around the world.* Champaign, IL: Stipes.

Kandel, J.L. (1933). *Comparative education.* New York: Houghton-Mifflin.

Kirsch, A. (1978). Research concept for sport pedagogy. In H. Haag (Ed.), *Sport pedagogy. Content and methodology* (pp. 111-114). Baltimore, MD: University Park Press.

Krotee, M.L. (1979). *Dimensions of sport sociology.* West Point, NY: Leisure Press.

Lotz, F. (Ed.). (1975). *Wissenschaft und ausbildung.* Schorndorf: Hofmann.

Lowe, B., Kanin, D.B., & Strenk, A. (Eds.). (1978). *Sport and international relations.* Champaign, IL: Stipes.

Meinberg, E. (1981). *Sportpädagogik. Konzepte und perspektiven.* Stuttgart: Kolhammer.

Menze, C.L. (1976). Die herauslösung der sportpädagogik aus der allgemeinen pädagogik. In G. Hecker et al. (Eds.), *Der mensch im sport* (pp. 72-84). Schorndorf: Hofmann.

Mester, L. (1973). Wechselbeziehungen zwischen sportpädagogik und erziehungswissenschaft. *Int. Zschr. f. Sportpädagogik, 20,* 1, 15-20.

Meusel, H. (1976). *Einführung in die sportpädagogik.* Müchen: UTB.

Morrison, D.H. (1971). The comparative approach to research in physical education and sport. *Bibliographies and techniques.* Champaign, IL: Stipes.

NCPEAM/NAPECW (Ed.). (1967). The nature of a discipline. *Quest IX.* Tucson, AZ.

NCPEAM/NAPECW (Ed.). (1968). Toward a theory of sport. *Quest X.* Tucson, AZ.

Nixon, J.E. (1970). Comparative, international, and developmental studies in physical education. *Gymnasion, 7,* 4-9.

Noah, H.J., & Eckstein, M.A. (1969). *Toward a science of comparative education.* New York: Macmillan.

Pooley, J., & Pooley, C.A. (Eds.). (1982). *ISCPES Halifax 1980.* Halifax: Dalhousie University.

Röhrs, H. (1969). *Allgemeine erziehungswissenschaft. Eine einführung in die erziehungswissenschaftlichen aufgaben und methoden.* Weinheim: Beltz.

Schmitz, J.N. (1973). Fachdidaktik und curriculumtheorie in der sportwissenschaft. *Sportwissenschaft, 3,* 251-276.

Schmitz, J.N. (1979). *Allgemeine grundlagen der sportpädagogik. Grundbegriffe-problemfeld-zielproblematik.* Schorndorf: Hofmann.

Simri, U. (1974). *Concepts of physical education and sport science.* Wingate, Israel: Wingate Institute.

Singer, R.N., et al. (1972). *Physical education: An interdisciplinary approach.* New York: Macmillan.

Toohey, D.M. (1979). Research in comparative physical education: Some interdisciplinary considerations. *Quest, 31,* 1, 6-11.

Vendien, C.L., & Nixon, J.E. (Eds.). (1968). *The world today in health, physical education and recreation.* Englewood Cliffs, NJ: Prentice-Hall.

Wehle, J. (Ed.). (1973). Lexikon pädagogischer Schlagworte und begriffe. 3 Bde. *Pädagogik aktuell.* München: Kösel.

Widmer, K. (1977). *Sportpädagogik. Prolegomena zur theoretischen begründung der sportpädagogik als wissenschaft.* Schorndorf: Hofmann.

Willimczik, K. (1968). *Wissenschaftstheoretische aspekte einer sportwissenschaft.* Frankfurt: Limpert.

Comparative Research in Education: What, Why, and How

John J. Cogan
University of Minnesota

> The comparative study of education is not a discipline; it is a context.
> (Broadfoot, 1977, p. 133)

The statement above reflects the position of this writer with respect to the field. This chapter will focus on three questions: (a) What is comparative education? (b) Why study education in a comparative fashion? and (c) How might this be done? In the limited space available only brief attention can be given to each of the three questions. However, where appropriate, reference will be made to more detailed sources of information for the reader.

Several caveats are also in order. First, I am not trained as a professional in the field of physical education and sport. My roots are in social science education and in international and comparative education specifically. Second, given my background, I will not be able to give many specific examples from physical education to illustrate points and, thus, will discuss comparative research in education in more general terms. I will leave others who are trained as specialists to draw specific relationships to physical education and sport.

What is Comparative Education?

In some respects the comparative study of education is very new, and yet, if one looks carefully its origins can be traced back as far as the Greco-Roman period. Greek slaves were carefully sought out by Romans to tutor their children. The Romans studied the Greek methods and gradually incorporated them into their system. Halfway around the world, the Japanese carefully studied Chinese education and, in the main, adopted the Chinese characters for their written symbol system. There are many other instances as well.

In colonial America, Horace Mann, generally regarded as the father of American education, studied Prussian schools seeking possible innovations for his Massachusetts schools. In the 19th century, comparative study was used in the development of basic educational institutions such as universities, teacher training schools, and technical institutes. In the

20th century comparison of educational practices aided in the universalization of particular institutions such as elementary and secondary schools. It also allowed educators, particularly in Europe and North America, to trace emerging educational trends on both sides of the Atlantic. Thus, early efforts in the area of comparative education were aimed at borrowing from one another, largely without regard to whether or not the borrowed practice actually fit into the cultural system adopting it.

Although the comparative study of education can be traced back over several centuries, it is only since World War II that the area has sought to regard itself as a specific area of inquiry. During the past 3 decades a great debate has focused on exactly how the field should define itself. The debate continues even today and is best summarized in the following statement (Kelly, Altbach, & Arnove, 1982, p. 505).

> Unlike other fields, such as history, sociology, economics, and psychology, whose subject matter and methodologies have been well defined, comparative education in the past thirty years has had to develop a rationale for existence as a scholarly endeavor as well as to define its content and methodological parameters. Because of this and the field's diverse and broad clientele, comparative education has been eclectic and has failed to develop one single, widely accepted method of inquiry; moreover it has not established a unitary body of knowledge. Rather comparative education remains a field characterized by methodological debates and diversity of opinion as to what constitutes its subject matter and orientation.

This debate might be characterized by the question: What is comparative education, a method or a content? Various scholars and leaders in the field have taken differing stances on this question (Anderson, 1961; Bereday, 1964; Carnoy, 1974; Holmes, 1965; Kazamias, 1972; King, 1968; Noah & Eckstein, 1969). In addition, two special issues of the most prestigious journals in the field of comparative education, both published in 1977, describe the current state of the field as it is viewed in North America and in Great Britain (*CIES*, 1977; *Comparative Education*, 1977). Both of these are necessary background reading to understand the nature of this continuing debate.

As noted at the outset of this chapter, this author characterizes the field as a context in which comparative study can take place. The strength of the field is that (a) it draws scholars from many discipline areas related to education; (b) it utilizes a host of methodologies, although it still depends primarily on those from the social sciences; and (c) it utilizes a variety of contexts for investigations. Thus, the comparative study of education is more general and doesn't suffer from the narrow constraints of specialization, which so many disciplines labor under today. This writer views this as a strength, not as a shortcoming. King (1979, p. 84) supports this view.

> Comparative education can provide an arena where representatives of different disciplines come together to their mutual benefit, forcing investigators out of their narrow specializations. The field has often been considered a natural

candidate for interdisciplinary work by reason of the particular problems and data it treats. Indeed, many of the important topics that fall to comparative education can be handled satisfactorily only in an interdisciplinary manner. . . . [No] study of education and national development is conceivable solely within the confines of a single discipline; it must draw from a wide range of behavioral and social sciences.

For the purposes of this chapter, then, the comparative study of education will be defined as a context in which research related to educational practice, planning, policy making, theory construction, and decision making takes place. A number of research methodologies are appropriate to carry out investigations.

This interdisciplinary approach should certainly incorporate the field of physical education and sport, which is such an integral part of nearly all societies. It is an area that seems to bring people together, the recent problems of Olympiads notwithstanding. The potential for cooperative research appears unlimited.

Why Study Education Comparatively?

Even if the question of the "what" of comparative education were adequately addressed, and it has not been, the more important question still remains. Why study education comparatively? When discussing what functions are served by comparative study, three are generally cited (King, 1979, p. 31).

1. [To] inform and sensitize people eager to study the workings of education in a variety of alternative contexts.
2. [To] aid analysis of educational phenomena, trends, and problems.
3. [To] guide educational decision and development with increasing recognition of socioeconomic and political repercussions.

During the past decade, educational decision makers have made increasing use of comparative education research results. The monumental International Educational Achievement (IEA) studies of the late 1960s and early 1970s are a case in point. Broadfoot (1977, p. 136) points out the advantages of such studies to educational decision makers.

Firstly, they can provide internationally consistent data on the effects of different educational practices where this can be obtained. Secondly, in providing detailed case-studies which reveal how the internal dynamics of education systems influence the idiosyncratic effects of educational practices in any particular context comparative studies can provide planners with ways of analyzing the likely outcomes of any innovation in their own society. Thirdly, and most fundamentally, comparative studies can stimulate questioning of the basic assumptions under which any education system operates. Any one of these three roles would be a sufficient justification for comparative studies in education. Taken together they are overwhelming.

Although the above statement provides a strong rationale for the comparative study of education, one must also consider the strengths and the problems inherent in such study. Among its strengths, it allows us to

- extend the range of variables of a theoretical interest beyond that which is possible in a study based only on one society,
- test the generalizability of a finding based on data from one society,
- replicate the findings based on one society or a small number of similar societies, and
- empirically test theories that specify societal-level characteristics as variables.

There are also specific problems in using the comparative method of which the researcher must be aware.

- What we see or understand in the phenomena of some other system of education may not be recognized in the same terms by alternative observers or the indigenous users of that system. We come to the situation with our cultural blinders firmly in place.
- Much will depend for its reliability and validity upon the value judgments of those involved in the educational action or decision we observe.
- When people plan education inside cultural situations different from their own, they suffer from cultural bias in their observations and even in their rational processes; this occurs not only because of indoctrination from childhood, but because they see a different map of what is feasible or normal within their system and its resources.

The latter point speaks specifically to the area of context. Researchers will approach comparative studies with varying degrees of sophistication and background about the "context" in which they will be conducting their study. For the researcher to truly carry out a quality study, it is essential that he or she understand the context, societally, culturally, and educationally, if the study results are to have merit and generalizability. King (1979, p. 52) elaborates on this point.

> The central and abiding need is to "get inside the context" by any means at the level required for the study contemplated, and to be true to it constantly. That means true factual knowledge, fidelity to the *system* understood by the natives, and empathy for the problems seen by them. There is no substitute for this kind of knowledge. No comparative analysis is true without it.

Having a thorough grounding, not only in the research methodology to be employed but also in the context of the study is critical to its success. Often this means spending an extended period of time in the other societal or cultural context before initiating a study. Collaborating with someone from within the context society can also help alleviate these difficulties.

What Kind of Methodology Should Be Employed?

As noted in earlier parts of this chapter, a number of different methodological approaches have been utilized in the comparative study of education. In the following pages three of the more common approaches will be discussed. I believe these approaches are most applicable to the field of physical education and sport.

Survey

The most common research methodology employed in comparative studies of education is the survey. It is a distinctive research methodology, which owes much of its recent development to the discipline of sociology. The survey is often used to determine present conditions or trends and compare present conditions with those of the past. The researcher makes use of direct observations or consults sources that can provide current, accurate data, such as statistical abstracts, primary records, and so forth.

In addition to direct observation, surveys make use of interviews, questionnaires, and tests. The survey method can help to gather factual data or to suggest cause-and-effect relationships; it cannot reveal what are necessarily optimum conditions. Thus it is descriptive rather than prescriptive.

There are two kinds of surveys that are commonly employed in comparative studies, the cross-sectional and the longitudinal. In a cross-sectional survey, data are gathered or measurements are made at the same time for all persons or groups being studied. This allows for large-scale sampling and has the advantage of economy of time. However, it assumes that all groups or individuals selected for the study are comparable. This may not always be an accurate assumption. The researcher will need to try and reduce this negative factor as much as possible through careful use of scientific sampling techniques.

In the longitudinal survey, data are gathered over an extended period of time so that growth and change within individuals or groups can be measured. The obvious strength of this type of survey is that because the same subjects are being observed or measured repeatedly, they are comparable; indeed, they are identical. Equally obvious are the negative factors in longitudinal sampling. First, there is the increased cost. Because measurements or observations are made over a period of time, the researcher must wait until the appropriate comparative data are available before being able to draw conclusions or develop hypotheses for further study. Second, there is the problem of keeping track of your research population. If too many of your sample move and can't be traced, you may be faced with an inadequate sample; thus, the validity and reliability of the conclusions could be questioned.

Case Study

The case study is an intensive study of an individual, group, institution, or issue at one particular point in time or over a period of time. It is descriptive in nature much like the survey. It is an attempt to gain a depth of understanding, whereas the survey often only describes people or issues at a surface level. The case study would seem to be very appropriate to the field of physical education and sport in the study of such institutions as the Olympics. It could be used to study the games historically in search of certain trends or recurring themes and, also, to study the relationship between sport and political issues, which has crept into the games during the past several Olympiads. Is this a new phenomena, or has this occurred throughout the history of the games? Similar case studies could focus on the amateur versus professional status of athletes participating in the games, issues surrounding World Cup play, or regional activities such as the Asian or Commonwealth games.

Cross-Cultural Study

This is generally a study that tests hypotheses designed to contribute to a theory. By testing hypotheses in a culture in addition to one's own, a greater degree of generality can be obtained. One must, however, be aware of the shortcomings of such a study; cultural bias can easily creep in if one is not careful.

In conducting such a study, one must first determine the theoretical structure to be employed. Then the selection of an appropriate cultural context in which to test the hypotheses must be made. The culture chosen should be distinctive and accessible. Again, time will be required to become familiar with the culture before subjects can be selected, and this familiarization period cannot be underestimated. Failure to understand the people, institutions, and cultural attributes of the society in which the study is being carried out could result in less than expected success or, perhaps, even a total breakdown of the research process.

Further, when reporting the results of a cross-cultural study, one must be careful not to interpret findings solely on the basis of one's own cultural perspective. One way to overcome this potential trouble area is to collaborate with a colleague in the context country.

These three methodologies represent only some of the more common approaches to comparative research endeavors. Other experimental and quasi-experimental designs are appropriate as well (Campbell & Stanley, 1963). Recently futurist models have been employed in comparative studies of education as well. They attempt to predict future trends and needs and are especially useful to educational planners (Poolpatarachewin, 1980; Textor, 1980).

Conducting a Survey Study

In the remaining pages I would like to take the first model discussed above, the survey, and describe how to approach such a study. As noted previously, this is one of the most commonly used research techniques employed in comparative studies.

Planning the Study

The value of a study depends largely upon how thoroughly the research problem has been thought out at the outset. Ideas take shape against the background knowledge one has; the more extensive that knowledge, the more likely the ideas considered will be of value.

The most effectively designed studies are an outgrowth of what others have already studied. The researcher should begin with a general idea and then widely discover how others have approached the topic issue. As one reads, he begins to form tentative questions or hypotheses which help to define the problem to be studied more precisely. Reading brings the general topic into sharper focus and shows how it may be best examined. Then the problem must be framed in a way that makes it accessible. It should be kept in mind that a conclusive finding on a relatively restricted aspect of a problem is of more value than an investigation that fails to reach a firm conclusion because it tries to cover too much. This planning stage obviously requires time, but pays dividends later. No amount of sophisticated analysis can derive worthwhile results from a poorly designed study, and the researcher should not underestimate the importance of this first stage of the research process.

Criteria for Problem Selection

There are several criteria that one might consider when selecting a research problem. First, is the problem or topic of interest? One should select a problem that not only interests the investigator, but has some probability of concerning other members of the scientific community as well. Second, can the study be carried out with the funds available? It is important to determine this before beginning a study. Third, is the study unique? Does it have the potential of adding new knowledge to the field? Fourth, do you, as a researcher, have the necessary skills to carry out the study?

Sampling

Once the research problem or topic has been selected, the investigator will have to select an appropriate population. Because of the difficulty of studying an entire population, one usually selects a population sample by means that ensure unbiased, suitably close estimates of the relevant characteristics of the entire population. A sample is unbiased when elements are drawn in some random manner. Unbiased samples approximate parameters as additional cases are drawn. Biased samples, on the other hand, consistently underestimate or overestimate parameters.

There are several kinds of sampling techniques, for example, simple random sampling, stratified random sampling, systematic sampling, and area or cluster sampling. The researcher should consult any basic, educational research-design textbook to determine which technique is most appropriate for the study being planned.

Data Gathering

After the sample has been drawn, the next step is to decide whether interviews or questionnaires will be used to gather the data. The researcher should be aware of the strengths and weaknesses of each technique.

Interview Schedule.   The interview is a direct, face-to-face measure for gaining verbal responses from respondents. It has a number of advantages as a data gathering technique.

- It allows the interviewer to clarify questions.
- It can be used with those who have reading problems, for example, young children or illiterates.
- It allows informants to respond such that they can enlarge upon, retract, or question items presented to them.
- It allows the interviewer to observe nonverbal, as well as verbal, behavior.
- It is a useful means of obtaining personal information, attitudes, perceptions, and beliefs.
- It reduces anxiety so that potentially threatening topics can be studied.

There are also some disadvantages to using the interview technique.

- Unstructured interviews often yield data that are difficult to summarize and/or evaluate.
- The cost of the study is increased by the necessities of training interviewers, sending them to meet and interview their informants, and evaluating their effectiveness.
- Interviews sometimes do not distinguish accurately between fact and opinion.
- Generally, only a small sample can be reached unless unlimited funds are available. It is a costly procedure.

In order to be reliable, interview sessions should be as constant as possible from respondent to respondent. Questions to be asked should be carefully thought out before the interviewing process begins and organized in the form of a schedule. This means that all respondents will be asked the same questions, in the same order, and under as uniform conditions as possible. In addition, if more than one person is going to be conducting the interviews, training sessions should be conducted to reduce and hopefully eliminate errors. All interviewers should do several trial runs, preferably with the same individuals, to ensure uniformity of style. Careful attention should also be paid to the recording of responses. If possible, interview sessions should be taperecorded to provide uniformity of recording and accuracy of reporting.

Interviewers should also be aware of biasing factors in using this technique. Because interviewers have to interact with informants, they may influence the direction and intensity of the informants' statements. Some variables that have been shown to influence the responses of interviews include the interviewer's age, educational level, experience in interviewing, racial background, religious background, sex, and socioeconomic level.

Questionnaires. The questionnaire is the best alternative to the interview and is widely used by scholars in a variety of disciplines. The technique has some distinct advantages as well as several serious shortcomings. Among the advantages are economy and standardization. Many more respondents can be surveyed for the same cost as that incurred in the interview, and if the instrument is carefully written and structured, each respondent receives the same set of questions phrased in exactly the same way. Even the best trained interviewers often have difficulty maintaining this kind of standardization.

The disadvantages of using questionnaires can present challenges to the researcher. These are not insurmountable, but they are something to consider when deciding whether to use the interview or questionnaire technique.

- Respondent motivation is difficult to assess, because the investigator doesn't always meet the respondents face-to-face.
- Language can present a problem, as there is an assumed ability of the respondents to read and write. Also assumed is an understanding of terminology cross-culturally, which may or may not be accurate.
- Sampling may be inaccurate, because if a random sampling of returns is not obtained, those that are completed and returned may represent biased samples.
- Lack of standardization in the conditions under which the respondents answer questions may exist, especially if the same person is not administering all questionnaires.
- The meanings of questionnaire items may differ for various respondents, who have no way to clarify the intended meanings.

Once the data is gathered the investigator must then select appropriate statistical measures to analyze the results and prepare a report of the findings. As noted earlier, surveys are descriptive, but they often raise questions or give the researcher background information that can be utilized in pursuing a more experimental study.

Summary

This chapter has been an attempt to briefly examine the nature of the comparative study of education, to review some of the more common research methods employed in comparative study, and to describe the conduct of a survey study. Comparative research is increasingly more common as colleagues from all over the world seek to solve common problems and learn from each other. The field of physical education and sport seems a rich, yet largely untapped, area for this kind of collaboration.

References

Anderson, C.A. (1961). Methodology of comparative education. *International Review of Education*, **7**, 1-23.

Bereday, G.Z.F. (1964). *Comparative method in education*. New York: Holt, Rinehart and Winston.

Broadfoot, P. (1977). The comparative contribution—A research perspective. *Comparative Education*, **13**, 133-138.

Campbell, T.D., & Stanley, C.J. (1963). *Experimental and quasi-experimental design for research*. Chicago: Rand McNally.

Carnoy, M. (1974). *Education as cultural imperialism*. New York: McKay.

Comparative education: Its present state and future prospects. (1977). *Comparative Education*, **13**, 75-132.

Comparative and International Education Society (CIES). (1977). The state of the art: Twenty years of comparative education. *Comparative Education Review*, **21**, 151-420.

Holmes, B. (1965). *Problems in education: A comparative approach*. London: Routledge and Kegan.

Kazamias, A.M. (1972). Comparative pedagogy. *Comparative Education Review*, **16**, 406-411.

Kelly, G.P., Altbach, P.G., & Arnove, R.F. (Eds.). (1982). Trends in comparative education: A critical analysis. *Comparative education*. New York: Macmillan.

King, E.J. (1968). *Comparative studies and educational decision making*. London: Methuen.

King, E.J. (1979). *Other schools and ours* (5th ed.). London: Holt, Rinehart and Winston.

Noah, H., & Eckstein, M. (1969). *Toward a sense of comparative education*. New York: Macmillan.

Poolpatarachewin, C. (1980). *Alternative futures of Thai universities*. Unpublished paper, University of Minnesota.

Textor, R.B. (1980). *A handbook on ethnographic futures research*. Stanford, CA: Stanford University.

A Comparative and Cross-Cultural View of the Study of the Quality of Life

March L. Krotee
William M. Bart
University of Minnesota

The study of comparative physical education and sport can be enriched by certain other fields of inquiry. Two such fields are the study of the quality of life and comparative and cross-cultural education. The purpose of this paper is to detail some of the prominent benefits for the profession of physical education and sport from the study of these two fields. To explore these benefits, a conceptual framework provided by Bart (1981) on the nature of the quality of life will be liberally utilized and augmented primarily by ideas of Krotee and LaPoint (1979) on the same topic.

A key concept being addressed is that of the quality of life, a vital attribute of human existence that serves not only as a common denominator of humanity, but also as an attribute that deserves to be improved in every human society. When viewed as a variable, the quality of life appears to be ordinally scaled. Thus, an individual or a people could be said to possess low, middle, or high quality of life, and the qualities of life of two individuals or groups may be ordinally compared. But more precise methods of quantifying the quality of life need to be investigated as to their conceptual merits in order to identify an acceptable method of measuring the quality of life that will permit any changes in that quality to be validly and precisely assessed. The nature of the quality of life thus needs to be scrutinized across peoples and cultures in order for effective procedures to be formulated that will permit its management and improvement.

As a step in such scrutiny, let us contend that the quality of life has three essential components—happiness, development, and adaptation—all of which are personal characteristics. In other words, if an individual has a high quality of life, then that individual primarily has experiences (a) that are enjoyable and pleasurable and that engender positive affect of various autotelic forms, (b) that permit the actualization and utilization of his or her physical and psychosocial needs, and (c) that permit the acquisition of new physical and psychosocial resources that allow adaptation to specific environmental situations. These three components of the quality of life are conceptually distinct to a great extent, but tend to overlap and be interdependent in nature.

But how are these essential components of the quality of life related to physical education and sport and comparative and cross-cultural education? How can these components be improved and increased? To probe these questions, alternative conceptions of the quality of life need to be examined in order to identify additional aspects of the nature of that quality, which may be embodied even in faulty or unorthodox conceptions and can only be revealed through critique.

The Money Principle

One widely held view of the quality of life is termed the money principle. According to this principle, *the quality of life is directly related to economic wealth*. Figure 1 graphically depicts this relationship.

The money principle has tremendous appeal, as it attributes an economic basis to the quality of life. It is a prominent guiding principle in social policy, which relates economics, the most influential social science in the 20th century, to utopianism, the belief in the perfectibility of human society.

One attractive feature of the money principle is that it is quantifiable in that it holds that an individual's quality of life is directly proportional to the sum total of the economic values of all of the marketable possessions of that individual. Marketable possessions consist of monetary possessions, material possessions, and occupational skills. Other attractive features of the money principle are its simplicity, practicality, and explanatory capacity.

According to the money principle, the quality of life is determined by the availability of material objects and experiences that provide happi-

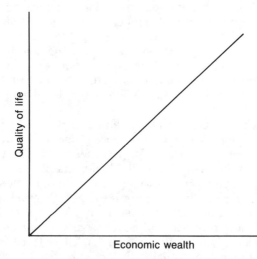

Figure 1   Relationship between the quality of life and economic wealth.

ness, development, and adaptation. Such material objects and exotelic experiences are only those that have specific monetary values. Thus, to increase personal quality of life, an individual should increase his or her marketable possessions so that he or she is better able to afford experiences that provide enjoyment, development, and adaptation. In fact, the economic technique of cost-benefit analysis can be used effectively to select courses of action that increase personal quality of life by comparing the costs to the benefits of various courses of action and, then, by choosing those courses of action in which the benefits exceed the costs to the greatest degree. In doing cost-benefit analysis, both the costs and benefits of actions can take the form of monetary items, physical objects, occupational skills, time, and other exotelic entities that can be readily translated into monetary value.

The consequences of the money principle for physical education and sport are that traditionally participants in physical activity and sport tend to learn and practice forms of physical exercise that are psychosocially related to economic wealth. Those forms would vary, of course, from one culture to another. In a country such as Brazil, soccer may be the sport most compatible with the money principle; whereas, in Japan, baseball may be the most representative, as would cricket in India, field hockey in Pakistan, football in Australia, and perhaps ice hockey in the state of Minnesota in the United States. Comparative and cross-cultural education could and should be consulted to identify those forms of learning and knowledge that would be crucial for the economic well-being and development of the state, and physical education and sport programs could be fashioned to enhance the economic productivity of the participants while complying with the economic growth plan of the state. But should all physical education and sports programs be directed to economic ends? A related question is whether the money principle is the best principle to guide efforts at improving the quality of life. Comparative physical education and sport must seek to attain a data bank to provide a basis for formulating and choosing viable models for the improvement of the quality of life not only in individual countries, but also across regions and cultures.

Sociologist Jacques Ellul (1964), in his book, *The Technological Society*, argued that contentment and not happiness is encouraged in contemporary technological societies. Psychologist Angus Campbell (1976), in a report in the *American Psychologist*, provided evidence that the quality of life does not lie in the objective circumstances of life. Hans Selye (1975) further suggests that "the secret of health and happiness lies in the successful adjustment to changing conditions, the penalties for failure in this process of adaptation are disease and unhappiness." There are sufficient instances of mental health problems and high cardiovascular risk among the wealthy and of high quality of life among certain groups with modest economic means to discredit the money principle in this context. In addition, compliance with the money principle guarantees neither happiness, the actualization and utilization of physical and social capabilities, the satisfaction of physical and psychosocial needs, nor the development of new physical and psychosociological resources. The human is not *homo faber* alone, but *homo festivus* and *homo fantasia* as well—one who not only works and thinks, but who also plays, pretends, dreams, celebrates, and dances (Cox, 1969).

The Possessions Principle

Another principle that retains many of the features of the money principle is that of the possessions principle. One needs to examine the relationship between the money principle and acquisitiveness, that is, the basic need among humans to acquire and hold possessions, in that the acquisition of marketable possessions enhances the quality of life. Acquisitiveness can be narrowly interpreted as the need among humans to acquire and hold marketable possessions, which have readily determined monetary values; or it can be liberally interpreted as the need among humans to acquire and hold possessions, which may be either marketable or not. The restricted interpretation of acquisitiveness, which emphasizes the accumulation of economic wealth, is a view most compatible with the money principle, as it equates the personal value of a possession with the economic value of that possession. The liberal interpretation of acquisitiveness is a view less compatible with the money principle, as it permits the personal value of a possession to be markedly different from its economic value. The liberal interpretation of acquisitiveness also provides the basis for an alternative principle underlying the quality of life. That alternative principle is termed the possessions principle, which holds that *the quality of life is directly related to the accumulated value of a total set of possessions.*

To clarify the possessions principle, one should examine the four domains of personal possessions. Figure 2 depicts these domains.

Personal possessions can be classified according to their form (physical or psychosocial) and position (external or internal). Personal possessions form four domains: (a) external physical possessions, which include money, food, shelter, and other tangibles; (b) external psychosocial possessions, which include friendships, acquaintances, and social relations; (c) internal physical possessions, which include senses, muscles, psychomotor skills, and other bodily entities; and (d) internal psychosocial possessions, which include cognitive skills, knowledge, affective states, and other entities of a psychosocial nature.

All external physical possessions have market values, but there are some possessions in the other three domains that do not have readily determined market values. Those possessions in the other three domains that do have market values tend to constitute occupational skills. Thus, in determining the quality of life, the possessions principle acknowledges the importance of possessions that do not have market values as well as those that do have market values.

The possessions principle is not as simple and practical as the money principle. It certainly is not readily quantifiable in that the personal values attached to certain psychosocial resources and capabilities are not easily

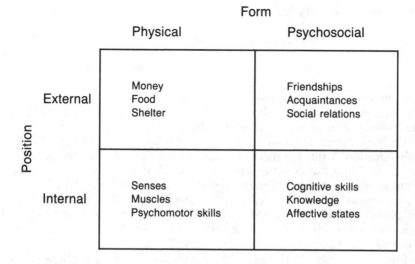

Figure 2   Examples of the four domains of personal possessions.

quantified. It is more explanatory than the money principle, however, in being able to explain why an individual with modest economic means can strive for and attain a high quality of life. There are many ways, many being of a psychosocial nature, in which the value of an individual's life can improve and increase, thus permitting an increase in that individual's quality of life.

The consequences of the possessions principle for physical education and sport are that participants should learn and practice as many forms across the physical education and sport continuum as possible. These forms may vary from one culture to another, but the more choices available the better. Comparative and cross-cultural physical educators should be consulted to identify additional forms of physical education and sport that could be assimilated into existing traditional programs. This course of action has tremendous implications for curricular innovation and coordination with other subject matter areas in the effort to enculturate the participant and to present a series of instructional learning experiences through the physical education and sporting process. But are quantity and variety the key ideas to guide physical education and sports programs? A related question is whether the possessions principle is the best principle to guide efforts at improving the quality of life. In other words, are the accumulation and diversification of possessions sufficient to guarantee a high quality of life? To answer that question, one must consider the nature and function of a possession. The personal value of a possession tends to lie not in its mere ownership, but rather in its usage in permitting the occurrence of worthwhile experiences. Continued accumulation of possessions tends to decrease the likelihood that any one possession will be used to provide some worthwhile experience.

Simplicity Principle

But if the possessions principle has explanatory inadequacies, what principle would be a better candidate to guide efforts to improve the quality of life? To answer this question, one should first consider more viable revisions of the previous two principles. The money principle could be reformulated into the following proposition: *Some level of economic wealth is a prerequisite to a high quality of life.* The possessions principle could also be reformulated into another proposition: *Some set of possessions from each of the four domains of personal possessions is a prerequisite to a high quality of life.*

In addition, acquisitiveness could be reformulated from a consideration of the fact that humans need sensory stimulation for survival. Acquisitiveness thus could be reformulated as the following: *There is a basic need among humans to receive various forms of stimulation on a regular basis in order for various cognitive, affective, and psychomotor capabilities to be practiced.* Possessions, then, serve as the basis for sensory stimulation of various sorts on a regular basis.

Possessions vary in the extent to which they provide desirable forms of sensory stimulation. Thus, being selective in choosing possessions becomes highly important. But what guidelines can be provided in the acquisition of possessions that will increase the quality of life? The authors recommend that the human body, which bears our biological heritage, provides many cues as to which possessions should be acquired. Internal physical possessions, such as the vital organs, are inherited and should be developed, exercised, and maintained. Internal psychosocial possessions, such as the cognitive processes of attention, encoding, self-monitoring, information retention, and information retrieval that constitute actualizations of human neurological and psychomotor capabilities, should also be developed, practiced, and maintained. All other possessions should be selected on the basis of their compatibility with the inherited internal possessions. In other words, humans are contended to have a basic nature established by biological evolution, and that basic nature is embodied in the structure of the human body, which provides a blueprint for an ideal society. Manmade environments are, then, inadequate to the extent to which humans are not happy, not fulfilled, and not fully developed; those environments should, then, be reconstituted to increase human happiness, fulfillment, and development. This contention should provide the profession of physical education and sport with transnational guidelines to better meet the needs of the individuals whom it serves.

The opportune utilization of inherited internal possessions can often result in experiences of enjoyment. For example, the utilization of analytic reasoning skills to solve a problem can lead to a positive feeling state associated with mastery and competence; whereas, the utilization of holistic reasoning skills to identify new phenomena or new relationships can trigger positive affective states of discovery and surprise (Bart, 1980; Krotee, 1976, 1977a). Each of the senses, when stimulated, can trigger peculiar forms of satisfaction. In fact, all forms of happiness result from the utilization of some inherited internal possessions. Thus, all programs directed toward improving the quality of life should have as their central goal the opportune and regular utilization and maintenance of inherited internal possessions. This goal is closely related to the goal of optimal brain stimulation or psychomotor functioning (Krotee, 1976, 1977b). Some internal personal possessions need to be used on either external or other internal possessions to produce desirable forms of stimulation. Personal possessions, then, form a system such that certain combinations of them can be used interactively to provide optimal brain stimulation. As can be determined by the domains of personal possessions, physical education and sport can be valuable in the development of the total human being, resulting in a more positive interrelatedness quality that would lay a foundation for the proper attitudinal framework that would permit awareness, appreciation, and understanding across and within cultures.

With these comments as background, a third principle, to be termed the simplicity principle, can be formulated to guide efforts at improving the quality of life for both individuals and societies. The simplicity principle states that *the quality of life is directly related to the extent to which personal possessions are used interactively to develop and maintain inherited internal possessions and to produce optimal brain stimulation on a regular basis.*

Although this principle is not as simple, quantifiable, and practical as the previous two, it is explanatory, as it accounts for how happiness, fulfillment, and development could regularly occur. The simplicity principle has certain interesting consequences. For example, it becomes important not merely to acquire possessions of any sort, but to acquire only those possessions that are compatible with the utilization of inherited internal possessions and that maximize personal happiness, fulfillment, and development. Each human, ideally, needs a limited set of personal possessions that have been carefully selected. A major task, then, is to identify which possessions each person needs to insure a high quality of life.

Given that many of our social environments are in harmony with the money principle, we will be encouraged to acquire possessions, many of which will not contribute to our quality of life. Thus, each of us must be highly selective and choose possessions that are compatible with the utilization of inherited internal possessions. In order to do that, we will have to become aware of our inherited internal possessions and their uses. To develop such an awareness, the authors recommend educational programs on the quality of life and a period of disengagement in which the individual withdraws from the many superficial and seemingly excessive culturally imposed dependencies, such as television viewing, video game playing, and cigarette and alcohol consumption. Through disengagement, the individual objectifies his or her inherited internal possessions and is liberated from false needs and superficial dependencies (Marcuse, 1964). After an awareness and understanding of inherited internal possessions is developed, the individual can be fully re-engaged into the cultural flux of society and again acquire and utilize possessions, but in a much more selective and rational manner than before disengagement. It is strongly contended that individuals who comply with the simplicity principle to improve their quality of life will be highly productive and contributive to society as a whole, and their activities will contribute to the quality of life of others. In addition, those technologies that will be compatible with and serve to facilitate the development of inherited internal possessions will most likely endure and be successful.

It is anticipated that quality of life programs will be developed that focus on the development of inherited internal possessions, and a step in that direction is the formation of health maintenance or wellness type programs that focus on the maintenance of inherited physical and psychosocial possessions. Viable quality of life programs will be developed to the extent to which the integrated scientific study of the quality of life can be promoted and research on the quality of life and its underlying complex systems of human-environment interaction is instituted and completed. Such inquiry requires now, and will continue to require, the services of many individuals who are willing, in the words of Thomas Merton (1973), "to concentrate more on the quality of life and its mystery, and thus to escape in some measure from the senseless tyranny of quantity."

The consequences of the simplicity principle for physical education and sport are that each student should learn and practice forms of physical exercise and sport that custom fit his or her unique set of internal possessions and that permit that student to experience happiness, adaptation, and development. Each student should be assessed to determine what his or her unique set of physical and psychosocial skills are, and then forms of physical education and sport could be prescribed for that individual that seem best suited to that set of internal personal possessions. With the advent of microcomputers and advances in physiological and psychosocial testing, such individualized programs of physical education and sport could be a reality for multitudes of people. It is hoped that, in accordance with the simplicity principle, programs of physical education and sport could markedly improve the quality of life of hosts of individuals throughout the world. It is also hoped that more comparative and cross-cultural inquiry will be instituted to explore how physical education and sport can improve the qualities of individual life and, in turn, the general quality of life in each society.

The ramifications for physical education and sport in the comparative context are to identify the cultural variations, similarities, and interrelations regarding the process and nature of physical education and sport, as well as to establish reliable data concerning the potential patterns of physical education and human societal function and interaction. A sound and systematic study of the physical education and sport phenomenon, the individuals it includes and excludes, and the underlying principles of the quality of life across cultures must be addressed in an accelerated fashion in order to keep pace with the global interrelatedness of human potential and the full realization of the development of humanity.

References

Bart, W. (1980). *Developmental and neurological implications for relating cognition and affect.* Paper presented at the meeting of the American Educational Research Association, Boston, MA.

Bart, W. (1981). Simplicity: A perspective on the quality of life. In G. Lasker (Ed.), *Applied systems and cybernetics: Vol. 1. The quality of life: Systems approaches.* New York: Pergamon.

Campbell, A. (1976). Subjective measures of well-being. *American Psychologist, 32,* 117-124.

Ellul, J. (1964). *The technological society.* New York: Alfred Knopf.

Hayes, H. (1928). *Our economic system.* New York: Henry Holt.

Krotee, M. (1976). *The psychological impact of movement education.* Paper presented at the Symposium on Sports Psychology, Philadelphia, PA.

Krotee, M. (1977a). *The effect of movement on the young child.* Paper presented at the National College of Physical Education for Men and Women, Orlando, FL.

Krotee, M. (1977b). *Perceptual motor performance and academic achievement.* Paper presented at the meeting of the Central District of the American Alliance for Health, Physical Education, and Recreation, Cheyenne, WY.

Krotee, M., & LaPoint, J. (1979). Sociological perspectives underlying participation in physical activity. In M. Krotee (Ed.), *The dimensions of sport sociology.* West Point, NY: Leisure Press.

Marcuse, H. (1964). *One-dimensional man.* Boston: Beacon Press.

Merton, T. (1973). *Contemplation in a world of action.* Garden City, NY: Image Books.

Selye, H. (1975). *The stress of life.* New York: McGraw-Hill.

Qualitative Aspects of the Comparative Study of Sport and Physical Culture

Martti T. Silvennoinen
University of Jyväskylä

Modern sports culture can be considered as a part of a larger whole, of physical culture, regardless of whether we are studying and analyzing the latter or not. Physical culture is a whole that embodies the relationship between the physical and the spiritual typical of our time, as well as a whole ethos of the body.

By means of the comparative study of sports and physical cultures, we can attempt to find functional equivalences in different communities. This pertains equally to both the quantitative and qualitative paradigms. These functional equivalences, however, must preexist as natural social phenomena. They cannot be created or manipulated.

The quantitative paradigm focuses on features and qualities that are measurable in terms of amounts. This presupposes the development of exact categories and/or pattern variables, which are functionally equivalent in modern sport throughout all industrialized cultures.

The qualitative paradigm, through its method of study, aims at an understanding and interpretation of processes. The most proper object of study of the qualitative method is physical culture—the social and cultural aspects of corporeality and the control over the body that it conveys. These aspects can be studied and compared (a) in communities that are at different levels with respect to their degree of "civilization" and (b) as a general genetic-historical process of "civilization." Without a historical understanding of corporeality, it is hard to develop a wide understanding of the physical activity of modern man.

Physical Culture as an Object of Study

In recent years, the Central European tradition of the social sciences has witnessed a new awakening of interest in the living body, in the nature of man. Attempts have been made to discover, behind the known and public history of Europe, the intellectual history, an unwritten, "underground" history of the "concealed" body. Interest has focused on the fate of the instincts and passions rejected and distorted by civilization.

"As the Western way of life has been largely based on (a) bodily ascetism and (b) mastery over nature by means of technology, man's mental ego was not far away from hatred and contempt for the body" (Sironen, 1982).

Discourses on the "forgotten" body have leaned, among other things, on Norbert Elias's (1939, 1978) long-ignored, socioanthropological study *Ueber den Prozess der Zivilisation* and on works published in the 1960s and 1970s by the French social scientist and philosopher Michel Foucault, who is, at present, perhaps the best known and most controversial figure in the field on the continent. With his "political economy of the body," Foucault has attempted to demonstrate how the knowledge hidden in the human body has, historically and through outside power, gradually and in a wide variety of ways started to produce "obedient bodies." Thus, an understandable body has simultaneously been a useful body to the outside power. The individual human being has, especially in modern times, been the object of constant individualizing, normalizing, observation, and rectification; and the soul, that is, the inward essence, has been the product and realm action of the intervention of knowledge and power (Foucault, 1980).

In his studies, Elias views body and soul, nature and history, as inextricably intertwined, and in this way attempts to undermine the long-lasting tendency in the history of ideas to consider the body to be the prison of the soul (Sironen, 1982).

An important epistemological and methodological principle is apparent in Elias's method of study: Man's psychogenesis cannot be understood independently of the sociogenesis of the era (Elias, 1978). Consequently, there must exist a specific "sociogenetic basic law" according to which the individual in his or her *short* life history undergoes some of the processes that his society had already passed by in its *long* (author's italics) history. Such development is apparent, for instance, in a decrease in impulsiveness and spontaneous aggressiveness, in a simultaneous increase in the control of affects, and in an embarrassment felt about one's own body and its functions. The direction of the process of civilization is such that corporeality has been increasingly hidden "behind the scenes" (Sironen, 1982).

Elias provides numerous examples of how the general developments of the civilization process are reflected in sport. For instance, he has observed how the tensions and aggressions of a soccer match are controlled in miniature in the audience and among the players in a way similar to that of the *larger* society; or how modern man substitutes mimesis for his feelings of tension, which used to show themselves and be released in ways different from the present ones (e.g., by watching a championship fight on television) (Elias & Dunning, 1970). Even today, participation in or being a fan of sports does not aim at releasing excitement; rather, it aims at experiencing excitement (Elias & Dunning, 1966). However, tension and aggression today are totally different from what they were in societies based on slave labor, for instance. Elias questions the equation of the Olympic ideal of ancient Greece with modern competitive sport. The amateurs (or professionals) of contemporary sports are "choirboys" compared to the Greek pancratium competitors. There must be a myth or an ideological objective here, based on an overestimation of similarities and an underestimation of differences (Elias [no date of publication]).

The difference in the aggressiveness and the control of affects between ancient or medieval man and modern man is, however, not explained away by changes in the nature of man, but rather by changes in the social figuration (Elias, 1978). The "internal control" of modern people is the product of the requirements of the civilization process (subordination in schools, factories, and offices).

Elias's concept of the sociogenesis of the body is widely similar to that of Marcel Mauss (Polhemus, 1978). "The human body cannot be understood independently of the structure of social reality. By learning, first, the fact that we do have a body, we can begin to learn something of our 'social body'!"

The Paradigms of a Comparative Study

When, in the social sciences, the quantitative and qualitative points of view are observed, these turn out to be much more than mere methods of data collection. They should be viewed as paradigms, which contain different interrelated assumptions about the social world (Filstead, 1979). In the history of philosophy, the difference between these two viewpoints is, to put it simply, the difference between the "realist" and "idealist" theories of knowledge (Filstead, 1979).

The qualitative paradigm is characterized by a phenomenological and enlightened view of its object of study. Compared to the quantitative paradigm, the qualitative one is expansive rather than reductionist, holistic rather than particularistic, sensitive rather than categorical, oriented towards processes rather than products, and considers social reality to be dynamic rather than static (e.g., Reinhardt & Cook, 1979).

If the quantitative paradigm is observed in terms of the two basic aspects of comparative study, cross-cultural and long-term comparisons, it can be considered categorical from the point of view of both of these. The object of study is categorized in terms of quantitative, classifiable, and measurable features.[1] In the tradition of modern sociology, the underlying idea of the quantitative paradigm is that social reality or various communities can be characterized by means of what are known as pattern variables.

In Elias's criticism of the sociological pattern variables is contained the idea of *establishing a theory through the qualitative paradigm*. Elias criticizes sociological thought particularly for its tendency to characterize quite different communities in terms of established and stated terminology. In his opinion, it is Talcott Parsons who has been responsible for endowing communities with certain permanent features. Tönnies's *Gemeinschaft*-community has been characterized by Parsons with the attribute "affectivity," and the *Gesellschaft*-community with the attribute "affective neutrality . . . instead of a relatively complex process whereby the affective life of people is gradually moved toward an increased and more even control of affects—but certainly not toward a state of total affective neutrality" (Elias, 1978).

Elias emphasizes the fact that social life and reality cannot be conceived of as suspended states, nor does development in social life take place as successive states of rest (Sironen, 1982), but rather in terms of long-term, unplanned processes. From the Middle Ages to modern times, the processes have changed the anthropology of man "from top to toe" (Elias, 1978).

Elias (1978) wants to refute Parson's assumption

> that every society normally exists in a state of unchanging equilibrium which is homeostatically preserved. It changes when this normal state of social equilibrium is disturbed; for example, by a violation of social norms, a breach of conformity. Social change thus appears as a phenomenon resulting from an accidental, externally activated malfunction of a normally well balanced social system.

With respect to Parson's ideas, Elias points out that his (Elias's) method of study "upholds the idea, based on abundant documentary material, that change is a *normal* (author's italics) characteristic of society." If *change* is a *normal* feature of social communities and of the whole process of civilization, studies should avoid emphasizing the value judgments of our time or our industrial civilization, particularly when the object of study is either our earlier history or a culture living and acting differently from us, for instance, an original culture.

> The structures of personality and of society evolve in a dissoluble interrelationship [cf. psychogenesis-sociogenesis-MS]. It can never be said with certainty that the people of society *are* civilized. But on the basis of systematic investigation referring to demonstrable evidence, it can be said with a degree of certainty that some groups of people have *become* more civilized, without necessarily implying that it is better or worse, has a positive or negative value, to become civilized. (Elias, 1978)

In the literature pertaining to comparative studies, one can, however, find a large number of descriptive units that can be assumed to reflect, to some extent at least, ethnocentric values. This ethnocentrism is obvious, at least when we are looking in one direction only—from our technological culture toward original cultures or from modern "civilization" toward the "barbarity" of centuries ago.

Berry (1969) has gathered together from the literature examples that are considered typical of modern communities. These include independence from traditional authorities, a belief in the power of science, an active life-style, the abandonment of fatalism, interest in one's own personality, family and civil issues, participation in mass communication, individualism, a low degree of integration with one's family, an egalitarian attitude towards the system of roles within the family, and so forth.

Similarly, we could identify "modernist" features typical of the sports culture of industrialized countries such as amateurism versus professionalism, elaborate organizations, strong achievement motivation, commercialism, the formalism of rules, the rationality of action, a wide variety of sporting activities, and so forth.

If we are able to discard our ethnocentric values, we can see on the basis of ample research findings that the physical culture of each community and of each stage in civilization is inextricably and naturally connected with the social figurations of that community or era; that is, with how corporeality is experienced and what significance physical exercise, the aesthetics of the body, and communication have to self-concept, that is, to the individual as well as social status of a person (Busch Hansen, 1981; Polhemus, 1978). We can hardly impose preconditions on the different content areas solely from our time or our world.

However, by means of the comparative study of the sports and physical cultures, we can attempt to find functional equivalences in different communities. This pertains equally to both the quantitative and qualitative paradigms. These functional equivalences, however, must preexist as natural social phenomena. They cannot be created or manipulated (Segall, 1979). Functional equivalence means, briefly, that the phenomena being studied (the concept, categories, and instruments) must be reasonably familiar features of the two cultures being compared, even though they may not play the same role in each. Instruments or methods of data gathering that satisfy this condition could be called "culture-fair."[2] By contrast, "culture-free" instruments and methods would be required to measure certain qualities and features *equally well* in all cultures. At least Segall (1979) regards these methods as questionable.

Conclusions

The comparative study of the sport and physical culture can focus on different communities and cultures (cross-cultural comparisons), or on different periods of time (long-term developments). The basis and method of the comparison, in terms of the theory of knowledge, may be quantitative, qualitative, or a combination of both (see Figure 1).

Keeping in mind the principles governing the methods of study described above, the following practical conclusions at least can be made concerning the comparative study of the sports and physical cultures:

Quantitative Paradigm
- The *quantitative* paradigm focuses on features and qualities that are measurable in terms of amounts, on a systematic and analytic comparison of these properties.[3] This presupposes the development of exact categories and/or pattern variables.
- In order to satisfy the condition concerning the adequacy of functional equivalences, the study must focus on products rather than on processes.

	Cross-cultural comparisons	Long-term developments
Quantitative	Empirical data Analytic comparisons ETICS/sports culture	ETICS/sports culture
Qualitative	Social and cultural aspects of body and games EMICS/physical culture	Genetic-historical Psychogenesis-sociogenesis EMICS/physical culture

Figure 1   Aspects of the comparative study of the sports cultures.

- The more industrialized and technological the societies under study, the greater the number of similar products of civilization that can be found in them; these include structured organizations, institutional division of labor, and formal and rational features of social life.
- Modern sport and organized physical education are subfields of the technological culture. They are also highly differentiated and rationalized, and many features can be found in them that are functionally equivalent in all industrialized cultures.
- The most proper object of study of the quantitative method is *sports culture*—the differences and equivalences that are to be found in it.
- The picture of social reality of sports culture formed by the quantitative paradigm is, however, particularistic and atheoretical. It can be used to test a theory, but not to find one.

Qualitative Paradigm
- The *qualitative* paradigm, particularly through its phenomenological and hermeneutical method of study, aims at an understanding and interpretation of processes.
- The most proper object of study of the qualitative method is *physical culture*, the social and cultural aspects of corporeality and the control over the body that it conveys. These aspects can be studied and compared (a) in communities that are at different levels with respect to their degree of "civilization," and (b) as a general genetic-historical process of "civilization" (Eichberg, 1978; Elias, 1978; Foucault, 1980). Without a historical understanding of corporeality, it is hard to develop a wide understanding of the physical activity of modern man.
- The qualitative paradigm presents an opportunity to view sports culture as a part of physical culture.
- Only by means of the qualitative method of study can an attempt be made to determine the relationship between the physical and the spiritual. Fresh avenues of thought are needed to account for the histor-

ical as well as contemporary dualism between spiritless corporeality (e.g., body-building) on the one hand, and incorporeal spirituality (ascetism, intellectualism) on the other. The possibility of a balance between the physical and the spiritual in spite of the adverse elements created by "civilization" (cf. hiding the body "behind the scenes") is what qualitative studies are concerned with. This is why, in my opinion, the qualitative paradigm in a natural way incorporates both a critical and an emancipatory point of view.

Notes

1. The *quantitative* paradigm has often been compared with the *etics*-type of study, for example, in cultural anthropology. The term "etics" originated in linguistics (phon*etics* = for example, developing a universal coding system for the comparison of different languages). The *qualitative* paradigm has been characterized as being of the *emics*-type (phon*emics* = for example, identifying the expressive units of a given language [see Pike, 1954]).
2. An example of attempts to achieve "culture-fair" measurement is the study on the achievement motivation of Navajo students carried out by Duda (1980). Achievement motivation is also encountered in the Navajo culture, albeit in a form different from that experienced by the student in the white control group. As an example of how failure is experienced by the Navajo, Duda states as follows: "Failure in general, to a Navajo, was a function of not working well with others or caring for one's family, not having self-respect and an understanding of life, and not being happy or healthy. Not being generous, well-educated, well-liked, or owning an abundance of property *were not* an indication of failure."
3. A good overview of the categories and indicators used in the comparative study of the sports and physical cultures is offered in the seminar report *Comparative Physical Education and Sport. Proceedings of an International Seminar 1978* (Wingate Institute, Netanya, Israel).

References

Berry, J.W. (1969). On cross-cultural comparability. *International Journal of Psychology*, **4**, 119-128.

Busch Hansen, F. (1981). Idraetsforskning—Tanker of perspektiver. Idraet i samfundsperspektiv. *Nordisk Forum*, **32**, 6-18.

Duda, J.L. (1980). *Achievement motivation among Navajo students. A conceptual analysis with preliminary data.* Unpublished manuscript, University of Illinois, Champaign, IL.

Eichberg, H. (1978). *Leistung, spannung, geschwindigkeit. Sport und tanz im gesellschaftlichen wandel des 18./19. Jahrhunderts.* Stuttgart: Klett-Cotta.

Elias, N. Sportens oprindelse som et sociologisk problem. Sportshistory nr. 19-20. *Den jyske historiker* (pp. 63-88). Arhus: Forlaget Modtryk.

Elias, N. (1978). *The civilizing process. The history of manners.* Oxford: Basil Blackwell.

Elias, N., & Dunning, E. (1966). Dynamics of group sports with special reference to football. *The British Journal of Sociology*, **4**, 388-402.

Elias, N., & Dunning, E. (1970). The quest for excitement in unexciting societies. In G. Lüschen (Ed.), *The cross-cultural analysis of sport and games*. Champaign, IL: Stipes.

Filstead, W.J. (1979). Qualitative methods. A needed perspective in evaluation research. In T.D. Cook & C.S. Reinhardt (Eds.), *Qualitative and quantitative methods in evaluation research* (pp. 33-48). Beverly Hills, CA: Sage Publications.

Foucault, M. (1980). *Tarkkailla ja rangaista*. Keuruu: Otava.

Kuhn, T. (1962). *The structure of scientific revolutions*. Chicago: Phoenix.

Lüschen, G. (Ed.). (1970). *The cross-cultural analysis of sport and games*. Champaign, IL: Stipes.

Polhemus, T. (Ed.). (1978). *The body reader. Social aspects of the human body*. New York: Pantheon Books.

Reinhardt, C.S., & Cook, T.D. (1979). Beyond qualitative versus quantitative methods. In T.D. Cook & C.S. Reinhardt (Eds.), *Qualitative and quantitative methods in evaluation research* (pp. 7-32). Beverly Hills, CA: Sage Publications.

Segall, M.H. (1979). *Cross-cultural psychology. Human behavior in global perspective*. Monterey, CA: Brooks/Cole.

Sironen, E. (1982). Ruumis ja sivilisaatio. Näkökulma ruumiinkulttuurin historiaan. *Liikunta ja tiede*, p. 3.

Current Issues and Trends in Comparative Physical Education and Sport

Donald Anthony
Center for International Sports Exchange

This paper addresses three major topics: (a) a brief history of development which I consider keynote in the evolution of comparative studies in this area, (b) an explanation of my professional involvement in this ongoing work, and(c) the identification of some major funds and issues in comparative physical education and sport.

The Evolution of Comparative Physical Education and Sport

I identify the following five major stepping stones in this history:

1. The Victorian era from 1850 to 1880.
2. The development of the international sports movement starting in 1881.
3. The international YMCA movement in 1904.
4. The League of Nations involvement in 1928.
5. The recent emergence of comparative physical education and sport as an academic discipline in its own right.

The Victorian Era

This was the age of colonialism with Britons, particularly, exporting their way of life throughout the world. Sport was an integral aspect of that way of life. Copies of the Hurlingham multisport club in London appeared in Cairo, Montevideo, Rio, Singapore, and other far-flung outposts of the Empire. The role played by sport in character development, as expressed in English public school education, became famous. Among others there arrived in England the French baron, Pierre de Coubertin; first as a teenager at a Catholic boarding school; later as a devoted anglophile anxious to visit the tomb of Arnold at Rugby; and finally, to the Shropshire town of Much Wenlock where he was eager to experience the "Olympian Games" established there since 1850.

Much Wenlock had inherited the Olympic tradition established in the Cotswolds since 1612, and its games set out to establish sport as a means of education, not only for the privileged classes, but also for agricultural laborers. The founder of these games, William Penny Brookes, was an astonishing man: doctor of medicine, magistrate, educator, and innovator, whose remarkable work has only recently been recognized in his home country thanks to the discovery of four bound volumes of minutes and press cuttings, which trace, intimately, the history of the Much Wenlock Olympian Society and the National Olympian Association that grew from it. This National Olympian Association held its first Games at London's original Crystal Palace in 1866.

The Games were organized by E. Ravenstein, President of the German Gymnastics Society in London. Both Brookes and Ravenstein had an international outlook, but neither were accepted members of the establishment; Brookes because he was neither a Londoner, nor from Oxford or Cambridge; Ravenstein because he was a foreigner. However, history will show that the fear of Brookes and his National Olympian Association triggered the formation of the Amateur Athletics Association, which then took on international responsibilities leading towards the foundation of the Olympic movement. I will also show that the "German Gymnasium" in London was the womb of the national gymnastic association and the national swimming association of Britain.

In the first Games at the Crystal Palace, now moved to Sydenham in southeast London, more than 10,000 people took part as competitors or athletes. In an address to the assembled gathering, Brookes dealt passionately with the virtues of colonial expansion and the export of Christianity, and he displayed an interesting familiarity with other systems of physical education. He explained the work of Gutsmuths and Jahn and the oppression suffered at the hands of the Napoleonic Empire. He referred to the work of Bigham of Boston and an article in the *New York Herald* that showed that "the physical degeneracy of the North Americans, of both sexes, was due to the want of athletic exercises and outdoor recreation." Turning to the French, he presented data showing that of 1,000 youths registered for conscription in 1863, 731 were deemed unfit to bear arms. This situation was thought due to two causes: excessive labor in the manufacturing districts and the lack of gymnastic training in the schools. Finally he called for a rejuvenation of the ancient Olympic Games of Greece.

I deal at some length with this matter, because I am sure it is new to many of you. It was certainly new to me, and I find it stimulating. These founding fathers of sport and physical education in the Victorian era were true comparativists fired by internationalism. Indeed, some historians would say that internationalism began at the Great Exhibition of 1851, held at the original Crystal Palace in Hyde Park.

The Development of the International Sports Movement

Once the idea of an international sports movement took hold, it grew with ferocity. The first international sports body was for gymnastics and was started in 1881 by a group of physical educationists with Jan Cuperus of Belgium at its head. By 1892 there were two more for skating and rowing. The first International Olympic Committee of 16 persons had 8 educationists, of whom Coubertin is the most famous. Coubertin, of course, discovered Olympism in his quest for a new education to excite French youth. A scholarship from the French government enabled him to travel widely in this quest. Other notable educationists in the first IOC were Victor Balck, the Director of the Gymnastic Central Institute in Stockholm, the mecca of Ling gymnastics, and William Sloane of Princeton University. Thus international sport was dominated in the early years by teachers who understood the principles of internationalism and the interconnections between sport, education, social life, and international understanding. The *intrinsic* folk festivals of sports, which have a very long history, were never connected internationally. It was these early "physical educationists" who understood the potential of sport as an *instrument* and gave the first real push to the international sports snowball.

The International YMCA Movement

No survey of this area can omit a tribute to the pioneering international work of the YMCA. The inventors of basketball and volleyball and initiators of a bachelor's degree at Springfield as early as 1904, the YMCA physical directors established a European training school at Geneva and centers all over the world. Their graduates were prominent in developing basketball in China and the Baltic states of the USSR, and their influence accounts, even today, for the high standards and traditions in those countries vis-à-vis basketball and volleyball. The founder and life general secretary of the International Amateur Basketball Association (FIBA), Springfield graduate William Jones, has a unique place in the history of comparative and international physical education. He established FIBA in 1932 and served it loyally until his death in 1981. Jones was also director of the UNESCO Youth Institute in Gauting and established there the first headquarters of the International Council of Sport and Physical Education. On mission for UNESCO in Africa, he drew up the principles for the establishment of the Supreme Council of Sport in Africa at Brazzville, Congo, in 1965. It was the YMCA movement that signposted the development of the *instrumental* use of sport in international relations.

The League of Nations

There are two comparative studies that I would like to repeat one day. The first is Coubertin's in the 1890s, and the second is Piasecki's study of 13 European countries for the Health Committee of the League of Nations in 1928. Eugeniusz Piasecki was a leading Polish physical educationist, and his work for the League heralded the emergence of international government interest in sports and physical education. It was not until 1952 that UNESCO took an interest in comparative physical education, but we should remember Piasecki's study as the first commissioned by world government. It appeared, coincidentally, in the same year that Coubertin established his Bureau International Pedagogy Sportive—an office dedicated, in his words, as the "weather vane of the international sports movement, able to predict trends." Switzerland thus has a unique place in sports study history as the birthplace of world government interest in sports and physical education and the host for the modern Olympic movement. It is also interesting to note that working in the League secretariat at this time was Philip Noel-Baker, an ex-captain of the British Olympic team who was later to become a Nobel Peace Prize winner, President of UNESCO's ICSPE, and doyên of the Olympic movement.

Comparative Physical Education and Sport

There was always a small place for physical education in the work of early comparative educationists, and for many years we all tended to lean heavily on *education* for academic credibility. In 1965 I published two articles on "Comparative Physical Education" and "Physical Education as an Aspect of Comparative Education," which traced this relationship. I tried also, in these articles, to elaborate a rationale for comparative physical education and sport in its own right. These were generally well received by the profession, I like to think, and since that time, those of us engaged in the *actual* work have categorized and catalogued our work with much greater care and a heightened sense of awareness.

I discovered "physical education" at Loughborough in 1946 to 1948 and then again in 1950 to 1951. Our major textbooks were American. Many, indeed most, of our students had returned after 5 years of war from countries far and wide. My own generation was the first group to go from school direct to university, and it was a very stimulating experience to be educated alongside those who had undergone such traumatic worldly experiences. Loughborough's Director, Herbert Schofield, was an international rotarian much taken by the developments in higher education and sport in the United States. Against all advice and with no encouragement from the establishment, he had created Loughborough College, now Loughborough University. The student faculty was enormously international, and I studied with Nigerians, Ceylonese, Chinese, other Africans, and Asians from many countries.

Between 1948 and 1950 I underwent national service and found myself teaching in Cyprus. Concurrently I was sports editor of the *Cyprus Sunday Times*, and I also learned a game called volleyball, which helped in my training for my major sports interest, athletics. At the 1948 Olympics we had all received a unique boost to our internationalism. London hosted many thousands of athletes from many countries, and the air was thick with aspirations for peace and international understanding. We gave a demonstration of athletics training to an international physical education conference held at the same time; our teacher was a Greek marooned in England because of the war.

Such early seeds of internationalism took root in me. I could not help but be an enthusiast for comparative studies. On the way back from Cyprus, I traveled by boat and train through Rhodes, Athens, Izmir, Bari,

Venice, Milan, and Paris. My journey took me through Gibraltar, Malta, and Egypt, and because my previous only travel abroad had been from Southampton to Jersey in a 12-seat, two-engined biplane called a De Havilland Rapide, these wonderful experiences, at a time when travel was not so common for everyone, had a significant effect on me.

After completing my last year at Loughborough I realized that "British *might* be, but was not necessarily best." I realized that I had merely climbed the hill of physical education and was peeping into the valley beyond. I thus took 2 further years of study at my own expense to satisfy my quest for nourishment in the valleys. I visited Berlin, Poland, and Czechoslovakia in 1951. In 1952 I sold my small car and used the proceeds to study for one semester at the Sporthochschule in Cologne. This evident self-sacrifice impressed the British Council so much that they awarded me a fellowship for study in Finland. However, I then found myself in Sweden as a member of the British athletics team; I managed to persuade the Swedes that they needed an English teacher at the National Sports Centre in Bosön and spent 3 delightful months in Stockholm prior to my study in Helsinki.

I returned to England only because an opportunity occurred to work at Manchester University. I was expected to undertake some research there, and I could see no reason why this should not have practical spinoff. "How about that game called volleyball?" I thought. A letter to the *Manchester Guardian* and the Amateur Volleyball Association of Great Britain and Northern Ireland was formed. At the same time I was still a member of the British athletics team, throwing the hammer. This took me to many countries, and arrangements were much more flexible than those today. I was able to link my athletics competition to my professional interest. I trained with the Polish team at their training camp, and I visited the physical education conferences at Melbourne and Vancouver in the 1950s when I wasn't competing. For 10 years as a British team member, I was able to consolidate my network of contacts throughout the world. I was also able to consolidate my reputation as an author and journalist. While representing both *The Guardian* and *Sports Illustrated*, I met William Jones at the 1959 UNESCO Conference on Sport Work and Culture, and he invited me to join in the work of the newly formed ICSPE. This, in turn, led me into a working relationship with UNESCO as a consultant on sport and physical education for many years.

During these years I was able to develop the idea of academic courses in comparative studies, and these grew in maturity as our complete degree courses in England developed. It was not until the early 1960s, remember, that it was possible to graduate in physical education in England; that is one reason why North America was able to rob us of so much brain power in those precious years. It was this actual robbery, however, that developed into another personal network internationally. I now get letters from ex-students and ex-colleagues holding high positions all over North America, who emigrated in those years in the pursuit of degrees. I know these people well; I can trust their powers of analysis and discretion, and it makes for a fascinating transfer of up-to-date information.

Lastly, I have translated a special interest in Third World sports problems into a network of personal and institutional contacts throughout Latin America, Asia, and Africa. I have been able to do this mainly through my association with the British Olympic Association. I now represent the national volleyball association on the national Olympic Committee, and because of my professional status, I was asked to chair a special unit on education. Among other responsibilities in this connection, I codirect, for the International Olympic Committee, international courses on sports administration. In 1976, 1978, 1981, and 1982 such courses provided me with associates in more than 70 countries. I was for 4 years, moreover, seconded halftime to develop the Centre for International Sports Exchanges at the Central Bureau for Educational Visits and Exchanges, and this was the hat I wore at this conference. The Central Bureau is the international office central to the Ministries of Education for Wales, Northern Ireland, Scotland, and England.

What does all this mean? Why is it relevant? I think it means that *no* experience has been wasted. I have, at last, created a situation professionally that works as a catalyst for all these experiences. Each strand in the experience can now be woven into a whole by creative thinking. All decisions, even bad ones, are important to the creative process. It also means that divergency and intuition are as valuable as convergency and rationality. Earlier I mentioned the history of sports with an axis moving from intrinsic to instrumental; I now cross this vertical axis with a horizontal axis moving from intuitive to rational. These twin axes help me analyze trends and issues in physical education. I am fortunate in that I have, at long last, created a working position in which I have one foot in university physical education and national sports administration, and the other in international education and comparative action. It is from this experience and from this professional position that I can now offer my views on trends and issues.

I have addressed myself to the question, therefore, as someone who has played some part, be it a modest one, in the development of comparative physical education and sport as an academic discipline; someone who has spent 35 years thinking and writing in the area and is currently engaged professionally in identifying trends and issues.

Current Trends

Some of you might remember how the multitude were fed with five loaves and seven fishes. I am restricting myself to those magic numbers—five trends and seven issues. I see these trends as five major explosions in

- knowledge,
- organizations,
- facilities and equipment,
- international access to sport, and
- mobility.

Explosion in Knowledge

Even 20 years ago it was difficult to find any text relating to the area. Articles were rare, and most material was purely descriptive and issued by official organizations, such as embassies, for promotional purposes. Today we have immense data banks. The flow of material is almost overwhelming. I subscribe at ridiculously low fees to the Council of Europe Clearing House filing cards system, and a random selection prior to preparing this paper gave me current information on the following matters:

- How sport for the disabled is organized in Australia.
- How professional leaders for sport are trained in Holland.
- How the churches are involved in sport in West Germany.
- How family sport and leisure rank in Finland.
- How sport for all is planned in Sweden
- How the Council of Europe wants international conferences to be supported financially.

It also provided a summary of a recent survey of 25 countries with regard to extracurricular school sport.

Not long ago I wanted to research the origins of the British Olympic Association. It was formed in the House of Commons in 1905, but there are no minutes for the first meetings. I thought of the *Times* reports of that period. To my delight I found that three libraries carry complete microfilmed records of *The Times*. In the space of one day I had formulated a problem, discovered a source, and, without prior arrangement, was sitting at a machine in Leicester Square Reference Library, reading the sports pages of *The Times* for the relevant period.

Let us not take such benefits for granted. I can receive translations and contribute to an international computerized store of information. All national Olympic committees issue journals; those for the GDR, Bulgaria, Rumania, and the USSR, among others, are also issued in English. At embassies in London I can find detailed explanations in written form about sport in more than 40 countries. I receive the journals of the major international organizations, such as the IOC, ICSPE, ICHPER, FIEP, and various specialized physical education research journals. At the embassies I can collect films about sport; I can attend more than ten European sports film festivals and study the latest developments. Together with many hundreds of millions I can follow the actuality of sport from the World Cup and the Olympic Games. I can videorecord my own programs and conduct audio research into sports history. I can assemble my findings in multislide-sound projections. I can visit sports museums in London, Madrid, Helsinki, Stockholm, Warsaw, and many centers in North America. In London, alone, I can visit the headquarters and archives of the international federations for tennis, athletics, and sailing, as well as for cricket and rugby football. In other parts of England I can visit the archives of international federations for badminton and table tennis. In

Budapest I can visit a physical education research institute and meet an international team of researchers who all speak English; in Warsaw, for many years, the research institute for physical culture has had a staff of over 80 persons and a full-time translation team, working with many languages. Today there is no shortage of knowledge. Our problem is how to handle the volume of information, categorize it, and process it.

Explosion of Organizations

Here again there has been enormous mushrooming. From three international sports federations and the IOC in 1900 we now have more than 150 international sports federations. Some, like basketball, have more members than the United Nations. National Olympic committees are associated in their own international federation. In physical education we have another proliferation. ICSPE, ICHPER, and FIEP are the largest, but they have spawned smaller specialized bodies for psychology, sociology, philosophy, and history. There are similar bodies for sports writers, the handicapped, women, Catholics, and others. Most try to relate to UNESCO for "consultative status" so that there is some coherence to the pattern. In addition to the Olympic Games and the Winter Olympics, there are regional sports organizations for Africa, Asia, Central America and the Caribbean, the South Pacific, the Indian Ocean, the Mediterranean, and elsewhere. There are Pan American, Commonwealth, Pan Arab, and other "sports cultural" groupings. There are some nationally based institutions that have developed powerful international profiles, and the United States Sports Academy is one of these. In Europe, Leipzig, Cologne, and Paris, specialized international programs have developed that attract worldwide support in the areas of teacher training in physical education and sports coaching.

In recent years the many multisport bodies in various countries have tried to form their own international association. An International Federation for Sports Film and Television has been founded in Italy, and sports shoe manufacturers have also formed an international coordinating committee. The President of the IOC has endeavored to provide a hub to this network by forming the Commission for the Olympic Movement which brings together the IOC, the National Olympic Committees, and the International Sports Federations in an attempt to develop a dialogue with UNESCO representing international governmental organizations in sport. Again our problem is not finding material, but organizing all that is readily available.

Explosion of Facilities and Equipment

Are there any countries lacking a national stadium? For some the provision of a stadium has been a budget-breaking exercise. In many it is the major sports expenditure. In the Middle East it is impossible to count the new stadiums, sports halls, and swimming pools under construction. In the United States last year Nike was assessed as having sold $470 million worth of equipment, whereas Adidas, in the United States alone, had the figure of $350 million. Even in the poorest and newest countries, sports equipment and facilities represent big business. A developing country needs a stadium just as it needs an airport as a symbol of modernity, according to Rene Maheux, the late Director General of UNESCO.

Are comparativists active in this area, assessing (a) how best countries might invest their money, (b) how best they might exploit their facilities, and (c) how they might make sport a job-creating area by manufacturing their own simple "sport for all" equipment?

Explosion of International Access to Sport

The idea of sport for all was first conceived by Coubertin when he called for "Every sport for everyone" more than 60 years ago. The slogan took on the possibility of actuality when governments started to invest, nationally and locally, in sports for all. The socialist countries saw sport on a par with art and science; it was considered socially desirable that access to sport and sports instruction should be readily available and that excellence should be fostered by the state. California state universities provide a model of dual-use by colleges and communities of their immense facilities. Earlier this year I visited a high school in Long Beach and mused on the thought that the acres of playing fields and sports centers at this one school could be matched by very few national centers in the developing countries of Africa.

This awareness of inequality has sparked the development of international aid schemes. Olympic Solidarity is the largest and most exciting. This world bank of sports expertise helps to redress the balance between rich and poor in sport; all Olympic sports are aided to enhance their growth in the Third World, and courses in sports medicine and sports administration are offered. This has proved to be a creative way of spending the Olympic movement's newfound wealth, accruing mainly from television royalties. Some of the larger international federations also mount aid schemes; tennis, athletics, football, and basketball are examples. Volleyball is also considering how it might now respond to worldwide needs. International sport now provides a most remarkable means of nonlingual communication between peoples. It is possible that a young man or woman, who is still denied access to a good education in a poor country, can yet win a gold medal in the Olympic Games. Let us not scoff at the symbol of opportunity and the glorious hope that this fact represents.

When we think comparatively let us think truly globally, recognizing that 65% of the world's countries are classified as developing. Despite unemployment, poverty, malnutrition, poor administration, lack of material resources, and the many other ills of underdevelopment, people recognize something in sport that catches their imagination and can help to develop their most precious resource—the human resource, which is their most valuable biological capital. Comparativists studying in this area can find their own problems brought into high relief and can help make the general arguments in our own sophisticated societies that will persuade governments to budget for sports expenditure.

Explosion of Mobility

It was no accident that Coubertin and Thomas Cook were contemporaries. One toiled for sports as an instrument of character development, a school for the emotions, a wedding of mind to muscle; the other saw travel as an instrument for education as well as enlightenment. Both sought to extend what was then a privilege to the masses.

Mass travel is a social phenomenon that we, again, tend to take for granted. There were not many Coubertins in the 1890s. There were not many Madame Osterbergs either. These and other individuals, expressing a firm belief and a skilled professionalism, provided the direction and the initial stimulus to the development of national gymnastic and sport systems. Osterberg came to London, de Paulli went to Moscow, and Olta started things off in the University of Helsinki. Travel was difficult and expensive. They were the few. We are the many.

Today travel is easy and relatively inexpensive. The range of travel opportunities for top sports people is clearly evident, and the world of tennis and golf are indicators. At lower levels there is a massive movement of school and youth sports teams in Europe and about the world. Spectators travel in their many thousands. As early as the 1960s a German soccer club brought 30,000 supporters to England for a European Cup final. I estimate that there are now 21 sports travel agencies in Britain specializing in general sports travel; these do not include the many more who concentrate on winter sports travel. We are talking about a movement of people in sports that amounts to many millions in all countries. Physical education professionals can join a number of educational institutes for Comparative Physical Education tours to China, the USSR, Romania, Switzerland, Sweden, and England and get official study credits. There are many other opportunities to travel and study in physical education today.

This year we made a major breakthrough in study opportunities within the European Economic Community. We sold successfully the idea that sport and music were two major components in a drive to develop European awareness. We, the Central Bureau, were allotted some $40,000 for 1982 to develop sports *links* among schools, colleges, and universities in the EEC. We had previously been able to help only a very small number of people take part in intensive study visits, but this was a new departure. A *link* is not just a study; it has to aim at developing long-term spin-off. Applicants have to spell out how they see the link developing over 3 or 4 years. In future years other EEC governments will help their nationals make visits back to the UK. I look down my list of successful applicants this year and I see such links as

- Loughborough with the University of Liège,
- Oxford Polytechnic with Ludwigsburg College of Education,
- the British Student Sports Federation with their Italian counterparts,
- the University of Liverpool with the University of Bonn,
- Brighton Polytechnic with the Sporthochschule Cologne,
- Bognor Regis School with a link in Paris,
- a London College of Education with the National Sports Institute in Eire,
- Ulster Polytechnic with Louvain University in Belgium, and
- Much Wenlock School with a school near Olympia.

Later this year we will call together the 60 plus people we are now helping to evaluate the projects individually and as a whole. We hope that this is only the beginning and that we will have at least 3 years to develop this comparative program.

British comparative physical educationists have never had it so good. In addition, over the last 4 years, we have sent an expert—at 3 weeks notice—to train the television teams for the South East Asian Games in Indonesia. We sent experts to Jamaica, and at Wembley Stadium, we organized the first-ever, international course in stadium management for stadium directors from 12 countries.

This is what we mean by a Center for International Sports Exchange. We cannot aid people to attend *all* the international conferences, but we do attempt to advertise them, monitor them, and publicize the results in our journal "Sports International." We organized, with the University of Zagreb, the first of an annual series of conferences under the title International Sports Dialogue-North/South/East/West. The 1983 problem was "The Development of Sport in Society."

For comparativists there are some key questions. Do we make best use of these occasions? When there are official, nationally organized delegations, do we brief our representatives properly; do they report back responsibly? How do we know they represent a truly "national" viewpoint? Who votes, for example, on what, how, and why at UNESCO's new Intergovernmental Committee for Sport?

Of the five explosions, I find this explosion in mobility the most astonishing. There is much to be said for the movement of documents, and even more to be said for the movement of people. The greatest advantage of travel, it is said, is that it enables you to find yourself.

Current Issues

Next to the *issues*, and I submit the following seven as being significant for comparativists in our area today.

- The control of world sport and physical education.
- The revival of the Olympic movement.

- The financing of sport.
- The elite/mass equation.
- The state/voluntary equation.
- The intrinsic/instrumental equation.
- The academic study of comparative physical education and sport as a university discipline.

Control of World Sport

The phenomenon of organized world sport is only 100 years old. It is not surprising that in its adolescence it should have problems. The media, especially television, pay heavily for sports programs; some would claim not heavily enough. Program sponsors and presenters have begun to demand a voice in even such matters as the rules of the game. Commentators take on roles quite outside their remit. They often undermine, publicly, the decisions of officials and pronounce off-the-cuff remarks on important ethical issues.

Commercial companies involved in the sports equipment market are another new and powerful force affecting sports decision making. Behind the scenes they can also be kingmakers. Relationships between politics and sport become more evident; the Commonwealth could break if sports teams ignore the governmental Gleneagles Agreement and flirt with apartheid sport in South Africa. The IOC seeks discussions with the United Nations organization with a view to seeking Red Cross status for world sport.

The Revival of the Olympic Movement

Every Olympics since 1896 has been the last, according to the pessimists. But at Baden Baden in 1981, the Olympic Congress showed that the Olympic movement was again to the fore in the leadership of world sport. It might not be, indeed it is not, perfect. But it has worked for the betterment of mankind, and public opinion seems to want to preserve it. The IOC can, it seems, still serve as the hub of a gigantic sports network. In addition to trying to keep the ship afloat, competitively speaking, the IOC can assist in rejuvenating the fine arts traditions of the Olympic movement in Los Angeles in 1984, Seoul in 1988, Barcelona perhaps in 1992, and certainly Athens, for the centenary, in 1996. The Olympic movement is a hub to which all other sports bodies can relate. The NOCs relate directly; the International Olympic Academy is now sparking the development of related National Olympic Academies. The international sports federations accept IOC leadership, even if unwillingly. UNESCO recognizes that an area of international voluntary service through sports should not be rudely interrupted without great thought.

Financing Sport

The basic question in all societies is the following: Is sport seen to be a human right, a social service, or a commodity to be bought, sold, and sometimes exploited? If it is to be both, is anyone to determine distinct areas of operation? When is sport to be health and education? How can amateur and professional sport relate to each other? When is it to be theater? These questions help to determine how society finances its sports and physical education. Is physical education to be integral to all schools? If so, what are the minimum conditions regarding facilities, programs, and leadership? Is sport to be allowed to be merely an unthinking area for advertisement, or are there certain conditions to be met? All countries have to face this question. How they face it makes for a fascinating and rewarding comparative exercise.

Elite/Mass Equation

Excellence and mass participation are ends of the same spectrum. Setting these principles as an either/or question is a misconceived approach in my opinion. Champions should nourish the masses and be nourished by them.

How countries provide for their outstanding young people and organize provision for all makes for another major and creative comparative area.

State/Voluntary Equation

How do we balance institutional backup represented largely by the state at local, regional, and national level—with individual and group initiatives? What models are there in the world? How does the North American college-based system compare with the German club-based system for sport? How do they both compare with a traditional school-based preparation for sport as is still found in the United Kingdom?

When sport is organized, is this best done by the "Sports Council" approach, by a Ministry of Physical Culture, by attaching sport to the Ministry of Education, or Health, or Conservation, or Culture, or Youth, or what?

Intrinsic/Instrumental Equation

There is much to be said for sports activities played entirely for fun and pleasure, with little structure and little need for any organization except self-organization. Such activities exist in all societies and always seem to have done so. Sport has its own intrinsic worth. But a sport as intrinsic as local wrestling has often taken on instrumental forms; it has been used, for example, to establish land rights or to find a bride. Sports festivals have developed ceremonies and rituals that seem to meet deep needs in mankind. Is it an accident that the 2 days that could be sold out again and again at any Olympics are the opening and closing ceremonies? We are concerned with both the conservation of indigenous games and dances in societies, on the one hand, and with the development of sport as an instrument in the promotion of health, education, community development, and national identity, on the other. We are concerned with establishing an ideology for sport; that is, creating a rationale for it that will persuade those who keep the public purse to invest in it. Surely this approach is better than abandoning sport entirely to those who only see the sports movement as a marvelous marketing mechanism.

If one puts into a hat the attitudes of the world's top political leaders towards sport, and into another their names, any random selection comes out with almost the same juxtapositions. They all believe firmly in the positive role that sport can play in society—sport being life as it could and should be.

The Academic Study of Comparative Physical Education and Sport

All problems in physical education can profit from the comparative strategy, and the art is to identify an order of priorities, which will vary from country to country. It appears to me in general, however, that in the last few years, while comparative sport and physical education has been trying to establish itself in universities, we have been perhaps too much engrossed in method and almost too pedantic in choice of topic and its treatment. We are also not established in enough universities in enough countries.

What we have *not* done is tackle, head-on, many of the major problems of the day, and try to play a leading part in their solution. The issues and trends that I am submitting as important call for just that exercise. If we can show that the comparative strategy really helps sports planners to solve problems and sports administrators to handle their budgets more wisely, the comparative movement will find more bases in higher education and more power to its elbow. We must make ourselves essential to the decision-making process.

I end with one further thought. If we happen to go over again and again some old chestnuts, it matters not if they are part of the basic formulas for comparing in physical education and sport. One of the most meaningful phrases I have ever heard emphasized for me the urgency of constant reinforcement of the basics. It was made by a Chinese Buddhist speaker, and I conclude my opening remarks in this same spirit. "No matter," he said, "if a tree grows to more than a thousand feet in height, each leaf, each day, must return to its roots for nourishment."

What's New Around the World in Comparative Physical Education and Sport?

Bruce L. Bennett
The Ohio State University

My presentation is taken largely from the concluding chapter of the second edition of our book on comparative physical education and sport and represents the combined observations and thinking of my coauthors, Maxwell Howell and Uri Simri, and myself. We can identify 12 trends and significant developments on the world scene that have occurred between the writing of the first edition in 1973 to 1974 and the writing of the second edition in 1980 to 1981.

We have examined Anthony's trends and issues in the previous chapter, and this chapter will further elucidate the dozen distinctive trends that have been identified by my colleagues and myself.

The People's Republic of China is moving swiftly to prepare its athletes for sport competition at the international level. This is a sharp reversal from their attitude toward international competition in the late 1960s and the first half of the 1970s during the Cultural Revolution. Efforts to achieve international success in sports were generally condemned, and Chinese teams and athletes made few appearances in world competition.

But following the demise of the Cultural Revolution in 1977, a nationwide meeting of physical educators and sport officials was held in January, 1978. At that time the objective of training athletes to compete with world champions was declared. Systems for grading athletes, referees, and coaches were reinstated. Also a system to commend those who established new records was formulated to be put into practice. All kinds of competition within the country and with foreign teams were to be scheduled, and invitations were to be extended to foreign coaches to come in and work with their athletes. The 2-year labor requirement was abolished. All these procedures were to take effect immediately (Sasajima, 1979).

There is every indication that the People's Republic of China will have an impact upon international sport comparable to that of the entry of the Soviet Union into the arena of international sport at the 1952 Olympic Games in Helsinki. The PRC was admitted to the Olympic Games by the IOC in 1979 but did not take part in the Moscow Games because of the boycott. They participated in the FISU Universiade in 1977 for the first time. Just 4 years later they captured the fourth highest total of medals of any country at these games. *China Sports,* an English language publication from Beijing, proudly reported that Chinese athletes captured 280 gold medals in international contests in 1981 alone. Their athletes won 25 world titles in 1981, compared with only 3 world titles in 1980 (*China Sports,* 1982). In this concerted drive for international superiority, will the famous Chinese slogan, "Friendship First, Competition Second," have to be revamped to put friendship in second place? I hope not.

The diffusion of sports among the various nations of the world has made remarkable progress. An increasing number of sports are making new friends in unfamiliar territory. Team handball, rugby, and orienteering are some recent examples of this. Even the American sports of baseball, softball, and football are finding greater acceptance outside the United States. Baseball is now played in over 40 countries, including the PRC, and was a demonstration sport in the 1984 Olympic Games. Eleven countries sent teams of 18-and-under youths to the First World Friendship Baseball Series in Newark, Ohio in July, 1981, where the championship was won by South Korea (Wulf, 1981); over 20 countries sent teams to participate in an international women's softball tournament in Taiwan the summer of 1982. American football is gaining popularity in Japan where a number of American college teams have traveled to play games in the past few years. An American football league began operation in the Federal Republic of Germany in 1980 and over 40 teams have been organized. A very significant development in the other direction geographically has been the spread of the Eastern arts such as karate, judo, aikido, yoga, tai-chi, tae kwon do, and others to Western countries. Television has had a powerful influence in making unfamiliar sports familiar to its viewers. It is no longer easy for a sport to remain indigenous!

The sport option and theory courses for secondary school students reflect an increased academic recognition for physical education and sport in the curriculum. Students have an opportunity to concentrate in the theory and practice of sports for 6 to 12 hours a week. However, the plan does have the possibility of abuse if the gifted athletes are favored over the less talented students.

The specialized schools for sport have demonstrated their value in the GDR and the Soviet Union and are now being copied by many other countries striving for international success in sport. In addition to the other socialist countries such as Cuba and the PRC, these schools now exist in such diverse nations as France, the FRG, Korea, Greece, India, Austria, and on a private basis, in the United States.

The practice of granting athletic scholarships to college students is an innovation from the United States that is beginning to appear in other nations, although as yet, on a modest scale. Most Canadian universities voted in 1981 to offer scholarships, and in the same year the University of Stirling became the first in Scotland to provide sport bursaries. The University of Bath in England began awarding athletic scholarships in 1976. These athletic emoluments also exist in Nigeria, Korea, the Philippines, and India. Perhaps other countries will have more success than the United States in avoiding some of the serious problems caused by these financial aids.

The development of national and international caliber athletes has become a stated priority objective for many countries. This fact is a primary reason for the granting of athletic scholarships to university students, for the spread of the specialized schools of sport, and, to a lesser extent, for the sport option courses. It is the reason why India gives a scholarship of $12 a month to 2,000 promising athletes. It is the reason the PRC awarded half or full scholarships to 295 primary and middle school students in Shanghai who were chosen as "good student-athletes" of the year (China Sports, 1981). This scholarship money presumably could be used to enable these students to attend a spare-time sport school to further develop their athletic abilities. Andre Van Lierde and Hilde Van Dun (1978), editors of the Council of Europe study, concluded that the sport clubs generally did not welcome the less skilled children as much as the talented ones. Consistently throughout the world, athletes with high potential get the use of the best facilities and equipment and receive the best coaching.

The mass media have continued to increase their coverage of sports through television, radio, and the press. In addition to more detailed coverage of major sporting events, such as the recent World Cup soccer tournament in Spain viewed by every third person on this planet, other lesser known sport competitions are receiving television attention. In a typical week the Entertainment and Sports Programming Network in the United States features college basketball, professional rodeo, college soccer, gymnastics, full-contact karate, auto racing, power boat racing, weight lifting, boxing, and soccer from England. The growth of cable television will provide additional fare for the sport addict to go with their radio and sport newspapers and magazines.

Mass participation in physical activities and sport has profited from organized campaigns carried on in a number of countries. Sample programs are "Participation" in Canada, "Life Be In It" in Australia, and TRIM or "Sport For All" in Europe. The media have been enlisted to sell these programs to the populace. It is difficult to know whether the increase in the number of participants has kept pace with the increase in population or not. Jung Hae Hahm, a Korean physical education student at Ewha's Women's University, puts the case for continued mass participation very nicely.

> In short, man now possesses the freedom to be weak. Few activities demand his speed, strength, endurance, and ability. To stay fit both in mind and body one should choose a lifelong sport that is suited for one's need. Lifelong sports is the process by which changes in man are brought about through his interesting movement experience. (1981)

Marathon running has become an attractive mass activity for men and women of all ages in a number of countries. In the 1981 marathon in New York City, 13,360 runners finished the race.

Olympic Games boycotts were very much in the news in both 1976 and 1980. At Montreal, 29 mostly African nations went home to protest a New Zealand rugby team's playing in South Africa. They wanted New

Zealand expelled from the Games. In 1980 the United States initiated a boycott of the Games to protest the sending of troops from the Soviet Union into Afghanistan in December, 1979. Only 81 out of 145 qualified countries sent athletes to Moscow, which actually was only 7 countries less than participated at Montreal 4 years before; but the absence of the United States, Canada, the FRG, the PRC, and Japan was particularly felt. The use of a boycott has been hotly debated, but if every country decides to boycott the Olympic Games every time it faces a political dispute or an international crisis, the Games will not survive. Writing in the *Christian Science Monitor*, Melvin Maddocks (1980) was critical of the U.S. boycott and feared that the next step might be a new version of SALT: a Sport and Arts Limitation Treaty. He stated:

> Whatever became of the argument that any relationship between people of two countries was better than no relationship at all. . . . Certainly in a world of nuclear warheads the boycott of a javelin thrower or two must measure as the most imperceptible of wrist slaps. (p. 22)

The rapid growth of soccer for girls and women has opened up a fine new sport opportunity for females. In 1979 there were 278 women's clubs in England and Wales. Taiwan hosted an international women's soccer tournament in 1981 for teams from France, New Zealand, West Germany, Finland, Switzerland, Norway, Holland, Thailand, and Taiwan. The Soviet Union has held back, because soccer (and wrestling) ''arouse unhealthy excitement among some spectators . . . and are harmful to a woman's organism in that they may cause damage to sexual functions, varicose veins, thrombophlebitis, etc.'' (Teoriya i praktika fizicheskoi kul'tury, No. 10, 1973, cited in Riordan, 1978).

Another significant development has been in the area of facilities. A major step forward is the new fiberglass-coated fabric dome for buildings, which is lightweight, relatively inexpensive, and quickly and easily erected. This technological breakthrough promises much for providing greatly needed indoor areas for all sports in many climates. There is one right here in Minneapolis, the Hubert Humphrey Metrodome.

As recently as a few years ago there was no organization where students and scholars of comparative physical education and international sport could get together and compare notes. Today there is a healthy and thriving International Society on Comparative Physical Education and Sport with the formidable initials combination of ISCPES. This third seminar and a membership of over 150 from 26 countries are proof of its vitality and vigor.

Several years ago we were apprehensive about the serious effects of the 1973 energy crisis upon physical education and sport. The effects turned out to be minimal after all, and sport continued unhampered in its growth and prominence. However, the potential for future energy crises continues to exist, and it cannot be wished away. The world often struggles, also, with severe economic recession marked by inflation, high interest rates, and widespread unemployment. Because sport is big business, it cannot be divorced from economic conditions in general.

Physical educators and coaches are part of the world community and should not remain oblivious to the enormous buildup of military personnel and weapons around this globe. The total military budget of all nations for 1981 was $550 billion, and $100 billion of that amount was spent to manufacture nuclear weapons. The world nuclear weapon stockpile in 1981 contained *over one million* times the explosive force of the Hiroshima bomb in 1945 (Sivard, 1981). The real possibility of nuclear disaster for mankind and the shameful and seemingly uncontrollable diversion of national resources into armaments and away from meeting basic human needs can no longer be ignored. We cannot forget that physical education and sport have little meaning or reality to the millions of people who are hungry and sick.

It is easy for one to be swept up in the glittering and glamorous world of sport with its tremendous media attention. But let *us* never forget that the essence of physical education and sport lies in that special relationship between a boy or girl and his or her teacher or coach at the school or club. Stephen Gooden, a school teacher in the United Kingdom, captured the beauty of this relationship in eloquent fashion.

> I teach rugby for two reasons. It offers a large number of boys what they need from education, apart from exam passes; the rough diamonds get some of their sharp edges knocked off and dull gems get a bit of polish. Secondly, I get enormous satisfaction out of something amorphous, without form and void, taking shape over the course of three or four years and becoming good to watch. I would not say that the under-15 "A" team is a work of art but, on the day that they put it all together, they are magic. (1981)

I conclude by inviting you and all physical educators and coaches around the world to try to bring a little of this "magic" into the lives of each and every one of our students and to keep it in an educational context.

References

1981: A bumper year (1982, March). *China Sports* No. 14, pp. 2-3.

China Sports. (1981). No. 12, pp. 13, 21.

Gooden, S. (1981, March). Please sir, Harwood is in detention. *Action— British Journal of Physical Education,* **12,** 36.

Hahm, J.H. (1981, October 20). Sports in modern society. *The ETHA Voice,* **27,** 3.

Maddocks, M. (1980, January 14). *Christian Science Monitor,* p. 22.

Riordan, J. (Ed.). (1978). Teoriya i praktika fizicheskoi kul'tury. *Sport under Communism.* Montreal: McGill-Queen's University Press.

Sasajima, K. (1979, December). Reforms in school education and sports in China under the Jua Kuo-Feng system. *Newsletter,* International Committee on Comparative Physical Education and Sport, No. 2, pp. 5-8.

Sivard, R.L. (1981). *World military and social expenditures, 1981* (p. 5). Leesburg, VA: World Priorities.

Van Lierde, A., & Van Dun, H. (1978). *The sport at school: Survey of the situation in eighteen European countries* (p. 164). Brussels: Clearing House.

Wulf, S. (1981, July 27). Taking 'roo hops in Nerk. *Sports Illustrated, 55,* 42-45.

The Role of Teacher Centers: Organizations for International Educators

Frederick V. Hayen
Gail Hughes
University of Minnesota Teacher Center

If you are an educator in Australia, Canada, Germany, Great Britain, Italy, Japan, New Zealand, Sierre Leone, or the United States, you are likely to have access to one of the teacher centers that can be found in these countries. Most of the credit for initiating the teacher center movement goes to teachers in British schools who organized the centers for social and professional needs.

Teacher centers are organizations established for the continuing education of practicing educators and to assist educators in the improvement and development of the educational programs in their institutions. Traditionally, teacher centers were organized to serve educators of young children, but have since developed into centers that collaborate with higher education institutions and are sometimes even sponsored by colleges and universities, with strong ties to the schools in their region. As might be expected, teacher centers differ widely in their structure, service systems, funding sources, and emphasis. However, they have a characteristic that is generally common to all; they tend to be *responsive* agencies, highly sensitive to the needs of their clients. They generally have the capacity to respond quickly and effectively to needs expressed by teachers for materials, new curricula,[1] training, and contacts with others who can serve as a resource.[2] The approach is from the bottom up rather than the top down. This simple, straightforward service approach, however, requires a new perception and skill on the part of the client. The client must know how to use a teacher center.[3] The client must often make the first move to cause a teacher center to respond effectively.

There are several types of assistance that a teacher center can generally provide. Most of them have a lounge, library, or other form of meeting place where new colleagues will be met. These spaces often serve as locations for conferences, workshops, seminars, and other learning sessions. When teacher centers are collaborative agencies, they provide formal and informal contacts between college personnel and school personnel. Often these new associations lead to cooperative ventures which benefit everyone.

Many centers contain special collections of materials, which are made available to its members through a distribution system of some kind. Some centers provide a systematic form of program dissemination to help teachers in one place adopt successful practices that have been developed elsewhere.

One of the most common pursuits of teacher centers is the development of professional training or in-service programs for its clients. These services are conducted in many ways, but their most common characteristics from center-to-center are the response to participant needs and the use of peer trainers. There is a strong emphasis in teacher centers on utilizing local talent in workshops and other training models. In addition, teacher centers emphasize follow-up and reinforcement so that new learning can be applied.

The responsiveness to individual clients is one of the most unique roles played by teacher centers. These centers can provide the power and authority of an organization to the professional needs and obligations of an individual. By bringing these forces together, individuals are appropriately supported by their peers through the teacher center structure. A recent example of this technique was the participation of the Teacher Center at the University of Minnesota in the Third International Seminar on Comparative Physical Education and Sport held July 21 to 23, 1982. The Teacher Center, which is jointly supported by the Minneapolis Public Schools and the University of Minnesota, responded to the conference director's request and organized an informal reception for early arriving conference participants, conducted a panel discussion session, and provided personalized campus orientation activities for participants. This teacher center role was undertaken as a response to the University faculty member who directed the conference, rather than from a role or function mandate dictated by policy or precedent. The response was to the individual's needs rather than the system's needs.

Many problems of practicing educators could be resolved by making contact with others who have faced and solved the same problem, or by gaining support and assistance to move through a more gradual problem-solving process. Teacher centers can help in both of these processes; however, individuals must initiate the contact. One must learn how to use a teacher center. The first step, of course, is to contact the center and talk with people there, observe its programs, and then develop a plan for how the center can help with your problem. Teacher centers are often willing to help, but they cannot become responsible for everyone's problems. The centers can only help you to help yourself.

Teacher centers have developed a rather wide-ranging network of resources. Most teacher centers not only have a local network of supporting members and human resources, but are also a part of a national and international network. Not all centers actively participate in these networks, but many do. The Teachers' Centers Exchange, associated with the Far West Laboratory in San Francisco, California, had actively managed a United States network of teacher centers for several years, but has now lost its funding; however, a directory of U.S. teacher centers and other valuable information can be obtained.

The international links that many teacher centers maintain can provide a contact point for professional educators who are interested in international education. With the help of teacher centers, contacts with schools and colleges can be made in other countries. Occasionally housing can be arranged for an extended or short-term study program and sites for visitation can be arranged in advance. Other agencies are available for these services, also, but often the attention that can be provided by a teacher center is more personalized.

There can be a great role played by the teacher center in regard to physical education and sport. Teacher centers and the development of their concept could, in many countries, provide pre- and in-service teacher training, as well as sport and teacher certification. As previously discussed, teacher centers are no strangers to some countries; however, in many areas, such as Central and Latin America and Africa, the teacher center concept is in its developmental phase. Certainly comparisons of the structure, function, funding, and role of the teacher center in regard to physical education and sport are needed; but more importantly, the global development of a network of teacher centers is needed in order to establish an educational link for the future of all education as it plays its crucial role in furthering the development of all nations.

Notes

1. British teachers' centers originated as places for teachers to make their own curriculum materials and are probably still more materials-oriented than are those in the U.S.
2. However, this approach does not hold for all centers or predominate in all countries with centers. In Japan, teacher centers arose to promote and improve science education, followed by other academic areas, and in New Zealand, centers train teachers to incorporate recent research findings ("The Teacher Center Experience Around the World" by Mary Crum and Joel Burdin, in U.S. Department of Health, Education and Welfare, 1977). Even where the "bottom-up" method predominates, as in the U.S. and England, teacher centers do oftentimes assist in disseminating information about innovative curricula that have had good evaluation results. For example, the MPS/UM Teacher Center is affiliated with The EXCHANGE, an organization that helps schools to implement validated nationally developed projects.
3. For more information and referral to consultants, readers may write or phone the Teachers' Centers Exchange, Far West Laboratory for Educational Research and Development, 1855 Folsom Street, San Francisco, California 94103, phone: (415) 565-3095. The Exchange also maintains two East Coast offices: Lorraine Keeney, Grange Avenue, Little Compton, Rhode Island 02837, phone: (401) 635-4817; and Gretchen Thomas, P.O. Box 1047, Amston, Connecticut 06231, phone: (203) 537-1306. The authors can be contacted at the MPS/UM Teacher Center, 101 Pattee Hall, 150 Pillsbury Drive SE, University of Minnesota, Minneapolis, MN 55455, United States, phone: (612) 376-4580.

References

Devaney, K., & Thorne, L. (1975). *Exploring teachers' centers*. San Francisco: Far West Laboratory for Educational Research and Development.

Feiman, S. (Ed.). (1978). *Teacher centers: What place in education?* Chicago: University of Chicago Center for Policy Studies.

Piper, B. (1982). *Teachers' centers exchange directory.* San Francisco: Far West Laboratory for Educational Research and Development.

U.S. Department of Health, Education and Welfare. (1977). *The commissioner's report on the education professions 1975-76: Teacher centers.* Washington, DC: U.S. Government Printing Office.

A Comparative Study on the Thoughts Between Japanese and Non-Japanese Physical Educators

Tetsuo Meshizuka
Shunichi Takeshita
J. Umemoto
Yokohama National University

Eigi Koshimizu
Tokyo College of Pharmacy

Makoto Sakai
Tokyo Metropolitan University

The purpose of this paper is to present an interim report on our survey of the pedagogical and philosophical thoughts of physical educators in the world today. The questionnaire, consisting of 10 questions, was distributed among professors and others in colleges and universities, teachers in schools of all kinds, and major students, including graduates of physical education.

So far, approximately 50% of those persons surveyed have responded to the questionnaire. Examination of the data at this time shows the following points to be sufficiently important to mention, even though lacking statistical significance at this time:

- Devotion to and excellence in sports are common denominators of physical educators without regard to their cultural, ideological, and religious differences as motivators in choosing the profession.
- Physical education is carried on in combination with moral and ethical teaching that usually coincides with Olympic ideology or Olympism.
- Teaching of physical activities is always placed above any form of physical punishment.
- More applicable research results are demanded by physical educators, but few, other than physical educators, present suitable questions.
- The lifetime health and fitness for adults has become the task of physical educators today, together with the school physical education program.

Hypotheses and Methods

The purpose of this study is to investigate whether there are common thoughts among contemporary teachers of physical education in Japan, as well as in other countries. Hypotheses on which this study is based are: (a) Japanese physical educators, including those receiving professional training, have become so liberated that they fail to apply appropriate behavioral student discipline and, as a result, have lost their pedagogical authority and charisma; (b) that teachers, since the end of World War II, have continued to emphasize complex thought while viewing the teaching and inculcation of ethics, morality, manners, and etiquette in the school as undemocratic; and (c) that those teachers located in countries having both compulsory military duties and compulsory schooling may differ in their thinking from teachers in Japan who have no compulsory duties.

It was determined that a questionnaire was needed to examine the aforementioned hypotheses of this study. A review of the literature revealed that there were no appropriate questionnaires of this kind except those assessing teacher psychosocial constructs.

This study is premised on the basis that such moral and ethical objectives as are raised in this study relating to sports and physical education at school can be achieved by adopting and placing more emphasis upon Olympic ideology and sportsmanship in physical education.

A questionnaire based on the hypotheses of this study included 10 questions prepared in both English and Japanese (Appendix A). Approximately 120 questionnaires were distributed at the International Olympic Academy session and among Japanese physical educators. To date, 50 questionnaires in English and 55 in Japanese have been collected and reviewed.

Table 1 Countries That Responded to the Questionnaire

Country	Number of responses	Country	Number of responses
Japan	55	Canada	2
United States	8	Austria	2
Taiwan	4	Malta	2
Philippines	2	Bahrain	1
Israel	3	Egypt	1
United Kingdom	3	Paraguay	1
France	4	Germany	1
Switzerland	3	Korea	1

Results and Discussion

On the basis of the questionnaire, it was found that those responding had, in some way, been involved in sports involving competition ranging from high to low. Five non-Japanese and seven Japanese had experience as national team members and had participated in international games. The remaining respondents had participated as regular members of university, high school, and club sports. Nearly all areas of sports were represented with the largest concentration in track and field.

Eighty-two percent of the Japanese and 96% of the non-Japanese believed that sport participation had a high positive influence on personality and morality (see Table 2). For example, perseverance, patience, self-confidence, spirit of cooperation, sportsmanship, fair play, and honesty all were believed to be expressions of one's personality as influenced by participation in different kinds of sports and, thus, human relations in sports participation. With respect to this, it is significant that sports have both qualities of internationalism and universality. However, one Japanese mentioned, "I became to have a trend of individualism and lack spirit of cooperation." In addition, three non-Japanese expressed the opinion that morality, as influenced by home discipline, is separate from sports discipline. Here it is interesting to note the divergency between teaching discipline in sports and strengthening spirit.

Eighty-three percent of the non-Japanese and 56% of the Japanese respondents stated that sports participation had positive effects on health (see Table 3, Appendix A). This big percentage gap showed that Japanese could not decide whether their health had been affected before or after sports participation. They also noted that poor health was the result of the overtraining they had, which was not true for the non-Japanese. Different points of view were expressed about prescribing sports to keep one's health and fitness.

Table 2 Influence of Sport Participation on Personality and Morality

Influence	Japanese		Non-Japanese	
Positive	33	60%	21	91%
Negative	0	0%	1	4%
Positive and negative	0	0%	1	4%
Not decisive	9	16%	0	0%
Personality only	0	0%	3	13%
Total influenced	45	82%	22	96%
Total not influenced	10	18%	1	4%

Table 3   Sport Participation Effects on Health

Effects	Japanese		Non-Japanese	
Positive	31	56%	19	83%
Negative	0	0%	1	4%
Positive and negative	4	7%	0	0%
Not decisive	19	35%	3	13%
No answer	1	2%	0	0%

With regard to both the respectability and trustworthiness of sportsmen and sportswomen, the Japanese showed antagonistic feeling toward indicating a criterion for both traits. Positive answers were given by 9% of the Japanese and 43% of the non-Japanese, while negative responses were given by 53% of the Japanese and 0% of the non-Japanese (see Table 4, Appendix A). Some Japanese mentioned that sportsmen and sportswomen should not only be evaluated in terms of their respectability and trustworthiness, but should be assessed in general. One Japanese stated that sportsmen and sportswomen are more respected and trusted than sports students; they can be better assessed due to their maturity than students whose personalities are still unstable. Another mentioned, "In employing people in Japanese companies or enterprises, sportsmen and sportswomen receive priority. They consider them of high caliber." Another respondent said, "People who have experienced sports participation understand (and even envy) the sportsman who always plays without working hard." It was also mentioned by Peter McIntosh that "Some are respected, for example, Sir Roger Bannister, some are not. Being good at sports is not itself a reason for trusting anyone." Janos Horvath, who teaches at a high school in Hungary, stated, "They are appreciated more

Table 4   Respectability and Trustworthiness of Sportsmen and Women

Responses	Japanese		Non-Japanese	
Positively affirmative	5	9%	10	43%
Rather negative	29	53%	0	0%
Both affirmatively and negatively assessed	19	34%	10	43%
Not decisive	2	4%	3	13%

than ordinary people, they are more popular than scientists and artists because many people are interested and involved in sports than in any other fields of culture.''

Generally speaking, Japanese opinions were vague compared to the direct views expressed by non-Japanese as to whether physical educators should teach skill or personality first to their students. This difference may be due to the fact that most non-Japanese served as administrative staff of the faculty. Non-Japanese mentioned that there is a direct influence in teaching both skill and personality, while Japanese said otherwise. One Japanese stated, ''I don't like my own personality so I cannot influence my students in a personal way.'' It is difficult at this point to classify the opinions statistically. However, those who believe that skills should be learned first consisted of 5% Japanese and 4% non-Japanese (see Table 5).

Forty-nine percent of the Japanese and 17% of the non-Japanese favored teaching personality first, while 42% of the Japanese and 75% of the non-Japanese believed that both personality and skill should be taught at the same time. One Japanese who believed in teaching sport skills first said, ''I always teach the calculated and systematic training for a promising youth to be a champion, teach a method of coaching for the hopeless competitor, and teach basic knowledge of training for a jogger of older age.'' Hillel Ruskin of Israel stated, ''I do not teach skills. However, theoretically, it should be blended.'' One Japanese mentioned a similar opinion on the influence of sport participation on personality and morality, that is, ''I hope students get willpower and passion to survive on their own feet.'' Moreover, McIntosh mentioned, ''My first action and words in the gymnasium project my personality, so this is what students learn first.'' One Japanese said, ''I think students are more influenced by things unseen and unspoken while teaching skills and knowledge. Thus it is also difficult to measure the depth of education because of the infinite connotations involved in teaching.''

Physical educators differed markedly in their acceptance of the use of punishment even though data were difficult to collate. Thirty-three percent of the Japanese and 91% of the non-Japanese responded in the negative to this question (see Table 6, Appendix A). Japanese cannot deny

Table 5   Student Expectation of Learning Skill or Personality First From a Physical Educator

Responses	Japanese		Non-Japanese	
Sport skill first	3	5%	1	4%
Personality first	27	49%	4	17%
Both	23	42%	17	75%
Not decisive	1	2%	1	4%
No answer	1	2%	0	0%

Table 6 Acceptance of Physical Punishments by Physical Educators

Responses	Japanese		Non-Japanese	
Never accept	18	33%	21	91%
Positively accept	32	58%	2	9%
Not decisive	4	7%	0	0%
No answer	1	2%	0	0%

the necessity of physical punishment because of their broader understanding of its meaning. For them it is necessary to use physical punishment to teach the child what cannot be given to the brain. McIntosh's statement may be representative of the non-Japanese when he said, ''Never. Physical punishment is educationally ineffective, socially undesirable and physiologically dangerous.''

About 61% of both Japanese and non-Japanese think that research products are useful to give physical education a scientific basis (see Table 7, Appendix A). Mequi, Dean of the University of the Philippines, said, ''Some yes, others no. I especially like to carry innovative techniques suggested by research studies.'' According to McIntosh, ''Much research is too specialized and done in order to gain a PhD and not to assist teachers and coaches. Findings of research are not made available in a usable form.'' John Lucas of Pennsylvania State University said, ''For 50 years this has been a serious problem in the U.S.A. Today researchers in sport and physical education are more sensitive to this matter and a certain percentage (20-30%) of them work directly to help teachers and coaches.'' According to August Kirsch, ICSSPE President-elect, ''Developing a new scientific discipline generally has difficulties to produce useful results for practical transmission by thinking in short terms. There is much further

Table 7 Usefulness of Research Products in Sports-Physical Education

Responses	Japanese		Non-Japanese	
Very useful	34	62%	14	61%
Useful and not useful	16	29%	6	26%
Not useful	0	0%	0	0%
Others	4	7%	0	0%
No answer	1	2%	3	13%

work to be done." There seem to be many situations where research products cannot suit the current social changes in the field of education.

Regarding the physical educators' inclusion of moral and ethical education, 49% of the Japanese and 65% of the non-Japanese felt it was their responsibility to provide moral and ethical education (see Table 8, Appendix A). Thirty-eight percent of the Japanese and 22% of the non-Japanese think that it is everyone's responsibility, both in school and outside school. According to one Japanese, "Who can teach students and pupils manners, politeness, patience or friendship in front of a desk inside the classroom? The physical education teacher should teach them by coming in personal contact face to face, body to body." Barolome, a former dean of the University of the Philippines, said, "Yes, you are in direct contact with them. Your association is more informal." While G. Alan Stull said, "No. Every teacher has this responsibility. It is extremely important for all teachers." Moreover, as McIntosh mentioned, "All teachers should teach modes of behavior but because physical activity, e.g., competitive sport and dance, are more highly charged with emotion than other subjects, teachers of physical education have special opportunities to teach control expression of emotion and we would practice sport rightly, the moral and ethical way, and thus absorb it."

Reasons given for the respondents' selection of physical education as an occupation or specialization were: (a) desire to pursue an essence of sports and physical education, (b) interest in sports and physical education, (c) teacher influence, (d) influence of relatives, and (e) use of their teachers as images, and so forth. Comments were generally common to both the Japanese and non-Japanese groups.

Conclusion

On the basis of this study, it was found that Japanese physical educators often mentioned other persons' viewpoints and not their own. This may

Table 8 Responsibility of Physical Educators for Moral and Ethical Education Relative to Other Teachers

Responses	Japanese		Non-Japanese	
Essentially responsible	27	49%	15	65%
Everyone's responsibility, or beyond school, for example, home	21	38%	35	22%
Miscellaneous	6	11%	3	13%
No answer	1	2%	0	0%

be due to the typical Japanese trait of not expressing too many feelings in words. In reference to the question of respectability and trustworthiness of sportsmen and sportswomen, the gap between the Japanese and non-Japanese was marked. The Japanese gave general answers, such as "respectability and trustworthiness depend on each human nature," while non-Japanese clearly stated a yes or no answer.

Respondents from both groups (Japanese and non-Japanese) expressed the thoughts that sports education should (a) aim at a totalized humanity through education and individual sports involvement and participation, and (b) encourage people who have gained experience in sports to become members of a community aimed at educating others just as they were educated.

The comparative study between Japanese and non-Japanese physical educators showed that the Japanese tended to use deductive thought, as is clearly seen in their acceptance of physical punishment. Non-Japanese, however, use inductive thought. For example, Japanese are apt to be satisfied to look for their own aim, ideology, and method of training; non-Japanese are not satisfied with aim and ideology unless they are practiced in sports, so that the life may become their own.

Because the responses that are still coming in are more detailed and individualized, other approaches may be necessary to assess this survey. At this time, we shall not dare predict any further conclusions.

Appendix A
The Questionnaire

1. What kind of sports competitions were/have you been involved in? Please write down your highest records or achievements, if any.
2. Do you think your participation in sports either as an athlete or a player has influenced your personality or morality? Please write both its positive and negative influences.
3. Do you think that your career as a top athlete or a regular player has helped your health? If so, please state in what aspects it has helped.
4. Are the sportsmen and women in your country respected and trusted more than others who are not involved in sports? Please tell why and why not.
5. What are the aims of school physical education in your country? Please list those according to primary, middle, higher, or other schools.
6. What do you expect your students to learn first, your sports skills or your character and/or personality? Why?
7. Do you use physical punishment when you think it is needed? Why or why not?
8. Are the research products on sports and physical activities very useful in your teaching of physical education or sports classes? Why and why not?

9. Do you believe that as a physical educator, you, more than other teachers, should teach students manners, politeness, patience, and friendship? Why or why not?
10. Why did you choose your occupation or your specialization?

References

Bennett, B.L., Howell, M.L., & Simri, U. (1975). (T. Meshizuka et al., Trans.). *Comparative physical education and sport*. Philadelphia: Lea & Febiger.

Suetoshi, H. (1967, March). *A study of attitudes of British students towards sports I. Construction of the scale*. (Reprinted from *Bulletin*, Series B., No. 30, Kyoto University of Education.)

Suetoshi, H. (1969, September). *A comparative study of attitudes towards sport between Japanese and British*. (Reprinted from *Bulletin*, Series B., No. 35, Kyoto University of Education.)

Suetoshi, H., & Cooper, G.E. (1968, March). *A study of attitudes of British students towards sports II*. (Reprinted from *Bulletin*, Series B., No. 32, Kyoto University of Education.)

Svoboda, B. (1977). Physical education teacher's personality and teaching performance. *Didactic studies in physical education* (pp. 1-41). Praha: Univezita Karlova.

International Sports and Games Expressed in Children's Creative Art

Thomas C. Slettehaugh
University of Minnesota

At a recent international children's art exhibition held on the University of Minnesota campus, March Krotee commented to me that many of the pictures had sport activity and games for their subject matter. This was a special exhibition of 77 paintings by children of The People's Republic of China and was the first exhibition of children's art from China ever held in the United States. The young artists, ranging in age from 5 to 15 years, were students from elementary and high schools geographically representative of several provinces in China.

Like children throughout the world, these Chinese children disclosed characteristic modes of understanding that showed through their artistic creations. They had made paintings of familiar things that they had directly experienced, like "Acrobatic Performance," "Physical Training," "Skating Game," "Relay Race," and other activities (see Figures 1-3). The diversity of their geographical locations and cultural and traditional

Figure 1 It's good to do physical training by Ge Yin (girl) age 12 (China).

Figure 2   Relay race by Zhou Quan-hong (girl) age 8 (China).

Figure 3   Skating by Wang Sin (girl) age 12 (China).

backgrounds is reflected in their works and brings a new level of understanding of Chinese culture to the world.

In the recent translations of another ancient culture, the 2,000 year old carved symbols of the Mayan civilization of Central America, indications are that individuals living in that culture were encouraged to "use their body to expand their mind," just as the Chinese children are doing today. These people had to make use of their various kinesthetic actions, reactions, and body movements to advance their civilization physically, emotionally, and intellectually. This was an early beginning in the use of inner imagery as it related to physical and sensory activity. Somehow, the Mayans were able to perceive that within each person is a secluded and personal flow of images and ideas. They probably realized that these interior environmental experiences are not just intellectual abstractions or emotional pleasurings but are occurrences that are as real to that person as any outward social event, like attending a sports activity or ball game. Today, the Chinese people are taking part in daily Tai-Chi Chuan exercises in which physical movements are done very slowly while inside mental and emotional dimensions are being exercised.

The process and production of an original visual picture reveal the "creative spirit" of a person and his or her personal mode(s) of expression at a specific given time period. In drawing or painting a picture, a person can create any original symbol to denote ideas; no specific degree of skill is needed. In the writing of creative ideas, preconceived written symbols must first be intellectually learned. This places a limit on what can be expressed creatively in a literary way in order to communicate with other people. Sport activity and visual artistic activity are similar in that the individual tries to be different from the established norm of an educational standard. This can be seen when a person is participating in an individual or group sport, dance, or game. The creative spirit signals to the person the specific movement(s)—a twist, turn, jump, stop, or change of body direction—that is needed to display his or her mode of individual expression. Examples of the physical and aesthetic growth process can be found in a visual and pictorial form in Viktor Lowenfeld's (1975) studies with gang-age children. This is the age and stage where children become more aware of themselves as a part of a peer group, and each is more conscious of his or her specific culture.

If the children's art from several cultures is examined for sameness or differences using the basic elements listed by Benjamin Lowe (1977), a visual analysis of the concrete items can easily be found. Elements or variables that are constant throughout the various cultures can be noted. These art elements of straight or curved lines, light or dark values, figurative or naturalistic shapes, and so forth can be seen and compiled for statistical analysis. As children use their own ideas to create game and sport symbols, like an abstract soccer ball, the cultural variables become inconsistent. This inconsistent factor is very noticeable when children from different countries, or subcultures within a country, express their ideas using geometric shapes and forms. The children from the People's Republic of China create the eye of a person using a different geometric configuration than children from the United States or other countries in the Western world. Other differences can be noted between the creative works from children living in Europe and those living in the Orient.

The creative mind needs the freedom to create original images and symbols that can play out inner environmental ideas. Originality is an important part of the creative act in art and in sports, and each individual possesses the ability to produce outward symbol(s) that no other person has made. The trained aesthetician/clinician can look at these creations and the processes used in achieving them and make many distinctions, not in terms of judging a skillful performance, but in terms of deciphering what the individual is doing and thinking. The results of a visual expression can be related to the PSIX analysis (Slettehaugh, 1981), and a graphic profile indicates where a person is during a certain time period. The PSIX program can be used for children 5 through 14 years of age and is designed to serve as a map or gauge to guide the child in personal creative expression.

Just as art expression can be analyzed for comparison in regard to creativity, the content of the picture as it reflects or mirrors society may be of interest to the International Society on Comparative Physical Education. As demonstrated by my showing of "Sport and Art Around the World" (see selected pictures, Figures 4-6) that was displayed throughout our seminar meeting room in Nolte Center, the role that art can play in revealing various comparisons of societal thought and activity has tremendous, yet unexplored, potential.

Acknowledgments

Photographs courtesy of Slettehaugh Studio, Minneapolis, MN 55414, USA. Title translations courtesy of Zheng Shengtian, Zhejiang Academy of Fine Arts, Hangzhow, People's Republic of China.

Figure 4 Bullfighting by J. Carlos Millan, age 11 (Spain).

Figure 5 Soccer by Roger Arvidsson, age 13 (Sweden).

Figure 6 Gymnastics by Renale Wieger, age 12 (Austria).

Note

1. If the reader wishes to send some representative children's art and sport works for the author's file, it will help further research into the comparative and international dimension of sport, physical activity, and art. Send materials to Thomas C. Slettehaugh, Art Education, University of Minnesota, Minneapolis, Minnesota 55455.

References

Lowe, B. (1977). *The beauty of sport* (p. 327). Englewood Cliffs, NJ: Prentice-Hall.

Lowenfeld, V. (1975). *Creative and mental growth* (3rd ed.) (p. 430). New York: Macmillan.

Slettehaugh, T.C. (1981, November). Relating the PSIX Program to the interior human environment. *INSEA Newsletter*, pp. 83-87. Adelaide, Australia: Fisnbury Press.

A Comparative Study of Physical Education Professional Preparation Programs in Brazil and the United States

Edilia Vieira da Rosa
Sharon Lee Shields
Vanderbilt University

A long history of government legislation, debates, professional programs, and conferences precedes the continual growth, development, and changes in physical education professional preparation programs. The issues and problems of physical education professional preparation are long standing and vary internationally. With increasing international exchange of students at master and doctoral degree levels, a comparative study of undergraduate professional preparation programs is needed so that program differences and similarities may be discovered. Through the discovery of such differences and/or similarities, it may be possible for a deeper level of international understanding to occur within academe, thereby enhancing and enriching postbaccalaureate degree offerings.

The purpose of this paper is the comparison of physical education professional preparation programs in selected colleges and universities in Brazil, South America, and the United States. In order to analyze and evaluate the evolution of the physical education profession in Brazil, one needs first to consider its legal aspects. The profession, itself, as well as the curriculum and facilities requirements have always been guided by a set of governmental laws and regulations.

Physical education curriculum has had its norms set by federal law ever since the first courses aimed at preparing physical educators were offered during the late 1930s and early 1940s. At that time, physical education classes at the elementary and secondary levels were directed by instructors and focused mainly on body building.

The 1960s brought a radical change to the system. As the schools for the preparation of the physical educator spread, laws were passed with the purpose of guiding and directing physical education activities at the elementary and secondary levels.

The first law passed ruled physical education a mandatory subject for all students up to 18 years of age. However, due to the increasing number of physical education teachers and students, this law soon had to be modified to include mandatory physical education activities at all school levels.

A definite statement came only in the 1970s. Decree 69.450, passed on November 1, 1971, is, in fact, responsible for the orientation and functioning of physical education in Brazil. This decree defines physical education as being an element directly related to national education. It regards physical education as a means of developing and improving physical, moral, civic, psychological, and social values, as well as setting the standards that rule professional preparation programs for physical educators.

A special branch of the Ministry of Education, the Secretaria de Educacao Fisica e Desportos (Secretary of Physical Education and Sports), is the national office responsible for ruling and supervising all physical education programs in Brazil. A national plan for physical education and sports, aimed at establishing the nation's priorities in the field, is elaborated for a period of 5 years. Program implementation and regional strategies are suggested; in other words, the national program is an action plan devised to serve as an orientation for all organizations involved in the process of offering physical education programs at all school levels.

Professional preparation in physical education in the United States enjoyed no general popular support or enthusiasm in the early part of the 19th century, but tentative beginnings were made. In view of the lack of teacher training for any subject in the public schools, the lack of recognition of teacher training for physical education was to be expected. Teacher training in physical education received its first genuine impetus from Dio Lewis when he established a Normal Institute of Physical Education in 1861.

Somewhat later in the 19th century, the rise of interest in public school physical education resulted in the passage of the first state laws regarding physical education. Ohio is generally credited with being the first state to pass a physical education law in 1892. The cause of professional preparation received a powerful boost when Dudley Sargent opened a private gymnasium in Cambridge, Massachusetts, and offered to give a one-year training course free to anyone who desired to teach. Sargent had projected a 2-year course in theory and practice of physical education, but this plan was not realized until 1892 because of the increasing demand for teachers. In 1883 gymnasia were reported in only 19 out of 119 public normal schools and in 16 out of 114 private normal schools. It was nearly 1900 before any general college added a professional curriculum in physical education to its course offerings.

A summary of the history of physical education between 1900 and 1930 shows that the greatest progress occurred after World War I (WWI). The number of physical education teachers decidedly increased as more colleges and universities offered professional curriculum. One significant effect of WWI was improved state legislation for physical education. By the postwar period (1921), 33 states had enacted physical education legislation. Because of the increased demand for trained professionals the number of teacher training schools in physical education reached 150 by 1930.

In the period that followed (1930 to 1950), physical education achieved a recognized place in general education. This was reflected in various ways: (a) teacher education courses were placed in the school of education, (b) academic rank was bestowed on the physical educators, (c) students in physical education courses earned academic credit, and (d) universities offered master and doctoral programs in physical education. Over 70 institutions inaugurated a master's program and approximately 20 began to grant a doctorate degree. In a 1945 study of graduate faculties at 49 institutions, it was disclosed that 54% of the staff members had a master's degree and 22% had a doctor's degree.

As we look to the 30 years following 1950, we find that prospective teachers in health, physical education, and recreation are graduated from approximately 940 institutions of higher learning each year. Legislation concerning physical education is present in all states. Professional preparation programs have shown a marked difference in the past century and a half.

Physical education undergraduate programs in Brazil are aimed at forming a generalistic/humanistic professional capable of teaching at kindergarten, elementary, junior, and senior high school levels. The teaching areas considered are physical education, sports, and recreation and leisure.

Foreign influences are still present in Brazilian programs. Because the programs were first built upon the European system, there is still a very strong trend toward the characteristics of that system; but, as the teacher exchange programs began to include other countries in the options for the attainment of advanced studies, influences began to vary accordingly. The American influence, for instance, is becoming a very definite one.

Environmental components, however, such as demographic conditions, physiological and anatomical characteristics of the population, climate and geographical locations, and economical and sociological aspects that differ from people of other countries, require Brazilian programs to be specifically designed for the population they serve. These environmental factors, called in the national program 80/85 ''The Ecology of Physical Activity,'' are definitely social forces that need to be taken into account when designing a program.

In order to gain a better understanding of the comparative nature of health and physical education professional preparation programs for physical educators in Brazil and the United States, the following areas are discussed: (a) selection requirements for students wishing to prepare for careers in physical education (undergraduate programming), (b) qualifications of the teaching faculty in these programs, and (c) curriculum requirements.

Student Selection

In order to be accepted as a physical education student in an under-graduate program in Brazil, a candidate must

- graduate from a federally accredited high school;
- undergo a series of health tests and shots (urinalysis, blood tests, chest x-rays, smallpox vaccination, etc.) before taking the specific ability test;
- before taking the nationwide examination, pass a test of specific ability for physical education that may vary from college to college, but generally includes (a) a medical examination at rest, (b) a coordination and sports ability test, (c) a speed test (40 meters), (d) an endurance test (Burpe 1-minute), and (e) a medical assessment after exercise; and
- take the nationwide examination, given over a 3-day period, in areas that are weighted differently according to a student's interest field, but generally include (a) Portuguese and either French, English, or German; (b) mathematics, chemistry, and physics; and (c) Brazilian government, general history, and general geography.

No specific tests are given on a national basis for the selection of students for admission to an institution of higher education in the United States. However, among the 77 institutions surveyed, the following methods were employed: (a) SAT scores; (b) IQ scores; (c) high school GPA; (d) graduation from an accredited high school; (e) leadership characteristics, as exemplified through extracurricular activity involvement; (f) letters of reference; (g) physical examination; (h) statement of future directions and personal goals; (i) skill proficiency examination; and (j) personal interview. In many institutions, students experience a formal screening process conducted by the faculty of the department after the second year of training, plus a final screening after the completion of all course work for the undergraduate degree. Table 1 presents the criteria used in the selection of students entering undergraduate professional preparation in physical education in Brazil and the United States.

Teacher Demand

The demand for teachers prepared at the graduate level in Brazil is very high. However, the number of graduate courses offered and the number of professionals with graduate degrees earned within the country or in foreign countries do not meet present needs. Thus, undergraduate programs are mainly led by physicians and physical education certified teachers who must meet college and university policies to enter the college teaching career.

Usually an entrance examination must be passed by the prospective teacher. Professors appointed by the university's administration form the examination committee and are held accountable for the exams. Their

Table 1   Criteria for the Selection of Students Entering Undergraduate Professional Preparation Programs in Physical Education in Brazil and the United States

Brazil	United States
Graduation from a federally accredited high school	Graduation from an accredited high school (also GPA)
Screened through a series of health tests and shots	IQ scores
	Physical examination
Nationwide examination on language, mathematics, chemistry, Brazilian government, general history, and general geography	National examination (SAT or ACT)
	Skill proficiency examination
Physical education examination: medical examination at rest, coordination and sports ability test, speed test, endurance test, medical examination after exercise	Leadership characteristics as exemplified through extracurricular activity and academic leadership roles
	Letters of reference
	Statement of future direction and personal goals
	Personal interview (either on site or by telephone)

duties encompass the decisions regarding personal and professional abilities of the candidate.

Teaching experience and a proven interest in self-actualization through participation in postbaccalaureate courses take care of the first part of the examination, the titles and experience portion. A second part is fulfilled after completion of a lecture and an interview. The lecture has a 2-hour duration, and the subject is drawn 72 hours prior to its realization. Upon completion of the lecture, an interview follows, focusing on general knowledge of the physical education field. Its duration varies from 1 to 2 hours.

After the entrance exam is passed, a nontenure track position is granted for 4 years. Further graduate work entitles the faculty member to the highest ranks in the college teaching career.

Selection of faculty is varied in the United States, but some basic selection procedures exist among most major institutions. Most candidates must (a) go through an exacting application procedure, which includes an in-depth personal report such as a vitae or resumé, (b) present confirmation of an education background that focuses on specific qualifications related to the job being applied for, and (c) undergo a personal interview at the site of prospective employment. In our survey of 77 colleges with a student population of 10,000 or more throughout the regions of the United States, it was found that the qualifications of the teaching faculty ranked extremely high.

Table 2   Faculty Degrees and Ranks as Reported Among 77 Colleges in a Nationwide Survey

Degree held by faculty member	%	Rank	%
PhD, EdD, or MD	77	Full professor	22
Ed. specialist	4	Associate professor	29
Master's	13	Assistant professor	32
Bachelor's	6	Instructor or other nontenure track	17

Note. N = 1,742.

As shown in Table 2, faculty members holding PhD or EdD degrees comprised 77% of the teaching faculty, specialists 4%, master degree members 13%, and bachelor degree members, the remaining 6%. Twenty-two percent of the faculty members had achieved full professor rank, 29% associate professor rank, 32% assistant professor rank, and 17% the rank of instructor or other nontenure track designations.

Physical Education Programs

Ninety-six percent of the undergraduate programs in physical education in Brazil are responsible for the preparation of approximately 2,000 physical education teachers yearly. The programs are rather evenly distributed throughout the country and are administered either privately or by the federal, state, or municipal government. There are 20 federal colleges, 11 state colleges, 11 municipal colleges, 50 private colleges, and 4 programs offered through the Army.

A minimum curriculum requirement is set by law. However, similarities stop there. The range of required credits set by the institution usually falls between a 10% and 50% increase. A total of 1,800 class hours taken in a minimum of 6 and a maximum of 10 semesters is necessary to fulfill the requirements for graduation.

The national conference of the American Alliance for Health, Physical Education, Recreation and Dance (held in New Orleans, March 1979) set forth competency areas that were to be used as guidelines in designing undergraduate professional preparation programs. These areas included (a) an historical and philosophical perspective of the profession, (b) administration, (c) curriculum, (d) adapted physical education, (e) scientific foundations, (f) health education, (g) teaching methodology, and (h) skill development. The areas serve as foundation guidelines for establishing professional preparation programs in physical education in the

United States. There is evidence to support the observation that a more varied and in-depth approach is taken in the training of teachers at the undergraduate level in the United States while skill development, skill proficiency, and preparation for the teaching of skill seem to be the primary focus of most undergraduate institutions in Brazil. Table 3 shows the courses that are required as part of the core curriculum in professional physical education programs found in 77 colleges in the United States. Table 4 presents a typical Brazilian professional physical education curriculum. Table 5 presents the minimum curriculum components of professional undergraduate physical education, an outgrowth of the National Seminar, Brazil, 1981.

As noted in this paper, the field of physical education in Brazil has changed and is changing significantly. Based on the belief that physical education contributes to the development of understanding and behavior needed by students throughout life, sound professional preparation programs for physical educators have always been sought.

Education as a means of total development is given high priority in Brazil. Therefore, the objectives and actions set forth by the National Plan for Physical Education and Sports for a given period of time are precise and seek to meet the nation's highest educational priorities.

It is our hope that, through the information presented, we can now observe the areas of need in professional preparation and continue to grow

Table 3   Required Courses in the Core Curriculum in Physical Education Professional Preparation Programs Among 77 Colleges in the United States

Area	%
Teaching and coaching	63.6
Health education	46.7
Recreation and leisure	38.9
Dance	25.9
Sports medicine/physical therapy	23.3
Physiology of sport	15.5
Adapted physical education	11.6
Philosophy/history of sport	10.3
Sports administration	7.8
Cardiovascular rehabilitation	3.8
Gerontology	2.5
Sports psychology	1.2
Sociology of sport	1.2

Table 4   Typical Curriculum in Brazilian Physical Education Professional Preparation Programs

Area	Program %
Sociocultural	4.9
Pedagogical	22.7
Biological sciences	15.9
Technical sciences	7.5
Skill development	46.6
Complementary	2.4
Total class hours = 2,445	100.0

Table 5   Proposed Minimum Curriculum Components (National Seminar/1981)

Area	Program %
Sociocultural	11.4
Pedagogical	17.1
Biological sciences	16.4
Technical sciences	15.2
Skill development	34.8
Complementary	5.1
Total class hours = 2,370	100.0

Note. Currently, the minimum curriculum components required by law involve the pedagogical, biological sciences, and skill development areas for a total of 1,800 hours distributed according to the schools' priorities.

as neighbors on adjoining continents, pooling our resources and knowledge to strengthen the professional preparation programs for the people of Brazil and the United States.

References

Albuquerque, L.C., e outros (1977). *As grandes diretrizes da universidade brasileira*. Belo Horizonte: Imprensa Universitaria-UFMG.

American Alliance of Health, Physical Education and Recreation (1972). *1972 New Orleans conference on health, physical education, recreation, safety, and dance. A guide to professional preparation*. Conference proceedings.

Bucher, C.A. (1972). *Foundations of physical education*. St. Louis: C.V. Mosby.

Decreto (1971, November 1). No. 69.450.

Decreto (1977, August 25). No. 80.228.

Gezi, K.I. (1971). *Education in comparative and international perspectives*. New York: Holt, Rinehart and Winston.

Goldberg, M.A. (1980). *Systematica de avaliaco*. Brasilia, D.F.: MEC.

Grillo, A.N., e outros (1978). Universidade Federal de Santa Catarina-plano de desenvolvimento. Florinaopolis, S.C.: Imprensa Universitaria.

International Council on Health, Physical Education, and Recreation (1967-1968). *Teacher training for physical education. Questionnaire report, part II, 1967-68*. Washington: ICHPER.

King, E.J. (1968). *Comparative studies and educational decision*. London: Methuen and Company.

Lei (1975, October 8). No. 6.251.

Machlman, A.H. (1964). *Comparative educational systems*. New York: Center for Applied Research in Education.

Ministerio da Educacao e Cultura, Secretaria de Educacao Fisica e Desportos (1980-1985). *Plano nacional de educacao fisica e desportos*. Brasilia: Circulacao Interna.

Ministerio da Educacao e Cultura, Secretaria de Educacao e Fisica e Desportos (1980-1985). *Politica nacional de educacao fisica e desportos*. Brasilia: Circulacao Interna.

Ministerio da Educacao e Cultura, Secretaria Geral (1980). *III Plano setorial de educacao, cultura e desporto*. Brasilia: MEC.

Monteiro, J.V. (1979). *Formulacao e avaliaco de politicas publicas—Manual de instrucao da disciplina*. Sao Paulo: EBAP/CIPAD—Fundacao Getulio Vargas.

Pelton, B.C. (1968, Spring). International programs of physical education for college youth. *Gymnasion*, **V**, 11-13.

Ribeiro, N.F. (1977). *Administracao academica universitaria: a teoria, o metodo*. Rio de Janeiro: Livros Tecnicos e Cientificos Editora S.A.

Rocha Filho, J. (1973). *Universidade para o desenvolvimento*. Santa Maria: Imprensa Universitaria-UFSM.

Secretaria da Educacao (1976). Fundacao Educacional de Santa Catarina. Universidade para o desenvolvimento do Estado de Santa Catarina. *Catalogo Geral 1976*. Florianopolis: SE/FESC/ODESC.

Van Dalen, D.B., & Bennett, B.L. (1971). *World history of physical education*. Englewood Cliffs, NJ: Prentice-Hall.

Vendien, C.L., & Nixon, J.E. (1968). *The world today in health, physical education, and recreation*. Englewood Cliffs, NJ: Prentice-Hall.

A Comparison of Children From the United States and The Netherlands on Selected Physiological Changes Related to Aerobic Exercise

Leon Greene
James D. La Point
University of Kansas

The interest in the relationship of physical fitness and daily physical activity to the general health status of elementary school-age children has dramatically increased among physiologists, epidemiologists, physical educators, and others who deal with the primary prevention of coronary heart disease (Saris et al., 1980). This interest has resulted in an increase of longitudinal studies and a wealth of data. Although much data are being obtained each day, many questions still exist when seriously analyzing the effects of physical activity upon the health of children.

Research dealing with the relationship of physical fitness and participation in regular physical activity (Armstrong & Davies, 1980) has focused primarily on adolescent and older populations. Specific longitudinal studies examining the effects of these variables on children are much needed.

For this reason a comparison of data obtained on children in the United States was made to data obtained on children from the Nijmegan area of The Netherlands, using the American children as an experimental group and the Netherlands children as a control group. Research of this type is important because of the curricular implications that administrators may be able to implement into the elementary physical education curriculum, and because it demonstrates the need for physical activity to improve the status of health in young children.

Methods

The study involving 43 American children was conducted during the course of a normal school year (1980 to 1981), or over a period of 9 months. The subjects were fourth, fifth, and sixth grade students of a public school located in the midwestern area of the United States. The children were from middle socioeconomic families.

The subjects participated in a specially designed aerobic activity program for a period of 7 months, 3 days per week, 20 minutes per day. Running, walking, movement exploration activities, exercises on Vitae Park Stations, and gymnastics composed the aerobic program.

The primary objective of the aerobic program was to keep the students moving continuously for a period of 20 minutes. A variety of movement activities was emphasized during each aerobic activity period in an attempt to create a more individualized environment, which would better promote the learning process.

The study (Saris et al., 1980) involving 54 children of the Nijmegan area of The Netherlands included students from three different schools and from lower to middle socioeconomic level families. All data were collected during school time. Children in this study were not subjected to an aerobic activity program, but physical activity levels were considered. Questionnaires were used to determine the physical activity (PA) indexes.

Results and Discussion

Variables under examination between the two studies included resting heart rate, total cholesterol, and triglycerides. Due to the similarities of both studies and the fact that one study tested an aerobic activity program whereas the other did not, a comparison of the normative data obtained on the variables was made.

The data presented in Table 1 show the differences in the findings of the two studies. Resting heart rates in the American children were considerably lower (9.8 b/m) than those of the Netherlands children. The Netherlands children had an average resting heart rate of 90.5 b/m, while the American children had an average rate of 80.7 b/m. The Netherlands children also had higher total cholesterol with a mean of 186.6 mg/100 ml than did the American children with a mean of 175.4 mg/100 ml. As for triglycerides, the American children had a mean of 62.4 mg/100 ml, and the Netherlands children a mean of 75.3 mg/100 ml, making the mean triglyceride level 12.9 mg/100 ml lower for the American children.

Table 1 Means for Resting Heart Rate, Total Cholesterol, and Triglycerides

Group	N	RHR B/M	Chol mg/100 m	Tg mg/100 ml
Netherlands	54	90.5	186.6	75.3
American	43	80.7	175.4	62.4
Variance	11	9.8	11.2	12.9

Armstrong and Davies (1980) reported that atherosclerotic coronary heart disease becomes manifest in adult life, but there is growing conviction that the disease is of pediatric origin. They also suggested that risk factors known to be associated with an increased incidence of atherosclerosis in adults have been recognized. Two of the risk factors associated with heart disease in children are obesity and physical inactivity, which, to some extent, may be interrelated. Because these particular risk factors do pertain to children and because, to a degree, the risk factor concept in children is speculative, the justification for comparing results of two separate studies becomes more evident.

Because the mean resting heart rate for American children was 9.8 b/m slower than that of the Netherlands children, it is possible to attribute some of the difference to the Americans' 6-month aerobic activity program. The results from the Netherlands study (Saris et al., 1980) indicated that children with a high physical performance capacity who were also highly active had a lower mean heart rate than children who were not as active. As this tends to support the results of the American study, it could be explained by the well-known observation that a better state of fitness coincides with a greater heart stroke volume and, therefore, a lower mean heart rate (Åstrand & Rodahl, 1970). It could be said that a reduction of physical activity in a contemporary civilized society brings about a decrease in physical fitness, which directly relates to the efficiency of the circulatory and respiratory systems (Seliger et al., 1980). As a result, an aerobic activity program for elementary school age children may well be the answer to decreasing the heart disease related risk factor of a higher than normal resting heart rate.

The mean cholesterol and triglyceride levels for the American children were considerably lower than those of the Netherlands children. The difference of 11.2 and 12.9 mg/100 ml of blood, respectively, for the two variables could certainly be reflective of what proper dietary habits and regular aerobic exercise can do for elementary school children. Early research suggested that total plasma cholesterol and total plasma triglycerides were important indicators of heart disease risk. In recent years there has been evidence that heart disease is more closely associated with decreased high-density lipoprotein cholesterol and elevated low-density lipoprotein cholesterol plasma levels (Parizkova, 1961; Rhoads, Kazan, & Yano, 1976; Scanu, 1978). Physical exercise has been associated with changes in the plasma lipid profile. From research findings in recent years, there is every indication that exercise intervention can affect the plasma lipid profile.

Cholesterol levels in blood tend to be lower during childhood than adult life, and although it is not certain exactly what level of cholesterol constitutes a risk factor for children, it is likely that the risk increases steadily with increasing levels of cholesterol. Intervention programs in nutrition and aerobic exercises for children may stabilize the cholesterol levels or at least cause far less than normal increase.

A decrease in the triglyceride count has often been described as a side effect, or possibly a direct result, of physical and/or aerobic activity.

Although dietary intervention quite effectively keeps the triglyceride level below the 150 mg% recommended by the National Institutes of Health, regular vigorous physical activity has been proven an equally effective method of control in some people (Lampman et al., 1978). This being the case, it certainly appears reasonable that an aerobic exercise program would aid in the reduction of this risk factor. This fact could certainly be supported by the difference observed between the means of the American children and the children from The Netherlands. This difference seems to be especially important, because the American children participated in an aerobic exercise program as well as having nutrition education.

Whether it is accurate to infer that exercise is responsible for the reduction of risks such as elevated serum cholesterol, triglycerides, and resting heart rates remains somewhat controversial. Until the evidence becomes conclusive with respect to the benefits of exercise, it still seems wise to implement aerobic exercise programs for children in order to establish good health habits. The existing evidence does not necessarily infer that physical and/or aerobic exercise has a negative effect upon children.

Conclusions

These points seem appropriate concerning the possible changes in children that may be a direct or indirect result of aerobic exercise programs.

- Children who participated in an aerobic activity had a lower mean resting heart rate than those children who had not been in such a program.
- Children who had not participated in an aerobic activity program had an elevated serum cholesterol and triglyceride level.
- Children in an aerobic exercise program to reduce heart disease related risk factors should undergo a recommended minimum training period of at least 7 months.
- Children in aerobic programs should participate at least 3 times per week for 15 minutes per experience.

From the results of the comparison, school administrators, curriculum specialists, and physical education teachers should certainly examine the amount of time used to teach aerobic activity to children.

References

Armstrong, N., & Davies, B. (1980). The prevalence of coronary risk factors in children—A review. *Acta Paediatr Belg*, **33**, 209-217.

Åstrand, P.O., & Rodahl, K. (1970). *Textbook of work physiology*. New York: McGraw-Hill.

Lampmann, R.M., Santinga, J.T., Bassett, D.R., Mercer, N., Block, W.D., Flora, J.D., Fors, M.D., & Thorland, W.G. (1978). Effectiveness of unsupervised and supervised high intensity physical training in normalizing serum lipids in men with type IV hyperlipidemia. *Circulation, 57*(1), 172-180.

Parizkova, J. (1961). Total body fat and skinfold thickness in children. *Metabolism, 10,* 794-807.

Rhoads, G.B., Kazan, A., & Yano, N. (1976). Associations between dietary factors and plasma lipoproteins. *Circulation, 54,* 11-53.

Saris, W.M., Binkhorst, R.A., et al. (1980). The relationship between working performance, daily physical activity, fatness, blood lipids and nutrition in school children. In K. Berg & B.O. Erikson (Eds.), *Children and exercise IX.* Baltimore, MD: University Park Press.

Scanu, A.M. (1978). Plasma lipoproteins and coronary heart disease. *Annals of Clinical and Laboratory Science, 8,* 79-83.

Seliger, V., et al. (1980). Functional demands of physical education lessons. In K. Berg & B.O. Erikson (Eds.), *Children and exercise IX.* Baltimore, MD: University Park Press.

Patterns of Social Participation Among Minnesota and Bolivian Youth: Cross-Cultural Perspectives

Dario Menanteau-Horta
University of Minnesota

A recurring finding in sociological studies is that urbanization and industrialization are generally accompanied by an increasing need of affiliation and participation. Economic and cultural changes, characterized by greater geographical mobility, higher occupational demands on men and women, and a more complex diversity of values and beliefs, have been seen as responsible factors contributing to the weakening of the traditional structure in which the family and other primary institutions played major roles in satisfying an individual's demand for social interaction.

The purpose of this study is to examine, from a comparative, cross-cultural perspective, the impact of industrial and economic development on patterns of social participation of adolescents in two cultural contexts: Minnesota and Bolivia.

The central question is the extent to which the nature and type of social participation of youth vary between social systems that present differences in structural conditions, levels of urbanization, and industrial growth.

An additional question is whether patterns of participation within each culture setting differ according to social factors such as sex, rural or urban residence, family characteristics, socioeconomic status, and value orientations held by individuals.

The Cross-Cultural Survey

Data presented in this report are drawn from a cross-cultural study initiated during the 1970s in Minnesota and in the Andean country of Bolivia, South America. The analysis is based on responses from a statewide sample of 2,861 senior students attending about 30 Minnesota high schools and a national sample of 1,110 Bolivian high school senior students. A basically identical questionnaire containing statements about participation of students in extracurricular activities was utilized in both cultural settings. Since high school students were the respondents, individual characteristics such as age, sex, and educational attainment were equivalent in the two samples. Structural differences of their societies, specifically those depicting varying degrees of economic and social development, population size, organizational complexity, urbanization, and other societal characteristics, are illustrated by figures in Table 1.

Bolivia, with a population of 5.4 million, a rapid rate of demographic growth (2.6% per year), high infant mortality, low levels of urbanization, high illiteracy, and a life expectancy still under 50 years of age, is one of the less developed countries of Latin America. In contrast, the United States of America has a larger and predominantly urban population, which enjoys better conditions of health and education, but also has a greater concentration of economic wealth and resources. Minnesota ranks 19th among the states in total population with over 4 million inhabitants in 1979, about one-third of whom live in rural areas. Although farming continues to be important to Minnesota's economic growth and development, the state's economy is today highly diversified with about 6,000 industrial firms. Manufacturing contributed a value of over $9.2 billion to the state's economy in 1977; by 1978, it accounted for 24.1% of all personal income.

Bolivia, with a total area of 537,792 square miles, is bounded on the north and east by Brazil, on the south by Paraguay and Argentina, and on the west by Chile and Peru. Her population is heavily influenced by the presence of a significantly high proportion of Indians with their culture and traditions. More than half of the Bolivian population is full-blooded Indian, compared with about 8% for the rest of Latin America. About 25% of Bolivians are mestizos, persons of mixed Indian and white blood.

Table 1 Selected Demographic and Social Characteristics of Bolivia and Minnesota

Characteristics	Minnesota	Bolivia
Total population (in millions, 1979 mid-year estimates)	4.0	5.4
Annual rate of population growth (%)	.6	2.6
Life expectancy at birth (years)	73.2[a]	48.6
Infant mortality (per 1,000 live births)	14.0	157.0
Urban population (%)	66.0	32.4
Literacy (%)	99.0[a]	63.2
Gross domestic product (in 1978 U.S. $ millions)	26,820[b]	2,709

Note. Data compiled from Statistical Abstract of Latin America (1978 and 1980); Economic and Social Progress in Latin America (1979); Statistical Abstract of the United States (1979); and Minnesota: Statistical Profile (1981).
[a]National estimates for the U.S.
[b]Minnesota gross state product.

Modern Bolivian history, particularly after the Second World War and the 1952 national revolution, has been characterized by political instability in conjunction with chronic inflation, economic crisis, rapid succession of military governments, and prolonged periods of social unrest. Despite some important attempts by the country to bring about changes over the last 3 decades, the Bolivian revolution of mid-century failed to achieve its goals of sustained industrialization, economic growth, and social development. Although some gains were accomplished to improve conditions for Bolivian miners and peasants through the nationalization of mineral resources and land reform, frequent unrest and military uprisings have severely curtailed major efforts to modify the traditional basis of Bolivian society. This political and social instability has been accompanied historically by violence, maldistribution of income, ineffective leadership, citizen insecurity, and problems of national integration, all of which hamper modernization and development.

Because of these structural constraints operating within the Bolivian society, one might expect individuals to look upon the family unit, as well as their extended but tightly closed circle of relatives, as their most stable, trustworthy community.

From the perspective of the individual in Bolivia, the family is a relatively large and wide network of relationships providing necessary benefits and privileges of companionship, security, and sustenance. At the societal level, however, the Bolivian family structure may be seen as a hindrance to the development of secondary associations and other organized groups, which are vital for the larger national community.

Sociologist Norman Dennis discusses the complexities of secondary group relationships in contemporary modern organizations, indicating that "in urban industrial society it is necessary to collaborate with one set of people in order to earn a living, with another to worship, with a third set to be educated, with a fourth for amusement, with a fifth in seeing to the affairs of the neighborhood, and so on." Minute differentiation of function, he concludes, is the secret of productivity.

Patterns of Participation Across Cultures

Social participation was measured in both cultures by the same questionnaire items, including the following dimensions: (a) affiliative behavior of respondents in school and community organizations, and (b) degree of participation and commitment in extracurricular activities.

Patterns of social participation differed substantially between the two samples (Table 2). Membership and involvement in various types of activities are proportionally higher among Minnesota students than among Bolivians. Affiliation and general participation in sports, social clubs, voluntary associations, political and religious groups, and academic and leisure activities were reported by 57% of Minnesota respondents as compared with less than 50% of the Bolivian students.

The most striking differences, however, correspond to participation in school-related organizations and in community activities by members of

Table 2   Patterns of Social Participation of Youth in Minnesota and Bolivia

Type of social participation	Minnesota (N = 2,861) %	Bolivia (N = 1,110) %
General	57	49
School organizations	52	6
Community activities	36	45

both samples. More than 50% of Minnesotans indicated some form of participation in extracurricular functions within their schools. These types of activities included only 6% of the Bolivian students. Most of the Bolivian respondents who participate (45%) tended to belong to organizations operating at the local and even at the national level of their society, while the proportion of Minnesota students involved in community activities was slightly larger than 33.3% of the respondents.

These differences in affiliative behavior between Minnesotans and Bolivian youth would appear to be consequences of both opportunity structures for participation of students within schools and some fundamental differences in the educational system of the two cultures.

Contemporary American society has delegated participation functions through a vast number of extracurricular activities to the institution of education, which has become increasingly involved in the total process of socialization of the young. The social space traditionally occupied by the family, the church, and other primary social institutions has been considerably reduced, contributing to an expansion of the role played by schools and other educational structures in the lives of children and adolescents.

In exchange for these added functions and services, and as a result of available resources to the once growing economy of the country, the American educational system received local, state, and federal support for developing facilities and implementing the new tasks. The strength of the national economy, particularly during the 3 decades following World War II, the improvement in the standard of living of the average American family, and increasing opportunities for individuals and communities were readily reflected in more and better facilities available to schools to assist the participation needs of their students.

Although differences in the distribution of these resources appeared, and inequality persisted among school districts serving the various sectors of society, the American educational system, in general, has been able to incorporate into its major functions those activities enhancing social participation of the young. What should be a matter of concern, however, is the relatively large proportion of Minnesota students who declared that they did not participate in any type of extracurricular programs or activities. About 43% of Minnesota respondents indicated no participation, compared to approximately 50% of the members of the Bolivian sample.

Education in Bolivia, as in most countries of the Third World, is severely afflicted by problems of social and economic development and limited means with which to serve the basic needs of the population. Lack of schools, shortages of qualified teachers, and insufficient resources result in an alarming deficit of schooling and other educational opportunities. Recent reports estimate that over 40% of school-age children (6 to 14 years of age) remain without the benefits of elementary education. At the high school level, the educational system is only accessible to less than 25% of the total population of Bolivian adolescents (Bolivian Ministry of Planning, 1970).

Under these circumstances, the educational system of Bolivia faces insurmountable challenges that limit its functions to traditional methods of teaching in pursuit of basic instruction. Extracurricular activities, therefore, constitute, at best, a marginal priority for most schools, as they do not have either the necessary facilities or the teaching staff to develop them. This situation would explain, in part, the low percentage of Bolivian respondents who held membership and had some participation in school organizations. Most of those who participated in youth programs had to seek opportunities elsewhere, outside the boundaries of the school system.

Levels of Social Participation

The degree of participation and student commitment to organized activities was assessed in both cultures by the same participation scale, which ranged from lack of affiliation to leadership roles, including two intermediate categories of membership and actual involvement. Students' responses to this scale were classified into four groups, which portray a basic typology of participative behavior of the respondents (Table 3).

The first category corresponds to "marginal" individuals, characterizing those students who did not belong to organized groups or associations. Approximately 4 out of 10 Minnesotans and about 50% of the Bolivians fell into this category of nonparticipants.

Three types of respondents also showed major differences as to the nature and levels of participation among members of both samples. More Bolivians (24%) than Minnesotans (17%) were classified as "passive" affiliates. They represent those students who claimed to belong to an organization but did not attend meetings or contribute in any other form to its organized programs.

The status of "active" participants corresponds to individuals with higher commitment to their organizations and regular attendance to meetings and other activities. About 25% of Minnesota students reported active participation, compared to 16% of Bolivians. Students who held, or have held, leadership positions in youth organizations or in other forms of

Table 3   Levels of Social Participation of Youth in Minnesota and Bolivia

Type of individual	Minnesota (N = 2,861) %	Bolivia (N = 1,110) %
Isolated	43	52
Passive	17	24
Active	24	16
Leader	16	8

Note. Isolated = does not belong to social organization; passive = student belongs to one organization but does not attend meetings; active = active participation and regular attendance at meetings; leader = in leadership position.

associations represented, as expected, the smallest proportion of the respondents from both samples. Still, the relative number of Minnesota students with opportunities to learn and exercise leadership roles (16%) is twice as high as among the Bolivians.

These differences in the extent of participation and actual involvement in students' activities, youth programs, and community affairs between Minnesotans and Bolivians depict deeper differences in the opportunity structure of social participation for young people in both cultures. Active participation and the attainment of leadership roles within organizations operating outside the school system in the larger community, as appears to be the case for most Bolivian students, is likely to be more demanding in time, skills, and other resources than participation in school-related activities. The lack of institutionalization of students' involvement in extracurricular activities as part of the educational system, rather than through private or other external agencies, may place Bolivian students at a clear disadvantage for the fulfillment of their needs to participate.

Characteristics of the Participants

In recent years, there has been increasing concern among sociologists and other scientists in studying social and cultural factors related to social participation (Babchuck & Booth, 1969; Coleman, 1961; Coleman et al., 1966; Cutler, 1973; Hausknecht, 1962; Smith, 1975; Smith & Freedman, 1972; Tomeh, 1973). Despite variations in scope, as well as in theoretical and methodological perspectives, research on this important area of social behavior has provided some useful generalizations about major characteristics associated with participation. Loy, McPherson, and Kenyon (1978) summarize contemporary research findings, indicating that

based on empirical studies to date, it appears that participation is related to (1) a higher socioeconomic status in terms of types of organizations joined, degree of involvement, and the holding of leadership positions; (2) age, with increasing involvement to about 50 or 60 years, followed by a decline (i.e., disengagement); (3) sex, with males being more affiliative in general and being more likely to join instrumental groups, whereas females are more likely to join expressive groups; (4) race, with blacks being more involved than whites at comparable social class levels; (5) religion, with higher Protestant involvement; and (6) availability of role models, with higher participation rates by those whose parents and peers are involved. Variables such as size of community and length and place of residence do not appear to be consistently related to affiliative behavior. (pp. 236-237)

Although most of these characteristics suggest a combination of individual attributes and structural factors related to social participation, it could be argued that they largely reflect conditions found in the United States, Canada, and western European countries. Comparative research, however, in which internal or intrasocietal variables are considered in conjunction with cross-cultural variations based upon the degree of modernization and development of the social systems, is still badly needed.

The following discussion gives attention to some characteristics of students who participate in social organizations and extracurricular activities in Minnesota and Bolivia, as compared with those respondents without participation. Selected variables include (a) sociodemographic characteristics such as sex, place of residence, and size of community; (b) family background regarding socioeconomic status of the respondent's family, parents' education, and father's occupation; and (c) school-related variables including type (private or public) and size of school, student's scholastic achievement, educational aspirations and occupational choices, and student's self-concept in relation to his peers.

A general inspection of the data reported in Table 4 shows a substantially higher intrasocietal variation in most of the selected characteristics among Minnesota participants than among their Bolivian counterparts, when both groups are compared to nonparticipants. This finding might suggest that factors that may help explain social participation in one cultural setting (i.e., the U.S.) differ from those factors necessary to explain similar behavior in another culture (i.e., Bolivia). In addition, the lack of internal variability in the Bolivian data may also be a consequence of a high level of homogeneity of the sample population, considering the process of extreme selection affecting Bolivian students throughout their 12 years of formal education. It has been estimated, for instance, that less than 33.3% of all Bolivian students entering the educational system reaches the fourth grade in elementary school, and less than 20% of them have access to high school education. By the end of the educational process, a proportion of less than 3% graduate from high school and have potential access to universities.

Sociodemographic characteristics. Comparisons between participants and nonparticipants among Minnesota students show a relatively higher proportion of females than males participating in extracurricular activities. In Bolivia, however, an overwhelming majority of the participants

Table 4 Characteristics of Students Who Participate in Social Organizations and Extracurricular Activities in Minnesota and Bolivia

| Students' characteristics | Participants | | | |
| | Minnesota | | Bolivia | |
	N	%	N	%
Sociodemographic				
Sex				
Males	1265	58	448	85
Females	1296	68	257	62
Residence				
Urban	1714	63	604	76
Rural	843	65	96	78
Size of community				
Small	848	70	81	80
Medium	828	59	246	74
Large	893	61	384	78
Family background				
Family SES				
High	605	69	91	75
Middle	818	66	343	78
Low	779	60	271	76
Father's education				
College	834	76	234	76
High school	1465	61	182	75
Elementary	71	44	247	78
Mother's education				
College	693	78	108	75
High school	1631	65	166	77
Elementary	50	42	363	76
Father's occupation				
Professionals and managers	842	72	200	78
Farmers	231	70	31	77
Clerical services	357	63	164	76
Laborers	960	57	216	76
Other	117	51	—	—
School-related				
Type				
Public	2309	63	488	78
Private	260	70	223	74
Size				
Small/medium	1059	70	310	74
Large	1508	59	392	78
Student's grade average				
A	921	84	16	63
B	1231	57	329	75
C or less	404	34	337	80

(Cont.)

Table 4 (Cont.)

Students' characteristics	Participants			
	Minnesota		Bolivia	
	N	%	N	%
Educational aspirations				
College	1543	76	563	77
Vocational	389	44	124	77
Get a job	445	41	15	80
Occupational expectations				
Professional	1352	76	648	77
Nonprofessional	1072	48	38	63
Self-concept				
High	1278	78	242	77
Low/average	1290	49	455	76

are males. Rural and urban residence appears to have no major impact in explaining differences between participants and nonparticipants in both samples. The size of community seems to show, however, a negative relationship among Minnesota participants. This is not the case in Bolivia.

Family background. The general trend in Minnesota depicts a positive association between social participation and each of the four variables describing socioeconomic status of the respondents. Correlation analysis between participation scores and parents' education of Minnesotans provided Pearson's coefficients of .20 and .18 for fathers' and mothers' educational attainments, respectively. Data on fathers' occupations also indicate a positive association with participation in Minnesota. However, these comparisons between participants and nonparticipants in Bolivia show neither the same differences nor direction as in Minnesota.

School-related characteristics. Regarding the type of school (public or private) among Minnesota participants, private education appears to offer a relatively higher advantage for students' involvement in extracurricular activities. The opposite was found in Bolivia. Also, students attending small and medium-size schools in Minnesota appear to participate more than those in larger schools. This trend is slightly reversed in the Bolivian sample.

Minnesota students' scholastic achievement, measured by respondents' GPA, shows a positive association with students' participation ($r = .43$). This finding is in agreement with results reported by other studies conducted in the United States showing a similar association between schoolwork and students' participation in extracurricular activities (Bend, 1968;

Schafer & Armer, 1968). In addition, a vast amount of empirical research in the area of the sociology of sports has supported this view, which suggests that athletes and adolescents who participate in sport activities tend to have a higher academic performance (Rehberg, 1969; Snyder & Spreitzer, 1977; Spady, 1970).

Within the same domain of achievement orientation, other studies have also found a relationship between participation in extracurricular activities and students' educational aspirations and occupational expectations (Otto & Alwin, 1977; Spreitzer & Pugh, 1973). Otto (1975) provides empirical support to Spady's hypothesis that participation in high school extracurricular activities has a salutary effect on educational attainment. His basic argument is that "extracurricular activities, like an academic curriculum, provide opportunity for acquiring, developing, and rehearsing attitudes and skills from which status goals evolve and upon which future success is grounded." Minnesota data in Table 4 appear to be consistent with these previous findings as suggested by responses to items dealing with students' grades, educational aspirations, and occupational choices.

Contrary to these United States results, in Bolivia, students' participation would appear to have a rather negative effect on schoolwork and no significant association with educational aspirations. A possible explanation for this pattern may be found in the fact that Bolivian students, as indicated earlier, tend to participate more in organizations outside the school setting. This situation may create competition and conflict of interest with school activities, rather than provide reinforcement to academic requirements and study habits. Despite these potentially adverse conditions, Bolivian respondents who participate in social organizations appear to be more inclined to have higher occupational expectations than nonparticipant students.

A final observation reported in Table 4 refers to students' self-concept in comparison with their classmates. In both cultural settings, it was found that participation appears to be generally related to high self-esteem, although the Bolivian data seems less conclusive on this point than the information obtained in Minnesota. It is worth noting, at least, that the trend found in Minnesota relating participation and greater self-concept coincides with similar results reported by other studies conducted in the United States (Schurr & Brookover, 1970; Weiner, 1977).

Social Participation and Youth Values

In many respects, extracurricular activities and youth programs have been seen as a microcosm of life and social reality (Sawyer, 1977). Moreover, as Sutton-Smith (1977) suggests, they have been largely supported and justified "by the contribution they are supposed to make to the individual's or group's socialization into the larger society."

These processes of personal and social integration are not only mediated by the more visible elements of social organization and material facilities provided by the structural components of a system, but they also receive the influential guidance of cultural values commonly accepted by the members of a society.

Values are defined as shared conceptions of what is good and desirable (Williams, 1965). They represent standards that guide relationships and influence the functioning of social institutions. Values, therefore, are conceived as necessary for establishing societal goals, norms, and guidelines required for achieving social integration. At the system level, they represent cultural goals and institutional imperatives (Menanteau-Horta, 1981).

From the individual standpoint, value orientations imply the direction in which behavior may be guided and also involve varying degrees of individual decision and choice. From this perspective, value orientations constitute the influencing criteria for behavior, and, therefore, refer to individual motivation to act in a particular way. It may be argued, then, that as adolescents join groups and associations and participate in organized activities, they carry with them some values usually learned from other socialization agents (i.e., family, church, school, and friends). Also, in contact with new acquaintances and relationships, they may expand, reshape, and change some of their initial values.

The concept of value orientation discussed here corresponds to students' concepts of the desirable in relation to participation in extracurricular activities and in situations involving specific decisions and choices. The following areas of decision, experienced by most youth in both cultures, were selected: (a) the selection of future career, (b) the choice of going to college or pursuing other activities after high school graduation, (c) occupational and job selection, and (d) the choice of a community or place to live.

For each of these four areas, respondents were asked about the most important quality desired in each object of their choice. Students were asked to select one among four values for each decision situation. Three of these value orientations, such as the desire to serve and help others, to be creative and humanitarian, and to be willing to assume responsibilities more than personal rewards, are considered here to represent *intrinsic values*. The others, including strong motivation to achieve status and social recognition, economic rewards, and material gains, are conceived as examples of *instrumental values*.

In relation to these two sets of value orientations, it was hypothesized that social participation of the young would be associated with intrinsic values rather than with instrumental orientations, as their involvement and commitment to extracurricular activities are largely voluntary in nature and focus on the noninstrumental aspects of social interaction. Table 5 shows the more prominent characteristics valued by Minnesota and Bolivian students regarding the four areas of decision.

Data reveal that a larger proportion of the respondents from both cultural settings favored intrinsic qualities more than instrumental values in each of the areas of decision making. This is contrary to popular assumptions that portray the younger generation as predominantly motivated by material achievement and economic rewards. Cross-cultural comparisons show that in three of the four areas of decision, with the

Table 5 Value Orientations of Participant and Nonparticipant Students From Minnesota and Bolivia in Relation to Selected Areas of Decision Making

Areas of decision making and value orientations	Minnesota		Bolivia	
	Participants %	Isolated %	Participants %	Isolated %
Future career				
Intrinsic	59	49	77	71
Instrumental	41	51	23	29
N =	1595	913	523	159
Going to college				
Intrinsic	86	75	91	85
Instrumental	14	25	9	15
N =	1587	909	521	156
Job selection				
Intrinsic	84	74	88	91
Instrumental	16	26	12	9
N =	1576	901	521	156
Place to live				
Intrinsic	65	62	64	58
Instrumental	35	38	36	42
N =	1591	917	523	159

exception of the choice of a place to live, more Bolivian students than Minnesotans tended to stress intrinsic values, rather than instrumental values. In both cultures, however, when students who participate in extracurricular programs were compared with nonparticipant and isolated respondents in terms of their value orientations, it was found that participants, in general, tended to favor intrinsic qualities over instrumental orientations. These results, however, provide support to the hypothesis that social participation of the young would appear to be positively associated with intrinsic and noninstrumental orientations for social action.

Concluding Remarks

Social participation, in general, has been recently defined as a basic human need in contemporary society. From a developmental standpoint, participation constitutes an active and decisive process by which the individual and his cultural milieu can meet in a constant search for balance and integration. Organizational arrangements of the social system, however, particularly those establishing institutional functions, patterns of stratification, distribution of power, and other resources, largely determine the structure of opportunities and mechanisms that facilitate or impede social participation.

This paper has attempted to illustrate from a comparative, cross-cultural perspective the impact of economic and institutional development on the social participation of youth in two cultural settings: Minnesota and Bolivia. In these two societies, it can be observed that there is still a substantial need to improve the amount and quality of student participation in extracurricular programs. In Bolivia, for instance, the main barrier to student participation in school activities is the lack of institutionalization of these endeavors within their educational system. In Minnesota, on the other hand, the issue appears to be one of student motivation to participate when confronted with competitive alternatives such as part-time jobs and, in some cases, other early acquired adult responsibilities. In conclusion, based on the findings of this research, it seems appropriate to underline the importance of school-related activities for young people to stimulate and prepare them for both participation and commitment in community affairs in their adult lives.

Acknowledgments

Information analyzed in this paper is part of a larger research project (Project Min/27/017) conducted under the auspices of the Department of Rural Sociology and the Agricultural Experiment Station, University of Minnesota. (Paper No. 1839-0)

References

Babchuck, N., & Booth, A. (1969, February). Voluntary association membership: A longitudinal analysis. *American Sociological Review, 34,* 31-45.

Bend, E. (1968). *The impact of athletic participation on academic career aspiration and achievement.* New Brunswick, NJ: National Football Foundation and Hall of Fame.

Coleman, J.S. (1961). *The adolescent society.* Glenco, IL: Free Press.

Coleman, J.S., et al. (1966). *Equality of educational opportunity.* Washington, DC: Government Printing Office.

Cutler, S. (1973). Voluntary association membership and the theory of mass society. In E. Laumann (Ed.), *Bonds of pluralism: The form and substance of urban social networks* (pp. 133-159). New York: John Wiley.

Hausknecht, M. (1962). *The joiner: A sociological description of voluntary association membership in the United States.* New York: Bedminster Press.

Loy, J.W., McPherson, B.D., & Kenyon, G. (1978). *Sport and social systems* (pp. 236-237). Boston, MA: Addison-Wesley.

Menanteau-Horta, D. (1981). Value orientations of Minnesota youth. *Sociology of Rural Life*, 4(3), 1-8. St. Paul, MN: University of Minnesota.

Ministerio de Planificación Coordinacion (1970). *Estrategia socio-económica del desarrollo nacional*, II, 503-542. Republic of Bolivia.

Otto, L.B. (1975). Extracurricular activities in the educational attainment process. *Rural Sociology*, 40, 162-167.

Otto, L.B., & Alwin, D. (1977, April). Athletics, aspirations and attainments. *Sociology of Education*, 42, 102-103.

Rehberg, R. (1969, April). Behavioral and attitudinal consequences of high school interscholastic sports: A speculative consideration. *Adolescence*, 4, 59-68.

Sawyer, K.C. (1977). Ultimate goalpost: The human spirit. In T. Craig (Ed.), *The humanistic and mental health aspects of sports, exercise and recreation* (p. vi). Chicago: American Medical Association.

Schafer, W.E., & Armer, J.M. (1968, November). Athletes are not inferior students. *Trans-Action*, pp. 21-26, 61-62.

Schurr, T., & Brookover, W. (1970). Athletes, academic self-concept and achievement. *Medicine and Science in Sports*, 2, 96-99.

Smith, C., & Freedman, A. (1972). *Voluntary associations: Perspectives on the literature*. Cambridge, MA: Harvard University Press.

Smith, D.H. (1975). Voluntary action and voluntary groups. In A. Jukeles (Ed.), *Annual Review of Sociology*, 1, 247-270. Palo Alto, CA: Annual Reviews.

Snyder, E., & Spreitzer, E. (1977, January). Participation in sports as related to educational expectations among high school girls. *Sociology of Education*, 50, 47-55.

Spady, W.G. (1970, January). Lament for the letterman: Effects of peer status and extracurricular activities on goals and achievement. *American Journal of Sociology*, 75, 5-31.

Spreitzer, E., & Pugh, M. (1973, Spring). Interscholastic athletics and educational expectations. *Sociology of Education*, 46, 171-182.

Sutton-Smith, B. (1977). Current research and theory on play, games and sports. In T. Craig (Ed.), *The humanistic and mental health aspects of sports, exercise and recreation* (pp. 1-5). Chicago: American Medical Association.

Tomeh, A. (1973). Formal voluntary organizations: Participation, correlates and interrelationships. *Sociological Inquiry*, 43, 89-122.

Weiner, B. (1977). Motivational psychology and sports activities. In T. Craig (Ed.), *The humanistic and mental health aspects of sports, exercise and recreation* (pp. 55-57). Chicago: American Medical Association.

Williams, R.M. (1965). *American society: A sociological interpretation*. New York: A.A. Knopf.

Government—Sport Policy—Politics

Thomas Bedecki
Canadian Association for Health, Physical Education and Recreation

In this century, the role of governments in sport has been evolving from an initial utilitarian one to one that is more complex and comprehensive. Several trends can be discerned in foreign governments' involvement in sports. One is the increased recognition of the responsibility to promote physical fitness and amateur sport programs. Others are a greater tendency to allocate public monies to support amateur sport programs and a growing emphasis upon participation and achievement in international competition. In spite of these similarities, each country's involvement has developed in its own economic, social, and political climate.

Government involvement in sport has historically been related to military fitness, education, national identification, and opportunity to participate in leisure activities. Recently, the extensive growth of national government participation in sport has been directed in accordance with national political objectives: The degree of involvement appears to be directly related to an expressed political ideology and political structure. It has generally been strong central governments that have reacted most effectively to the value of sporting success in building national identity.

There has been a substantial increase in resources allotted to sport by public and private organizations to raise the level of athletic performance. Allocations toward technical, scientific, and medical research have made vital contributions.

The main factor responsible for the intensifying national interest in sports is a heightened interest in international sport as a means of promoting an international image, understanding, and prestige. Emerging nations have the viewpoint that achievement in sport represents a means of attaining world recognition. The apparent decision by the socialist nations in the early 1950s was to project, for political reasons, a positive image based on athletic excellence.

In the past 3 decades especially, national governments have considered and increased their role in relation to the world sport movement. The amount of interest respective governments take in the structure of sport domestically has affected the global standing of "sporting" nations. In many countries sport has become an instrument of national policy and subsequent foreign policy. Western countries have gradually accepted government involvement in sport but have made efforts to exclude politics from sport. Policy formulation is still a principal task of government.

Over the past 20 years sport has occupied an increasingly important role in Canadian society. Direct participation in sport by the federal government is a fairly recent development expressed initially in Bill C-131, an Act to Encourage Fitness and Amateur Sport.

In the late 1960s the federal government began a more direct excursion into the realm of sport with "A Proposed Sports Policy for Canadians," produced in 1970, calling for an increased emphasis on the development of elite athletes as a form of official policy. Subsequently, a document entitled "Towards a National Policy on Fitness and Recreation" was released in 1979. The latest policy statement was articulated in "A Challenge to the Nation: Fitness and Amateur Sport in the 80's," a document issued in 1981.

During the past decade, divergent opinions have been presented in federal sport policy papers on the extent of government involvement in Canadian sport. More recently, views have been expressed that there is a necessity for a renewed national effort to make sport an integral part of the Canadian lifestyle and that excellence must become a national goal in sports. Increased government involvement has resulted in a desire to focus attention and direct resources to such immediate areas of national concern as unity and identification.

This changing emphasis and trend towards increased government involvement will affect the future direction of sport. The sport policy objectives the government adopts will determine its role and influence. We are living in a period in which we can look forward to an ever-increasing involvement by governments, as well as by the public sector in sport. The purpose of this paper is to identify the specific relationship between sport and the political system, as well as public policy considerations emanating from this relationship and its ramifications.

Sport as a Public Policy

It is important to make the following distinction between the terms *polity* and *policy*. Polity, in this paper, refers to the type of government or structure and its makeup. Policy refers to the management of government. Increased government involvement with the variety and number of nongovernment agencies involved in sport leads to the conclusion that there is a dependent character of sport on both public and private agencies in many countries. This interdependence suggests that any development of a national sport policy within these nations will necessitate a structure consisting of a complementary mix of government and nongovernment agencies.

The issues of sport are issues of public policy, the outcomes of which, unfortunately, are too often decided by the political process. The sport public, despite its great interest in sport matters, needs to understand clearly the process of voicing its policy preferences in an attempt to influence policy decisions. Too often sport has turned to a government when it has not been able to solve its problems. Government involvement has been justified in public sport policy under the assumption of the public's intense interest in sports. Sport policy is a result of the frequent utilization of the political process. The belief that sport and government are independent of each other does not stand up to careful scrutiny. The growing recognition of the need for government encouragement and assistance in the development of sport and recreation has enabled government agencies to shape public sport policy. The desirability of, and the reduction of, government involvement in sport are policy questions still in need of debate.

In many western countries public sport policy has been made by government when the issue has not been resolved favorably in the nongovernmental sector, and government has been successful in gaining perceived public support. Sport questions of integration and priority then have been referred to government. Participation in international competition is now of public interest, if not concern. Policy proposals to further government involvement in amateur sport have been, and will continue to be, considered seriously by policy makers, that is, White Paper. Policy makers, wishing for government involvement, attempt to expand issues from federal policy to sports public policy (i.e., Green Paper, hockey reports, etc.). As issues in sport gain visibility and public support, sport enters the political arena.

In reviewing the knowledge of the public on policy, it is important that we recognize the distinctions between policy making and policy decision. Generally, a policy in government terms is an expression of a stance in relation to issue situations formed by government with a legitimate concern in such situations. This policy can be about intended future action or activity. The act of declaring such a stance through some formal political channel can be described as the taking of a policy decision. Previously released policy papers by the Canadian government have been interpreted as policy decision, and the distinction between act and stance has not been made.

Such policy implementation has been interpreted as responding to a perceived demand to reduce a state of uncertainty about intended future action or activity. The issue of specificity or ambiguity is crucial in any articulation of policy statements; for, whatever the mode of expression, there is considerable scope in the way issue situations are distinguished and in the prescription of the stance to any particular problem situation. For many, these issue situations have a wide impact within a society where several government and nongovernment agencies claim a legitimate concern as either accountable authorities or as interest groups with a right to be consulted. This will become more evident, particularly, if and when sport policy becomes part of a sociocultural policy.

The legitimate concerns and responsibilities of government have been identified between health and sport (exercise—fitness). Health is an area in which governments have a universally accepted responsibility, and every government will wish to take all possible steps to encourage its citizens to live healthy lives. Public policy by governments in identifying and assessing the benefits and risks of various forms of sport and exercise in the context of its overall policies on preventative medicine and health is readily accepted.

It is evident that the distinction between the roles of government organizations in the field of national and international sport is being eroded. Government has recognized that reasonable achievement in sport is important to the national psyche. More than other aspects of our international relations, competitive sport touches the emotions of many Canadians. The government perceived that the public wanted someone to do something to bolster our national pride. However, insofar as the pursuit of excellence in sport policy, the machinery of government is badly equipped to make the individual case judgments necessary to separate the potentially outstanding from the good, the bad, or the mediocre.

The role of government has generally been accepted in the selectivity of controls and administration of penalties, but selectivity in the granting of rewards and incentives has been somewhat limited. Essentially, policy and programs to foster participation in sport demand personal involvement, whereas sport performance and/or competition encourage delegated involvement. The future direction of public policy toward sport with increased government involvement will determine what federal presence is appropriate and desirable.

Sport public access to participation in government policymaking is diminished as federal and provincial bureaucracies overshadow the policymaking role of the elected representatives. Since public policy is mainly formed by the Cabinet and the public service, sport groups must sharpen their awareness about where they can best attempt to influence government decisions. Government discussions with sport interest groups have been more concerned with the application than the formulation of policy. In Canada, the present mechanism indicates the access of members of the public interested in sport to policy formulation and application by government (Figure 1).

Political sport participation has been considered a closed activity. Where policy sometimes seeks the truth, politics usually seek the public good. This participation process is based on the belief that the sport public has a right to acquire a degree of legitimacy and thereby gain access to government processes.

It is to the development of the sport policy *system* that we in sport must direct our attention and commitment. These processes are especially complex in many western countries like Canada, where there are multiple constituents of the public sport interests to be represented. As sport policy choices become more difficult, the need for active, rather than reactive policymaking, becomes evident. Government and nongovernment agencies must establish and guarantee serious and regular consultation in the formulation of national sport policy.

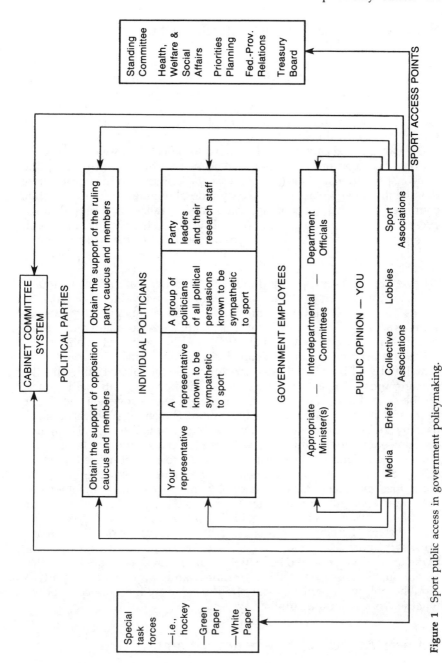

Figure 1 Sport public access in government policymaking.

Sport and the Different Political Systems

The extensive growth of national government participation in sport has been directed in accordance with the national policy objectives. The degree of national government involvement appears to be directly related to an expressed political ideology. Some political systems focus on the development of the individual, while others place their emphasis on the function of service to the country.

The two general categories often used to reflect the largest number of sociopolitical features of nations have been constitutional democracy and nonconstitutional systems (both federal and unitary). In the world, more than a billion people are governed by federal regimes, and in almost all countries of enormous geographical area, federalism is accepted; however, it is not the predominant political system in the world. Most countries are authoritarian and have unitary systems (those with only one major level of political authority), as illustrated in the following diagram (Figure 2).

Reviewing the sport policy statements of individual nations generally indicates the degree or nature of government involvement. Such statements provide the predominant motives or functions governments see sport as serving. These may include individual development and participation, national prestige, socialization, and international relations.

There is usually, among the constitutional democracies, a concern for individual well-being, national and international competition, and the ensuing prestige it may bring a nation. The nonconstitutional regimes, on the other hand, have as their major objectives sport as a socializing agent and an image enhancer for the nation. The term "physical culture" used by socialist countries, is a significant element in their social progress. In such centralized countries, sport has placed itself within the national framework and has become institutionalized and/or nationalized. In many other countries sport is increasing its permanent pressure on public authorities and is seen as falling naturally under government involvement.

Authoritarian governments have influenced the practice and organization of sport. Sport is increasingly being integrated into the existing political system, thereby increasing the politicization of the decision-making process in sport. Many more ministries of sport and youth are appearing in the form of a centralized agency. It is important that we are aware that a relationship exists between government and sport and that sport, as a public policy concern, is most often decided by the political process, whether in a federal or unitary system.

Political Aspects of International Sport

The political nature of sport is often demonstrated by examples from international sport events. Visible major sport events increase our awareness and understanding of world interactions. These events are not only contests, but international social and political events; for, if the Olympic

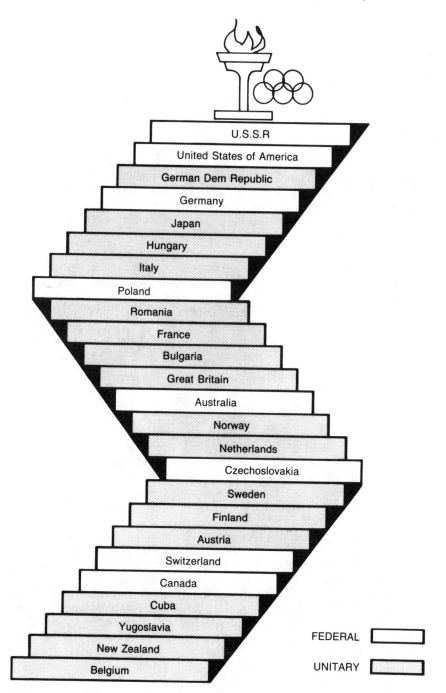

Figure 2 Leading Olympic sport nations and their political systems as indicated by total medals at the Olympic Games 1964-1976.

Games were designed in part to influence nations in terms of understanding, it was to be expected that international politics would penetrate the Games and influence sport.

National political objectives of sport, as mentioned previously, have been employed in changing domestic physical activity lifestyles, national psyche, and social integration. International political objectives of sport appear to fall into four main categories in which government has a legitimate concern.

- Identification-visibility (athlete, nation, government).
- Prestige in the international sphere (nation's stature or image).
- International understanding and cooperation (international sport relations).
- Promotion of particular political ideology (reflection of political system and public sport policy).

A serious form of political intervention in international sport has been the boycott of the major Games, more recently over racially discriminatory policies. As a promising means of advancing domestic or foreign policies, the media coverage associated with such international sport events provides the medium to pursue political objectives. It is reasonable to assume that as a sporting event begins to draw support from the majority of nations, that event will become the focus of government and political attention.

Interpretation of Sport and Politics

To date, we have had only a few historical, sociological, and journalistic analyses of a descriptive nature in understanding the reciprocal relationship between politics and sport. Any sports event that brings together athletes from two or more countries is bound to have political implications beyond the question of performance. Athletes, themselves, reflect the social and political milieu of their country. Political expression at the Olympic Games has produced a contradiction. On the one hand, it has advocated that politics should not intrude; on the other hand, the political role of promoting understanding and cooperation between nations is highly stressed.

Baron de Coubertin, the reviver of the Olympic Games, believed that they would lead to the development of positive political relationships between the nations represented. If sport was to influence nations, then interaction would demand that politics influence sport. Apolitical proponents of such Games appear to demand that certain kinds of, but not all, politics be kept out of sport.

The point may well be made that what such events as the Olympics need is not less politics, but better politics. The expansion of international sport participation by a number of countries is related to the political emphasis and government involvement in sport policy. It is evident that sports and politics cannot be separated. Government and its subsequent public sport policy statements have intertwined sport and politics, especially in the international arena. Politics, we are told, have intruded into sport, and these do not mix. This proposition may be reasonable, but it is supported by neither history nor logic.

Sport is not free of politics, nor are politics free of sport. Strong central governments have intentionally and, perhaps effectively, utilized sport as an instrument for the achievement of national goals. The relationship between sports and international affairs will continue to be reflected in the role of sports and world politics. Evidence is lacking, at the present time, for determining whether this two-way interaction is a negative or a positive association. As long as sport is an element of social reality attached to the political-economic system in which it has developed, this relationship between sport and politics has serious national and international consequences as we continue to nationalize sports.

The intent of this paper has been to bring to the attention of the sport public the need to participate in the formulation of national sport policymaking. As sport takes its place in Canadian culture, government will be continually pressed for a clearer statement of future policy. Public sport access to government policy must be provided so that flexibility, adaptation, and change can be ensured in any sport development policy. In the past, the social and political dimension of sport has suffered from too little attention. Sport, as a sociocultural phenomenon, should be protected as a national public interest.

Bibliography

Anthony, J. (1978). Introduction. In J. Riordan (Ed.), *Sport under communism* (pp. 2-11). Montreal: McGill-Queens University Press.

Ball, D.W., & Loy, J.W. (1975). *Sport and the social order: Contributions to the sociology of sport* (Social significance of sport series). Reading, MA: Addison-Wesley.

Bedecki, T. (1971). *Modern sport as an instrument of national policy.* Unpublished doctoral dissertation, Ohio State University, Columbus.

Bennett, B.L., Howell, M.L., & Simri, U. (1975). *Comparative physical education and sport.* Philadelphia: Lea & Febiger.

Bouet, M.A. (1968). *Signification du sport.* Paris: Editions Universitaires.

Broom, E.F., & Baka, R.S. (1979). *Canadian governments and sport* (Sociology of sport monograph series). Ottawa: CAHPER.

Burgener, L. (1977). *Sports and politics: A selected bibliography* (Culture Series, Vol. 4[2]). Switzerland: UNESCO Press.

Cheffers, J. (1972). *A wilderness of spite or Rhodesia denied.* New York: Vintage Press.

Corran, R. (1980, November, December). Federal government, sport and physical activity. *CAHPER Journal,* **47**(2), 7-14, 40-41.

Council for Cultural Cooperation of the Council of Europe. (1964). *Physical education and sport: A handbook of institutions and associations*. Strassbourg: Librairie Berger-Lavrault.

Douglas, S.A. (1975, March). *Uses of sport in domestic politics*. Paper presented at the Popular Culture Association Annual Meeting, St. Louis, MO.

Douglas, S.A. (1978). Policy issues in sport and athletics. *Policy Studies Journal, 7*(1), 137-151.

Fitness and Amateur Sports Program. (1970). *A proposed sports policy for Canadians*. Ottawa, Canada: Ministry of Health & Welfare.

Fitness and Amateur Sports Program. (1971). *Sport Canada: Recreation Canada*. Ottawa, Canada: Ministry of Health & Welfare.

Fitness and Amateur Sports Program. (1973). *Report prepared for the fitness and amateur sports program: The first ten years and after*. Ottawa, Canada: Ministry of Health & Welfare.

Fitness and Amateur Sports Program. (1977). *A working paper: Toward a national policy on amateur sport*. Ottawa, Canada: Ministry of Health & Welfare.

Fitness and Amateur Sports Program. (1979). *Toward a national policy on fitness and recreation*. Ottawa, Canada: Ministry of Health & Welfare.

Fitness and Amateur Sports Program. (1981). *Challenge to the nation: Fitness and amateur sport in the 80's*. Ottawa, Canada: Ministry of Health & Welfare.

Gear, J.L. (1973, December). Factors influencing the development of government sponsored physical fitness programmes in Canada from 1850 to 1972. *Canadian Journal of History of Sport and Physical Education, 4*(2), 1-25.

Goodhart, P., & Chatway, C. (1968). *War without weapons: The rise of mass sport in the twentieth century and its effect on men and nations*. London: W.H. Allen.

Goodhue, R.M. (1974, May 10-12). Politics of sport: An institutional focus. *The Second Annual Convention of the North American Society for Sport History* (pp. 34-35). London, Ontario.

Guldenphenning, S. (1978, August). *The necessity of sport politology*. Paper presented at the World Congress of Sociology, Uppsala, Sweden.

Hanna, W.A. (1962). *The politics of sport*. Washington, DC: American Universities Field Staff.

Hoberman, J.M. (1977, Summer/Fall). Sport and political ideology: Relating sport and ideology. *Journal of Sport and Social Issues, 1*(2), 80-114.

Johnson, A.T. (1978, January/February). Public sports policy: An introduction. *American Behavioral Scientist, 21*(3), 319-344.

Kolatch, J. (1971). *Sports, politics and ideology in China*. New York: J. David.

Kropke, R. (1974, June). International sports and the social sciences. *Quest* (Monograph XXII), 25-32.

Lapchick, R.E. (1978, Spring/Summer). A political history of the modern Olympic Games. *Journal of Sport and Social Issues,* 2(1), 1-12.

Lund, A. (1972). Sport and politics. In M. Hart (Ed.), *Sport in the sociocultural process* (pp. 482-485). Dubuque, IA: W.C. Brown.

Mandell, R.D. (1971). *The Nazi Olympics.* New York: Macmillan.

Maynard, J. (1966). *Sport et politique.* Paris: Payot.

McIntosh, P.C. (1963). *Sport in society.* London: C.A. Watts.

McIntosh, P.C. (1978, November). Sport and politics have always been mixed. *Sports Digest,* 355, 11-13.

McKelvey, G. (1972, March). Sport and politics in Canada. Presented at *Symposium on Sport, Man, and Contemporary Society.* Queen's College of the City University of New York.

Mitchelson, B., & Slack, T. (1979, May 6-9). *Government involvement in sport: A comparative analysis between Canada and the United States.* Paper presented at Smarts Conference, Amherst, MA.

Molyneux, D.D. (1962). *Central government aid to sport and physical recreation in countries of Western Europe.* Birmingham, UK: University of Birmingham.

Morton, H.W. (1963). *Soviet sport.* New York: Cromwell-Collier.

Nafziger, J.A., & Strenk, A. (1978). The political uses and abuses of sport. *Connecticut Law Review,* 10(2), 259-289.

Natan, A. (Ed.). (1958). *Sport and society.* London: Bowes and Bowes.

Natan, A. (1969). Sport and politics. In J.W. Loy & G.S. Kenyon (Eds.), *Sport, culture and society.* Toronto: Collier-MacMillan Canada.

Noll, R.G. (Ed.). (1974). *Government and the sports business.* Washington, DC: Brookings Institution.

Petrie, B.M. (1975). Sport and politics. In D.W. Ball & J.W. Loy (Eds.), *Sport and social order.* Don Mills, Ontario: Addison-Wesley.

Pooley, J.C., & Webster, A.B. (1972, March). Sport and politics: Power play. Paper presented at *Symposium on Sport, Man and Contemporary Society.* Queen's College of the City University of New York.

Redmond, G. (1977). I: English works. Sports and politics. *Culture* (Vol. 4(2), pp. 17-25). Switzerland: UNESCO Press.

Sands, R. (1976, June). International sport is politics. *The Australian Journal for Health, Physical Education and Recreation,* 72, 7-10.

Semotiuk, D.M. (1970). *The development of a theoretical framework for analyzing the role of national government involvement in sport and physical education and its application to Canada.* Doctoral dissertation, Ohio State University, Columbus.

Shaw, S.M. (1976, September/October). Sport and politics: The case of South Africa. *CAHPER Journal, 43*(1), 30-38.

Strenk, A. (1978, Spring/Summer). Back to the very first day. *Journal of Sport and Social Issues, 2*(1), 24-36.

Strenk, A. (1978, Summer). The thrill of victory and the agony of defeat: Sport and international politics. *Orbis,* pp. 453-469.

West, T.J. (1973, December). Physical fitness, sport and the federal government 1909 to 1954. *Canadian Journal of the History of Sport and Physical Education, 4*(2), 26-42.

Wohl, A. (1953). The problem of development of physical culture in a socialist system. *Kultura Eizycgna,* pp. 182-187.

Wright, S. (1978). Nigeria: The politics of sport. *Round Table,* N272, 362-367.

National Government Involvement in Amateur Sport in Australia 1972-1981

Darwin M. Semotiuk
University of Western Ontario

Keith Dunstan, in his book *Sports*, suggests that Australia is obsessed by sport and proceeds to develop support for the theme that "sport has moved Australia—often more than anything else" (1981, p. x). Sociologists, historians, philosophers, and journalists would argue that sport is one, if not *the*, national obsession of Australians. The existence of an Australian sporting ethos suggests that sport occupies a uniquely important, if not enshrined, place in Australian society. The difficulty in objectively measuring the degree of obsession, or even the importance of sport to a nation is self-evident. Any meaningful assessment would have to rely upon the subjective judgment of the observer, despite the fact that quantifiable data such as government expenditures, available human and physical resources, sport participants, and sports performances can be identified. The *Report of the Australian Sports Institute Study Group* (1975) concluded that Australians "spend an enormous amount of time and money on sport—thinking, talking, reading and writing about it, saving and spending for it, watching and doing it and above all 'loving it' " (p. 4).

An attempt to deify the theme of sport and its fundamental significance in Australian culture is contained in the following statement from the same report.

> Sport is the Australian religion—is the ultimate . . . is the only thing Australians believe in passionately . . . has no knockers . . . has become the God . . . has moved Australians more than anything else . . . helps unify Australia as a nation . . . can do no wrong . . . in Australia carried the Christian message of muscular Christianity. (p. 5)

One author has commented that "never have we been so moved by our work, our music or our literature, and perhaps the passion we have spent on sport explains the dull history of our politics" (Dunstan, 1981, p. 10). It is within the context of this theme that the following questions need to be addressed and reflected upon. How important is sport to Australia and its people? How does one measure its importance and its significance? What responsibility does the government have in sport? Should the government control and direct sport? Should the sport policy deal with the issue of mass sport participation versus elite athlete performance? These are fundamental questions that require some form of resolution in both the short- and the long-term.

It is within the framework of these broad, yet extremely significant questions, that the issue of the national government's involvement in amateur sport in Australia will be examined. The study will encompass 1972 to 1981 and investigate several areas including sport policy philosophy, administrative structure, budgetary allocation, programs, personalities, and future trends.

Australia has always taken considerable pride in its sporting successes in the international arena. It is interesting to note that in the 1956 Summer Olympic competitions held in Melbourne, Australia amassed 36 medals and ranked third in the world in the unofficial points standing. Twenty years later in Montreal, the Australian Olympic effort accumulated 5 medals and ranked 32nd in the world standings. The estimated expenditure of the Commonwealth Government for the 1980 to 1981 fiscal year was approximately 36 billion Australian dollars. Of this total, $383.1 million, or 1.06% of the total budget, was earmarked for support of culture and recreation. The 1980 to 1981 budget for the Sport and Recreation Branch within the Ministry of Home Affairs was $8.2 million or .0023% of the total federal expenditure. Based on a total population figure of 14.5 million, this would represent a per capita expenditure of 52.91 cents per person for sport and recreation. Another comparison worthy of note is the appropriation assigned to the arts and to sport. The data suggest that small groups of elite artists receive significant amounts of assistance compared to a much wider group of sports persons. The Australian Opera ($3.0 million), the Australian Ballet ($1.5 million), and the Elizabethan Trust Orchestras ($2.5 million) are, indeed, well supported by the federal government. A document (Budget Information Papers, 1973-1981) that undertakes an analysis of government spending observes that a comparison of "like" figures reveals that general support for the arts represents a $17.2 million item, as compared to a $2.9 million expenditure for the Sports Development Program. These data clearly suggest that sport does not receive a high priority in terms of financial support provided by the national government. These examples serve to illustrate that, perhaps, sport is not as important to the Australians as they believe it to be.

Australian Government Involvement in Sport—
Historical Perspectives

Programs Prior to 1972

Despite the fact that sport plays such a prominent part in the lives of so many Australians, it is surprising how little attention has been given to sport by governments, particularly at the federal level. Prior to the 1970s the federal government's involvement was minimal, at best. In response to the conflict of World War II the *National Fitness Act* was passed to deal with the fact that significant numbers of Australian men and women had been classified as unfit for military service. An overriding objective of the program was to improve the standard of fitness of Australian youth. The program operated through state education departments, university physical education courses, and state national fitness councils. A second program, which was instituted in 1951 by the federal government, provided grants towards the cost of Life Saving Assistance programs. As one might expect, the support of both of these programs involved a minimal expenditure on the part of the government. Apart from these two programs, the only contributions to sport by the federal government were ad hoc grants towards the cost of sending representative teams to international competitions, specifically the Olympic and Commonwealth Games. Prior to the formation of the Federal Department of Tourism and Recreation in 1972, funding for sport and recreation was primarily the responsibility of the sporting organizations, themselves, and state and local governments. By the early 1970s, departments of sport and/or recreation were in operation in most states.

The Labor Government 1972 to 1976

The election of Gough Whitlam and his Labor Party in 1972 represented the beginning of a new era in Australian sport. Clearly, the Labor Party platform had within it a strong view on the commitment that the government should have towards sport and recreation and the use of leisure time.

> There is no greater social problem facing Australia than the good use of leisure. It is the problem of all modern and wealthy communities. It is, above all, the problem of urban societies and thus, in Australia, the most urbanized nation on earth, a problem more pressing for us than for any other nation on earth. For such a nation as ours, this may very well be the problem of the 1980s; so we must prepare now; prepare the governments of the 80s—the children and the youth of the 70s—to be able to enjoy and enrich their growing hours of leisure. (Whitlam, 1972)

The election of the Australian Labor Party in December, 1972, led to the creation of a Federal Ministry of Tourism and Recreation under the guidance of the late Frank Stewart. The Labor government embarked upon a program that provided two main forms of assistance: (a) a Capital Assistance Program to help provide sporting facilities at the local level, and (b) a Sports Assistance Program to assist national associations with travel, coaching, and administrative costs. The Capital Assistance Program considered the funding of any project that increased the range of leisure activities available within a local region. The formula was such that the grant represented 25% of the total costs, and the annual expenditures for the years that Labor remained in power appear in Table 1. The aim of the Sports Assistance Program was to support sports associations at the national level to supplement and strengthen the work of the association.

Table 1 Capital Assistance and Sports Assistance Program Expenditures ($ Million)

Program	Year		
	1973 to 74	1974 to 75	1975 to 76
Capital assistance	4.00	4.60	6.30
Sports assistance	.60	1.15	1.20

Note. Data compiled from Australia Budget Information Papers, Ministry of Tourism and Recreation, Ministry of Environment, Housing, and Community Development, Ministry of Home Affairs, Canberra, 1973-1981.

The Minister for Tourism and Recreation, Frank Stewart, stated that while his government viewed the pursuit of excellence in sport as being as worthwhile as the pursuit of excellence in the arts, and national and international success as a stimulation to mass participation "we have no intention of imitating some countries which regard success in sport as some sort of proof of the superiority of their way of life, ideology and race. Our task lies clearly elsewhere, in meeting more basic needs, in catering for masses, not just a small elite" (1975, June). This basic philosophical position came through by way of an increased expenditure under the National Fitness Act and the introduction of a nationwide fitness awareness campaign—Fitness Australia.

During this time, the Department of Tourism and Recreation undertook initiatives that examined issues in sport and recreation. The discussions and documents they produced have laid the basic foundation for the present day program of the federal government. These reports include *Recreation in Australia—Its Role, Scope and Development* by Professor John Bloomfield (1973); *The National Seminar on Leisure* (1974); *The National Coaches Seminar* (1974); and *The Report of the Australian Sports Institute Study Group* (November, 1975), chaired by Alan Coles. This latter document represents a landmark publication on Australian sport and performs a useful function in clarifying the status of the Australian sport delivery system. The 30 recommendations that came from the report clearly gave philosophy and direction to Australian sport in general and the concept of the Australian Sports Institute (TASI) specifically. The increased activity, mostly of an introspective nature, certainly gave further clarification to the role that the federal government should play in sport and recreation. The pieces of a national sports policy had been isolated.

The Liberal Government 1976 to 1981

With the defeat of the Labor Party, the Liberal-Country Party coalition returned to power in 1976 under the leadership of Malcolm Fraser. Sport and recreation was one of the first victims of this party's return to office, the Sport Assistance Program was abolished, and the Capital Assistance Program was continued only insofar as it honored commitments previously entered into by the Labor Government. The reaction from the sporting community was predictable, and after considerable pressure was put on the government, the Sport Assistance Program was reintroduced in the 1977 to 1978 budget.

The change in government certainly illustrates the profound difference in philosophical approach to sport between the present Liberal-Country Party government and the Australian Labor Party opposition. These differences are evident in the level of funding and the relative significance given to different aspects of the program. A further examination of the positions on sport taken by both political parties provides additional insights into national government intervention in sport.

Barry Cohen, a member of Parliament and Shadow Minister for Sport, Recreation, Tourism, and the Environment, prepared a *Green Paper on Sport and Recreation*. In making reference to the Liberal-Country Party philosophy, he states "when questioned on sport, Mr. Fraser (The Prime Minister of Australia) gives the impression that all that is required to produce a fit and healthy nation is a pair of sandshoes and running shorts" (1980). Cohen maintains that this approach fits in well with the Liberal-Country Party view that success is up to the individual. Cohen, in speaking for his political associates, maintains that such an approach was relevant 50 years ago when sport was primarily the domain of affluent gentlemen. He further suggests that it represents a "naive, unrealistic approach these days when wealthy nations are able to provide top quality coaches and less wealthy but politically motivated countries are prepared to devote considerable time and money to produce world class athletes." The Labor Party maintains that if Australia wants to have a fit and healthy nation and regain its position as a top sporting nation, it will have to be prepared to commit its financial, physical, and human resources to achieve those ends.

The Australian Labor Party—Position on Sport

The Australian Labor Party has developed a comprehensive position statement on sport and recreation. Fundamental to its position is that "the Federal Government has a responsibility to provide national leadership in making sport and recreation available to everyone who wishes to participate." A most progressive position is taken by suggesting that "part of the funding for sport and recreation should be appropriated from the health budget." The sport policy includes further initiatives in the creation of a National Sports Institute, the development of a national coaching scheme, the expansion of the athlete assistance program, the provision of support for national sporting associations, a commitment to funding sports medicine research, and a provision of funds under a cost-sharing arrangement to build facilities in cooperation with state and local governments.

The Liberal-Country Party—A Position on Sport

The Liberal-Country Party, during its most recent tenure as the governing party, has formulated a general philosophical position on sport. The federal government accepts as its role that suggested by the Confederation of Australian Sport in its *Master Plan for Sport*, March, 1980; namely,

• the provision of international standard facilities,
• the servicing of the development programs of national sporting associations, and
• the education of administrators.

The federal government's stated policy in relation to sport has two broad objectives: (a) the encouragement of the pursuit of excellence in sport, and (b) the improvement of general health and enjoyment of life through involvement in sport. Through its policies the government promotes both these objectives, and it regards several principles as basic to their achievement.

• Maintenance of the voluntary nature and autonomy of sporting bodies.
• Assistance, in general, for only the nonprofessional aspects of sport.
• Provision of equal opportunities for the handicapped in sport.
• Encouragement of private sponsorship for sport.

It is interesting to note that both political parties have considered sport important enough to develop a policy position on it. Philosophically, both positions are quite similar, in that both have indicated that the pursuit of excellence and mass participation in sport are important policy objectives. However, fundamental and significant differences exist in (a) defining the degree of importance of sport within the overall policy of the government, and (b) assigning the primary responsibility for the promotion, encouragement, and development of sport. The evidence examined suggests that the Australian Labor Party would assign a higher priority to sport than would its Liberal-Country counterpart. One also gains the impression that the Labor Party would favor a stronger intervention and control over sport on the part of the federal government. The privatization of sport position adopted by the Liberal-Country Party has been consistently enunciated by party officials. R. Groom, Minister for Environment, Housing, and Community Development, in a policy statement on June 1st, 1978, indicated that "clearly, the major responsibility for development rests with the sports themselves, with the Government assisting and encouraging this development."

Personalities appear to have had a large impact on the extent of government commitment and support provided to sport. In this connection, Minister Bob Ellicott stood out in recent years. Ellicott had taken an extremely keen interest in sport, and by virtue of his strong position within the Cabinet, had argued successfully for a greater share of government dollars for sport. The initiatives that he was responsible for have laid the foundation for present day federal government programs in sport. Of particular significance are the Australian Institute of Sport, the Sports Development Program, the National Coaching Accreditation Scheme, and the International Standard Sports Facilities Program. Ellicott's decision to resign his post as Minister of Home Affairs in 1981 meant that sport had lost one of its most supportive politicians at the federal level.

It was during Ellicott's tenure that the government undertook the task of formulating a comprehensive, long-term, national sports development policy. In February, 1979, Ellicott charged the Sports Advisory Council with preparing a report aimed at providing a policy framework for sports development within which all levels of government, sports bodies, and organizations with responsibilities for sport could cooperate to meet these needs. The report, entitled *Towards a National Sports Program*, identified possible areas of government involvement for discussion with state governments and highlighted areas for action by the Commonwealth. It also identified the problems facing Australian sport.

- Administrative deficiencies.
- Insufficient international competition.
- High cost of competition within Australia.
- Lack of sufficient opportunities to develop top caliber coaches.
- Lack of facilities of international standard.
- Difficulties facing individual athletes through career disruption and foregone educational opportunities.
- Lack of coordinated sports research.
- Failure to identify and nurture talented young sportspersons.
- Insufficient emphasis on sport and physical education in schools.

The report emphasized the need for governments to cooperate in the development of a national sports policy. In so doing, it also recognized and fully supported the role of the private sector and the self-help principle followed by voluntary sporting associations.

The distinguished members of the Sports Advisory Council saw the need to develop a comprehensive national sports policy that would provide a framework for the planned development of sport in Australia on a continuous basis. This policy would set national objectives, offer the opportunity for coordinated action by all levels of government, realize the implications of sport for other government policies, transcend political affiliation, and not be interrupted by changes of government or ministers. It was within this spirit that the report was submitted to the government for its consideration in April, 1979. The report was considered by an interdepartmental committee consisting of representatives from Home Affairs, the Prime Minister's Office and Cabinet, Finance, Health and Social Security, Industry and Commerce, Foreign Affairs, and Defense. The committee, chaired by Home Affairs, met over a period of 8 months, redrafted the council report and submitted the document for consideration to the Cabinet. The Cabinet made the decision to continue its funding support for numerous sport programs, but was reluctant to commit itself to establishing a national sports policy. The failure of the government to come to grips with putting such a policy on paper has meant that sports program support will continue on an ad hoc basis with the government's action reflecting a response to pressures being placed on it.

Commonwealth Expenditure on Sport and Recreation (1973 to 1980)

Table 2 outlines the federal government's expenditure on sport and recreation from 1973 to 1974 to 1980 to 1981. A detailed examination of the 1980 to 1981 budget and its programs is presented later in the paper.

Sport and Recreation Branch Organization, Budget, and Programs 1981

The Sport and Recreation Branch within the Ministry of Home Affairs is the administrative unit of the federal government responsible for directly supporting programs in the area. The Commonwealth Sports Advisory Council consists of nine members, appointed by the Minister, and is responsible for advising the Minister on all matters relating to sport. Specifically, this body makes recommendations on priorities for the development of sport and sets criteria for the allocation of funds. In addition, the Council is the agency responsible for monitoring developments in sport in Australia and overseas with a view to advising on future policy decisions. The Sport and Recreation Branch, headed by an assistant secretary, consists of a staff of 25 who work in one of the four sections: sports

Table 2   Commonwealth Expenditure on Sport and Recreation (1973-74 to 1980-81)

Year	Program support ($m)
1973-74	5.74
1974-75	6.88
1975-76	9.21
1976-77	12.05
1977-78	5.87
1978-79	3.29
1979-80	5.99
1980-81	8.17

Note. Data compiled from Government of Australia Budget Information Papers 1973-74 to 1980-81.

SPORT AND RECREATION BRANCH

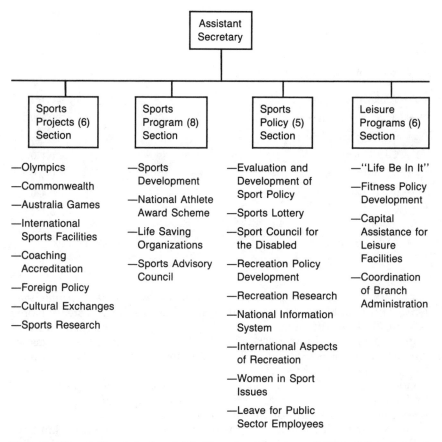

Figure 1   Organizational chart and definition of section responsibilities of the sport and recreation branch within the Ministry of Home Affairs. *Note.* Chart prepared in consultation with Geoff Strang, Sport and Recreation Branch, Canberra, ACT, April, 1981.

projects, sports programs, sports policy, and leisure programs. An organizational chart of the Branch, along with an identification of the various programs, is presented in Figure 1. Given the wide scope of program involvement, it is readily apparent that the unit is understaffed.

A breakdown of the 1980 to 1981 budget of the Sport and Recreation Branch serves to highlight the program activities of the federal government (see Table 3). One of the more controversial initiatives undertaken by the federal government in recent years has been the creation of the Australian Institute of Sport and its study course developed in cooperation with the Canberra College of Advanced Education. The seeds of the

Table 3   Sport and Recreation Program Budget 1980-1981

Program item	Support ($ m)
Sports Development Program	2.885
1982 Commonwealth Games	
Facilities	2.500
Pre-event competition	0.115
1980 Olympics—alternate competition	0.500
Australian Institute of Sport	0.902
AIS/CCAE Course	0.130
"Life Be In It" Program	0.700
Life saving organizations	0.440
Total	8.172

Note. Data compiled from the Australian Budget Information Papers, 1980-1981.

concept were planted with *Report of the Australian Sports Institute Study Group* (1975) and brought to fruition by the efforts of the Minister of Home Affairs, Bob Ellicott. According to Geoff Strang (personal communications, April, May, June, 1981), Ellicott's interest in the Institute was increased by overseas visits in 1979 and 1980. In 1979 he visited the People's Republic of China, where he saw the sports schools system in action, and London, where he saw Crystal Palace in its role as a national sports center. In 1980 he visited European and North American centers and further strengthened his vision of the Institute.

The Australian Institute of Sport was established in Canberra in January, 1981, and gives young Australians the opportunity to pursue their interest in their sport to the highest level without interruption or risk to their educations or careers. The aims of the Institute are

• to provide top level, specialist coaching and training for athletes who have shown great promise, at the same time offering them complementary and attractive education and career training opportunities, and
• to support these athletes with world-class facilities and sports science and medicine backup.

The 4-year pilot project commenced in January, 1981, with facilities and training provided for basketball, gymnastics, netball, soccer, swimming, tennis, track and field, and weight lifting. Australian athletes of both sexes, all age levels, and representing all states are presently working under the guidance of full-time national and international coaches employed by the Institute.

Concluding Observations and Comments

An overview of the Australian national government's involvement in sport has led to the following observations and comments:

- The sport system of Australia is extremely complex and fragmented with communication among agencies representing the public, private, and shared sectors not being as effective as it can be.
- The government of Australia has not, and does not, appear ready to make a firm philosophical and practical commitment to develop sport. The attempt by the Young Liberals to remove sport from the Liberal Party policy platform, along with the government's failure to adopt the Sport Council's *National Sport Program* proposal suggests that sport is, indeed, vulnerable in the present political environment.
- There is a need to articulate national, state, and local plans for sport that can deal with the short- and long-term needs of Australian sport. Such documents must be formulated by individuals representing all sectors of Australian sport and should reflect a cooperative spirit in making decisions for sport for the good of all. Needless to say, the vested interest mentality must be regulated in the preparation of these important planning materials.
- Consideration should be given to adopting a more professional approach to sport development. To this point in time, there has been an overreliance on the volunteer and the work that he does on behalf of Australian sport. The employment of full-time individuals with administrative and technical expertise can only strengthen existing amateur sport programs.
- Sport leadership will be a critical factor for Australian sport in the 1980s and 1990s. Leaders possessing vision, courage, energy, and enthusiasm must emerge from the political scene, from sports administration, from the teaching and coaching professions, and from the corporate sector.
- The sporting community must recognize the need and the potential for an effective sports lobby at the national level. Australian sport has been both negligent and naive in its failures to make an effort at understanding the political process and affecting change from within (Semotiuk, 1981, June).

Australian amateur sport has yet to realize its full potential. The outstanding sports tradition, the human and physical resources available, the magnificent climate, and the economic infrastructure provide Australia with the basic framework needed to become one of the greatest sporting nations in the world in both mass and elite sport. The challenge lies in convincing the government that such a goal is important to Australia and all Australians.

References

Bloomfield, J. (1973). Recreation in Australia—Its role, scope and development. Parliament of the Commonwealth of Australia. Canberra, Australia.

Cohen, B. (1980). *Green paper on sport and recreation*. Canberra, Australia.

Confederation of Australian Sport. (1980, March). *Master plan for sport*. Melbourne, Australia: Author.

Daily, J. (1981, May). Personal interview with Sports Advisory Council member in Adelaide, Australia.

Darlison, L. (1980, February). Has sport got a future? [Keynote address]. *First A.L.P. National Seminar on Sport and Recreation in Australia*. Q.E. II Jubilee Sports Centre, Brisbane, Australia.

Dunstan, K. (1981). *Sports*. Melbourne, Australia: Sun Books.

Groom, R. (1978, June). *Policy Statement on Sport and Recreation*. Ministry of the Environment, Housing and Community Development. Canberra, Australia.

Hartung, G. (1979, January). Sport and the Canberra lobby. *The Australian*.

Home Affairs, Ministry of. (1981). *The Australian Institute of Sport*. Canberra, Australia: Author.

Jobling, I. (1974, January). *A Ministry of Recreation and Sport at the national level of government*. Paper presented at the International Conference on Health, Physical Education and Recreation, Christchurch, New Zealand.

Pyke, F. (1981, May). Personal interview with Director Pyke, Sports Studies Program, Canberra College of Advanced Education, Canberra, Australia.

Report of the Australian sports institute study group. (1975). Department of Tourism and Recreation, Canberra, Australia.

Semotiuk, D. (1970). *The development of theoretical framework for analyzing the role of national government involvement in sport and its application to Canada*. Unpublished doctoral dissertation, Ohio State University, Columbus.

Semotiuk, D. (1981). Motives for national government involvement in sport. *International Journal of Physical Education*, **XVIII**(1), 23-28.

Semotiuk, D. (1981, May). *Notes* from lecture delivered at the Canberra College of Advanced Education, Canberra, Australia.

Semotiuk, D. (1981, June). *Notes* from lecture delivered at the School of Human Movement Studies, University of Queensland, Brisbane, Australia.

Stewart, F. (1975, June). Press release statement on sport and recreation. Canberra, Australia: Ministry of Tourism and Recreation.

Talbot, D. (1981, May). Personal interview at Australian Institute of Sport, Canberra, Australia.

Tourism and Recreation; Environment, Housing, and Community Development; and Home Affairs, Ministries of. (1973-1981). *Budget information papers*. Canberra, Australia: Author.

Towards a national sports program. (1979). Canberra, Australia: Sports Advisory Council.

Whitlam, E.G. (1972, November 13). *Australian Labor Party policy speech* at Blacktown Civic Centre.

The 1981 South African Springbok Rugby Tour of New Zealand and the United States: A Case Study

Dale P. Toohey
California State University, Long Beach

Well before the South African Springbok Rugby Union Team had even set foot on New Zealand soil, opposition to the tour had begun to simmer, both inside and outside of New Zealand. Public opinion polls within New Zealand had shown an increase in the local opposition to the proposed tour; 34% were against the tour in September, 1980, and this increased to 43% in June, 1981. "The increased opposition, however, is considered more a reflection of a fear of violence, rather than a substantial swing away from the tour on antiapartheid grounds" (*The Daily Telegraph*, June 16, 1981, p. 5). In anticipation of any violence, antiriot squads had already trained in army camps as a part of the $1 million "peacekeeping operations." Outside of New Zealand there appeared to be little support for the tour. The Australian government, in keeping with their foreign affairs policies with South Africa, had refused the team landing rights en route to New Zealand. However, this was also done so as not to "taint" the meeting of the Commonwealth heads of government in Melbourne in September and the 1982 Commonwealth Games scheduled for Brisbane by any involvement with South Africa (*The Australian*, July 6, 1981, p. 1). A consensus, taken by the Commonwealth Secretary-General concerning the Commonwealth Finance Ministers' Conference, showed mounting opposition against Auckland as its venue, especially from the African, Asian, and Caribbean nations.

Finally, in a 10-minute television and radio broadcast on July 6, 1981, the Prime Minister of New Zealand, Robert Muldoon, restated his government's position. "The individual sporting bodies had a fundamental freedom to decide who they would and would not be involved with, which he agreed to, in his interpretation of the Gleneagles Agreement" (*The Australian*, July 7, 1981, p. 1).

The tour was on, and within hours of the announcement, countries all around the world echoed their approval and disapproval. In Bridgetown, the Barbados Olympic Association announced it would boycott the 1982 Commonwealth Games in Brisbane if New Zealand's athletes competed. The West Indies Cricket Board of Control said that "they would not play the forthcoming series against New Zealand, if the tour went ahead."

Morgan Naidoo, President of the South African Council of Sport, said that "they had already instituted action to have New Zealand isolated from international sport." On the other side of the coin, Danie Graven, President of the South African Rugby Board, said that "they were delighted and grateful for the bold stand taken by the New Zealand Rugby Union" (*The Sydney Morning Herald*, July 11, 1981, p. 1).

New Zealand (July 19 to September 13)

While the Springboks flew from Johannesburg to Auckland, via New York, Los Angeles, and Honolulu, because Australia would not grant them landing permits, 2,500 demonstrators awaited their arrival. "How to make a petrol bomb" leaflets were distributed in Christchurch, venue of the first international on August 15. A 24-hour security guard was placed around Prime Minister Muldoon, and New Zealand was polarized into rugby supporters against protestors and protestors against South Africa. However, a well-executed plan had the Springboks out of Auckland and into Gisbourne, the site of the first match, without incident.

A capacity crowd of 19,000 was expected to turn out for the Springboks' first match. What wasn't expected was the vigor with which the demonstrators carried out their plans to halt the match and, subsequently, the entire tour. Extra guards were assigned to reinforce the police members, in a concerted move by the government to ensure that the South African Rugby Union tour continued. The next scheduled match against Taranaki in New Plymouth was expected to draw only token protests. An estimated crowd of 20,000 was treated to some rugby by the Springboks' "first strings" as they accounted for the local Taranaki side by 34 points to 9 (*The Australian*, July 29, 1981, p. 3; *The Sydney Morning Herald*, July 30, 1981, p. 31).

In the wake of police baton beatings of the antiapartheid demonstrators outside the South African Consulate in Wellington on July 30, the day after the Taranaki game, more violence was anticipated several miles away in Palmerston North, site of the next Springbok match. That following Saturday a police squad of 1,200, wearing protective riot gear and brandishing batons, stood three deep outside the Palmerston North showground to confront the 3,000 anti-Springbok tour protestors. A long 14 minutes of "eyeball-to-eyeball contact" between the groups finally ended with the protestors dispersing, having made no attempt to breach the police lines and storm the showground. The South Africans beat the national provincial champions, Manawatu, by 31 to 19.

Prime Minister Muldoon called for a round table peace conference between the New Zealand Rugby Union, the police, the antiapartheid protestors, and his government to trade off a shortened tour for an end to the civil disobedience campaigns. Speaking for HART (Halt All Racist Tours), John Minto said that "their objective is to end the tour and put them straight on a plane back to South Africa" (*The Australian*, August 3, 1981, p. 1). Thus, there appeared to be little hope of a compromise.

The much-heralded summit conference, chaired by Prime Minister Muldoon, ended without any real decision, except that the Springbok tour would continue. While there were several suggestions offered, nothing was agreed upon. Some of the suggestions were that (a) all sporting bodies be asked to reaffirm the principles of the Gleneagles Agreement, but with the onus for observing them on the individual sporting bodies rather than the government; (b) the antiapartheid movement be allowed to address the crowd before each match; and (c) members of the crowd be invited to observe a minute's silence before each game to mark their opposition to apartheid.

Meanwhile, the Commonwealth Games organizers in Australia convened a special conference in Canberra, Australia, to discuss the implications of the Springbok tour. Pressure for the conference had emerged after a meeting of international Olympic bodies in Milan. Uganda had already stated that it would not participate in the games if New Zealand were present. However, a consensus among African and Caribbean members was that while they did not wish to compete against New Zealand, they did not feel that they should be penalized because of New Zealand's actions (*The Sydney Morning Herald*, August 5, 1981, p. 8).

In Auckland, just 36 hours after the summit conference, violence again flared. Five hundred protestors headed for a brewery and a liquor distribution company, both of which supported the tour financially. Police repulsed a "main gate" charge at the brewery, but the protestors entered the distributing company, smashing bottles and a plate glass window. Meanwhile, the Springboks cruised to an easy win, 45 to 9, over a mediocre Wanganui side.

The leaders of HART were extremely pleased at the news that the New Zealand Rugby Union had called off the Springbok-South Canterbury match at Timaru on August 19. The decision was a bitter disappointment in Timaru, a city of 30,000. The South Canterbury Rugby Chairman, N.E. Wakefield, said that the fence of Fraser Park was partly wire, partly tin, partly hedgerow, and partly private homes, and not intended to withstand a siege.

The threats by HART to make New Zealand unpoliceable every time the Springboks played were taken very seriously by the government and the police. Prior to the Springboks' next game against the Southland at Invercargill, the army rolled out barbed wire along one sideline and the out-of-play lines to try and stop the field's being invaded. Because of these precautions, no major incidents occurred with the protestors. The Springboks looked less than convincing, though, beating the Southland 22 points to 6.

The next game was in Dunedin, deep in the south island of New Zealand, and this normally peaceful city became the scene of further violent confrontations between police and demonstrators. The police bus, transporting the Springboks to Dunedin, was involved in 110 km/hr pursuits as the demonstrators tried to roadblock the entries into Dunedin, but several detours allowed the protestors to be shaken off. However, they regrouped outside the Southern Cross Hotel, where the Springboks were staying, to launch another offensive. When the Springboks arrived, they entered through a rear door while a large contingent of police blocked the demonstrators who were attempting to prevent their entry. Police formed a wall and pushed the demonstrators back; when the demonstrators refused to disperse, the police forced them back a further 100 meters, using knees and elbows in a rhythmical motion and chanting "move, move, move." Five arrests were made throughout the day. In Wellington, the capital of New Zealand, there was a surprise move by the local council to cancel, in the interests of public safety and civil order, the second rugby international to be played between the Springboks and the New Zealand national team at Athletic Park in Wellington on August 29.

Across the Tasman in Canberra, Australia, Peter Ouu, speaking for the Organization of African Unity, launched a scathing attack on New Zealand's Prime Minister Muldoon. Ouu accused Muldoon of "sheer hypocrisy" over the tour and called for the people of New Zealand to oust the government that had given their country "the stigma of supporters of apartheid." "We will see to it that New Zealand is excluded from the 1982 Commonwealth Games in Brisbane, and if we cannot exclude them, we will not participate," Ouu said (*The Sydney Morning Herald*, August 11, 1981, p. 1). The O.A.U. represented 50 African countries, of which 14 were Commonwealth countries.

On the same day in Christchurch, police arrested 126 people during a protest, which blocked a major traffic intersection for more than an hour. In Dunedin, 27 were taken into custody when they tried to disrupt the contest between the Springboks and the Otago team by maintaining a barrage of whistleblowing. Despite the protestors' efforts, the South Africans defeated Otago 17 points to 13.

The strain of events was beginning to show on the South Africans, both on and off the field. Two games had been canceled, their training program had been jeopardized by Christchurch hotel workers who refused to serve them, and there were grave uncertainties as to whether or not the tour would continue past the first international match. Nelie Smith, the Springbok coach, explained that the team's lackluster performances were a result of waning match fitness and team morale.

Speaking for the New Zealand police force's "Operation Rugby," Chief Superintendent Brian Davies said that they had learned a great deal since the beginning of the tour and the cancellation of the Hamilton match. Now they were better briefed and ready to move much more quickly, and as far as the first international match in Christchurch was concerned, the plans were complete. "We're satisfied that we have the capacity to deal with it" (*The Sydney Morning Herald*, August 12, 1981, p. 11).

Lancaster Park, Christchurch, the venue for the first Springbok and New Zealand "All Black" international on Saturday, August 15, looked secure behind a 3-meter-high, corrugated iron fence with a 24-hour police guard. The army arrived with rolls of barbed wire, which would be stretched inside the grounds and at vulnerable points outside. The police had additional help in Christchurch, retired policemen who were sworn in as special constables to assist police during the Springbok tour. The increased precautions had been made as a reaction to the fire that destroyed a large grandstand at a Christchurch field where the Springboks had trained prior to the international. Secret travel arrangements were also necessary; the Springboks had been forced to sleep on the floor of a local rugby club prior to the first rugby union international, because police could not guarantee their safety in any of the city hotels, despite the deployment of 2,000 men. More than 5,000 antiapartheid demonstrators were expected to march in an attempt to stop the international, in what could be the biggest and most violent confrontation of the tour.

Feeling was running high on both sides. Rugby supporters were enraged at the burning of the grandstand at a local rugby club, and the anti-tour movement in Christchurch was the most determined and disciplined in the history of New Zealand.

On the day of the international, a day most New Zealanders would prefer to forget, the worst fears were realized. Fifty protestors stormed onto the field, spreading broken glass and tacks in a last-minute effort to stop the game between the two countries. They occupied the field for some 3 minutes before they were hurled off by 200 riot police. The start of the game was delayed several minutes while groundsmen cleared up the debris. Outside the grounds, another 5,000 demonstrators made repeated assaults on the 2,500-strong, riot police squad. Twice they broke through police lines, and a third time, just before halftime, managed to get onto the No. 2 field adjacent to the main field. Police advanced into the protestors with their batons stabbing and jabbing, and at least 20 people reported injuries. Police said that 25 arrests were made.

The violence around the grounds also crept onto the playing field. Near the end of the match, when the New Zealand All Blacks led by a score of 14 to 3, the crowd of 45,000 witnessed an all-in brawl between both teams. The final score was a well-deserved 14 to 9 points win by the New Zealand All Blacks, who outplayed their larger counterparts in almost every facet of play, scoring three tries to one.

On the same day there were other tour-related incidents throughout New Zealand. In Auckland, eight protestors boarded an Air New Zealand Boeing 737 jet bound for Wellington, and 2,000 demonstrators blocked the north, south, and western motorways into Auckland in an afternoon of cat-and-mouse chases with police. In Wellington, 1,000 demonstrators marched from the city center to Athletic Park, the venue of the second international, and a group of 200 blocked the entrance to the Mt. Victoria tunnel. Meanwhile, two other events relating to the tour had occurred. The New Zealand Prime Minister, Muldoon, was labeled a "fascist" by a dozen children who invaded the public gallery of Parliament, screaming, "amandla" (Zulu for freedom). Security guards forcibly removed the children, aged 9 to 16, throwing some to the floor immediately outside the gallery. Meanwhile, in New York, a coalition of more than 100 antiapartheid groups announced plans to picket the New Zealand mission to the United Nations each time the Springboks played a game in New Zealand. They were also determined to stop the Springboks playing any of their scheduled games in the United States (*The Australian*, August 14, 1981, p. 1). While these demonstrations were going on in New York, a World War II pilot was jailed in Auckland for 3 months for threatening to crash a plane into a packed grandstand during the Springboks' earlier scheduled match in Hamilton, which was subsequently canceled. In 1976, the same pilot was fined $400 and disqualified from flying for 18 months for dropping flour bombs from an aircraft onto a South African softball team (*Los Angeles Times*, August 19, 1981, p. 10).

The Wellington council's fears were well founded when the Springboks played the All Blacks in the second international match at Athletic Park on August 29. More than 125 arrests were made across the country, including several people who seized the New Zealand Television Control Center, briefly interrupting the live coverage of the match in Auckland. Twenty-six people were arrested as demonstrators tried to invade the Wellington rugby international, police were pelted with water bombs and fruit, and several smoke bombs went off during the game. Despite the protests, the South Africans defeated the All Blacks 24 points to 12, making the series between the two countries even at one win each.

The third and deciding Springbok-All Black rugby international was played at Eden Park in Auckland on September 12, after almost being canceled due to an aerial bombardment of flour bombs, flares, smoke bombs, and flattened cans with razor edges, which were thrown like frisbees. Altogether, 148 people were arrested in Auckland, including a group of 43 who formed a human chain on the city's harbor bridge, blocking one of the main access points to Eden Park. HART was involved in the cutting of the microwave cable near Auckland that was to beam the game live to South Africa. Another group was intercepted on its way to Auckland Airport, where members had planned to storm the fields and prevent the landings of aircraft carrying rugby fans.

The South African Springboks were given a noisy sendoff from New Zealand as they headed for the United States, on the second leg of their rugby tour, amid fears of further violence, civil disobedience, and possible 1984 Olympic boycotts.

Prior to the Springboks' departure for the United States, Los Angeles Mayor Tom Bradley, worried about a possible boycott by African nations of the 1984 Summer Olympic Games, had urged the State Department to withdraw visas granted to the South African rugby team for a scheduled tour of the United States. The United States State Department had held talks with "interested parties" on the Springboks' three-match visit to America, and the Reagan administration had reiterated its policy not to interfere with private sporting exchanges. However, a black American civil rights leader vowed civil disobedience to stop the Springboks' first match in his hometown of Chicago. Meanwhile, a neo-nazi group in the city said that it would mount a 100-man squad and "use violence if necessary" to protect the South African team (*Los Angeles Times*, September 12, 1981, p. 1; *New Zealand Herald*, September 12, 1981, p. 3).

The United States (September 15 to September 28)

As in New Zealand, the United States was preparing for a torrid time as the Springboks flew into Los Angeles. Young black and white demonstrators carried signs reading, "we don't play with racism," "crush apartheid, don't play with it," and "stop racist rugby" as the Springboks arrived at Los Angeles International Airport.

City councils began meeting to discuss the Springbok tour. In Los Angeles, the county supervisors were split 2 to 2 on a motion calling for the cancellation of a planned exhibition game by the Springboks, while in Chicago, the city council adopted a resolution denouncing any local appearance of the Springbok rugby team.

In New York, Governor Carey canceled the Springbok rugby match on the grounds that potential violence by demonstrators threatened public safety. Meanwhile, the Tass Press Agency carried a statement by the Soviet Olympic Committee charging the United States government with violating the Olympic charter by inviting South African athletes to compete in the United States. The statement stopped short of a Soviet move to the International Olympic Committee Congress to have the 1984 Summer Games taken away from Los Angeles (*Los Angeles Times*, September 17, 1981, p. 1).

A new twist to the Springbok tour was uncovered when it was learned that partial financing of the South Africans' visit to the United States had been made by a South African businessman. The idea of the Springbok tour to America began in December, 1979, when a South African businessman with close ties to his government contributed $25,000 to the Eastern (U.S.) Rugby Union, which hosted the Springbok's American tour and arranged games during their stay.

In Washington, the House Foreign Affairs Committee approved, without opposition, a resolution that would express the "sense of Congress" that the Springboks should not play in the United States, although some members expressed reservations about it. The Reagan administration had taken the position that it was a private sporting matter, not within the jurisdiction of the federal government (*The New York Times*, September 18, 1981, pp. A35, D15).

The Organization of African Unity called on its members to boycott sports events with the United States because of the current Springbok rugby tour (*Los Angeles Times*, September 19, 1981, p. 1). In Northglenn, Colorado, the National Conference of Black Mayors denounced the United States visit by the Springboks, calling it a back-door attempt "to create an aura of respectability around South Africa." However, under strict secrecy, a rugby match between the Springboks and an all-star team from the Midwestern rugby clubs was played in Racine, Wisconsin. The South Africans ran out winners 46 points to 12. Two persons were arrested when a small protest erupted 15 minutes before the end of the match (*The Los Angeles Times*, September 20, 1981, p. A32).

Powerful, closed-door speeches by the President of the International Olympic Committee and the United States Olympic Committee in Baden-Baden, West Germany, appeared to have squelched the immediate threat of an African-Soviet Bloc boycott of the 1984 Los Angeles Olympics. Meanwhile, in New York, a federal judge overruled the governor of New York, ordering that the South African rugby team must be allowed to play in Albany, despite threats of violence. In an oral decision, a United States district judge ruled the team deserved the "protection of the court, no matter how 'repugnant' that nation's racial separation policies might be." The threats of violence and the need for extra security "failed to justify the Governor's unilateral ban" (*Independent Press-Telegram*, September 21, 1981, p. 1; *The Los Angeles Times*, September 21, 1981, p. 1; September 22, 1981, p. 5).

The second match of the Springbok minitour of the United States was played in Albany, not without incident, however. There was an appeal to the Supreme Court by New York's governor to have the match outlawed; this was subsequently turned down. There was an early morning explosion in the building housing the Eastern Rugby Union, which did only minor damage to the club, but caused a neighboring dairy-products company some $25,000 worth of damages. Despite these deterrents, plus a small group of antiapartheid demonstrators, as well as 15 opposing players, the Springboks won the match 41 points to 0.

In Baden-Baden the President of the Association of African National Olympic Committees declared at the World Olympic Congress that there would be no boycott of the 1984 Los Angeles Olympics because of the current tour of the United States by the Springboks (*Independent Press-Telegram*, September 23, 1981, p. 14; *The Los Angeles Times*, September 23, 1981, p. 6).

The South Africans' final game in America, again held in secrecy, was played against the United States national rugby team on September 25. The game was scheduled to be played on September 26, and after the match officials said that they had "lied to the media only for the protection of everybody concerned" (*The New York Times*, September 26, 1981, p. A35). The "secret" international, played at Evansville, Indiana, was won by the South African Springboks 34 points to 7.

The South African Springboks left the United States on September 28 amid further tight security arrangements. Five persons were arrested on Saturday, September 26, in a "mini-riot" when demonstrators arrived at Kennedy Airport in the mistaken belief that the Springboks' team was preparing to depart for South Africa. They did leave, however, on Monday, September 28, thus bringing to a close the 1981 South African rugby union tour to New Zealand and the United States.

References

Australian, The. (1981, July 6). p. 1.

Australian, The. (1981, July 7). p. 1.

Australian, The. (1981, July 29). p. 3.

Australian, The. (1981, August 3). p. 1.

Australian, The. (1981, August 14). p. 1.

Daily Telegraph. (1981, June 16). p. 5.

Independent Press-Telegram. (1981, September 21). p. 1.

Independent Press-Telegram. (1981, September 23). p. 14.

Los Angeles Times. (1981, August 19). p. 10.

Los Angeles Times. (1981, September 12). p. 1.

Los Angeles Times. (1981, September 17). p. 1.

Los Angeles Times. (1981, September 19). p. 1.

Los Angeles Times. (1981, September 20). p. A32.

Los Angeles Times. (1981, September 21). p. 1.

Los Angeles Times. (1981, September 22). p. 5.

Los Angeles Times. (1981, September 23). p. 6.

New York Times. (1981, September 18). pp. A35, D15.

New York Times. (1981, September 26). p. A35.

New Zealand Herald. (1981, September 12). p. 3.

Sydney Morning Herald. (1981, July 11). p. 1.

Sydney Morning Herald. (1981, July 30). p. 31.

Sydney Morning Herald. (1981, August 5). p. 8.

Sydney Morning Herald. (1981, August 11). p. 1.

Sydney Morning Herald. (1981, August 12). p. 11.

The Impact of the 1981 South African Springbok Rugby Tour on New Zealand Society: A Participant Observation Study[1]

Garfield Pennington
University of British Columbia

During the 1981 calendar year I taught on exchange at North Shore Teachers College in Auckland, New Zealand.[2] This period of time overlapped the South African Springbok Rugby Team's tour of New Zealand (July 19, 1981 to September 13, 1981) by several months. This stay allowed me to witness many of the events leading up to the tour; to observe the tour and the protests and demonstrations that surrounded it; and to monitor its effects and aftermath. Additionally, I visited New Zealand in March and April of 1982 and was able to gain perspective on the delayed reaction of New Zealanders to tour issues.

This work is based upon personal participation in antitour marches and demonstrations; attendance at organizational meetings of MOST (Mobilization to Stop the Tour) and HART (Halt All Racist Tours); tape-recorded interviews with protestors; maintenance of an extensive news-clipping file related to tour affairs;[3] attendance at pertinent lectures; examination of New Zealand Government Hansards and related books and documents; and responses to newspaper notices from me that appeared in leading New Zealand newspapers asking for personal experiences and opinions from tour supporters and tour protestors. A primary source of data was my involvement, on a continuing, day-by-day basis, in the discussions and debates that occurred on this topic at my workplace and in virtually all social settings throughout the year.

Method

The methodology employed in this study was essentially naturalistic. Little of the information and analysis is quantitative. Naturalistic and qualitative approaches appear to be well suited to this work, in view of the complexity of the issues at hand, because of the dichotomous perceptions and opinions of those involved in tour matters and the difficulty in forming questions prior to the events under consideration.[4]

The presentation of findings here is thematic and episodic rather than chronological.[5] I have elected to present and analyze only those events and circumstances wherein I have had either personal experience or have interacted with others who have been directly involved in tour matters. Primary sources have been used wherever possible.

Reaction of Physical Educators to the Tour

College and school physical educators with whom I came in contact in New Zealand during 1981 were generally noncommittal about the Springbok tour; many preferred not to discuss the issue. This was particularly true of student trainees at North Shore Teachers College (NSTC) in Auckland. There appeared to be an unspoken pact among students not to discuss the tour openly either in class or in informal college social settings.

A large number of the male students at the college play club rugby.[6] Several play, or have played, at the first-division level. During the year, one student was selected for trials with the Maori All-Black Team, and another toured Japan with the Ponsonby Rugby Club. The standard of rugby skills and knowledge among male students is very high. Given this standard, the broad allegiance to rugby, and the fact that rugby is perhaps the most common topic of discussion among students in pubs on Friday afternoons and in college cafeterias on Monday mornings, I was surprised at the apparent moratorium on debate or discussion of the Springbok issue. It was simply not discussed among students or between students and staff. Moreover, during the year that I spent in Auckland, I did not come across one article or position paper on this issue written by a New Zealand physical educator in an academic, professional, or trade journal.

Thirty-five third-year students, whom I taught at North Shore Teachers College, were given the option to study racial discrimination in sport as part of a Sociology of Sport unit. None of this student group elected to study this topic. At various times during the year, I approached individual members of the teaching staff and study group to suggest that representatives of the New Zealand Rugby Union and the protest movement be invited to participate in a college-sponsored debate on the Springbok issue. There was little support for the idea; it was suggested that a debate would be "divisive."[7]

In early August I arranged for a group of 14 visiting Canadian university students and teachers to be addressed by HART spokesman Tom Newnham at Auckland University.[8] Because the Canadian party was being billeted and transported by NSTC students, several of them came to Newnham's lecture. A letter from me to a friend who coaches rugby at Palmerston North Teachers College provides an insight into the elements at play in each quarter:

> Listen, we met with Tom Newnham. I think you're wrong in labeling him as a kook. He gave us a very organized, moderate lecture on the history and

current status of the problem of racist sport and politics as they relate to New Zealand. Some strong pro-tour people from NSTC accompanied us and while they didn't change their opinion they did appear to alter their view of Newnham and appreciate the other side of the question more fully. I think you would enjoy talking with him.[9]

Testimony regarding the attitudes and involvement of teachers and school-age students is seen in excerpts of a letter to the writer from the principal of a remote, rural school on the North Island:[10]

The staff at our school were fairly evenly divided on the issue and I mean *divided*—really polarized. Three of us felt committed enough to join the pro-testers at Whangarei . . . there was a tremendous feeling of unity, warmth and solidarity with the 3,000-4,000 people in the march; although only one of the onlookers[11] actually tried to perpetuate any violence on us there was an unmistakable feeling of bemused contempt. We were flanked by a column of police on either side, 30-40 of them in front, and a bus-load behind . . .

On the way back we bumped into some of the pro-tour teachers in the Mangamuka Pub. . . . We were still euphoric from the march; they were (presumably) still reliving the match: there was a sudden embarrassed silence and the two groups moved to opposite corners of the pub.

In my observation the secondary teachers are more inclined to be actively anti-tour than their primary counterparts. The kinds at our school were almost 100% pro-tour.

It was surprising how little the issue was discussed in social gatherings. In my experience what happened was that there was a deliberate unspoken understanding *not* to talk about it—I'm sure it must have ruined quite a few social gatherings before this universal understanding was arrived at.

I'm always very slow to react on matters of conscience, i.e., where I have to take a stand. After having played rugby 25 years, I've belatedly decided never to have anything to do with coaching it at school (or anywhere). I used to think that the violence *wasn't* really part of the game, but of course it is . . . I told you about the incident at school where I refereed a junior game and our boys got a bit frustrated when they lost—so four or five of them went and found a quiet, inoffensive boy who happened to be working in the library and bashed him—bleeding nose, black eye, the lot. That's it, in a nutshell![12]

A Meeting of MOST (Mobilization to Stop the Tour)

I accepted an invitation from Tom Newnham to attend a CARE meeting at the Auckland University Workers' Education Centre on Sunday, October 7, in order to gather information about the tour and to inform CARE members that I was in the process of studying the tour issue and would welcome suggestions from them for questions concerning the subject that needed to be asked of New Zealanders. At the meeting I circulated the beginning of a list of questions, which I had secured from Teachers College staff and students. It was my hope that the questions contained therein, many of which were of a pro-tour persuasion, would be expanded and balanced by the introduction of other questions. As the CARE meeting was an executive meeting involving only nine people, it was recommended that I attend the forthcoming meeting of MOST in order to ask for the help of that group in the formulation of significant questions.

As a consequence, on Wednesday evening, October 10, I attended the regular bi-weekly meeting of MOST at the Trade Union Centre on Great North Road in Auckland. MOST, whose meetings are open to the public, acts in a coordinating capacity for a number of antitour and anti-apartheid groups, including CARE. Prior to the meeting I approached the chairman, Andrew Bayer, to ask if I might circulate a notice of my intentions and needs on two clipboards with an invitation for those present to provide key questions and the names of any persons who might be willing to complete a questionnaire once the questions had been worked through to questionnaire format. Bayer agreed that this would be fine. I was introduced at the meeting, my purpose was explained, clipboards were circulated from each end of the hall to the group of about 60 persons, and other MOST business got underway.

Many of the tensions, frustrations, and suspicions of the antitour group surfaced in the next hour as a result of this seemingly innocuous act. As the meeting was in progress, a small number of women protestors arrived belatedly. It seemed to be understood by those present that their late arrival had to do with court appearances related to earlier protests. They gave short, but graphic accounts of the feelings of power they had gained as a result of representing themselves in court, the onerous conditions they had to face in order to appear in court, and the incompetency that they felt characterized the prosecuting authorities, their witnesses, and the judiciary.[13]

Shortly after their arrival, one of the women interrupted other MOST business to ask whose lists were being circulated and on what authority. She was enraged and profane in her remarks and insisted that the preliminary questions contained on the sheets were "echo" questions and failed to attack the real issues. I was called upon to address the meeting and stated among other things that, while I was opposed to the tour and had taken part in marches and other forms of protest, I nonetheless felt that the questions being asked in both conservative and radical quarters of the community needed to be assembled and answered. Several people at the meeting spoke to this issue, some in support of the woman's view, a smaller number in support of my rights. Her final retort was that she felt I was at the meeting under false pretenses and that I was likely a CIA agent. She advocated that, in future, the membership look very carefully at whom they let attend meetings.

This example is offered not only to illustrate the volatile level of debate at such gatherings, but also to show that members of the antitour movement were extremely suspicious and fearful of infiltration into their ranks by local and overseas, undercover police agents and informers. A number of such infiltrations were cited by HART and MOST during the antitour campaign.

Police Action

Charges and countercharges about the actions of police and special police squads were levied during and after the Springbok visit. Among the most controversial aspects of the policing that occurred were the introduction and use of special "long batons" for crowd control, the alleged failure of the police to display badge numbers, the introduction of special civilian police corps, and the actual tactics that certain of the police force employed. On the other hand, many people, including some protestors, felt the police showed remarkable restraint throughout the tour in the face of extreme provocation and violence by front-line tour demonstrators.

The following lengthy statement by one protestor was echoed time and again by those involved in the antitour campaign. It is offered here to show the height of fear, anger, and violence that existed on many occasions throughout the country for a period of 7 weeks:[14]

> Rintoul-Riddiford Street Intersection—Saturday, August 29, 1981.
>
> My mother, my sister, and my friend . . . thought that the "Green Squad" was a passive-resistance, family group of protestors against the tour. We were keen not to get involved in a group which ran the risk of any confrontation with the police or rugby supporters. We marched until we arrived at the Rintoul-Riddiford Street intersection where the front of the march came face to face with a line of police. The front of the march veered to the right and curved back the way we had come underneath the shop verandas. To our shock we found our row was parallel and facing opposite the line of police.
>
> We sat down and there was some light friendly conversation with some of the policemen. Many of the policemen were silent and uncommunicative. They seemed tense.
>
> Suddenly, a bus load of police arrived and without warning rushed us and attacked the section of demonstrators standing under the shop verandas. The police attacked demonstrators with fists and feet in what was an unprovoked and very violent assault. Helmets of demonstrators came flying through the air as did one police helmet which demonstrators sitting down returned at the repeated request of the officer standing in front of us. This line of police remained silent and impassive and ready.
>
> The glass window front of a fruit shop was shattered by police pushing demonstrators through it. Protestors watching screamed, "Shame! Shame! Shame!" For a while we could not understand the reason for the police assault but it soon became clear—a police protected space under the verandas was made for rugby supporters to pass through the undersection to test the march . . . The displaced and injured protestors made their way through the protestors sitting down to the other side of the undersection . . . For me this episode was like watching television. At this point we felt angry but still relatively detached.
>
> After about five minutes, in which rugby supporters passed along the police protected footpath, the officer in front of us suddenly requested us to move to one side. Some demonstrators did this reluctantly after he asked several times but we decided it was a matter of conscience and we would passively

resist. We were prepared to be arrested . . . we were not prepared for premeditated assault by police.

I could not understand the insistence of the offer that we move. He almost pleaded with us to move—but not once did he tell us that they would attack us and assault us. We decided to move when a COST marshall told us to do so.[15] We did not have time to move to the side before we were charged by the police with small knee kicks and punches. We got together in a small huddle and put our arms around each other for support and comfort.

We were charged again. This time there were riot police as well as white helmet police. We were kneed about the groin and stomach and punched about the chest and face. The police tried to pull off helmets.[16] I think the police said, "Move! Move!" My mother said, "We can't. There are people behind us." One policeman was punching and kneeing her with such vigor that she was being pushed deeper into the crowd . . . My sister and I . . . screamed "Don't you dare hit our Mother!" . . . Several police expressed concern although others continued hitting like programmed automatons. The officer said, "Where is your mother? You can still get out of here." Reluctantly, my mother and I left the front line to a rather chaotic area behind the police assault line. We heckled police from behind. We were outraged at their unprovoked attack on passive demonstrators and we were worried about those still being assaulted.

From behind lines we saw some police obviously slow to get into the attack while others were being thugs. We saw at least one policeman take running kicks at the unhelmeted head of a young protestor being dragged away by his legs. We saw a flying wedge of white helmeted police run over a section of demonstrators passively sitting-down at the intersection. Protestors were kicked in the face and stomach . . . Not once did we see a protestor initiate violence or retaliate with violence.[17]

The aborted match scheduled for Hamilton between the Springbok and the Taranaki Rugby Union was the scene of unparalleled violence by vigilante groups of rugby supporters. Cancellation of this match occurred due to the protest action at Rugby Park and, more primarily, to the unpublicized fact that a private plane had been commandeered by a protestor and was en route to the field.[18] Police feared the possibility of a "Kamakazi-like incident" and prevailed upon rugby officials to cancel the match. Following this, many rugby fans took what they considered to be the law into their own hands. N.Y. Warren of Rotorua writes of the terrifying experiences that she and her husband suffered:

Remember: SOWETO? Yes, I heard about it.

Remember: Hamilton? Yes, I was part of it.

This was to be my last march . . . We marched from Garden Place to Rugby Park at the rear of the procession . . . We were in the rear, chiefly because my husband, with an artificial leg, caliper on the other, and the use of one hand only could not keep up a very brisk trot. We arrived outside the Park, and were thrilled *and* terribly scared to find that 300 of the advance guard were inside. My most urgent desire was to go through the fence and join them . . . but somehow a grey-haired grandmother leaving a disabled husband and battling the police lines hardly seemed my role.

We crossed the road to a reserve beside Rugby Park. A man was painting a sign . . . He stood up, holding his sign between two heavy sticks. THE GAME HAS BEEN CANCELLED!!!!

We started to move. Spectators came across the road. One man walked into the sign, smashed at it, and then threw the bearer on the ground. Another joined him in the attack . . . my husband swung his walking stick on someone's back—was tackled from behind—and fell to the ground. Suddenly the group was separated. I helped my husband to his feet, and was told, ''Get him out of here, quickly.'' As we walked away, I turned and saw our passive protestor, blood pouring from his nose, holding his sign aloft.

Yes, I do remember Hamilton, and it was *not* my last march.[19]

Perhaps the most devastating consequence of the thug-like actions of this group of rugby supporters was that it escalated the level of protest and violence surrounding the town to new and often unintended levels.[20]

Impact on Family and Friendship Patterns

The marked division of the general populace in New Zealand was seen in microcosm and experienced by families, couples, and friends throughout the country.[21] The family with whom I lived for a month in Oratia, a suburb of Auckland, was fractured by their conflicting interpretations of the tour and what constituted justice. In this case two brothers and their families, who live next door to each other, ended up being openly hostile to one another.

A woman in Wellington writes of how these kinds of differences affected her personal life.

I have recently broken up with my boyfriend of three years. He went to the Rugby Test in Wellington. *One* of the reasons we broke up was that political differences . . . had finally come to the surface . . . we could no longer ignore them. I know of at least two other couples who have broken up—one is a Maori woman with a marriage of over seventeen years. Her husband disagreed with the tour but would not participate actively against it.

Space limitations prohibit a fuller consideration of the impact of the tour on social and interpersonal relations. There is little doubt that the effect of the tour was profoundly negative at these levels.

Pro-Tour Perspectives

Because my sympathies in the Springbok question lay on the side of peaceful protest against the tour, it was logical that my interactions in New Zealand would be more frequent with tour protestors than with tour supporters. This is evident throughout this paper. In an attempt to introduce a degree of balance to the current discussion, I have compiled a list of excerpts from letters by individuals who have written to me to express either their protour sentiments or opposition to the tactics used by protestors. Following are arguments that appear to have considerable face validity or at least represent a sizable viewpoint in the country.

• The most alarming thing about the tour was . . . the violence which erupted in the more vigorous of the demonstrations. This violence was caused by and added to by both the antitour and the protour factions. The reason for such violent clashes, particularly on the antitour front, is due to the sincerity of the movement's beliefs. On closer investigation, however, it will be seen that both sides were arguing on subtly different premises. While the overall cause was human rights, the antitour faction based its argument on human rights in South Africa and the protour on human rights in New Zealand . . .

. . . the final game at Auckland. By this stage and at others before this game, elements of the protest movement appeared to change the object of its protest from being against apartheid to being against the police.

The Springbok Tour has left its mark on New Zealand forever—domestically and internationally.[22]

• I agree with peaceful protest which is every New Zealander's right so long as it doesn't interfere with others, who also have lawful rights. But, at three out of four games I attended . . . no way were the protests meant to be peaceful. But, so many times they infringed on the rights of the majority—

Palmerston North	5,000 protestors	28,000 supporters
Napier	300 protestors	25,000 supporters
Wellington Test	6,000 protestors	35,000 supporters
Auckland Test	6-8,000 protestors	48,000 supporters

Okay, it may be argued that some people were frightened to attend the protest because of "trouble" (only created by protestors), but so were the thousands of school children and women frightened to attend the games because of *foul* tactics used by protestors. What started as legitimate and legal marches became illegal when they arrived from the routes allowed on permits and challenges to the law became violent.[23]

• The words "hypocritical" and "frightened" were used by Bjelke Petersen, Premier of Queensland, Australia, to describe Prime Minister Fraser's (of Australia) attitude toward New Zealand over the Springbok tour.

We have just returned from living in Australia. Not long after our arrival there in March, we saw proudly shown on television Australian surfers competing in South Africa. Because of this and other blatant sporting contacts Australia has with South Africans, why didn't the Black African countries boycott the Olympic Games in Moscow even though the British Lions had played or were playing the Springboks at that time? (They say individuals do not represent their country. But

I bet if you told Australians that Alan Jones, the Grand Prix driver, did not represent Australia they would be most indignant.)[24]

- If the population of Auckland was 100,000 pakehas and one million Maoris and Islanders, how long would our hotel bars, restaurants, buses, trains, etc. remain desegregated? Not for very long, if not legally, then certainly socially. It happens now. Yet we have the effrontery to point the finger at South Africa.

Australia legislates against the Aborigine and for years after the last war adopted a "White Australia" policy in their attitude to war refugees. Yet they look down their nose at S.A.[25]

- Between 1965 and 1981, the South African Rugby Board and that country's politicians had to make a number of concessions to New Zealand before tours of either country. Firstly, the Maoris-No Tour movement forced the NZRU to insist that it would send only its best team to South Africa. Until then the understanding was that while in New Zealand the Springboks would conform to this country's custom and play Maoris both in representative and in a special Maori versus Springbok fixture that has invariably caused comment on "apartheid with a difference."

But the concessions were made: South Africa allowed New Zealand to pick its best side; it eventually agreed to break down apartheid in rugby in South Africa and to send a "merit selected team" to this country . . .

So in issuing the invitation the NZRU was being completely consistent. It had asked for merit selection, Maoris to be allowed to tour, in 1976 had played matches against Colored sides in South Africa. It was not going to dabble in politics. You could hardly blame the New Zealand body for not telling South Africa that a prerequisite of its agreeing to continue playing rugby with that country would be a change in its political system. After all, no one does that to anyone else in the world no matter how abhorrent Communism, fascism, dictatorship or whatever are to those wanting to meet on sports fields.[26]

- The antitour affair was primarily political in organization and wholly irrational in execution. Although the majority of those who paraded sincerely believed, even if they hadn't thought things through, that they were striking a blow against apartheid yet the whole concept was fatally flawed. The demonstrations were based on nothing better than a detestation of apartheid translated in a spurious equation that supposed the following:

—Apartheid is clearly wrong and immoral.
—The South African government practices apartheid; therefore, to attack citizens of South Africa is to attack apartheid.
—This also applies to South African citizens even if they are government opposed.
—New Zealand citizens are entitled to resort to violence and to break laws to show how much we hate apartheid.

—The police try to stop us breaking the law, therefore, we are entitled to defy them.

—The Blacks will have a better life if South Africa doesn't play rugby.

What right has any citizen got to forcibly prevent another citizen from doing that which he is legally entitled to do?

If you claim that your conscience authorizes you to interfere with another's lawful activities, then presumably you agree that any other citizen who conscientiously objects to *anything* that *you* do is entitled to forcibly stop you?

With 300 protestor-rioters on the ground at Hamilton surrounded by 40,000 rugby fans, understandably enraged that their civil rights were being denied, who were the police actually protecting?[27]

- Why did the so-called moderates allow the disaffected elements to take over the movement so that instead of 5,000 peaceful chanters carrying banners we, at times, had 2,000 or 3,000 "troops" carrying shields that had protruding bolts, wearing helmets to protect them from the consequences of their "peaceful protests"? And who continually assaulted the police verbally and physically?

And what about poor old John Citizen taxpayer? He is going to foot the bill, not for "the rugby tour," which many suggest, but for the cost of fending off the protest movement.[28]

- In my view, the unfortunate circumstances surrounding the Springbok tour were largely due to a clearly expressed bias by the media, particularly the electronic media . . .

It would be hard to develop a rationale by which one could support the antitour protestors other than on a principle, and unless one supports such principles at all times and covering all similar situations (and this is hardly possible), there would be no valid reason to pick out just this one particular situation as a model of inequality or injustice.

With tempered and unbiased reporting, and firmer police action . . . the entire incident could have been kept within reasonable boundaries.

What, in my view, was missing entirely . . . was a strong representation by the media as to the restrictions and infringements to the individual by the antitour actions . . .[29]

Summary

Something as complex as the controversy surrounding the 1981 Springbok Tour is difficult to assess. Varying interpretations have been applied. Interpretations of a simplistic nature, while attractive to their advocates, deny the wide variance in perception, motivation, and experience found among the New Zealand populace. It is likely that the passage of time will provide greater clarity on the array of moral, legal, and utilitarian questions that have arisen in connection with this political and sporting contact between New Zealand and South Africa. In the meantime, it may be helpful to provide tentative judgments as to what the fundamental issues were that divided the nation like nothing before had done and to offer perspectives that ultimately may aid in the reduction of racial inequality, intolerance, and violence.

K.T. Matthews, responding to my letter to the Secretary General of the New Zealand Law Society, identifies the following as having been raised as fundamental issues in many areas of public life:

- The policies and behavior of the New Zealand Rugby Football Union.
- The policies (both declared and undeclared) of the New Zealand Prime Minister and the members of his Cabinet.
- The nature of the divisions in New Zealand society surrounding this subject and, in particular, the differences between town and country.
- The handling of the matter by the New Zealand police

  1. preceding Hamilton;
  2. following Hamilton;
  3. in setting up the Riot Squads;
  4. in managing the Riot Squads;
  5. in employing New Zealand Army personnel to set up barbed wire entanglements to impede protestors;
  6. in wearing headgear and unnumbered uniforms, making it difficult to identify the many policemen who used excessive violence;
  7. in crowd managing techniques, which in most instances were satisfactory but in some instances were appallingly bad; and
  8. in reacting as a government department to complaints made by individuals who were injured by police.

- The part played by the Race Relations Conciliator regarding

  1. the effect of the tour on the General Election held in November, 1981;
  2. the reactions and behavior of members of the Labour Opposition Party;
  3. the effect of the tour on sport in New Zealand and rugby football in particular;
  4. the effect of the tour on HART and other protest groups in the community;
  5. the effect of the tour on New Zealand's relationship with other Commonwealth countries and with the Commonwealth Office in London;
  6. the continued use by the New Zealand police of methods and equipment seen for the first time during the tour; and
  7. the reactions to the tour by different classes of this society with marked differences between churchgoers, middle class and professional people, organized trade unions, Maoris, Pacific Island groups, and so forth.[30]

Other conclusions and implications may be drawn from the 7 weeks of batons, barricades, and barbed wire. Whereas previous social disputes in New Zealand have been equally as intensive, the Springbok issue was certainly more widespread throughout the country and more protracted than the earlier protests.[31] Also unique to the tour issue is the fact that division of opinion about the tour cut across political party and social class lines. Even the National Party, led by Prime Minister Rob Muldoon, had members who dissented from the main party line.[32]

The tour saw the emergence of feminine leadership among antitour groups. The dangerous, front-line work of protest marshalls was frequently assumed by women. The ranks of protestors exhibited roughly equal numbers of men and women. By stark contrast, the leadership of the rugby union and the great majority of rugby spectators were male. In what has been traditionally a society strongly dominated by men, it is likely that the emergence of strong female leaders and new cooperative relationships between men and women members of the protest movement were an added, if unconscious, insult to those representing the rugby establishment.

Increased racial sensitivity is a probable consequence of the tour issue. On my return to New Zealand in March, 1982, it was obvious from participation in Bastion Point Maori land dispute rallies that many Pakehas (whites) and Maori leaders, who had worked hand in hand in an attempt to halt the tour, were now working in concert to return land to the Maoris. Obviously, many New Zealanders on both sides of the issue have been politicized through tour involvement. It is also likely, in the view of Waikato University sociologist Jeff Pugere, that the sport of rugby will no longer be able to symbolize the country's national aspirations.[33]

Serious questions remain, too, for citizens who believed in participatory democracy. What do people have to do in order to effect change? How can the positions that government leaders take be altered? What are some of the byproducts and implications of increased police powers in a democratic society?

An immediate and observable political result of the tour affair was seen in the national elections held in New Zealand in November of 1981. Whereas a common belief of political pundits *prior* to the Springbok visit was that the National Party and Robert Muldoon were committing political suicide for not interceding to stop the tour, the National Party was returned to office. It has been suggested that in times of crisis many voters identify with paternal, authoritarian leadership rather than more democratic and egalitarian forms of government. This appears to have been the case in New Zealand in the recent spring elections.

The final words in this interpretation of the 1981 South African rugby tour belong to a 17-year-old student at New Plymouth Boys' High School. His sensitivity to tour-related matters contrasts markedly with references made to college groups and rural school students earlier in this paper. The following three poems are selected from several that Darryl Ward wrote about the tour.[34]

What's it all worth?
Division, Repression, and Long-baton beats,
A Springbok Tour, Rugby, Racism, And Fear
Overseas loss of face for bringing apartheid here,
It wouldn't be stopped, a "strong leadership" defeat,
Was all this worth six marginal seats?

Freedom
Freedom.
What is freedom?
Is it being free to vote
Or to gamble at the tote?
Or to watch a racist rugby game,
Despite the suffering and the shame,
Those wanting our individual rights
Will go to such great pains,
But we never can be really free while our brothers are in chains.

Individual Rights
Tell my why the tour went on,
Because of Craven, Blazey, Couch, or Don?
Or because the Government thought
That it should preserve racist sport.
Did I hear a murmur about individual rights
When a Taiwanese Scouts' visit was banned?
Or did I hear complaints from SPIR fanatics
When "Death of a Princess" was canned.
We need freedom-sure, but tell me this,
Which would be a better aim?
The right for all to freely live or marry,
Or to watch a rugby game.

Notes

1. This paper is limited to a discussion of the *internal* impact of the Springbok rugby tour on New Zealand. Dale P. Toohey's paper, which preceded this presentation, provides an international perspective on tour affairs and also considers the United States segment of the South African tour agenda. This discussion extends and provides further insight into matters raised by Toohey. It should be considered as supplemental and complementary to his work.
2. In view of the nature of my personal involvement in tour affairs and the context of this paper, I have chosen to write in the first person throughout most of this paper.
3. One barometer of the strength of public opinion on the tour issue is that my file of news cuttings related to the tour, which I maintained for a 12 month period, is 12 inches thick. This file was drawn primarily from three Auckland area newspapers and includes items ranging from short letters to the editor to page-one news stories and multi-page feature articles.
4. See Lee J. Cronbach, "Choosing Questions to Investigate," in *Designing Evaluations of Educational and Social Programs* (San Francisco: Jossey-Bass, 1982) for a discussion of naturalistic research methods.
5. Unless otherwise indicated, all dates given are in 1981.

6. As is the case in all primary teachers colleges in New Zealand, the ratio of male to female students is about 1:4. Gender did not appear to play a significant role in student opinion on these issues.

7. An evening address on South African-New Zealand sporting relations and apartheid by banned, former South African newspaper editor, Donald Woods, at NSTC Hall on June 23 was given to an audience of 600 persons. No more than a handful of staff and students from the college attended this function, which was widely advertised, conveniently located, and free to the public. Woods is the author of *Biko* (London: Penguin, 1978), the story of black leader Steve Biko who died in prison under violent circumstances at the hands of his captors.

It should also be noted that the reluctance of Teachers College staff and student groups to engage in open dialogue and debate about the tour was not mirrored in the country's universities. Active social protest emanated from many university groups.

8. Newnham is perhaps the best known, antiapartheid spokesman in New Zealand. A secondary school teacher by occupation, he has written *Apartheid is not a game* (Auckland: Graphic, 1975); *A cry of treason: New Zealand and the Montreal Olympics* (Palmerston North: Dunmore, 1978); and *By batons and wire: A response to the 1981 Springbok tour of New Zealand* (Auckland: Real Picture, 1981).

9. The writer to Grant Jones, PNTC, August 14.

10. Letter to the writer from Allan Watkins, principal, North Hokianga Primary School, October 2. It is generally recognized that the north as well as most rural and farming areas of New Zealand are strongholds of support for rugby, and that most people residing in these regions were in favor of the tour.

11. Throughout the tour protest marches were chaperoned by large contingents of police officers who acted in a peacekeeping role and provided a buffer zone between marchers and the public. It was not uncommon for onlookers, particularly pub patrons, to be verbally abusive to march members. This is the "onlooker" situation to which Watkins refers.

12. It seems that dramatic productions involving sport such as "Kes" and "Tom Brown's School Days" may be more accurate in their portrayal of attendant intolerance and brutality than might be thought.

13. A colorful description was also afforded regarding the wearing of brown paper bags by accused protestors. See accounts of these attempts to disrupt judiciary procedures in newspaper acounts of the day, for example, "Two-year Tag on Protest Hearing," *N.Z. Herald*, October 14, 1981, p. 2.

14. Letter to the writer from J. Antill, October 12.

15. Coalition to Stop the Tour.

16. After initial confrontations with the police in the first two weeks of the tour, most frontline protestors wore motorcycle helmets, faceguards, and improvised padding and shields. Their appearance was most akin to a goalkeeper in ice hockey.

17. Protests in the early stages of the tour, which were nonviolent in nature, rapidly escalated to a point where flagrant violence was perpetrated by both police and protestors; however, it is also true that restraint was shown by the majority of police and antitour followers.

18. See Shears, Richard and Isabelle Gidley, *Storm Out of Africa! The 1981 Springbok Tour of New Zealand* (Auckland: Macmillan, 1981) for a detailed account of the plane threat issue.

19. Letter to the writer from Mrs. N.Y. Warren, Rotorua, December 2.

20. For pictorial accounts of the tour, see Newnham, *Ibid*, 1981; McCredie, Athol. The Tour—Photographs. (Wellington: Author, 1981).

21. Antill, *op.cit.*

22. Letter to the writer from Andrew Little, New Plymouth, undated (received December 5, 1981).

23. Letter to the writer from N.B. Lyons, Hastings, December 2.
24. Letter to the writer from "One Angry New Zealander," Auckland, December 4.
25. Letter to the writer from J.S. Lanham, Dunedin, December 12.
26. David Gardiner editorial, "The unpalatable facts must now be faced," *Dannevirk Evening News* (undated).
27. Letter to the writer from Austin B. Ward, Nelson, October 1981.
28. David Gardiner editorial, "Who were winners, losers?" *Dannevirk Evening News*, October 6.
29. Letter to the writer from Gerhard Ammermann, Karori, November 30.
30. Letter to the writer from K.T. Matthews of Trip, Matthews, and Feist, Barristers and Solicitors, Wellington, July 9, 1982. Matthews affords a further perspective on the law and order question in his letter when he writes, "Some of us from this office were involved in peaceful protests against the tour and later in lodging complaints with the New Zealand Police in regard to the conduct of some of their members. Those complaints were rejected and the Ombudsman has been requested to enquire into the manner in which they were carried out by the police."
31. Reference here is to the waterfront confrontations of 1913 and 1951 and riots between police and unemployed workers in 1932. In the 1913 riots one striker was killed. The use of guns by police was part of these earlier scenes.
32. According to public accounts, Marily Wearing, MP, was the most fervent antitour government member.
33. Radio New Zealand special report on the Springbok tour, September 14.
34. Letter to the writer and copies of poetry from Darryl Ward, New Plymouth, December 6.

References

Access report on the 1981 Springbok tour. (1981, November). *Arena Review*, pp. 36-45.

Cronbach, L.J. (1982). *Designing evaluations of educational and social programs.* San Francisco: Jossey-Bass.

Edwards, J. (1981). *Racist rugby: Front line poets respond.* Auckland: Author.

Gardiner, D. (1981, October 6). Who were winners, losers? *Dannevirk Evening News.*

Gardiner, D. (undated, c. 1981, November). The unpalatable facts must now be faced. *Dannevirk Evening News.*

McCredie, A. (1981). *The tour—Photographs.* Auckland: Author.

Newnham, T. (1975). *Apartheid is not a game.* Auckland: Graphic.

Newnham, T. (1978). *A cry of treason: New Zealand and the Montreal Olympics.* Palmerston North: Dunmore.

Newnham, T. (1981). *By batons and barbed wire: A response to the 1981 Springbok tour of New Zealand.* Auckland: Real Pictures.

Radio New Zealand. (1981, September 14). *Special report on the South African Springbok tour.*

Shears, R., & Isabelle, G. (1981). *Storm out of Africa! The 1981 Springbok tour of New Zealand.* Auckland: Macmillan.

Toohey, D.P. (1982, July 22). The 1981 South African Springboks' rugby tour of New Zealand and U.S.A.—A case study. Address to the *Third International Seminar on Comparative Physical Education and Sport*, Minneapolis, MN.

Two-year tag on protest hearing. (1981, October 14). *New Zealand Herald*, p. 2.

Woods, D. (1978). *Biko*. Auckland: Penguin.

The Variety of Interpretations
of Olympism and the Olympic Idea

Uriel Simri
Wingate Institute

In the annals of modern sports, it is hardly possible to find a term that has been interpreted in so many different ways as the terms Olympic Idea or Olympism, as the founder of the modern Olympic movement, Baron Pierre de Coubertin, used to refer to the Idea. Coubertin, himself, never tried to define those terms unequivocally, at least until the last years of his life; even then his attempts were not very clear.

At the conclusion of the Olympic Games of 1908, Coubertin stated (1908, p. 20) that the Olympic Idea was a concept of "strong physical culture" based upon the spirit of chivalry and upon aesthetic sensitivity. However, 12 years earlier, when the Olympic Games were first held in Athens (1896), Coubertin (1896, p. 39) considered the contribution of the movement as "a potent factor in securing international peace," the core of the Idea. At least as far as this statement is concerned, I hope that you will agree with me that the Olympic movement has been a total failure.

In his last years of life, Coubertin made a few more efforts to define Olympism. In a speech in Paris in 1929 (Coubertin, 1929, p. 124), he referred to Olympism as a doctrine based on a philosophical and religious theory; in 1931 he referred to Olympism as a school of nobility, moral purity, endurance, and physical energy (Coubertin, 1931, p. 208); and in a radio message broadcast from Berlin in 1935, Coubertin (1935, p. 150) stated that the main feature of Olympism, in ancient as well as modern times, is that it forms a religion—a "religio athletae." Never bothering to explain precisely the sense in which he used the term religion, Coubertin added that Olympism included religious emotions aggrandized by humanity and democracy (1935). It was indeed ironical to speak of Olympism, humanity, and democracy in the same breath in Berlin one year before the Nazi Olympics.

Coubertin's reference to the relationship between sports and religion has led the New Left of recent years to paraphrase Marx in claiming that "sport is the opiate of the masses" and "Olympism distracts the masses from genuine political aims in class struggle" (Hoch, 1972). On the other hand, Avery Brundage has followed in Coubertin's footsteps and has referred to Olympism as the modern, true, exciting, virile, and dynamic religion of the 20th century (Brundage, 1964). Nissiotis, IOC member for

Greece and professor of the philosophy of religion, disagrees with Brundage on this point. To Nissiotis (1976), Olympism is not a religion, but an ideology, which contains hidden religious elements and can possibly cooperate with religion because of a common goal: love and fraternity among people, and promotion of world peace.

To come back to the vagueness of Olympism definitions, even Lucas, one of the strongest supporters of Coubertin and Olympism, has to admit that "Coubertin defined Olympism in scores of different ways" and that Coubertin's "habitual 'pollyanna' view of sport was a fortress, as well as a continuing puzzle and weakness" (1980). Lenk goes further in claiming that this vagueness or even ambiguity of definition has led to a multiplicity of interpretations and has made possible relatively flexible changes without changing the aims of Olympism themselves. He further points out that the terms Olympism and Olympic Idea are not mentioned in the Olympic Charter of the IOC at all, and this charter only refers once, in a vague manner, to the Olympic Ideal (Lenk, 1976).

Coubertin's cofounders of the IOC were not better off when they tried to explain the Olympic Idea. William Milligan Sloane tried to do so in an article published in 1912; all he really did, besides reporting the achievements of the young Olympic movement, was to speak in disconnected generalities such as the Olympic Idea "purifies sports" and "aims to create and strengthen bonds of friendship" (Sloane, 1912, p. 408).

Leaders of international sports are, however, as confused as they were 70 years ago when it comes to the definition of Olympism. Roger Bannister, for instance, prefers to refer to the Olympic Ideals alongside the term Olympism, as if they were separate entities, and admits that "the Olympic Ideals have developed separately from the Games themselves and are not entirely dependent on them" (Bannister, 1980). Should this mean that the Ideals are dependent on the Games, or could one rather expect that the Games be based on the Ideals? In any case, it is nothing but a convenient escape to separate the Olympic Ideals and the Olympic Games, as if the Games had nothing to do with the Olympic movement and its Ideals. Yet, at the same time, Bannister quotes the aim of the Olympic Games, as stated in the Olympic Charter of 1979, claiming that this represents the Olympic Ideal.

Thoughts along a similar line, although in a much clearer manner, have been expressed by the dean of the International Olympic Academy in Greece, Otto Szymiczek. Szymiczek claims that Olympism is a perfect idea that has been carried out, accompanied by human faults, in the Olympic Games, which are only one part of the Olympic Movement. To Szymiczek the "Olympic ideals were passed on to us by the ancient Greeks," and "their final goal is harmonious growth and perfection of the individual" (1970, pp. 51-53). In short, Szymiczek sees in modern Olympism a revival of the ancient Greek principles of "Kalokagathon" and "Arete." He further adds that "the first and fundamental principle of Olympic ideology is honest competition among amateurs on equal terms" (Szymiczek, 1970, pp. 51-53), but here he veers away from ancient

Greece, for the ancient Greeks were neither aware of the term amateurism nor bothered by this issue.

This, by the way, is not the only essential element of modern Olympism that had no parallel in ancient Greece. There is also the maxim that taking part is more important than winning and the aim of promoting peace and understanding among nations (Laemmer, 1977).

On another occasion, Szymiczek, who has tried more than anybody else to explain Olympism to the world in recent years, refers to Olympism as "an international institution, fully independent and free of any national, political, economic or other constraints" (1977, p. 58). While the second part of that statement may be considered wishful thinking by a philhellene, the first part echoes a statement made by Coubertin (1920, pp. 94-95) in 1920. It may, however, not be easy to bridge between the approach that Olympism is an institution and the approach that Olympism is an idea.

Szymiczek, at the same time, realizes that "the disadvantage of the multiformity of Olympic principles lies in the fact that a great number of people are given the opportunity to exploit a part of these principles by channeling them towards a direction which conforms with and is adapted to their particular aims and pursuits" (1976, p. 52).

It is only natural that the French are the stoutest supporters of Coubertin's Olympism, for they take great pride, often bordering on chauvinism, in the Baron's deeds. Henri Pouret, the late laureate of the French Academy, saw in Olympism "a pedagogical system oriented both towards the body and the spirit in order to create a man of perfection" (1971, p. 73). While this definition is clearly along the line of Greek thought, thereby representing one approach to Olympism, it is much harder to comprehend another rather unique statement by Pouret, that Coubertin "had hoped that through Olympism every individual would be able to enjoy: Bread, dignity and knowledge" (p. 74).

Anyone who is familiar with the cultural and societal developments in the post-World War II Federal Republic of Germany should not be astonished that the most severe, skeptical, and even cynical criticism of Olympism has its roots in this country. This criticism ranges from von Rezzori's remark that "the Olympic Idea is an outdated concept of the 19th century" (1960) to the fact that a leading German TV sports personality, Manfred Bloedorn (1980), has devoted a book to this criticism and has named it *The Olympic Perjury*. The German criticism is often aimed at the claim that Olympism is a humanistic ideal. One leading German writer referred, for instance, to the Olympic Games as an "idiotic record factory and the organization of a superbusiness in which only a fool could perceive the existence of a humanistic ideal" (Andersch, 1960). Even former IOC Vice-President Willi Daume (1976) of Germany had to admit in a press interview that the Olympic slogan of "citius, altius, fortius" may lead, through excesses, to inhumanity rather than humanistic ideals. The most cynical of all definitions of Olympism was made by Karl Adam, who has coached a number of German Olympic rowing champions. To

Adam, who called his book *Competitive Sport-Sense and Nonsense,* "the idea of the Olympic Games is very simply that once every four years a number of selected sports arrange their world championships in one and the same place at a given time" (1975, p. 35).

The time has now come to cast a glimpse at the attitudes of the communist countries of Eastern Europe towards Olympism. Before doing so, one has to remember that until 1945 the Soviet Union did not want to have anything to do with the "bourgeois-capitalistic games" organized by the "aristocratic and capitalistic degenerates of the IOC." The Soviet Union, as well as the communists and social-democrats of Western Europe, even organized anti-Olympias as a condemnation of the Olympic Movement and its Games. All this changed from one extreme to another after 1945, according to Bloedorn (1980) as a result of political expediency at the eve of the imminent cold war, but such changes in the communist world should not surprise anyone.

Thus, it was not difficult for East German State Secretary for Sports Guenter Erbach (1972, p. 409) to define, at the Olympic Scientific Congress in Munich (1972), the Olympic Idea as an expression of the "unity between top athletic performance and physical culture of the people in a deep humanistic sense." According to Erbach, the humanistic significance is revealed by the fact that the Olympic Idea has created the foundations for mutual respect, recognition, and understanding among peoples. May I draw your attention to the term recognition, which in this case indicates the importance assigned by the German Democratic Republic to sports as a means for political recognition. It is, at the same time, satisfying to know that a bourgeois-capitalistic idea can contribute at all towards humanistic ideals, even according to Marxist, materialistic dialectics.

In a recent statement Soviet Minister of Sports Sergej Pawlow came up with a more complex definition of Olympism. According to Pawlow, "Olympism is a complex of philosophical, moral, ethical and organizational principles that determines the content of the Olympic Movement, is based on the universal, cultural and humanistic values of sports and the Olympic Games as its climax, and is a means for the harmonious development of man as well as for the strengthening of peace, of friendship and of mutual understanding" (Gitter, 1982, pp. 1-2).

Praise of Olympism, however, does not seem to disturb the communist countries in attempting to undermine the Olympic Movement through a so-called policy of democratization of sports, which aims at an upgrading of UNESCO activities in sports and greater government influence on sports (Holzweissig, 1981).

Two aspects of Olympism remain to be discussed, even if only briefly. I refer to the issues of elitism and amateurism. In the earlier mentioned 1935 radio message of Coubertin, the French baron considered a physical nobility and elite, combined with will power, the second characteristic feature of Olympism. As such a physical elite or aristocracy is to be found primarily at the Olympic Games, it may well be that even Coubertin failed, on this occasion, to differentiate between Olympism and the Olympic Games. In any case, the elitist approach is far from the approaches of either Szymiczek or Erbach, who see in the Olympic Games only one aspect of Olympism and believe that, through the Olympic Movement, Olympism should also cater to the masses, who definitely are not elitist. Although Coubertin claims in his message that the physical aristocracy should be, and is, completely egalitarian from a social point of view, one has to remember his approach to the matter of amateurism and his early recognition of the fact that the elite required immense amounts of training. Would all social classes have an equal chance to excel physically were we to adhere to Coubertin's brand of amateurism? Obviously the answer to this question is negative. May I further remind you that as late as 1948 a Swedish team was disqualified because one of the riders was only a non-commissioned officer, and equestrians were supposed to be "gentleman-officers" (Kamper, 1972). Indeed social equality! This elitist approach has led Bloedorn to define Coubertin's Olympism as "a social-political lightning rod that can blur class differences but not eliminate them, and which aims to educate the masses towards physical and moral hygiene, in order to render them more controllable by the ruling classes" (1980).

So much has been said and can be said about the issue of amateurism that a few more brief comments cannot be avoided here. First, no paragraph in the Olympic Charter has been changed as often as paragraph 26 which deals with eligibility. Second, Olympic champion Christopher Brasher hit the nail on the head when he spoke, as early as 1968, of "money professionalism" and "time professionalism." In recent years the first brand of professionalism has been emphasized at the expense of the second, perhaps under the pressure of the communist countries, which claim that only sport that has assumed the nature of a commodity should be described as professional sport. The problem of amateurism is, nowadays, as far as ever from finding a solution, and the fact that the term amateur has disappeared from the Olympic Charter has not created a less hypocritical situation. It is also not by mere chance that at the last Olympic Congress in Baden-Baden, a representative of a communist country suggested reinstating the term in the Charter (Gitter, 1982). Allow me to summarize this point by quoting Finnish sport sociologist Kalevi Heinilä who refers to a "detachment of the official ideology of amateur sport from reality" (1972, p. 352).

In conclusion, this paper never attempted to define or explain Olympism. At present we do not possess a definition of Olympism accepted by one and all, and the argumentation goes on over whether it is a doctrine, an idea, an ideology, an institution, a pedagogical system, a religion, and so forth. If I have clarified the various positions and attitudes towards, and interpretations of, Olympism and compared them, in as far as possible, this paper has achieved its goal.

References

Adam, K. (1975). *Leistungssport-sinn und unsinn* (p. 35). Munich: Nymphenburger Verlagshandlung.

Andersch, A. (1960, September 1). Der literarische Olympia. *Frankfurter Allgemeine Zeitung*.

Bannister, R. (1980). The Olympic Games: Past, present and future. In J. Segrave & D. Chu (Eds.), *Olympism* (p. 140). Champaign, IL: Human Kinetics.

Bloedorn, M. (1980). *Der Olympische meineid* (pp. 139, 152). Hamburg: Hoffmann & Campe.

Brasher, C. (1968). *Mexico 1968* (p. 8). London: Stanley Paul.

Brundage, A. (1964). *I.O.C. Bulletin*, No. 88, p. 30.

Coubertin, P. (1896). The Olympic Games of 1896. *Century Magazine*, No. 53, p. 39 ff.

Coubertin, P. (1931). *Memoires Olympiques* (p. 208). Lausanne: Bureau International de Pedagogie Sportive.

Coubertin, P. (1966). Les trustees de l'Idee Olympique. *Der Olympische Gedanke* (p. 20). Cologne: Carl Diem Institut. (Original work published 1908).

Coubertin, P. (1966). Philosophischen Grundlagen. *Ibid*.

Coubertin, P. (1966). La victoire de l'Olympisme. *Ibid*. (pp. 94-95). Ibid. (Original work published in 1920).

Coubertin, P. (1966). Olympie. *Ibid*. (p. 124). Ibid. (Original work published 1929).

Coubertin, P. (1966). Die philosophischen Grundlagen des modernen Olympismus. *Ibid*. (pp. 150 ff). (Original work published 1935).

Daume, W. (1976). Interview in *Sueddeutsche Zeitung*, pp. 3, 27-28.

Erbach, G. (1972). High-performance sport as a social problem. In O. Grupe et al. (Eds.), *Sport in the modern world* (pp. 409, 417). Heidelberg: Springer.

Gitter, W. (1982). Zum XI Olympischen Kongress 1981 (Quotation translated by author). *Theorie und praxis der koerperkultur* (Vol. 30, No. 1, pp. 1-3).

Heinilä, K. (1972). Sport and professionalization. In O. Grupe et al. (Eds.), *Sport in the modern world* (p. 352). Heidelberg: Springer.

Hoch, P. (1972). Rip off the big game. *Soziologie der Olympischen spiele* (p.25). Munich: Hauser. (Reprinted from Prokop, U., 1971, pp. 20-21. New York: Doubleday).

Holzweissig, G. (1981). *Diplomatie im trainingsanzug* (p. 119). Munich: Oldenbourg.

Kamper, E. (1972). *Enzyklopaedie der Olympischen spiele* (p. 346). Stuttgart: Roemer.

Laemmer, M. (1977). The nature and function of the Olympic truce in Greek antiquity. *History of sport and physical education—Research and studies* (Vol. 3, pp. 37-52). Tokyo: ISCPE.

Lenk, H. (1976). Toward a social philosophy of the Olympics. In P.J. Graham & H. Ueberhorst (Eds.), *The modern Olympics* (pp. 111-112). Cornwall, NY: Leisure Press.

Lucas, J. (1980). *The modern Olympic Games* (pp. 22, 78). Cranbury, NJ: Barnes.

Nissiotis, N. (1976). Olympism and religion. *Report of the International Olympic Academy* (pp. 59-70).

Pouret, H. (1971). The Olympic philosophy. *Report of the International Olympic Academy* (pp. 73-74).

Sloane, W.M. (1912, June). The Olympic idea—Its origin, foundation and progress. *Century Magazine*, p. 408 ff.

Szymiczek, O. (1970). The fundamental principles of Olympic ideology. *Report of the International Olympic Academy* (pp. 51-53).

Szymiczek, O. (1976). The Olympic movement and the Olympic Games. *Report of the International Olympic Academy* (p. 52).

Szymiczek, O. (1977). Olympism in a process of constant evolution. *Report of the International Olympic Academy* (p. 58).

von Rezzori, G. (1960, September 7, 14). Ein mayhrebinier in rom. *Der Spiegel*.

Funding the Development of the Olympic Athlete: A Comparison of Programs in Selected Western and Socialist Countries

Eric F. Broom
University of British Columbia

A cursory examination of records in amateur sport since the first modern Olympic Games in 1896 would confirm that athletes striving for excellence have worshiped at the altar of the Olympic motto, "citius, altius, fortius"—swifter, higher, stronger. Levels of achievement have risen inexorably; slowly until midcentury, but with increasing momentum since then.

The pursuit of ever rising standards requires ever increasing effort; today's amateur athletes preparing for top-level competition maintain that the demands of training, both time and energy, are no longer compatible with a full-time job or full-time study combined with employment to earn university fees and subsistence. At the highest levels amateur sport has become far more than a spare-time occupation. In more and more countries, elite athletes are receiving financial assistance to compensate for loss of earnings. This paper will examine programs of funding assistance to elite amateur athletes in selected western and socialist countries.

The first financial assistance program to elite athletes was the athletic scholarship developed by American universities. Since the early years of this century, athletic scholarships have been the means by which American athletes, until very recently exclusively males but now females in rapidly increasing numbers, have combined training for excellence in sport with a university education.

The budding, highly talented young athlete and the university intercollegiate athletic program have maintained a longstanding symbiotic relationship, which has been cemented by the athletic scholarship. Scholarships have enabled student athletes to utilize university athletic programs as stepping stones to professional sports careers, particularly in football and basketball, and to develop excellence as amateurs in such sports as track and field, swimming, basketball, volleyball, wrestling, and so forth. Professional football and basketball in the United States have reveled in the free-farm system, which annually offers a supply of highly trained, highly motivated players, and every 4 years the United States

Olympic effort has been launched with a team made up of athletes primarily developed and prepared by the universities.

In the absence of such scholarships, a large proportion of student athletes would be unable to attend university, and the time devoted to sport would be drastically reduced. A full scholarship, which officially provides room and board, tuition fees, and required books, can at present be worth between $8,000 to $10,000 per year. The total number of scholarships awarded annually is unknown, but in 1980, following an NCAA imposed 33% reduction in the number of football scholarships, there were in that sport alone over 4,000 signings by major colleges and twice that number by the so-called smaller schools (Rooney, 1980).

Traditionally, athletic scholarships in the United States have been funded primarily from gate receipts and alumni donations. In the last few years, however, television fees have increased dramatically in size and importance, and university athletic programs have become increasingly dependent on television revenue, particularly as gate receipts have fallen overall. More recently, legislatures in at least two states, Arizona and Wyoming, have appropriated funds specifically for athletic scholarships.

Funds for athletic scholarships are highly dependent on the success of the team. In order to maximize gate receipts and/or television fees the team must win; in order to win, a team must recruit the better athletes. Academically eligible, better athletes are in short supply because of the high demand for their services, so coaches and administrators violate the eligibility rules. The necessity to win is thus the root cause of the ills that plague the United States intercollegiate sports system today (Axthelm, 1980; Underwood, 1981).

When viewed strictly as a system to produce world level amateur athletes, the American intercollegiate athletics program has three major weaknesses. First, it officially makes no provision for highly talented athletes who cannot meet established university academic standards, and not all elite athletes have that particular ability. Second, much of the cream of pure athletic talent is enticed into only two sports, football and basketball, with the promise, and in some cases the realization, of a professional playing career. Third, intercollegiate regulations limit the athlete's university playing career to 4 years. In consequence, university athletes either turn professional, retire, or at least considerably reduce their involvement in amateur sport by the age of 22 or 23.

High schools in America offer a wide range of sports, but their interscholastic athletic programs, in the image of the universities, promote the same relatively few sports to elite levels. Sports such as swimming and gymnastics at elite levels are frequently coached in clubs outside the school system, and annual fees in the region of $5,000 in the latter sport, for instance, impose major financial barriers to universal participation.

The American system is very successful up to a point. However, economic barriers to universal participation; academic barriers to coaching and competition in the university system; and the retirement of participants before athletic maturity, which is encouraged by the paucity of opportunities for continued active involvement in amateur sport after leaving the university, make it a wasteful system in comparison to that of socialist countries.

In Canada almost all universities have a small number of long established awards associated with sporting prowess, but the sporting component is subservient to the academic criteria. The only university in Canada to offer athletic scholarships, as such, is Simon Fraser University, which, since its inauguration in 1966, has offered scholarships that cover tuition only. As a consequence, the university has been ineligible to compete in Canadian Intercollegiate Athletic Union (CIAU) competition.

Although, with the exception of SFU, Canadian universities have not offered sports scholarships, the question of financial aid to student athletes has been regularly debated by the CIAU membership for the past 20 years. During that time a number of special committees have been struck to report on university athletic awards, and at the 1980 CIAU Annual Meeting a motion that:

> financial awards which recognize athletic participation and are administered through the Awards Office of a member institution shall not be in violation of CIAU regulations (Bayer et al., 1981)

received the required two-thirds majority. However, because of concerns expressed by the meeting, it was unanimously agreed that the effects of this change not be implemented for a period of one year.

In addition to the one-year delay, a committee was struck to investigate possible solutions to any conflicts that might develop when the new regulations came into force at the beginning of the 1981 to 1982 season. Although the principle of financial awards to student athletes had been ratified by the CIAU membership, the mandate of the committee was to develop a solution to the athletic awards impasse which still existed within the association. The committee's specific task was to present proposals to the CIAU Annual Meeting in June, 1981, which would be supported by at least 80% of the members of each regional conference.

Of the five unions comprising the CIAU (Atlantic, Quebec, Ontario, Great Plains, and Western), all but Ontario supported the implementation of university athletic awards as passed at the 1980 meeting. Ontario supported second party awards, those funded and administered by provincial governments, and third party awards, those from the federal government and approved outside agencies. They opposed first party awards, which are given directly by a CIAU member institution, although these awards must be approved by the senate, printed in the calendar, and limited to the amount of fees, plus 15%.

Since June, 1981, first party financial awards to athletes have been recognized by the CIAU but there is no apparent increase in the number of awards. Discontent still smolders in Ontario, and to a lesser extent in Quebec. The major bone of contention would appear to be concerned with problems of controlling scholarship violations. This concern is, no doubt, stimulated by the plethora of violations reported in the United States during the last 2 years (Morford, personal interview, June 10, 1982).

British university sport contrasts markedly with sport in American institutions of higher education. Participation is considered to be very important, and large numbers of students play regularly at both elite and recreational levels. It would be naive to suggest that sporting prowess has no influence on university entry, but it is always subservient to academic achievement.

In Britain two small, new universities offer sports scholarships or bursaries. The University of Bath accepted its first sports scholar in 1977, and the University of Stirling offered its sports bursaries in 1980. Up to now there have been seven sports scholars at Bath and three at Stirling. The scholarship permits a student to extend his or her degree program by one year, and each sports scholar decides which year to take off from academic studies. Each scholarship is used to meet tuition fees, half the maintenance costs of the extra year, and the costs of a planned program of training at home and abroad.

All scholarships are fully sponsored by such disparate sources as a national office cleaning company, a national mail order firm, Compari, the Scottish International Education Trust, and the International Year of the Child Fund. There is no direct cost to the university. Each scholarship is valued at between $15,000 and $18,000. The first sports scholar at Bath graduated with an honors degree, made more than 50 international appearances during his university career, won the British championship, and placed fourth in the World Canoeing Championships. Other sports scholars are achieving comparable academic and sporting achievements (Wyatt, 1982).

The second major category of financial assistance to athletes is state aid, initially developed by the USSR and later adopted by its satellites. Socialist bloc countries have eliminated the weaknesses of the basic American model by having no professional sport, by extending at both ends the career of the student athlete, and by providing equal opportunities for working athletes. Sporting talent, in a full range of Olympic sports, is systematically identified before children reach their teens, and then concentrated in sports day and boarding schools under the guidance of highly qualified coaches. In the latter type of school, which caters to those with the highest sports potential, the general education schedule is flexible in order to meet the time demands of sports training and competition. Students selected to attend both day and residential schools do so without charge.

At the university level an athlete's academic program may be, and usually is, extended to 10 years or more. The university athlete, providing satisfactory academic progress is made at the slower rate, has all fees paid by the State, irrespective of the length of the program. Other adult athletes in military service or any other occupation are also able to devote unlimited time to training and competition without loss of salary or privileges. The socialist state amateur elite athlete thus has a financially subsidized sporting career from adolescence to competitive retirement (Gilbert, 1980).

In the western world the first country to develop state aid to athletes was Canada. A program of government assistance to elite athletes was first mooted in the 1969 Report of the Task Force on Sport for Canadians, which recommended

> that the Federal Government provide its Fitness and Amateur Sport Directorate (Sport Canada) with sufficient funds to give bursaries to outstanding athletes in a program comparable to that of the Canada Council for outstanding musicians and painters. (Rea et al., 1969)

To Canadian university physical educators, no doubt made wary by developments in the United States, athletic scholarships or awards made on the basis of athletic excellence, have long been an anathema. This opposition notwithstanding, the Student Athletes Grants-in-Aid program was implemented in 1970 to enable student athletes to continue their education while remaining financially free to pursue excellence in their sport. The program is administered by Sport Canada, a federal government department, and grant recipients are chosen from the applicants by a national selection committee after being ranked by the appropriate national sport association. With the grant-aided athlete free to attend the educational institution of his or her choice, many problems associated with recruiting in the United States are avoided.

Student athlete grants-in-aid were first made in 1970 to 1971 in small numbers, but for the next 3 years, approximately $1 million was allocated each year from the federal government's summer student work program. Annual grants to athletes in this program were for $1800, $1200, $900, or $600, depending on the educational level of the student athlete. University students were eligible for the larger amount and high school students the lower amount. At the height of this program in 1973 to 1974, some 600 grants were made annually. However, since the introduction of the Athlete Assistance Program in that year, the grants-in-aid program was gradually reduced in scope as the new program expanded, and was discontinued in 1981 to 1982.

The Athlete Assistance Program was introduced as part of Sport Canada's Game Plan in 1973 to 1974. The overall objective of Game Plan was to place Canada in the top 10 nations on a total points basis in the 1976 Olympic Games. To achieve this end, the athlete classification program, as it was first called, was designed to increase significantly the number of world-class, Canadian athletes.

Athletes are classified in relation to their world ranking. "A" athletes are those ranked in the top 8 in the world in individual events, or top 4 in team events; "B" athletes are those with an individual ranking between 9 and 16, or a team ranking of 5 to 8; "C" athletes are those who have demonstrated the potential to achieve A or B card status in Olympic sports only. In 1973 Canada had 47 carded athletes; by 1976 there were 126; and in 1981 there were approximately 660 classified athletes with 99 at A level, 108 at B level, and 452 at C level (Athlete Information Bureau,

1982). As of June, 1982, Sport Canada provided financial assistance to some 850 amateur athletes in 43 sports.

As of April 1, 1982, basic grants available for levels A, B, and C through the Athlete Assistance Program amounted to $2640 per year for working athletes and students alike, who were living at home, and $5820, $5520, and $4620 for those living away from home. Student athletes at A and B levels also received tuition fees, which were approximately $600 per year. In addition, athletes could receive 50% of the cost of books or instruments up to a maximum of $300, costs of equipment transportation, and up to $20 per day for baby sitting expenses to enable an athlete to attend approved training or competition. The combined budget for the Grants-in-Aid and Athlete Assistance Program was $2.47 million in 1979 to 1980, $2.024 million in 1980 to 1981, and $2.537 million in 1981 to 1982.

In 1980 the Athlete Assistance Program, which had been confined to athletes in the 35 Olympic sports, was extended to include 35 non-Olympic sports. Up to now Canadian athletes attending American universities have received grants, but that eligibility will be phased out as current recipients graduate.

In April, 1982, the federal government introduced the Extended Athlete Assistance Program, which is designed to assist retiring Canadian athletes who have fulfilled a long-term training commitment and have represented Canada in international sporting events. Retiring or decarded athletes, who have been carded for a minimum of 3 years, are eligible for tuition fees for up to two semesters at a Canadian educational institution, plus a living allowance for a maximum of 8 months. Athletes who have been carded for five or more years are eligible for special consideration for extended assistance (Charbonneau, 1982).

A requirement introduced in 1980 is the drawing up of an agreement between the national governing body and the athlete, which clearly spells out their respective obligations. The revised program is expected to produce superior athletic performances from Canada's amateur athletes, and only results will keep an athlete carded.

In addition to the federal government's Elite Athlete Assistance Program, all 10 Canadian provincial governments have established similar programs, usually, but not always, with the intent of assisting athletes who have the potential to attain Sport Canada carded status. The budgets for the year 1981 to 1982 were: $800,000 in the province of Quebec, $400,000 in Ontario, $100,000 in Manitoba, $140,000 in Saskatchewan, $185,000 in Alberta, and $386,000 in British Columbia. The remaining four maritime provinces had very small budgets.

In addition to the high-performance Athlete Assistance Program, the three western provincial governments have established programs of university sports awards or scholarships. The British Columbia program, which was started in 1980, makes available each year 550 awards of $1,000 to student athletes competing in intercollegiate programs. The awards are made on the recommendations of the three provincial universities. Alberta and Manitoba established similar programs in 1981, and Saskatchewan plans to introduce its program in 1982. In 1981 Alberta made awards of $1,000 to university students and $500 to junior college students for a total budget of $800,000; Manitoba made 150 awards, ranging from $600 to $1,000, for a total budget of $100,000.

In British Columbia the total 1981 to 1982 budget for all awards to athletes was $937,000 ($1 million in 1982 to 1983), in Alberta it was $985,000 ($1.1 million in 1982 to 1983), and in Manitoba $225,000. In total, some 3,660 awards were made by the provinces in 1980 for a total budget of $3.5 million. Federal and provincial governments assisted 4,310 athletes in 1981 to 1982 with a combined budget of $6.07 million (personal correspondence with provincial government offices, 1982).

Among Western European countries, only France has state aid. Late in 1978 the Minister for Sport announced that $10 million annually was to be made available for assistance to elite athletes. Subsequently, athletes with potentials to reach the finals at the Moscow Olympic Games were offered contracts by the national government. Under the contract the government pays training, educational, medical, and other sundry costs in exchange for a commitment by the athlete to adhere to an intensive training and competition schedule. The amount of the grant is dependent on the color of the athlete's medal prospects. A potential gold medalist would receive up to $18,000 a year from the contract and other sponsorship from the national sport association.

In announcing the program, the Minister said, not without irony when viewed against the credo of his illustrious countryman Baron Pierre de Coubertin, that "the essential thing is no longer to participate but to win. I no longer want athletes for whom the trip to Moscow is a reward" (Raphael, 1979). To the Minister, success was clearly the destination, not the journey.

In general, Western European countries favor a third approach to providing financial assistance to elite athletes—the autonomous foundation. It was the vast potential of the socialist system of state financial aid to elite athletes, as demonstrated by the GDR (East Germany) in 1964 during the last Olympic Games in which the two Germanies competed as one team, that prompted the FGR (West Germany) to develop the Deutsche Sporthilfe (Sports Aid Foundation). This autonomous body, completely free of state control, was established by the Deutscher Sportbund (DSB) and the German Olympic Committee in 1967. The foundation

> serves exclusively and directly the common purpose of compensating sportsmen and women both ideally and materially for being employed in the service of society and for participating in national representative teams. (Neckermann, 1977)

Sporthilfe rejects categorically the concept of the "professional amateur" and offers grant assistance to partly compensate for the costs of loss of salary, diet, education, transportation, equipment, and sports medicine. It attempts to remove monetary worries and provide a degree of security for athletes who are striving for excellence, and, above all, to provide equality of opportunity for the attainment of excellence for all, irrespective of economic or social status.

Sporthilfe obtains its funds from a variety of sources: a surcharge on Olympic and other sports stamps, lotteries, donations, commercial sponsorships, and special events such as an Annual Sports Ball, which is a highlight in the German social calendar. Aid is given to three major categories of elite athletes. Category A indicates international top class, category B national top level, and category C the talented rising young athlete. In addition, category S covers assistance in recovery from sports injuries, and educational allowance following retirement from competition.

During the years immediately prior to the 1972 Olympic Games in Munich, when national sports fervor was at its height and public support was very generous, it is reported that individual grants in excess of $5,000 per year were not unknown. Today, grants are much smaller. In 1980 approximately 2,500 athletes received assistance, and the average grant was close to $3,000, for a total outlay of $7 million. Athletes are recommended for assistance by the national sport association, and grants are channeled through mentors, usually regional head coaches, who ensure accountability.

In addition to individual grants, Sporthilfe sponsors the Federal School Games, an annual multi-sport festival with 500,000 participants each year, under the banner of Youth Trains for the Olympics. Since 1978 it has also supported 200 school-age athletes in residential sports schools (Pelshenke, personal interview, 1980).

In the image of Sporthilfe, the Sports Aid Foundation in Britain was established in 1976. It is an entirely independent organization, managed by a voluntary board of governors, whose function is to assist individual competitors, according to their personal needs, towards the cost of legitimate, out-of-pocket expenses incurred during preparation and training.

The foundation, which raises its funds in much the same way as Sporthilfe, gives three major types of grant. Elite grants are given to athletes who have a chance of a medal at Olympic Games or World Championships. These awards more or less pay the athlete's way for up to 12 months before the competition, and recipients have been able to engage in full-time preparation either in Britain or abroad. International grants are for competitors of proven ability, who are expected to compete in Olympic, World, European, or major international competition at senior or junior level. National grants are for athletes who are expected to compete internationally within the next 2 years. Each level of grant may be awarded for a maximum of 2 years, subject to review every 3 months.

In 1980 some 800 athletes received grants totaling $1.25 million. In addition to the three basic awards, there is a single memorial award annually of $20,000. This award in 1979 to 1980 enabled Robin Cousins, the 1980 Olympic Men's Figure Skating gold medalist, to meet the costs of training in Denver, Colorado, under the supervision of Carlo Fassi. The award for 1980 to 1981 went to Sebastian Coe, the 1980 Olympic

Games victor in the 1,500 meters, who prepared for the competition by training in seclusion in Spain for 6 months (Middleton, 1980).

The British Sports Aid Foundation established nine regional foundations in 1979. They function on exactly the same lines as the parent body, and the funds they raise are used to assist athletes in the tier immediately below the national level.

From the review of current practices, it is clear that financial assistance to elite athletes is now commonplace, and that the three major sources of funding are university athletic scholarships, state aid, and private foundations. In the intense competitive arena of today's international sport the prerequisites for a comprehensive funding assistance program would appear to be (a) assistance to all talented athletes, (b) assistance throughout the total duration of the competitive career, (c) integration of the sports career with education and working careers, and (d) assistance to help retiring athletes to refocus their lives.

When viewed against these criteria, the university athletic scholarship is seen to be restricted to those who meet university academic standards and to be limited to the middle years of an athlete's competitive career. In the United States widespread circumvention of academic requirements has placed the credibility of athletic scholarships in serious jeopardy. State aid, as practiced in socialist countries such as East Germany, is the most comprehensive of existing programs, meeting all the above requirements. The Canadian system of state aid is weak for preuniversity age groups, and lacks complete integration with universities and more so with the work world. Assistance from private foundations is probably the purest of all programs but tends to be isolated from both education and work careers, and assistance is confined to a relatively small number of established elite athletes.

Financial assistance to athletes is currently widespread in both socialist and western countries, although such assistance is erroneously still fairly widely regarded as something only provided by socialist states. The gap between available funding in the two worlds is rapidly narrowing, and in some instances it may well have closed.

References

Axthelm, P. (1980, September 22). The shame of college sports. *Newsweek*, pp. 54-59.

Bayer, J., et al. (1981, March 19). *Report of the CIAU Special Committee on Student Athletic Awards* (p. 1).

Champion Newsletter. (1982, February). Sport Canada carded athletes. Ottawa: Athletic Information Bureau.

Charbonneau, J.P. (1982, February 18). Increased assistance to Canadian carded athletes. *Fitness and Amateur Sport*, Ottawa.

Gilbert, D. (1980). *The miracle machine* (p. 239). New York: Coward, McCannand Geoghegan.

Middleton, C. (1980, December). *Sports and leisure* (pp. 26-27). London: Sports Council.

Neckermann, J. (1977). *Introduction to the activities of the German Sports Aid Foundation*. Frankfurt.

Raphael, B. (1979, August 5). *The Observer*, London.

Rea et al. (1969). *Report of the Task Force on Sport for Canadians* (p. 64), Ottawa.

Rooney, J.F., Jr. (1980). *The recruiting game: Toward a new system of intercollegiate sports* (p. 8). Lincoln, NE: University of Nebraska.

Underwood, J. (1980, May). The shame of American education: The student athletic hoax. *Sports Illustrated*, pp. 37-72.

Underwood, J. (February, 1981). A game plan for America. *Sports Illustrated*, pp. 62-80.

Wyatt, D. (1982, January 20, 21, 22). Sports scholarships. *The Times*, London.

China Returns:
A Preliminary Prospectus for a Study of Potential Chinese Sporting Success at the 1984 Olympic Games in Los Angeles

Brian B. Pendleton
Vancouver Community College

Following a lengthy period of isolation from involvement with and membership in the International Olympic Committee (IOC), the Chinese Olympic Committee of the People's Republic of China was readmitted to the IOC on November 26, 1979.[1] Three months later, a small contingent of Chinese athletes participated at the 1980 Winter Games in Lake Placid, and preparations were well underway for the Moscow Summer Games until China joined the boycott to protest Soviet action in Afghanistan.

Although Chinese athletes have entered individual competitions, multinational events, and major world championships with predictable regularity in recent years, they have yet to be tested in the demanding arena of the Olympic Summer Games. Among observers of the international sport scene are those who ask: "Will China emerge as another USSR or GDR at the Olympics?" Barring unforeseen developments, China's athletes will take the first step toward answering this question when they participate for the first time in 3 decades at the 1984 Summer Games in Los Angeles.

Background Considerations

The study outlined in this paper is seen as the first part of a three-phase investigation, which will conclude following the 1984 Games. The limitations of such an approach are acknowledged at the outset. As a preliminary *prospectus* on China's return to the Olympic Games, this first phase of the study endeavored to

- review previous empirical studies on national success at the Olympics to determine if and to what extent these investigations had generated models or identified parameters that might be applied to studies on Chinese sport;

- identify the level of sporting success recently attained by Chinese athletes in international competition; and
- provide background information and a research perspective on "things Chinese," which would enable completion of subsequent phases of this and other studies on Chinese sport and physical culture.

A review of the literature on national success at the Olympics indicates that, not surprisingly, China has been excluded by previous investigators for two reasons. First, China did not hold IOC membership and, thus, was ineligible to participate in the Games. Second, the majority of researchers felt that data on sport in China was unavailable. On the latter point, this investigator has argued that data is indeed available (Pendleton, 1981). As to the former limitation, China is now a member of the Olympic family and is expected to enter the 1984 Games.

On these two points, then, the present study appears to hold promise in making a contribution to the analysis of international sport, in general, and to furthering extant Sinologist methodology, in particular.

Furthermore, in undertaking the project, this investigator is making no small plea for a reconsideration of the *micro*-aspects of research within the comparative discipline. While acknowledging the need for broad, conceptually-based research that transcends mere description in search of theoretical framework, it is this writer's contention that much of what appears in the recent literature and on the programs of symposia such as this speaks in generalities and restates, in simplistic terms, the obvious while often ignoring or dismissing adequate mastery of what may be called *basic facts, roots,* or *networks.*

One example, drawn from recent reports and papers on Chinese sport, that may serve to illustrate this point is the question of Chinese names. Even after a decade of interaction with China, and certainly 5 years of significant sporting contact with Chinese athletes and teams, the recording of names such as *Deng Xiaoping, Chen Xiaoxia, Rong Zhihang,* and *Ji Zheng* still causes confusion in both the press and academic circles. With some attention to detail, this problem is easily overcome; one need simply remember that the *surname* comes first, while two major forms of transliteration, *pinyin* and *Wade-Giles,* assist with spelling and pronunciation. Table 1 may serve to clarify the issue.

The time frame covered in this initial phase of the study was 1978 to 1981, with several factors influencing the selection of 1978 as a starting point. First, 1978 saw the convening of a major National Physical Culture and Sport Work Conference, which outlined a new course for sport development. This occurred after the death of Chinese Communist Party Chairman *Mao Zedong* and the 1976 overthrow of the politically radical group, referred to as the Gang of Four, who were held responsible for the disastrous 1966 to 1976 Cultural Revolution. Second, 1978 saw China capture 56 gold, 60 silver, and 51 bronze medals to finish second overall to Japan at the Eighth Asian Games in Bangkok.[2] Third, 1978 saw relative order and stability return to the sport delivery system, as several

Table 1   Transliteration From Chinese to English

Chinese characters	Transliteration		English name
	(Pinyin)	(Wade-Giles)	
邓小平	Deng Xiaoping	Teng Hsiao-ping	*Mr.* Deng (Vice-Chairman)
陈肖霞	Chen Xiaoxia	Chen Hsiao-hsia	*Miss* Chen (diver)
容志行	Rong Zhihang	Jung Chih-hang	*Mr.* Rong (footballer)
纪政	Ji Zheng	Chi Cheng	*Ms.* Chi (sprinter)
			Taiwan

decisions were made that reaffirmed China's commitment to high performance sport.

- Restoration of the national sport ranking and awards system and the national certification program for coaches and officials.
- Restructuring of the occupational categories for sport personnel and cadres at the national, provincial, regional, and county levels.
- Revival of extensive sport science research.
- Introduction of a popularity poll for the selection of the nation's "top-10 sport stars."

In addition, renewed emphasis on the promotion of the *National Physical Fitness Test Standards*[3] and sponsorship of sports meets throughout the country heralded growth patterns that have continued into the 1980s. Table 2 depicts these growth indices.

Table 2   Growth Indices of Chinese Sport

Year	National fitness test (number reaching standards)	Sports meets held (county level and above)
1978	4.22 million	19,019
1979	6.25 million	20,948
1980	8.56 million	22,000 (est.)
1981	10.00 million	23,000 (est.)

Note.   Data from Zhongguo Tiyu Nianjian, Tiyu Bao, China Sports.

Findings

Previous Studies of National Success at the Olympics

Much of what has appeared in the literature to date has been generated by sport sociologists, who, in addressing questions of Olympic Games success, have noted the comparative, cross-national perspective underlying their inquiry (cf. Ball, 1979, p. 190; Kiviaho & Makela, 1978, p. 6; Seppanen, 1981, p. 94). The majority of these studies were macro-analyses of international sporting success, which sought to go beyond mere descriptions of continued success by selected nations in search of explanations for these occurrences (Levine, 1974, p. 353).

The common feature of these analyses was the attempt to isolate and identify correlates that might account for past success and permit prediction of future medal winning.[4] For example, using data from the 1964 Tokyo Games, Ball (1972) identified several demographic, economic, and political indices of the successful Olympic nation, while Novikov and Maximenko (1972) noted a positive relationship between the level of socioeconomic development, as viewed from a Marxist-Leninist perspective, and the nature of the socialist state system. Subsequent studies, which focused on the 1972 Munich Games, sought to develop socioeconomic models (Grimes, Kelly, & Rubin, 1974) and further determine the significance of such variables as gross domestic product, area size of the country, economic system (socialist or capitalist), newspaper circulation, and educational level as major determinants of Olympic success (Levine, 1974). Later, Shaw and Pooley (1976) examined the relationship between Olympic success and selected socioeconomic, politico-military, and educational variables and noted the importance of the grouping of nations (e.g., western-developed, socialist, or Third World) on the variables of population size, gross national product, military expenditure, and number of Olympic sports taught in school.

In a longitudinal study of the Games from 1896 to 1972, Seppanen (1981) focused on Olympic success as a function of ideational superstructure (i.e., religious tradition), while a similar approach was taken by Gillis (1980), who included data from the 1976 Montreal Games. In an attempt to connect the findings of several of these studies, Kiviaho and Makela (1978) analyzed the effect of material and non-material factors on Olympic success, as measured in both absolute and relative terms.[5] More recently, in a cogent summary of these previous Olympic success studies, Colwell (1981, pp. 247, 257) suggested that a major shortcoming of these investigations was the lack of an underlying "theoretical framework incorporating the rationale for the selection of variables and for the predicted relationships between these." The author then outlined a tentative framework for the analysis of sociocultural determinants of international sporting success (Figure 1) and concluded with a number of questions, of which the most pertinent to the present project on China was: "If socialist countries achieve greater success in general, what accounts for the variation within socialist countries?"

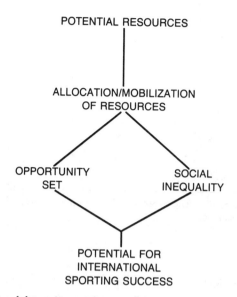

Figure 1   Sociocultural determinants of potential for international sporting success. *Note.* From "Sociocultural Determinants of Olympic Success" by J. Colwell. In J. Segrave and D. Chu (Eds.), *Olympism* (p. 257), 1981, Champaign, IL: Human Kinetics. Copyright by J. Segrave and D. Chu. Reprinted by permission.

On the Level of Chinese Sporting Success

Analysis of China's international sporting success for the years 1978 to 1981 suggests that, although progress is being made in reaching international levels, development is uneven, and attempts to predict possible future success are hazardous. For while national records continue to be broken in most sports, world record-setting performances are few and far between, and the number of world championship titles that are won varies dramatically from year to year. Table 3 highlights these recent fluctuations. Of specific interest to this study of potential Chinese success at the Olympics is a breakdown by sport of these world record and world championship titles (Table 4).

On "Things Chinese" and Perspectives for Further Study

Completion of the prospectus phase of the study has identified two issues worthy of consideration during the subsequent two phases of this project and by researchers who, in future, choose to undertake studies on sport and physical culture in China.

First, the present study is a hostage to time in three main aspects.

1. It must be acknowledged that some athletes and teams, identified as having potential in the years 1978 to 1981, may be nonparticipants in

Table 3   Success Indices of Chinese Sport

Year	National records	World records	World titles
1978	113	3	4
1979	159	12	11
1980	120	7	3
1981	124	8	25

Note. Data from Zhongguo Tiyu Nianjian, Zhongguo Baike Nianjian, Tiyu Bao, China Sports, China Reconstructs.

Table 4   Success Indices of Chinese Sport (World Records and Titles by Sport and Number)

Year	World records		World titles	
	Sport	Number	Sport	Number
1978	Archery	1	Badminton	4
	Shooting	2		
1979	Aeromodels	6	Badminton	5
	Archery	1	Gymnastics	1
	Shooting	4	Table tennis	4
	Weight lifting	1	Weight lifting	1
1980	Aeromodels	2	Gymnastics	2
	Model ships	2	Table tennis	1
	Parachuting	1		
	Shooting	1		
	Weight lifting	1		
1981	Aeromodels	1	Acro-gymnastics	4
	Model ships	1	Badminton	4
	Shooting	5	Diving	3
	Weight lifting	1	Gymnastics	2
			Model ships	1
			Shooting	2
			Table tennis	7
			Volleyball	1
			Weiqi chess	1

Note. Data from Zhongguo Tiyu Nianjian, Tiyu Bao, China Sports.

1984, having become, to use what might be a typically Chinese expression, "the 3 outs"—dropouts, burnouts, or leftouts.
2. Allowance must, also, be made for the emergence of new faces, not only in Chinese sport circles, but worldwide. Therefore, the identification of individual Chinese athletes with Olympic potential will occur in the second phase of this investigation, covering the two years prior to the 1984 Games.[6]
3. Political and organizational changes, both within China and globally, must be considered in these times of international instability. Notwithstanding the political significance of the decision, China's boycott of the 1980 Moscow Games was undoubtedly a blow to her dedicated athletes and coaches.

Second, the influence of the polity on sport in China is a critical factor in three major aspects.

1. Any marked change in China's current focus on its Four Modernizations program, the tenure of leadership of Vice-Chairman Deng Xiaoping, and the anticipated promulgation of a new constitution in the near future would most likely impact on sport from local to international levels.
2. China's recent sport rapprochement with the Soviet Union, ending nearly 2 decades of mutual vituperation, cannot be ignored when considering the long-term development of sport in the People's Republic.[7]
3. The perceived affinity between Marxist-Leninist concepts of dialectics and Confucian doctrines of *yin* and *yang*, as well as the state's astute, albeit dramatically less than decisive, melding of the two, should not be overlooked. Perhaps our western, occidental "worldview" requires rethinking. It would be a serious error to see China as merely another socialist state.

Discussion

Although several of the previously identified studies on national success at the Olympics provided informative data and insights on the diverse and complex nature of the question, only two raised issues immediately applicable to the present project. The question that arises from the Shaw and Pooley study in respect to any planned investigation of Chinese international sport is: What outcome could be expected from the interaction of selected variables in a country which is both socialist and Third World? Similarly, the theoretical framework proposed by Colwell offers several new avenues for the analysis of Chinese sport, which will be explored in the second phase of this project. It is, however, interesting to speculate at this juncture on the impact of selected economic, political, and social variables on sport in a country that is composed of 55 different ethnic groups, that has a population of 1 billion people, that has developed the world's eighth largest economy, and that generates a per capita gross national product of only $300 per year.

Turning to the issue of China's recent international sporting accomplishments, several points merit consideration. Clearly, Chinese success in paramilitary events and sports not yet on the Olympic program requires careful scrutiny. Researchers may also be interested to know that more than half of the 100 world records set by Chinese athletes since 1956 have been in shooting, parachuting, and model ships and planes, while only 3 have come in track and field and swimming. At the same time, it should be noted that table tennis is scheduled to be added to the 1988 Games' program, while badminton, another sport in which the Chinese excel, is under consideration for future inclusion. Moreover, China's most successful year ever, 1981, cannot be dismissed out of hand, as early indications are that 1982 and 1983 will be equally rich in gold medals and world titles.

Having raised these points, and considering the probable impact of "things Chinese" on subsequent studies on sport in the People's Republic, one might well ask if any study of potential Chinese Olympic success is possible at this time. One preliminary hypothesis can, however, be advanced: *Based on recent international sport performances, Chinese athletes will achieve relative rather than absolute success at the 1984 Games in Los Angeles.*

Susequent phases of this project will analyze China's potential for success at Los Angeles and, following the Games, measure the validity of these predictions. These results will, it is to be hoped, make a further contribution to the study of comparative and international sport.

Notes

1. For an account of the dispute surrounding the "two China" question, see Brian B. Pendleton (1978), "The People's Republic of China and the Olympic Movement: A Question of recognition," unpublished PhD dissertation, University of Alberta. Although the question of participation by two Chinese delegations at the Olympic Games appears to have been resolved (*Vancouver Sun*, March 24, 1981), the "two China" issue continues to be problematic in certain international sport governing bodies. For example, in July, 1982, the PRC refused to participate in the 5th World Women's Softball Championships held in Taiwan when, in apparent contravention of the International Softball Federation's ruling on the use of national flags, emblems, and anthems, the organizing committee permitted the Taiwanese entry to use the Nationalist (Republic of China) flag and emblem, rather than those approved under the agreement that saw Taiwan's team recognized by the ISF under the name China Taibei Softball Association (*South China Morning Post* [Hong Kong], July 15, 1982).
2. Chinese analysts have noted that a key to Japanese supremacy in 1978 lay in the fact that Japan captured 25 of 29 swimming medals. See Xia (1982) for an overview of Chinese and Japanese strength on the eve of the 1982 Asian Games.
3. Guojia Tiyu Duanlian Biaozhun Tiaoli, 1975, *Xin Tiyu*, **5**, 10-12. An English translation of the test standards appears in Pendleton (1977).

4. Recent work by Stefani (1982) identifies a successful model for the prediction of winning performances in Olympic competition. The author's tabulation of the percent improvement per Olympiad from 1952 to 1976 enabled him to predict with 97% accuracy the performance required to capture the gold medal at the 1980 Moscow Games, as well as extrapolate predictions for 1984 and 2000.
5. Absolute success (i.e., total points or medals won) does not control for differences between nations in area size or population, but is a measure of basic resources available. Conversely, relative success (i.e., medals won in proportion to population) is biased against larger nations, which are restricted in the number of participants they may enter, but does measure the effective use of available resources.
6. Chinese researchers have, in preliminary and somewhat unsophisticated studies, identified 10 factors thought to contribute to the success of an athlete: passion for sports, good physique, motivation, hard work, creativity, favorable background, early start, competition, systematic training, and coaching (see Lin and Zhu, 1981).
7. A small Soviet delegation participated at a Beijing (Peking) track and field meet in June, 1982, marking the first time since October, 1965, that Soviet athletes had competed in China. The numerous exchanges and cooperative agreements in sport, which characterized Sino-Soviet relations in the 1950s and contributed greatly to the development of the Chinese sport system in the early years after the founding of the People's Republic, were canceled in the wake of ideological disputes in the 1960s. Although far from certain at this time, renewed Soviet assistance would most likely hasten China's drive to become a sporting giant.

References

Ball, D.W. (1972). Olympic Games competition: Structural correlates of national success. *International Journal of Comparative Sociology*, **13**, 186-200.

Colwell, J. (1981). Sociocultural determinants of Olympic success. In J. Segrave & D. Chu (Eds.), *Olympism*. Champaign, IL: Human Kinetics.

Gillis, J.H. (1980). Olympic success and national religious orientation. *Review of Sport and Leisure*, **5**, 1-20.

Grimes, A.R., Kelly, W.J., & Rubin, P.H. (1974). A socioeconomic model of national Olympic performance. *Social Science Quarterly*, **55**, 777-783.

Guojia tiyu duanlian biaozhun tiaoli. (1975). *Xin Tiyu*, pp. 5, 10-12.

IOC solves China problem. (1981, March 24). *Vancouer Sun*, p. C7.

Kiviaho, P., & Makela, P. (1978). Olympic success: A sum of non-material and material factors. *International Review of Sport Sociology*, pp. 2, 5-7.

Levine, N. (1974). Why do countries win Olympic medals? Some structural correlates of Olympic success: 1972. *Sociology and Social Research*, pp. 58, 353-360.

Lin, S., & Zhu, D. (1981). Bashiyiming yundongyuande chengcai zhilu. *Xin Tiyu*, **10**, 2-4.

Novikov, A.D., & Maximenko, A.M. (1972). The influence of selected socioeconomic factors on the level of sports achievements in the various countries. *International Review of Sport Sociology*, pp. 7, 22-44.

Pendleton, B. (1977). What can we learn from the Chinese? *Coaching Review*, pp. 1, 4-7, 44-56.

Pendleton, B. (1978). *The People's Republic of China and the Olympic movement: A question of recognition.* Unpublished doctoral dissertation, University of Alberta.

Pendleton, B. (1981). The People's Republic of China: Sources and topics for sociocultural investigation. *Comparative Physical Education and Sport,* 7, 7-12.

Segrave, J., & Chu, D. (1981). *Olympism.* Champaign, IL: Human Kinetics.

Seppanen, P. (1981). Olympic success: A cross-national perspective. In G. Luschen & G. Sage (Eds.), *Handbook of social science of sport.* Champaign, IL: Stipes.

Shaw, S., & Pooley, J. (1976). National success at the Olympics: An explanation. In *Proceedings Sixth International Seminar on the History of Physical Education and Sport.* Quebec: Trois Rivieres.

Stefani, R.T. (1982). Olympic winning performances: Trends and predictions. *Olympic Review*, pp. 176, 357-364.

Taipei games were "a farce." (1982, July 15). *South China Morning Post,* Hong Kong, p. 9.

Xia, W. (1982). Asiad preview: Who'll be the cock-o'-the-walk? *China Sports*, pp. 7, 9.

Zhongguo baike nianjian. (1980). Beijing: Zhongguo Dabaike Quanshu Chubanshe.

Zhongguo tiyu nianjian. (1981). Beijing: Renmin Yiyu Chubanshe.

A Comparison of Soviet Soccer and Hockey With the Major American Sports

Victor Peppard
University of South Florida

For several decades soccer and hockey have been the most popular sports in the Soviet Union and, therefore, occupy a position that is analogous to that of the three major sports in the United States: football, basketball, and baseball. While Soviet scholars of sport have recently begun to pay attention to several of the questions related to the spectacular roles of sport (Matveev, Milshtein, & Moltchanov, 1980, pp. 5-26; Ponomarev, 1978, pp. 7-27), there does not appear to be any scholarship that attempts to explain why soccer and hockey should occupy such a prominent role not only in Soviet sport, but also in Soviet culture as a whole. The purposes of this paper are first, therefore, an examination of why soccer and hockey play such an important and popular role in the Soviet Union; second, a comparison of soccer and hockey in the Soviet Union with the three-part major sport system of the United States, which both illuminates the situation of Soviet sport and raises several provocative issues of comparative culture.

According to one of the major tenets of structuralism, the various communication systems may be considered "secondary modeling systems," which have as their primary model the structure of language (Lotman, 1971, pp. 13-28). Among the communication systems that scholars have treated as such secondary modeling systems are art, literature, and sport. Implicit in the structuralist view is the notion that these different secondary modeling systems or areas of culture are organically and profoundly interrelated with the overall culture. Perhaps no better example of this could be found than the relationship between Soviet soccer and hockey and Soviet culture in general. For instance, in any consideration of Soviet life, one must take into account a basic factor that has tremendous practical, psychological, and cultural implications—the climate. In much of the Soviet Union, and certainly in most of Russia, there are, for all practical purposes, two seasons, winter and nonwinter. Because soccer and hockey are each firmly identified with their own time of the year, the alternation between these two sports has become ingrained in the minds of players and spectators as two poles of a natural cycle. In fact, a recent attempt in 1976 to divide the soccer season into spring and fall halves met with failure. Such an arrangement violates the natural rhythm of the sporting seasons and has never met with success in the Soviet context.

The early history of Russian and Soviet soccer contains important keys to the sport's enduring popularity. In a rough and primitive form, the sport was first known to Russian spectators as a diversion during the intermissions at bicycle races in the early 1890s. The first soccer clubs were founded around the turn of the century, and by 1911, in the short space of about a decade, soccer had become the most popular sport in Russia (Perel', 1969, p. 100), which it remains to this day. In addition to the intangible attractions inherent in soccer, perhaps the single most important reason for its rapid growth in Russia is its association with things European and European culture. Indeed, soccer in Russia had an international flavor from its very inception, because its first players and teachers were the British living in Russia, with whom the Russians came to have a complex and stormy rivalry that lasted up until the eve of the first World War. There were cases of English players who continued to play on in Russia, even after the revolution and civil war. In 1921 Swift played for the Moscow club, *Sokolniki*, in the fall championships, and as late as 1923, Tikston played for the Moscow fall champions, *Krasnaya Presnya* (Esenin, 1974, pp. 36, 38). In Russia's first years of soccer, there were teams that called themselves by such names as "Germany," "Prussia," and "Russia" (Riordan, 1977, p. 23).

The early, true international matches between Russian teams and touring teams from Britain and Europe greatly helped to stimulate interest in soccer. The first of these, a visit to St. Petersburg by a Czech team called "Corinthians" in 1910, was both a sellout and a real sensation. When the Petersburg select team beat the Czechs, the *Petersburg Leaflet* (*Peterburgsky listok*) proclaimed in a burst of hyperbole that "the Russians have taken the world championship away from the Czechs." After the Czechs had left, Russian soccer players began to imitate their style of dress by wearing striped jerseys and white shorts (Korshak, 1975, pp. 39-46).

During the early years and, in fact, well into the 1920s, the majority of Russian soccer players were from the small, but dynamic, urban middle class. This middle class was particularly susceptible to the blandishments of European cultural modernity and technological novelty. In reading the memoirs of early observers of Russian soccer, such as the writer Yury Olesha, it becomes apparent that in the minds and imaginations of Russian middle class youth, soccer was somehow associated with the speed and motion of the new technology represented by bicycles, automobiles, and airplanes. For these young people soccer became nothing less than a symbol of the "new culture" (Olesha, 1979, p. 125). Soccer became the first great Russian sport of the 20th century because it was modern and European, and because the first Russian soccer players wanted to play *the* European game.

The Russians' urge to compete on an equal footing with their European neighbors reasserted itself almost as soon as the civil war came to an end. In 1923 a Soviet combined team, consisting of Moscow and Petrograd players, made a remarkably successful Scandinavian tour, which may be considered a harbinger, if not a progenitor of future sport diplomacy. The journal *Sport* considered this tour to be nothing less than "a definite transformation in the history of Russian sport. . . . The recent victorious performances of our soccer players in the West . . . have shown that the Russians are no worse, that they are international class players" (Korshak, 1975, p. 118). Subsequently, in the 1920s the leading role of soccer in Soviet sport is signaled by the fact that it was the only sport in which the Soviet Union engaged foreign competitors on a regular basis.

Soccer was also played, before the turn of the century, in the South in Odessa, Kharkov, and Kiev. By the teens the intercity rivalries, and especially the competition between Petersburg and Moscow, gave great impetus to the game's growth. After the capitol of the Soviet Union was shifted from Leningrad to Moscow, Moscow gradually became the center of Soviet soccer; in the 1950s the Soviet national team was made up almost exclusively of players from the Moscow clubs (Esenin, 1974, pp. 100-102). Subsequently, however, the Soviets have come to draw on the immense reserves of talent in the other national republics, so that the Soviet national team now contains not only Russians and Ukrainians, but also Georgians, Armenians, and other nationalities. Despite this infusion of multinational personnel and its longtime position of precedence in Russian and Soviet sport, Soviet soccer has yet to reach the heights of achievement attained by Soviet hockey since the second World War.

While soccer is somewhat cramped by a relatively short season in most of the Soviet Union, hockey is in its natural element. The Soviets actually play two different kinds of hockey. The first they call "Russian hockey." This is the game of bandy, which is considered indigenous to Sweden, Norway, Finland, and Russia. Bandy is played out of doors on a surface of ice the size of a soccer field. The game involves 11 players using soccer-size goals, a small ball, and sticks resembling those used for field hockey. The Scandinavian countries and the Soviet Union contest an international bandy championship yearly, and bandy has had its avid proponents since the first official game was contested in Moscow in 1946 (Kochalov, 1969, p. 164). The Soviets, however, have placed greater emphasis on what they call "Canadian hockey," the game played with a puck, in order to better compete in international ice hockey. The history of hockey in the Soviet Union serves in some respects, therefore, as the epitome of Soviet sport, where the stress has deliberately been placed on international forms of sport at the expense of Russian and other national folk games.

Outwardly, soccer and hockey appear to have little in common, for the accoutrements of the two games are radically different and they are played at different times of the year on different surfaces. Nevertheless, the two sports are, in essence, almost one and the same thing, and they present the spectator with a similar, if not identical, situation. The purpose of both sports is to propel an object past a goalie into a goal. In front of the goal, players assume both attacking and defensive roles, which are thought to be interchangeable or overlapping in nature. Both games are played for specific lengths of time on well-defined surfaces with specially designated zones, and both have an offsides rule, which is designed to prevent attackers from scoring easy goals merely by hanging around the goal. The number of skaters in hockey is exactly half the number of field players in soccer. In a conceptual sense, the game of bandy is virtually halfway between soccer and hockey, incorporating as it does the major aspects of both sports.

For training purposes during the winter, Soviet soccer players now sometimes play "minifootball" or what is called in North America, indoor soccer. While the Soviets hold occasional tournaments in minifootball, they have not reached the stage North American teams have with regard to full-length schedules. In the North American version of indoor soccer, as in bandy, the affinities between soccer and hockey become very apparent. Not only is indoor soccer usually played in an actual hockey rink with five field players and a goalie, but the tactics of hockey are also emulated, and there are now penalties that involve sending players off temporarily, as in hockey.

In the Soviet Union it has long been considered natural for athletes to alternate between playing hockey in the winter and soccer during the rest of the year. Before the advent of all-out specialization and the 11-month season for the major sports at the highest levels, it was even possible for an athlete to compete in the "big-time" of both sports. One of the last of the great all-arounders in Soviet sport was Vsevolod Bobrov, who at one time in the 1950s was considered to be not only the best footballer in the Soviet Union, but also the best hockey player with either the ball or the puck (Esenin, 1974, p. 198).

The prominence of soccer and hockey in the Soviet Union is bound up with a wide range of interconnections between these sports and the society as a whole. If one examines the history of the development of the two sports in the Soviet Union, one may observe a remarkable confluence between official policy and popular desires. A case in point is the emergence of the star system in Soviet soccer in the 1920s and 1930s, and the very designation of soccer as the first Soviet "big-time sport." During the 1920s competitive sport, even at the international level, was still officially called simply "physical culture." Certain elements of the public, however, were already clamoring for recognition of star players and big-time sport. The official policy finally caught up with popular demand in 1934 when the title of Merited Master of Sport was created (Riordan, 1977, p. 131). It should be noted here that the creation of this title reflected the desire of the Soviets to include sport as an element in the general implementation of the cult of "Stalin, the Master." At that time workers who performed outstanding feats were given special rewards. Virtually no area of culture and society was unaffected by the desire to cultivate heroes and masters. In 1934 Zhdanov promulgated the doctrine of socialist realism in literature and encouraged the "heroization" of literature; no longer would literature focus on the deeds of life's little men, but rather on the exploits of true heroes (Clark, 1978, pp. 189-206). In retrospect, the official approval of the star system in sport in 1934 may be considered the beginning of official awareness of the tremendous potential inherent in sport for shaping culture.

In the present day, the team sports of soccer and hockey provide convenient showcases for the official policies of collectivism and teamwork. It might even be argued that sport is the one area of Soviet society in which the consistent application of collectivist principles has produced indisputable and dramatic results. It should be noted, however, that official policies and preferences in no way deter contemporary Soviet spectators from making stars out of their favorite players. It is in the actual playing and management of Soviet soccer and hockey that the tension between the needs of the individual and those of the collective is felt most strongly. Based on the results of international competition, it appears that, so far, Soviet hockey has better solved the old dilemma that it takes teamwork to set up goals but an individual to score them than has Soviet soccer.

There are a number of levels on which it is productive to compare Soviet sport with sport in the United States. One of these concerns the ways in which both cultures have treated and developed imported forms of sport. The typical pattern for North Americans has been to modify games imported from foreign sources to suit their own tastes and requirements, so that they ultimately produce new and separate forms of sport. The most outstanding example of this is the adaptation of British rugby into American football (Riesman & Denney, 1972, pp. 152-167). Subsequently, basketball was developed as a winter surrogate for football. Although there is a rich tradition of indigenous folk games among both Russians and other Soviet nationalities, the Soviets have virtually supplanted these games with ones borrowed from Europe, particularly the games of the modern Olympics. In sharp contrast with earlier American practice, the Soviets have steadfastly adhered to the traditional rules of modern imported games. This does not mean, though, that the Soviet approach has been one of passive acceptance. The Soviets have, rather, concentrated their energies on trying to perfect the possibilities inherent in previously existing modern games. The innovative contribution of the Soviets has sometimes been in the development of new tactics and techniques within the framework of traditional rules. In one instance this had led to fundamental changes in the way a sport is played throughout the world. This is, of course, the case in international ice hockey, where Soviet passing and team tactics have revolutionized the game, one might add, even among certain North Americans, who were reluctant at first to admit the merit of Soviet innovations.

The conservative Soviet treatment of imported sport might seem surprising at first glance, unless one remembers that with the exception of the early 1920s and the period between 1928 and 1931 known as the cultural revolution (Fitzpatrick, 1978), Soviet culture has been characterized by a marked conservatism. The official rejection of proletarian culture, as espoused by the so-called *proletkultists*, represents a deliberate refusal by the Soviets to move in the direction of outright revolutionary culture. The proletkultists opposed competitive sports such as soccer on the grounds that they were inherently bourgeois, and they would have instituted in physical culture and education a kind of leftist collectivism

(Riordan, 1977, pp. 101–105), when compared with Soviet practice, the traditional American approach of making or remaking, into their own image, the idiosyncratic sports of football, basketball, and baseball (which, nevertheless, have historical connections with other sports) is at once more chauvinistic and more revolutionary.

There are several important contrasts between the Soviet two-cycle system of major spectator sports and the three-part system of the United States. First of all, soccer and hockey are continuous motion games, and as already noted, share many basic functional and conceptual similarities. American football, basketball, and baseball on the other hand are more markedly distinguished from one another than are soccer and hockey. Whereas soccer and hockey have long been international sports, the three American sports are far more regionalized in their practice, although basketball and baseball are acquiring an ever greater international status.

For all of their obvious differences, American football, basketball, and baseball do share some significant points in common. The greatest of these is the pronounced tendency towards frequent stoppages of play. Baseball is, by its very nature, a stop-and-go affair. Basketball and football, on the other hand, could be played theoretically at least, with a minimum of interruptions. Whereas American football has indulged itself in an overdosage of play stoppages by encouraging all sorts of deliberations and clarifications at every possible moment, basketball has occasionally struggled to become the continuous motion game it was intended to be. Unless the high number of allowable timeouts is reduced or eliminated, however, basketball will never become a genuinely free-flowing game.

Lately much has been made, and rightfully so, of the fact that commercially motivated timeouts interrupt the normal flow of action, such as it is, in televised sport in the United States. It should be remembered, however, that the traditional American penchant for managerial control long ago caused the introduction of timeouts and other stoppages designed to regulate more closely the course of play. This overt and constant managerial control guarantees that competitive sport in the United States is structured to suit the needs and purposes of managers rather than those of players and spectators. Perhaps the most fundamentally paradoxical result of the American tradition of overmanagement, especially given the professed American belief in the primary role of the individual, is that individual players are often deprived of the opportunity to make choices and decisions for themselves when they engage in organized sport.

In the United States the urge to engage in individual sports manifests itself most dramatically after the completion of formal schooling, when Americans tend to gravitate toward such sports as running, swimming, bicycling, tennis, squash, and racketball. One explanation for this phenomenon is the indisputable fact that postgraduate sport in the United States lacks any specific or well-defined structure for amateur team sports such as is found in most of Europe. One might well wonder whether the preference for individual sports is not, to some degree, also a reaction against the overmanaged conduct of team sport found in schools and colleges.

As opposed to the stop-and-go sports of the United States, soccer and hockey in the Soviet Union are continuous motion sports that preclude certain kinds of constant meddling by managers, and, consequently, give players the responsibility for making most decisions during the course of play. Particularly in soccer, while he may bellow all he likes, the coach does not have the opportunity to counsel regularly with his players when play is stopped. In Soviet soccer and hockey the bulk of the coaching must take place before a contest is played and not so much during its course.

While there are clear differences between Soviet and American sport with regard to the relative prominence of different sports and the overall structure of sport, there are also some important similarities. Two of these are the star system and the victory-at-all-costs mentality, which prevail in both the Soviet Union and the United States. There is now also the further possibility that if certain recently emerged tendencies continue to develop, an even greater confluence between the two systems will occur. Of special relevance in this connection is the performance of the United States hockey team in the 1980 Winter Olympics. One of the greatest ironies of this famous victory is that it was made possible by adopting a modified Soviet model of training. By living, training, and playing together for several months prior to the Olympics, the United States team was in effect imitating the practice of Soviet national teams, which spend most of the year training and playing together. Imitation, especially by one's arch rival, must not only be the sincerest form of flattery, but also eloquent testimony to the effectiveness of the Soviet model for competition in international sport. Indeed, lacking many of the resources for mass recreational sport that are found in most Western countries, the Soviets have been remarkably successful in concentrating their efforts on the production of world-class athletes in both team and individual sports.

The recent success of the United States national hockey team, which relied on Soviet style preparation, raises the possibility that Americans will, in the future, adapt certain features of the structure of Soviet sport in order to enhance their performance in international competition. The creation of Olympic training centers in the United States, for example, appears to be an attempt to match the Soviets' system of year-round training. The possibility has also been broached that both the United States and Canada may field national teams in the North American Soccer League sometime in the near future. Whether or not such developments actually take place, it is significant that many important questions now being raised about the structure of sport are being defined and debated using the models and concepts typical of Soviet sport.

In other ways, however, sport in North America continues to follow the logic of its own historical development. Even professional hockey has succumbed to the baleful influence of sports such as football and basketball by resorting to timeouts at certain supposedly crucial moments, for example, 2 minutes before the end of a period. Hockey in North America has also begun to show a tendency toward the high scoring that is increasingly characteristic of baseball, football, and basketball. This high scoring is one area in which the American spectators' need for constant gratification of their desires is certainly being met. The recent surge of interest in indoor soccer, where scoring is much more frequent than in the outdoor game, is further proof that the American spectator lacks patience and requires a constantly high level of excitement. At the same time, indoor soccer is nothing less than the latest example of the Americans' urge to restructure sports to suit their own ends.

In the Soviet Union soccer and hockey remain, for the most part, relatively low-scoring games. The Soviet spectator has to be more patient and attentive than his American counterpart lest he miss a decisive score. As the bourgeoisification of Soviet society gradually increases, one wonders whether Soviet spectators of sport will begin to demand the higher scoring that is now characteristic of American sport. Spectator dissatisfaction with the low scoring of Soviet soccer already points in that direction.

In summary, a comparison of Soviet and American major sports yields some paradoxical conclusions with regard to the role of individual players. While the Soviets place great emphasis on subordinating the individual to the cause of collective teamwork in their coaching and preparation, the nonstop character of soccer and hockey gives players the opportunity and the responsibility to make significant decisions for themselves as the game is played. In American football, basketball, and baseball, constant interruptions by management during the course of play ensure that players' chances to make crucial decisions for themselves are severely restricted. Since there is no end in sight to the victory-at-all-costs mentality, which prevails in both the United States and the Soviet Union, it is reasonable to assume that management control, in both countries however it is expressed, will only increase at the expense of player initiative.

Perhaps the most appropriate image one could choose to describe Americans in their dealings with sport is that of a tinker, who is never satisfied with the current shape of things and constantly patches and fixes them until they come to look only vaguely like their original selves. The Soviets, for their part, might be described as an overachiever-student, whose occasional flashes of inspiration allow him or her to leap ahead of the rest of the class. If the Americans wish to compete more successfully with the Soviets in international sport, they will probably have to apply their aptitude for tinkering not to the forms of games, but rather to the structure of sport itself by borrowing and adapting from the structure of Soviet sport. If they come to use different names and terminology than the Soviets, it will be no surprise. The great task awaiting the diligent Soviets is the creation of a foundation for mass participatory sport that will compare with that of the West and be a worthy complement to its own system for outstanding competitors.

References

Clark, K. (1978). Little heroes and big deeds: Literature responds to the first five-year plan. In S. Fitzpatrick (Ed.), *Cultural revolution in Russia 1928-1931*. Bloomington, IN: Indiana University Press.

Esenin, K. (1974). *Moskoviskii futbol* [Moscow soccer]. Moscow: Moskovii Rabochii.

Fitzpatrick, S. (1978). *Cultural revolution in Russia 1928-1931*. Bloomington, IN: Indiana University Press.

Kochalov, A. (1969). Starateli ledovych aren [Prospectors of the ice arenas]. In V. Zholdak (Ed.), *Stranitsy moskovskogo sporta* [Pages from Moscow sport]. Moscow: Moskovskii Rabochii.

Korshak, Y. (1975). *Staryi, staryi futbol* [Old, old soccer]. Moscow: Fizkul'tura i Sport.

Lotman, Y. (1971). *Structure of the artistic text* [Struktura khudozhest vennogo teksta] (Slavik reprint IX). Providence, RI: Brown University Press.

Matveev, L., Milshtein, O., & Moltchanov, S. (1980). Spectator activity of workers in sports. *International Review of Sport Sociology*, **15**(2), 5-26.

Olesha, Y. (1979). *No day without a line* (J. Rosengrant, Trans.). Ann Arbor, MI: Ardis.

Perel', A. (1969). Pravoflangovye otechestvennogo futbola [The pointmen of native soccer]. In V. Zholdak (Ed.), *Stranitsy moskovskogo sporta* [Pages from Moscow sport]. Moscow: Moskovskii Rabochii.

Ponomarev, N. (1978). About system analysis of sport. *International Review of Sport Sociology*, **13**(1), 7-27.

Riesman, D., & Denney, R. (1972). Football in America: A study in culture diffusion. In E. Dunning (Ed.), *Sport: readings from a sociological perspective*. Toronto: University of Toronto Press.

Riordan, J. (1977). *Sport in Soviet society*. Cambridge, MA: Cambridge University Press.

A Comparison of Players' and Coaches' Attitudes Toward Little League Baseball in the States of Oregon and Washington and Taiwan, Republic of China

Hu Cheng
National Taiwan Normal University

Little League Baseball is baseball that has been modified for boys between the ages of 8 to 12. It began in the United States in 1939. Since the 1969 World Series, Little League Baseball also has become a very popular sport in Taiwan, Republic of China. This is probably due to the fact that the Republic of China team won the series that year. However, the game seems to have different meanings for the people of the two countries.

Generally in the United States, parents enthusiastically support their children's participation in Little League Baseball. They believe that Little League Baseball develops individual qualities of citizenship and manhood in young boys.

In Taiwan, Republic of China, Little League Baseball takes on a different value. The government, the society, and the family are constantly favorable toward Little League Baseball as a participant sport. They are anxious to see their Little League Baseball teams do well and win the World Series. They believe that winning the championship will bring the society together and gain worldwide recognition and a positive image for their country.

The purpose of this study, then, is to examine and compare the attitudes of Little League Baseball players from the United States and from Taiwan, Republic of China. To accomplish this, a questionnaire based on Kenyon's (1968a) and Simon's (1973) research was developed, translated, pilot tested, and administered to Little League Baseball players.

Kenyon (1968a) perceived that physical activity could be logically reduced to six possible instrumental values for the participant:

1. As a social experience by providing a medium for social intercourse, that is, a way to meet new people and perpetuate existing relationships.
2. As a health and fitness improvement.
3. As a medium for pursuing the "thrill" sensation.
4. As an aesthetic experience in perceiving the beauty or certain artistic qualities of some physical movements and activities.

5. As a catharsis, a way of releasing the tension precipitated by frustration through vicarious means.
6. As an ascetic experience deriving from the strenuous and often painful training and difficult competitions that demand a determent of many individual gratifications.

In his study of attitudes toward sport and physical activity among adolescents from four English-speaking countries (the United States, Canada, Australia, and Great Britain), Kenyon (1970) expanded his physical activity scale to seven rather than six dimensions by including the dimension of physical activity as a chance.

Research by Alderman (1970), using Kenyon's six-dimensional scale to measure attitudes of Canadian championship athletes at the 1967 Pan American Games, and Simon (1973), who developed an instrument for assessing children's attitudes toward physical activity, served as a model for this study. Simon's instrument was a multidimensional, semantic differential scale based on Kenyon's conceptual model for physical activity. Her findings indicated that the multidimensional CATPA (Children Attitudes Toward Physical Activity) semantic differential scale is appropriate for group testing with fourth, fifth, and sixth grade children (Simon, 1973).

The instrument developed in this study for measuring players' and coaches' attitudes toward Little League Baseball was based on Simon's study. The title of each of Simon's dimensions was changed from physical activity to "Little League Baseball." For the purpose of this study, the seventh dimension—Little League Baseball as the pursuit of victory—was modified from Kenyon's scale (Kenyon, 1970). All seven dimensions of attitudes toward Little League Baseball were measured and compared.

- Little League Baseball as a social experience, providing a chance to meet new people and be with friends
- Little League Baseball for health and fitness, improving an individual's health and body condition
- Little League Baseball as a thrill, deriving from the game's risk and danger and the excitement of moving and changing directions very quickly
- Little League Baseball as a form of beauty in human movements, such as pitching, catching, and batting
- Little League Baseball for the release of tension, getting away from problems through participating in the game or watching other people play
- Little League Baseball as long and hard training, often necessitating that players give up other things they enjoy
- Little League Baseball as the pursuit of victory, attempting to accomplish the game's primary purpose of one team's players being as good or better than another team's players, as shown by a winning score

Method

The instrument used in this study consisted of two parts. The first was a semantic differential scale designed to assess the players' and coaches' attitudes toward Little League Baseball. The second was a questionnaire intended to obtain general information on subjects such as the goal of competition and the length of the baseball season.

Efforts were made to determine the validity, reliability, and feasibility of the instrument. Since attitudes, as a behavior disposition, are nonobservable, validity cannot be directly determined. Validity can be addressed by showing items to be logically representative of the attitude universe in question (Kenyon, 1968b). Two procedures were applied to check the content validity of the instrument.

First, the questionnaire was examined by Edwin Strowbridge, EdD, School of Education, Oregon State University. Strowbridge is a specialist in elementary teacher education. His examination verified that the concepts of each dimension and the meaning of the eight adjective pairs of wording were appropriate and understandable for children aged 8 to 12.

Second, in order to have an equivalent meaning on the two forms of the questionnaires (English and Chinese), the questionnaire was translated from English into Chinese. Mu Ming-Chu, an Oregon State University Chinese language instructor, then translated it from Chinese back into English. The results demonstrated that Kenyon's concept of the physical activity and also the words on the instrument were acceptable in Chinese culture.

For the face validity, the tests were personally administered. The United States tests were monitored by this researcher. Those in Taiwan were administered by a Chinese-speaking associate, Lin Chin-Ho. When the attitude questionnaire was administered to each subject in the four different study groups, the subjects all volunteered and showed a high degree of interest in participating.

A pilot study was conducted both in Taiwan, Republic of China, and in the state of Oregon by the researcher and his associate. In the process of administering the test, the subjects were observed to have no difficulties with the questionnaire. In summary, the results showed that the subjects understood the concepts being assessed and did not have any difficulty with the directions, mechanics, or wording of the questionnaire.

The study involved 20 randomly selected Little League Baseball teams, 10 from the United States and 10 from Taiwan, Republic of China. The United States teams were located in the states of Oregon and Washington, west of the Cascade Mountains. The Chinese teams were located throughout the island.

In order to test for any statistically significant differences between the attitudes of American and Chinese players and coaches, a two-tailed t test was employed at the .05 level of significance. For the questions resulting in nominal data, a Chi-Square test was employed.

Results and Conclusions

The results of this study seem to indicate that Chinese and American players and coaches give different meaning to Little League Baseball. Cross-culturally, this study found that both American players and coaches have a more positive attitude than Chinese players and coaches toward Little League Baseball as a social experience. Chinese players and coaches, however, have a more positive attitude than do their American counterparts toward Little League Baseball's contribution toward health and fitness, and toward Little League Baseball as a thrill involving some risk, a form of beauty in human movement, a release of tension, long and hard training, and the pursuit of victory. Chinese players and coaches, then, have a more positive attitude toward the sport on all dimensions except for playing as a social experience. The Americans view Little League Baseball as more positive only on this dimension.

According to the procedures for checking content validity and the results of the research, the Chinese players and coaches apparently understood the questionnaires very well. Kenyon's conceptual model for characterizing physical activity with a semantic differential scale is based on the culture of English-speaking countries, and physical activity in the Republic of China has been deeply influenced by western countries. Physical education in China was almost unknown until toward the end of the Ching Dynasty (1644 to 1911 AD), when new ideas about physical education were introduced to China from the west. After the establishment of the Republic (1912 AD), the Republic of China began to feel the need for a strong athletic program to insure a strong country. As a result, sports activities began to flourish.

Sport is a part of a culture. Different cultures view sport from different perspectives; thus, the culture affects the sport, and, often, the sport reflects cultural traits. The results of this research seem to indicate that both American and Chinese cultures have affected the players' and coaches' attitudes toward Little League Baseball.

Traditionally, the Chinese have emphasized the group. That is, they have socialized people to sacrifice for the group and have emphasized discipline and patience. These characteristics have been carried over into sports in Taiwan, Republic of China. In order to meet the physical education objective of the government, sports in the Republic of China have tended to guide the child toward learning basic skills and thus toward developing athletic abilities and cultivating such virtues as fairness, obedience, responsibility, honesty, friendliness, cooperativeness, courage, and decisiveness as firm bases for their later participation in community life.

In contrast, the United States, although a competitive society, seems to place more emphasis in elementary school sports on developing the child's self-realization and individual excellence. These characteristics can be seen in American Little League Baseball, which emphasizes individual interests and benefits. According to the results of the research, Little

League Baseball seems to reflect the cultural traits of the two countries (the United States and the Republic of China) very precisely.

References

Alderman, R.B. (1970). A sociopsychological assessment of attitude toward physical activity in champion athletes. *Research Quarterly, 41*(1), 1-9.

Heath, E.H. (1963). *A semantic differential study of attitudes relating to recreation as applied to a bicultural setting.* Unpublished doctoral dissertation, University of Wisconsin, Madison.

Kenyon, G.S. (1968a). A conceptual model for characterizing physical activity. *Research Quarterly, 39*(1), 96-104.

Kenyon, G.S. (1968b). Six scales for assessing attitude toward physical activity. *Research Quarterly, 39*(3), 566-573.

Kenyon, G.S. (1970). Attitudes toward sport and physical activity among adolescents from four English-speaking countries. In G. Luschen (Ed.), *The cross-cultural analysis of sport and games* (pp. 138-154). Champaign, IL: University of Illinois Press.

Simon, J. (1973). *Assessing children's attitudes toward physical activity: Development of an instrument.* Unpublished master's thesis, University of Washington, Seattle, WA.

Delivery and Receipt: Judo Instruction in Cross-Cultural Context

Mark W. Clark
University of Montana

There seem to be several major recurring questions that face the field of comparative physical activity and sport. One of them—Is the participation in and meaning of activity and sport culturally specific, or does it transcend culture and have some inherent meaning of its own?—forms the basis of this particular study.

Socialization processes tend to normalize behaviors and attitudes, which in turn lead to greater social orderliness within the given culture. In Japan, there is a stated priority on the cultural norms of obedience and group-directed behavior. In the United States, there is a stated priority on the cultural norms of independence and individualistic-directed behavior. Given this difference of cultural norm, this study used interviews and participant observation in a heuristic attempt to:

- determine whether "Judo" is perceived as the same activity for both American and Japanese participants
- determine whether American teaching of sport skills differed from the Japanese teaching perspective
- determine whether American students found difficulty assimilating sport skill instruction from the Japanese perspective (assumes a difference between U.S. and Japanese teaching modes)

Observable behaviors and ritual during Judo instruction and practice were investigated and analyzed to ascertain the participants' understanding of where and how they fit into the cultural context of Judo. Additionally, "bull sessions" with participants immediately before and after each session were used as a means to gain insight and meaning in regard to the observed behavior.

Background

Judo, as a participatory event, was developed in Japan by J. Kano around the year 1880 (Draeger & Smith, 1969). Kano's stated principles for participating were to develop cooperative learning, "Jita Kyoei," to develop a totally inclusive discipline based on integrated education and efficient energy usage, "Seiryoku Zenyo," and to promote Olympic Internationalism (Smith, 1958).

Contemporary Japanese judo seems to have taken a three-pronged attack to advance these principles. First, Japanese Judoka espouse judo as an intrinsically oriented way of living life and viewing the world. They view their participation as a way to gain self- and sensory awareness, as a means of creative expression, and as a way to guide and understand human interaction. These orientations toward life, when combined with traditional Japanese values, are viewed as helping form the inclusive discipline of judo. Second, participation is acknowledged as a way to instruct and reinforce ways of self-defense, familial type human relationships, rank-order hierarchies, courtesy, and respect to others. Additionally, it seems to reinforce the Japanese neofeudalistic, rank-order hierarchy in terms of associations and rituals. These values and orientations to life and society seem consistent with traditionally expressed Japanese values (see selected readings on Japanese culture and values). Lastly, to promote Olympic Internationalism, judo participation is viewed as competitive sport.

The first two orientations are stressed in Japan (Clark & Clark, 1980). Judo, as a way of life, is based on traditional Japanese values of "Bushido." Competition is not the end goal, but merely a way to gain insight into the living of a more perfect life. As one Japanese Judoka explained to me, "The ultimate in judo is death." I do not totally understand this statement, but interpret it to mean that when all is learned, the job of learning, feeling, and living is finished, and only the unknowns of death await.

In the United States, we seem to focus on the third aspect of judo, that of competitive sport. Western life seems compartmentalized rather than holistic, and with the American bent toward competition, it is interpreted that judo participation will reflect this trait. With these suspected differences in mind, the remainder of this article will be a presentation, analysis, and discussion of the observed and recorded behaviors. The collected data has been divided into five categories—bowing, language and counting, status and rank ordering, male/female interaction, and student/teacher interaction.

Bowing

Bowing is a formalized part of Japanese life. Bowing took many forms when the teacher and various participants interacted in situations both verbal and physical. Bowing helped set the hierarchy standards (bow-in and bow-out ceremonies from each session). Bowing together in time and place also seemed to acknowledge the idea of group unity often mentioned in the literature about Japanese behavior. Judo beginners were appraised of the "meaning" of bowing, and class time was spent telling us why it should be done correctly.

> You should always bow to your partner before and after you work with them, whether it is for a drill, mat work, or a match. Be sure to put some feeling into it. You are showing them respect, so show it.

The stress the teacher put on proper bowing is seen as an effort to transfer the Japanese cultural norm through judo participation. When the teacher was present, this norm was acknowledged by all class members. When the teacher was absent, there was an apparent lack of bowing from all the participants, regardless of longevity or rank status. This pattern would seem to indicate that this Japanese behavioral norm was not totally transferred to the American students of judo.

The socialization of beginners to this value on respect and group unity (through bowing) was done through role modeling of the teacher and advanced judo participants. The demand that beginners bow also reinforced this process of learning; for example, a more advanced participant followed a beginner across the mat and faced him until he bowed, as he had forgotten to do when they finished practicing together. The formal lesson at the end of a class on the importance of bowing was interpreted as a formal structured educational attempt to reinforce this value and its practice. This was in contrast to most instruction, which was more informal and role-model related. It is interesting however, that this formal lesson in bowing did not take place until the third week. Before that time, I feel the teacher wanted to rely on a more informal approach. It could also be that he did not feel the beginners serious enough or "worthy" of this knowledge until this later period. The teacher may have been saving this lecture for those of us who were more likely to "stick with" the participation. Beginning participants were never directly taught the mechanics of bowing, but only taught about its meaning. Observation of the more advanced members was the way beginners were to learn the mechanical technique.

An interesting example of break in ritual was also expressed in the bowing. During a drill designed to exhaust the participants and create endurance/skill, the advanced people were told not to bow to their partners.

> During this exercise, I don't want you to bow between each partner. We will switch partners on command. The important thing is to get going with the next partner without taking a rest. Bowing would be time for resting. The workout in this instance is more important.

This statement assumes that the advanced people were socialized to the ritual behavior of bowing and would have bowed unless told not to do so. This break in ritual is seen as a conscious intent to move toward the competitive aspect of judo (or more reflective of the American orientation). It would be interesting and useful to know if this also happens in Japan.

Language and Counting

Language usage and comprehension is important in understanding a cultural value. Thus, it would seem vital that some Japanese language was used and expected in our participation. A degree of cultural transmission of value was achieved through the ritualistic use of language and counting.

Counting, initially in English, but later in Japanese, was expected of all participants. The teacher expected the Japanese-Americans to be able to count in Japanese from the beginning (this higher expectation for this group was interesting in that several of them could not do it). No formal lessons were held on how to count. Class members learned informally from listening to others.

Japanese language was again evident during the teaching of "holds" and "counterholds." The teacher always used the Japanese word for these situations. After several sessions, he expected that all participants remember the Japanese word. Again, no formal lessons were held about language, but we were expected to pick up the terms (informally it seems, through the instruction and practice). It was never stated that we had to memorize these Japanese terms, it was just expected. This condition of learning seems similar to ballet, where French becomes a medium for learning the expected movements.

Advanced judo participants used more Japanese words and phrases than the beginners during the judo participation. My interviews and talks with Americans, who were advanced performers or teachers in judo, also had heavy reference to Japanese language and Japanese cultural values.

Status and Rank Ordering

The rank order process, and its identification by belt color, was a clear indicator of the Japanese value toward a stated and standardized hierarchical system. Upon seeing the belt, there was an immediate expectation of status, experience, and "things" in common to talk about. Little interaction took place between people of different ranks. This would seem to contrast to the American "experience." One clear example of this lack of interaction was demonstrated as follows. A woman with a beginner's white belt repeatedly asked questions of other male white-belted participants about a promotion tournament when other women who were present, but were wearing the more advanced brown belts, could have better answered her questions. The questions were heard all over the practice area, but neither the first woman or the other two women broke the belt boundary to interact with each other. In most cases, an affinity by sex should hold stronger in this type of situation (this is also true in Japan).

However, in this instance, one's ability (and the "visibility of rank") may have over-ridden sexual differences (she questioned the men, who were considered more "equal"). The three women in this situation had participated in judo for several years. Their behavior might tentatively be interpreted as socialization to a "foreign" status system. It would be interesting to see how these same people might act in a similar situation outside of the judo setting, or, if this same behavior would be observed in the Japanese setting.

The "bow-in" and "bow-out" ceremonies at each session also seemed directed toward a specifically defined status and rank-ordering system. We all acquiesced to the teacher's desires and dictates on positioning and lined up by peer rank (higher ranks to the teacher's right). The most advanced person present called the commands. There was full agreement as to who was the highest ranking person, since belt color was a major means of visual stratification. Beyond this overt identity, the brown and black belts seemed to intuitively know who was senior.

Often, exercises and drills tended to denote rank. The exercises introduced to and done by white belted beginners were often different from those performed by more advanced white, brown, and black belts. Some of these exercises and drills related to skill ability, but some (such as "warm up exercises") had little to do with skill level. In such differential cases, the creation and reinforcement of rank differences are interpreted as the primary objective.

Male and Female Interactions

During practices, the men would often hesitate or subtly refuse to work with the women (i.e., quickly choose a male partner). This behavior was observed for both the Asian and caucasian men in the class but, especially so for the Asians. Men and women wore different types of belts for the same rank levels, after the initial white belt rank. Reading and interviews indicated that females tended to participate and perform more in "Kata," almost a dance-like exhibition, than in the freestyle grappling contests. This is interpreted as a function of social "channeling" by sex role.

On several occasions, the teacher was concerned with whether a man had hurt a woman during a "rough" practice. There was no occurrence of similar concern when two men went at it very strenuously, and someone might have been hurt. This behavior may indicate some difference of performance expectation by sex role.

Student and Teacher Interaction

Throughout much of this paper I have presented material on student and teacher interaction. What will be focused on here is teaching style in relationship to this interaction.

Judo is an activity that consists of many types of movement. Holds, counterholds, strikes, blows, retreats, jumps, and "flows" of motion are often combined in some manner. The teaching of these types of movement forms the basis of much judo instruction. Aside from these "physical" aspects of performance, there is a "mental" sense that is also taught as vital to performance.

Holds and so forth were quickly demonstrated, and then we were asked to practice them. Often we were told not to worry so much about the mechanics of the hold; "think about the flow," we were told. This tends to differ from sport skill instruction in the United States where technique is highly stressed at the beginning stages. Little individualized interaction or specific instruction took place between teacher and student. Basically, we observed the demonstration as a group and were then left in pairs to practice, experiment, and find (or "feel") the moves ourselves. There was however, some concession to the individual in these practice periods. Occasionally, a "nice throw" or similar comment was heard from the teacher across the room. Many of the beginners expected and desired more formal and specific "teaching" in the presented techniques from the teacher.

Discussion and Conclusions

From the data collected, it does seem reasonable to state that some degree of Japanese values were cross-culturally transmitted through judo participation. How strongly they might have been transferred and accepted was not ascertained in this study. Concepts of Zen and Bushido are at the core of values in both Japanese society and judo participation. The rank-ordering structure, style of teaching, and ritualization of certain practices were seen as the vehicles of cultural transmission. The use of Japanese language, the explanation of the "essence" of behavior (i.e., bowing, movements), and the constant and consistent referral to "respect" and "obligation" were seen as ways to socialize participants toward accepting judo (and thus Japanese) values. The interpretation here is that the hope was to get the participants to "think" Japanese, and this would make them better able to perform a Japanese activity. The longer a person participated (and gained friends who participated or used the participation as a point of life focus), the more that participant seemed socialized to the "new" set of values. The insistence that people not bow in the advanced drill spoke to this "fact" of some degree of socialization. Constant use of Japanese language and referral to "things" Japanese by advanced performers also point in the direction of some degree of successful socialization. Conversely, the observation that class members did not bow when the teacher was absent might indicate that socialization was not all that successful. Many of the beginners expected more individualized, specific, formalized, and in-depth technique instruction from the teacher. This lack of acceptance of teaching style may have hurt early socialization in the activity of judo.

I felt that the Americans (both Asians and caucasians) viewed judo as competitive sport rather than as a way of living life in the same sense that the Japanese do. This perception seems to agree with previous literature in this area (Jacobs, 1970; Lomen, 1974; Pyecha, 1970). Participants showed a desire to "get to it," without wanting the long hours of learning the "correct feeling" of the movements. Respect and obligation shown overtly while practicing (bowing to the teacher and to fellow participants) were not observed in the before and after class "bull sessions." Beginning participants often spoke condescendingly about both the teacher's and the more advanced participants' manners, personalities, and skill levels in these outside talks.

This study was limited primarily to the beginner stages of participation in this sport. More exposure to advanced American Judoka could possibly yield different results. The study consisted of approximately 100 hours of observation done over a 4-month period.

Like many other exploratory studies, this one seemed to raise more questions than it answered. Obviously, more study is needed before definitive conclusions can be made, and there are several possible areas that future studies might pursue. People with some judo experience or background could be utilized to set up categories and take counts (as known or participant observers) about certain defined ritualized behaviors. For instance, How do participants bow (i.e., do inferiors bow deeper than superiors)? When do participants bow, or not bow? Does bowing style change with regard to rank? To sex? What usage of Japanese language exists during participation, and is this affected by rank or sex? Does the nationality of the teacher effect teaching style (i.e., one caucasian brown belt stressed how to do specific techniques, while the Asian teacher and an Asian brown belt stressed rhythm and body flow)?

It has been reported elsewhere (Altmann, 1971; Korsgaard, 1973; Lomen, 1974; Pyecha, 1971; Speakman, 1958) that few judo instructors have formal physical education backgrounds or advanced educational degrees. Without this background, they must still teach judo in physical education programs within organized schooling. Does this mean that there might be a difference in what is taught, and what methods are used, between the private "dojo" and the formal physical education setting? Both settings could be observed to determine what might be important factors in regard to learning and socialization.

Questionnaires and field methods could be used to investigate whether advanced attitudes differ from beginner attitudes in regard to the transmission of the various cultural values presented here. Questionnaires and/or interviews might be used to determine whether advanced participants were socialized to a specific set of values, or whether they already had these values and merely gravitated to judo because of a similarity in value orientation.

Further background study into the "innards" of judo and its social structure could be undertaken. Does the rank-order system for men and women truly differ in content, and if so, how? What kinds of ethnic and social class backgrounds do participants have? Does this change with the level of participation? How might judo participation fulfill other Japanese values (i.e., "amae"—obligated sponsorship; "onjoshugi"—parental obligation; "chugi"—loyalty; "mintai"—reserve), and how might these values relate to Americans' participating?

On an even larger scale, it would be interesting and useful to see what form judo participation takes in Europe and South America as compared to Japan and the United States. Similarly, how do judo participants compare and contrast in attitude and behavior with other martial arts participants?

Through the procedures of expanded study, professionals interested in whether physical activity and sport are "culturally specific" or "inherent in their own right" might truly investigate on a comparative and international scale.

Notes

1. The perspectives toward contemporary judo participation reported here are a synthesis from four interviews with advanced "Judoka," previously reported in Clark and Clark, 1980.
2. Bushido is the nonwritten code of ethical, philosophical, and military standards that formed the feudal Japanese samurai "way of the warrior." Passed on from leader to follower, it formed the strict definitions of "right" and "wrong" ways of conducting one's life.

References

Altmann, P.N. (1971). Martial arts in physical education: Fulfilling physical education objectives. *Journal of Physical Education, Recreation and Dance*, **42**(3), 32-35.

Boycheff, K. (1974). Judo as an intramural sport. *National Collegiate Judo Handbook*.

Bula, M.R. (1971). Judo for young people. *Journal of Physical Education, Recreation and Dance*, **42**(3), 38-39.

Clark, M.W., & Clark, R. (1980). *Cross-cultural analysis of ritual: A look at judo participation in Japan and the United States*. Unpublished paper presented at the Eastern District Association of AAHPERD, Lancaster, PA.

Draeger, D.F., & Smith, R.W. (1969). *Asian fighting arts*. Palo Alto, CA: Kodansha International.

Jacobs, G. (Ed.). (1970). Urban samurai: The karate dojo. *The participant observer*. New York: Braziller.

Kano, J. (1958). Judo: The Japanese art of self-defense. In R.W. Smith (Ed.), *A complete guide to judo*. Tokyo: C. Tuttle.

Korsgaard, R. (1973). A martial art: Individual offense. *The Physical Educator*, **30**(1), 3-5.

Lomen, L.D. (1974). Promoting the martial arts. *Scholastic Coach*, **43**(8), 73.

Min, K.H. (1967). Correlations among factors in judo contest performance. *Perceptual and Motor Skills*, **24**, 1243-1248.

Min, K.H. (1971). Martial arts in physical education: Organization at the
college level. *Journal of Physical Education, Recreation and Dance*, **42**(3),
36-37.

Norwood, W.D. (1973). *The judoka*. New York: Knopf.

Paul, W.W. (1974). *The social significance of Asian martial arts*. Unpublished
master's thesis, San Francisco State University, San Francisco, CA.

Pyecha, J. (1970). Comparative effects of judo and selected physical education activities on male university freshmen personality traits. *Research
Quarterly for Exercise and Sport*, **41**, 425-431.

Pyecha, J. (1971). Judo: A brief historical sketch. *Journal of Physical Education, Recreation and Dance*, **42**(3), 26-31.

Smith, R.W. (1958). *A complete guide to judo*. Tokyo: Tuttle.

Speakman, D.E. (1958). *A status study of the sport of judo in American
colleges and universities*. Unpublished master's thesis, Ohio State University, Columbus.

A Model for International Education Comparison: Middle East Perspective

Earleen Helgelieo Hanafy
St. Cloud State University

March L. Krotee
University of Minnesota

The field of comparative education seems to have no universal method or approach to describe, analyze, and explain. There are numerous methods and approaches by which each researcher puts forth his or her own model to meet the needs of each particular study.

The researcher's most critical consideration is to select a model that is appropriate for the task at hand. The model in Figure 1 is being used for this study.

The model spells out the system variables employed in this study. The remainder of the study is devoted to the model and its application. We hope it will provide information and stimulate others to follow up.

We strive to achieve normative standards. The test of any academic model is the acceptability of the model under different environments. We will always face adjusting and adapting our model to different areas of study.

A healthy nation is a productive one, and physical education is one of the variables that contributes to a healthy nation. Scientific planning, budgeting, and selection of the proper human resources reflect the needed input. Organization, ideology, management, know-how, and supporting environment ensure achievement of the desired output. Output is the fruit that a nation can enjoy from a system that is well designed, organized, controlled, and evaluated with the right incentive measured.

System Input

Geography

Kuwait is the gateway to the Arab Peninsula. The country is bounded on the east by the Arabian Gulf, on the southwest by the Kingdom of Saudi Arabia, and on the north and west by the Republic of Iraq.

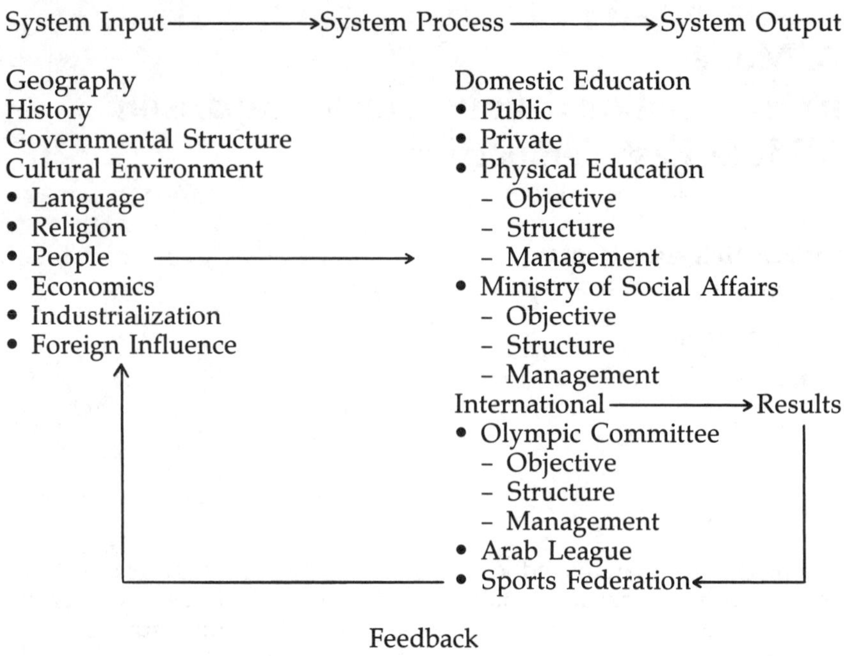

System Input ————————→ System Process ————————→ System Output

Geography
History
Governmental Structure
Cultural Environment
• Language
• Religion
• People ————————————→
• Economics
• Industrialization
• Foreign Influence

Domestic Education
• Public
• Private
• Physical Education
  – Objective
  – Structure
  – Management
• Ministry of Social Affairs
  – Objective
  – Structure
  – Management
International ————————→ Results
• Olympic Committee
  – Objective
  – Structure
  – Management
• Arab League
• Sports Federation ←——————

Feedback

Figure 1 Comparative physical education distribution.

The total area of the State of Kuwait is approximately 6,177 square miles, including 120 miles of gulf coastline. The population of Kuwait in 1980 was 1.34 million.

The principal geographic feature is the large bay. Kuwait consists of flat, rolling desert and mud flats. Some ridges rise from 150 to 900 feet above sea level. Kuwait is dry, hot, and typical of desert land lacking rivers and streams. Its climate is characterized by extreme temperatures and little rainfall.

Kuwait is a modern, dynamic, industrialized state with a high standard of civilized, democratic living. Modern Kuwait is, of course, identified with oil and possesses an estimated one fifth of the world's oil reserves.

History

The history of Kuwait may be traced back beyond the Christian era. It was part of the world powers of Assyria, Babylonia, Persia, the empire of Alexander the Great, and the Ottoman Empire.

Kuwait was a strategic point for the different Arabian powers. Until the 1950s when the country began exporting oil on a large scale, the Kuwaiti people depended for their livelihood on the sea. They built ships for fishing, pearl diving, and trading. Kuwaitis sailed their ships along the coast as far as Africa and Asia, thus forming a link in world trade between Europe and the Far East.

Oil drilling began in 1938 during the administration of Sheikh Ahmed al-Jaber 'al-Sabab (1921-1950). After Sheikh Ahmed's death, Sheikh Abdullah al-Salem al-Sabah became the new emir. Under his leadership, Kuwait was transformed into a modern developed state. He used the oil revenue to serve the country and the people and gave the nation the political importance it has in the world today.

Governmental Structure

Since its beginning, Kuwait has always been a self-governing state. It has always been ruled by its people—notwithstanding the protection treaty with Great Britain, which was in effect from 1898 until its termination in June 1961. After the termination of the treaty, Kuwait chose a democratic, parliamentary form of government that is retained to this day.

The Constitution of the State of Kuwait was promulgated in 1962 and declares that

- Kuwait is an independent, sovereign Arab state, and the Kuwaiti people are an integral part of the Arab nation;
- the state guarantees equal opportunities to all citizens;
- ownership, capital, and work form the basic elements of social structures of the state, as well as the national wealth;
- freedom of the individual is guaranteed;
- freedom of faith is absolute;
- freedom of the press, printing, and publishing is guaranteed; and
- freedom to form societies and trade unions naturally and peacefully is guaranteed (from *A View of Kuwait*, 1976, p. 5).

The constitution also clearly divides the government into executive, legislative, and judicial branches.

Islamic law, Sharia, is the foundation of the judicial system and is implemented directly in cases of personal status. In all other cases, public law as enacted by the state remains supreme.

Cultural Environment

A comparative study of any country must examine its cultural environment. Comparative analysis depends on these variables, and the roots of most human activity are couched within its culture and that of its immediate environment.

Language. Arabic is the official language of Kuwait. Arabic has an alphabet of 29 letters and is read from right to left. English is the second basic language taught in the public schools.

Religion. The Ministry of Religious Affairs controls religious funds and their use. The overwhelming majority of Kuwaiti citizens are Moslems. There are also non-Moslem groups, but the majority of the population is Moslem. The Constitution of Kuwait guarantees full religious freedom. At present, there are two Protestant, two Roman Catholic, and one Orthodox Church in Kuwait.

The Koran is the holy book of Islam. It explains how its followers should pray and conduct business, how marriage should be conducted, and how wars should be waged. The Koran describes the entire organization of life. Knowledge of the Koran is necessary to gain any perspective on Middle Eastern culture and society.

People. After the war between the Persians and Turks in 1776, Kuwait became a major stop on the East-West trade route. The population of Kuwait has gradually increased over the years, with today's population estimated at more than 1.34 million.

Many foreigners in the international labor force are attracted to Kuwait by the high salaries offered by the government, oil companies, and world of business. Jordanians and Palestinians constitute the largest group of foreign laborers, while others from Lebanon, Egypt, Syria, Yemen, Oman, Iran, India, Pakistan, Europe, and the United States create a truly international mix.

Economics. The economic planning of Kuwait is determined by various priorities and projects. The nation has guidelines for its economic development. The following five guidelines influence the government's economic planning:

> As in other countries, economic planning in Kuwait emphasizes the steps that must be taken if the per capita income level is to rise constantly. The second overall objective is to ensure a more suitable distribution of income in order to achieve a reasonable degree of social justice and to secure a continuously dynamic economy. The third goal is to gain a greater degree of diversification in the sources of the national income of Kuwait, increasing the relative contribution of the non-oil sector of the economy. Fourthly, Kuwaiti citizens must be educated in order to create specialized human skills in science and technology that will be able to round out the development boundaries of the Kuwaiti economy. The last objective is to coordinate the needs of economic development within Kuwait and the Arab countries in particular and other developing nations in general. (*A View of Kuwait,* 1976, p. 22)

The per capita income of Kuwait in 1980 was $18,338. The country's economy is now at par with many of the highly developed countries of the world.

In view of the increasing international demand for oil and petroleum products, Kuwait's future looks bright. The projected economic growth will apparently continue to break its own record. The only factors that might impede the country's progress are renewed warfare in the Middle East and, of course, a lower demand for oil.

Industrialization. Specifically designed domestic industries provide the population with many jobs. The industries include a fertilizer company, a flour company, and the Kuwait National Industries Company. The government has a 40% share in a piping factory, a 75% share in an asbestos factory, and a 30% share in a cement works. Kuwait has a bank on almost every corner, as well as large insurance companies.

Kuwait still exports goods that it has traded for centuries, including fish, Eastern carpets, goat and sheep skins, and ships. Large shrimp are also exported to the United States and Europe. The country has a fleet of old sailing ships, traveler fleets, and its own fleet of supertankers.

The Kuwait Airways Corporation (KAC), founded in 1965, flies its Boeing jets to European, African, and Asian cities. KAC has grown so rapidly that personnel are now being trained in Kuwait, and staffing of the new airport will soon be completed. Through planned industrialization the Kuwaiti people are being rapidly trained to the ways of development.

Foreign influence. The modern state of Kuwait emerged in the later part of the 19th century. The emergence of Kuwait was strongly influenced by the British interest in the Persian Gulf and Kuwait in particular. The British interest was the result of increased Russian, German, and French influence in the Persian Gulf area.

Kuwait's legal status prior to 1896 was confusing. British protection of Kuwait began in 1896, and Kuwait has received British naval protection in the Gulf since 1899. In 1914 Kuwait signed the British Declaration of Protection and was recognized as an independent government under British protection. This was the turning point in the legal status of Kuwait.

On June 19, 1961, the Treaty of Independence was enacted. Kuwait assumed full control of its own governmental processes and equal partnership in the community of nations.

Kuwait is a member of the League of Arab States, United Nations, and 21 other international organizations. Kuwait carefully guards her independence and sovereignty but also supports cultural and social movements aimed at achieving Arab unity and world peace.

System Process

Domestic Education

Public education. Before 1912 when Kuwait's first school was opened, the country had the type of education that was common throughout the Middle East at that time. Children visited the home of their teacher, who converted one room into a classroom. The master wrote his own textbooks, and the subjects taught were mainly the Holy Koran, arithmetic, and writing. The curriculum was broadened in the 1930s, and history, geography, and drawing were introduced. This remained the only educational delivery system for over 25 years.

In 1936, Kuwait established a Board of Education, and the government began to levy a special tax for the needed expansion of education. Girls attended school for the first time in 1937. In 1941 there were 41 schools.

In 1955, two leading Arab educators were invited to study the educational system and make recommendations for its reorganization. "The two experts proposed that there should be three stages in a child's education: primary (or elementary), intermediate, and secondary. Each stage would last for four years so that a primary school pupil starting at about the age of six left school at 18" (Ministry of Education, 1977, p. 7). Their suggestions were accepted and today form the basis for the public school system.

Kuwait began to expand its educational system on a massive scale. The Department of Education became the Ministry of Education in 1962. Budget expenditures for education have increased from year to year. Today the total expenditure on public education is about 24 percent of total government expenditures. The government provides free education from kindergarten through the university level.

Kuwait's education system was started from scratch, and few nations have achieved what Kuwait has achieved in education in less than 70 years.

Private education.   Private education has also grown rapidly in recent years. The expansion of private education has occurred in response to the needs of the large and varied expatriate community. During the academic year 1975-1976, the total number of private school students reached 46,382, compared with 37,750 in 1973-1974. The Ministry of Education supervises the private schools, most of which, unlike the public schools, are coeducational.

Physical education.   In conformity with the government's policy of popularizing and supporting sports in the life and conduct of its citizens, the concerned educational authorities introduced physical education into the schools. Physical education has been incorporated in the curriculum and regular timetable of all levels of formal education. Physical education was added to satisfy the psychosocial and physical needs of the youth and to promote a healthy and productive life-style.

Objectives.   *Mental activities* are one dimension of physical education. Mental activities teach students to discover new ideas, think conceptually, solve problems, and understand the individual environment in order to strengthen their capacity for innovation and creativity. *Spiritual activities* add to the individual's spirit, comfort, and happiness and allow the person to relieve tension and maximize development in order to participate fully in society. *Physical activities* directly affect the physical structure of the body as well as the nervous, circulatory, and respiratory systems. De-

Boys

Primary
- Group activities: basketball and soccer for youth.
- Individual activities: gymnastics, table tennis, and conditioning.

Intermediate
- Group activities: soccer, basketball, volleyball, and team handball.
- Individual activities: conditioning, gymnastics, and table tennis.

Secondary
- Group activities: soccer, basketball, volleyball, and team handball.
- Individual activities: conditioning, gymnastics, table tennis, and squash.

Girls

Primary
- Group activities: basketball for youth.
- Individual activities: conditioning, gymnastics.
- Contemporary training.

Intermediate
- Group activities: basketball, volleyball, and team handball.
- Individual activities: conditioning, gymnastics, and table tennis.
- Contemporary training.

Secondary
- Group activities: basketball, volleyball, and team handball.
- Individual activities: conditioning, gymnastics, and table tennis.

Figure 2 The structure of physical education in domestic education.

veloping physical fitness creates healthy individuals who can rationally take care of their responsibilities, understand the value of their society, and develop and update those values to modern times (Mater, 1979).

Structure.   The structure of physical education in domestic education is illustrated in Figure 2.

Management.   The Undersecretary of State for Social and Physical Education makes the decisions related to the entire educational process and its relationship to physical education. He also provides direction to the Department of Physical Education according to basic policies.

In the Physical Education Department, a general manager makes the technological and administrative decisions. The general manager also offers direction to staff working in the department and works as a liaison to all other departments and external groups.

The technical director is responsible for the physical education program for boys and coordinates physical education in the schools. He directs, assists, and evaluates the physical education teachers. Under him are general directors who oversee the physical education program and its direction. The first general directors are responsible for physical education in their own areas of elementary, intermediate, or secondary education. They provide recommendations to the general director for improvement and updating the general program. The physical education program for girls is similarly structured.

All school buildings in Kuwait are modern and impressive. Many schools have their own mosques, cinema theaters, libraries, dormitories, gymnasiums, clinics, classrooms, laboratories, sports stadiums, and swimming pools. Educational and physical education facilities for the most part are excellent and provide an environment conducive to learning.

University level.   The office of the Dean of Students at Kuwait University seeks to integrate formal academic opportunities with personal experiences that will positively influence the total behavior of the student. The University provides students with a healthy atmosphere and extracurricular activities that are conducive to personality development and self-realization.

Objectives.   As outlined in the Youth Guidance Administration's *General Plan for Activities Academic Year 1978-1979* (p. 6), Kuwait University's objectives for physical education include the following:

- Concentrated preparation for sports groups to participate in international university competitions scheduled throughout the years.
- Continued development of physical education in different facilities in order to provide students with a well-rounded physical activity program.
- Organization of and preparation for different tournaments and championship matches with outside organizations.
- Participation in physical education activities with selected groups within the University and with other universities.
- Free or elective activities.

Structure.   The University's physical education program utilizes the following structure outlined in the 1978 *General Plan* (p. 10):

Sport Supervision	Permanent Instructor	Part-Time Instructor
Faculty of Science	Soccer	Judo
Faculty of Education	Basketball	Table Tennis

(Cont.)

Sport Supervision	Permanent Instructor	Part-Time Instructor
Faculty of Commerce	Volleyball	Fencing
Faculty of Law	Handball	
Faculty of Engineering	Tennis	
Faculty of Girls College	Squash	
Faculty of Medicine	Swimming	
	Athletics	

Management. The office of the Dean of Students serves as a link between the University's structure and the students' needs. All activities in the physical education programs are the responsibility of the Youth Affairs Department. Activities are supervised for the most part by instructors with University training.

Ministry of Social Affairs and Labor. Many recreational facilities exist in Kuwait. Soccer is the most popular game. Sport stadiums, tennis courts, boat clubs, swimming pools, and facilities for other sports such as basketball, team handball, volleyball, bowling, karate, judo, and table tennis provide Kuwait with a variety of activities for both sport spectators and participants. In addition, public gardens, cinemas, and theaters as well as approximately 30 organizations provide various cultural and recreational outlets for the population.

Objectives. The following objectives for the Ministry of Social Affairs are described in the 1977 *Annual Report* (pp. 4-5). In the Youth and Children's Department:

- Supervising youth centers, children's gardens, camps, scout programs, and youth hostels.
- Planning programs and projects that help achieve the objectives of the State and that benefit the physical, psychosocial, and emotional development of Kuwaiti youth.

In the Private Sector Department:

- Cooperating with sport institutions and associations in the public interest and providing assistance to achieve their objectives.
- Following the activities and needs of these institutions and working to achieve their aims and objectives.
- Studying problems that face these institutions and providing recommendations to solve problems.
- Preparing periodic reports for the activities of the institutions, along with the necessary maintenance and facility requests.

In the Research and Guidance Department:

- Preparing research relating to the private sector as well as the youth and children's sector.
- Preparing plans and developing projects for these sectors.
- Preparing monthly and annual reports, booklets, and publications concerning studies related to these sectors.
- Preparing statistics and data for these sectors.
- Preparing balance sheets, accounts, final reports, and budget follow-up analyses for these sectors.
- Studying basic organization and management techniques related to sports organizations and new public interest organizations.
- Studying adjustments and changes suggested for sport organizations before submitting recommendations to the Ministry.
- Attending General Assemblies for legal guidance.
- Preparing sport leaders in all areas, including research studies, in connection with physical education and sport.

Structure. The following structure of the Ministry of Social Affairs is described in its 1977 *Annual Report* (p. 3):

Private Sector Department	Research and Guidance Department	Youth and Children Department
Public Interest	Financial and Legal Guidance	Scouting, Camping, and Youth Hostels
Maintenance of Institution	Legal Guidance	Youth Centers and Gardens
Sport Associations and Clubs	Preparing Sports Leaders	
	Research and Statistics	

Management. The Ministry of Social Affairs and Labor of the Kuwaiti government has the task of managing the Youth Sports Activities. All activities are supervised by specialists. A Leadership Center for training, officiating, coaching, and sports medicine was established in 1966 and offers courses to raise the standard of sport coaching, training, and officiating in Kuwait.

Kuwait National Olympic Committee, Arab League/Asian National Olympic Committees, and International Sports Federations

In the 1950s, organized sports were virtually nonexistent in Kuwait. In 1950-1951, however, several sports clubs opened, and the Sports Federation was formed. In 1957 the Kuwait Olympic Commission was formed and met for the first time in 1958. Kuwait also belongs to the Arab League and has gradually earned a place in many international competitions, mostly in the Middle East and Asia. Kuwait has also played a leading role in the establishment of the Asian National Olympic Committees and is being considered as the host country in that regard.

Objectives. Al-Hajji (1978) indicates that these Olympic and international organizations in Kuwait have the following objectives:

- Cooperating with sports clubs and other organizations within the limits of the organized sports activities; safeguarding sport games from evil and harmful factors.
- Promoting and developing organized sports games within Kuwait.
- Outlining and setting up the rules and regulations to be applied to the conduct of the games.
- Arranging local matches and competitions with international teams in Kuwait and abroad.
- Seeking affiliation with international sports federations and participation in international and regional sports tournaments.
- Organizing and strengthening sports relations between Kuwait and other countries, particularly Arab and Asian states (pp. 115-116).

Structure. Within Kuwait's collaboration in support of the Asian National Olympic Committees (ACNO) structure, of which Sheikh Fahed Al-Almad Al-Sabah of Kuwait is Vice President, the Kuwait National Olympic Committee has structured itself in a manner similar to the other Middle East representatives to the ACNO. The following are the federational structures of the Kuwaiti sporting community:

- Kuwait Basketball Association; member of the International Basketball Federation, Asian Association, and Arab Basketball Federation.
- Kuwait Football Federation; member of International Football Federation, Asian Association, and Arab Football Federation.
- Kuwait Amateur Athletic Federation; member of the International Amateur Athletic Federation (IAAF), Asian Amateur Athletic Association (AAAA), and Arab Amateur Athletic Federation (AAAF).
- Kuwait Volleyball Association; member of International Volleyball Association, Asian Association, and Arab Volleyball Federation.
- Kuwait Handball Federation; member of the International Handball Association, Asian Handball Federation, and Arab Handball Federation.
- Kuwait Gymnastics Association; member of the International Gymnastics Association and Asian Gymnastics Federation.
- Kuwait Swimming Association; member of International Swimming Association, Asian Swimming Association, and Arabian Gulf Swimming Federation.
- Kuwait Judo Federation; member of International Judo Federation and Arab Judo Federation.
- Kuwait Tennis Federation; member of International Tennis Association, Asian Tennis Association, and Arab Tennis Federation.

- Kuwait Fencing Association; member of International Fencing Association (Al-Hajji, 1978, pp. 113-114 and Kuwait Olympic Committee Constitution, 1982, pp. 21-38).

Management. The Ministry of Education furnishes the federations with financial support, but recently the Ministry of Social Affairs and Labor has assumed sponsorship and general responsibility for controlling and directing sport activities within Kuwait.

The cost of activities such as the organization and management of the Asian National Olympic Committee is being defrayed by the Kuwait National Olympic Committee, which submitted a plan for Kuwait to host the permanent headquarters. Essa Al-Dashti, Secretary General of the Kuwait Olympic Committee, has played a prominent administrative role under the leadership of Sheikh Fahed Al-Ahmad Al-Sabah. Most federations and sport in Kuwait are funded by the Ministry of Education, and most recently the Ministry of Social Affairs and Labor has assumed a leading role in controlling, directing, and sponsoring this domain.

It is clear to the authors, however, that the Kuwaiti government has made many combined and cooperative efforts in regard to physical education and sport and that the health and welfare components of sport and physical education are a high government priority. It is evident that Kuwait is taking a leadership role in regard to physical education and sport within Asia as well as the Middle East.

System Output—Results

Oil brought newfound riches to Kuwait and bestowed social benefits on the Kuwaiti people that are the envy of many today. Modern Kuwait is sprawling with office buildings, residential areas, industrial sites, and recreational facilities.

Kuwait is a modern state that compares very favorably with many western countries. It may even be ahead of some western nations in areas such as road building, social security, and, above all, per capita income. In visiting Kuwait, it is hard to believe that everything was built in the span of about 25 years.

Modern education has greatly improved the welfare of Kuwaiti youth, as well as other aspects of life. The youth are prepared to meet the challenges of modern life, and the development of body and mind has been emphasized. The last few years have witnessed a great expansion of various academic and physical education programs. However, the setting of goals to be attained at each level and the identification of activities suitable for various age levels are lacking. The physical education program is adequately staffed, trained, and provided with facilities, equipment, and a budget to obtain the best program possible. The Kuwaiti physical education system could have more detailed aims and objectives, however, and curriculum change for the primary and intermediate levels is needed. The present program is mainly a program of conditioning, team sports, and practicing for the National Day events.

Kuwait University does not have a Department of Physical Education, but it does have a Youth Affairs Department. The objectives of this program are to meet the needs and interests of the residential and day students. The program provides them an opportunity to join and participate in various activities and is much like recreational and extramural sports programs in United States universities. The Youth Affairs Department has several guest lectures each year and is keeping abreast of the latest research.

The aim of the government is to give the Kuwaiti and other sectors of the population a wealth of leisure facilities that will keep them at home in the hot summer months. The government is preparing several beaches, new sports arenas, greenbelt regions, sporting complexes, and amusement centers. The government is providing the leadership for the leisure pursuit of the youth and citizens of Kuwait.

Kuwait and other Middle East countries are trying to accomplish in a few years the kind of excellence in sport that took Europe and the United States many years to develop. They are beginning to realize that money cannot buy talent. They cannot buy a team; they must build it. They cannot gather a team together, practice for several weeks, and expect to win in international competition. Training is now being undertaken among the young children—wait for the "kids" of today because tomorrow they may be winning on the national teams. It takes a program that prepares youth at a young age in a wide range of activities to achieve this goal.

At the present time, the physical education in the schools, university, and recreation and sport programs lack coordination. In the Arab League, each country has its own structure and organization. The same structure and organization applies to the Olympic Committee. A new organizational structure will need to be developed at the top governmental levels in order to initiate the plans that ensure coordination between the different educational and recreational offices. These areas should include the police, army, university, Ministry of Education, Ministry of Social Affairs and Labor, and all other interested parties. Currently, there seems to be very little return from the funds that are being committed.

The Kuwait Olympic Committee is studying a proposed sports-control draft that deals with various sport aspects and definitions. With cooperation between physical education, sports and recreation programs, and the Olympic Committee, there could be great progress in the future of physical education and sport in Kuwait. Kuwait has climbed the ladder step-by-step, and we are sure that the Kuwaiti will accomplish their objectives.

Summary

The absence of a unified, analytical model makes it extremely difficult to study the Middle East and make a series of meaningful comparisons.

The authors perceive that using Kuwait as a developmental model for physical education and sport will help the reader to understand the place, role, and function of physical education and sport in a proper societal context. One needs only to follow the World Cup soccer development of Kuwait and Saudi Arabia to perceive that sport holds a valuable key to a measure of well-being and social development in this region of the world. The leaders of the Middle East, however, have not lost sight of their citizens, as evidenced by the club and recreational facilities that are being designed, built, and staffed to provide the people of the region with a physical and psychosocial foundation through physical education and sport. Again, one needs only to consider Saudi Arabia's Youth Welfare Five-Year Plan or Bahrain's Sport Institute development to see coordinated efforts to link the physical education and sporting processes of their respective countries together to improve the life-style of all citizens. These are encouraging efforts that deserve careful study by those of us interested in comparative studies to promote global understanding through physical education and sport. The Middle East picture seems bright. Tremendous strides need to be taken, but if the last decade is any indication, this region could well develop model programs to coordinate the health, physical education, recreation, and sport professions to contribute to the full realization and potential of humankind. A goal that has not been reached must be studied and certainly holds significance for those of us in the International Society of Comparative Physical Education and Sport.

References

Al-Hajji, A. (1978, January, February). *Sports features*, Nos. 75, 76. Kuwait: Kuwait Olympic Committee.

Mater, F. (1979). *Report: Physical education organization and structure in Kuwait*. Trans. of unpublished report, The Ministry of Education, Physical Education, Kuwait.

Ministry of Education. (1977, September). *Schooling . . . The comprehensive approach*. Kuwait: Author.

Ministry of Social Affairs and Labor. (1977). *Annual Report 1977 for Youth Children Administration, Private Sector Administration, Research Guidance Administration* (Trans.). Kuwait: Author.

A View of Kuwait. (1976). Washington, DC: Middle East Services.

Youth Guidance Administration. (1978). *General plan for activities academic year 1978-1979* (Trans.). Kuwait: Kuwait University Press.

North-South Dialogue: Sport, A Vital Ingredient

Janice A. Beran
Joao Piccoli
Frank Fang
Iowa State University

A commission chaired by Willi Brandt, former chancellor of the Federal Republic of Germany, was mandated to study the interrelationship of the world's peoples in terms of the dimensions of development, disarmament, hunger and food industrialization, and world trade. Their findings and recommendations are found in the book *North-South Dialogue: A Program for Survival.* We suggested that sport, too, is an essential ingredient in that dialogue, and in this panel presentation we dialogued regarding sport in Brazil, Taiwan, the Philippines, and Nigeria. The focus of the discussion was twofold, covering (a) the role of government in sport and (b) nongovernment agencies participating in sport.

The government of Brazil has an official position regarding the role of sport in Brazil, and the Brazilian public education system supports sport and physical education as part of that policy. Both the federal and state governments provide money for sport competition that is collected through the Sports Lottery. The Ministry of Education and Culture contains a Sports and Physical Education department that is in charge of sport instruction with a budget of approximately 3.7 U.S. dollars. The Sports and Physical Education department receives 35% of the 6.5% of Sports Lottery monies allocated to the Ministry of Education and Culture.

Taiwan, too, has compulsory education. From the primary school through the high school, college, and university levels, physical education and sports are part of a program that promotes health and the learning of sport techniques for later recreation purposes. Sports are very important in the total education system, and the government also gives some support to private schools. There is very little sport at the primary level. A few areas have primary school sports competitions, but they are only in volleyball, soccer, and baseball; the players on these teams are in the fifth and sixth grades. Taiwan has a highly integrated instructional physical education program at the elementary or primary school level. In the primary and junior high schools, students spend 2 hours per week in sport activities, and there are afterschool sports opportunities, in addition. Besides school sports, the government also supports or supervises individual sports associations.

In the Phillipines there is strong support from the government for a sports program. Both the private and public schools have competitions that culminate in a national sports competition. Because of the geography of the Phillipines, that means that a great deal of an athlete's time is involved in traveling from place to place. It is not unusual for athletes to lose a solid 4 to 5 weeks during the latter part of a school year. As one excellent softball player explained, ''It is really hard to finish the work and get good grades when you are an athlete. When we come to college we have to work to make up for lost time.'' This type of information doesn't appear on surveys completed from other countries. However, we feel it is essential to understand some of the barriers to total performance, both academic and athletic, that are present in countries of the southern hemisphere. Perhaps there are similarities in other parts of the world.

In Brazil, physical education is required of all students, and within it, they receive sports initiation in natural activities, games, stunts and tumbling, recreational gymnastics, rhythmical activities, and health and hygienic habits.

Sports participation in primary school is voluntary. Educators think that elementary children should learn, get the skills, and then compete. Physical education teachers may introduce an activity, for example, for the first time in the sixth grade. Students who show some ability are then asked if they want to join the school varsity team. If they accept, they talk to the coach, who is a physical education teacher from the school, and then participate in a tryout. If the coach accepts them on the varsity team, they are exempted from the physical education classes, but are required to attend all training sessions. Physical education is required of all secondary students, and sports that were introduced in primary schools are then taught on a more complex or advanced level. Students who want to participate on the school teams attend training after school, but such participation is voluntary.

The system in Nigeria is somewhat similar to the Phillipines. The private schools do not have elementary school children participating in interschool competition, but children in public schools compete in the upper grades.

In Brazil, the coaches must be physical education majors. Generally, a high school student, who is interested in becoming a coach, must pass the university entrance exam and enroll in the School of Physical Education as a physical education major. This person may coach during the period as an undergraduate, but will be considered a coach only after the completion of the program. People who are practitioners of their sport and coaching as a sideline are not frequently seen in Brazil.

In Taiwan, most of the coaches in the schools are physical educators who have graduated from physical education colleges or universities and have received 2 to 4 years of physical education training. There are some coaches, however, who are former athletes in a particular sport and have not received physical education training. They usually coach a team that is more like a sports club.

In the Phillipines there has not been much approval of girls who are competitive in sports. The role models for active women would usually be found in the area of dance, both ballet and Filipino folk dance. This is still true in the Moslem area of the Phillipines where women are not encouraged to participate in athletics. This was also very true of the Moslem culture in the northern part of Nigeria where we lived and taught.

In Brazil the Roman Catholic religion has burdened women's participation in many sports (e.g., basketball) that were considered masculine and, therefore, improper for women. In Catholic schools the sports emphasis for women is on dance and other activities that will not harm the beauty, grace, or femininity of the students. This view was popular with the Brazilian people for many years, perhaps because of the church's influence over their thinking. Nowadays, however, women are participating in many sports, even soccer. While women's soccer is not yet fully accepted and may never become truly popular, acceptance is growing as the people become used to it.

In the Phillipines, great care was taken to be certain that girls were adequately supervised and that no improper behavior would result from their participation in sports. In Nigeria, however, there was a great openness in relationships and this contributed to some negative attitudes toward women in sports among the general populace.

In Taiwan most people would say it is fine for a woman to be a sportswoman. The achievements of Chi Cheng encouraged women to participate in sports. Because she held the world record and was a recipient of a bronze medal in the Olympic sprints, Chi Cheng became a famous athlete and has since served as a role model for women. She is now a very respected congresswoman and was chosen as one of the outstanding women of the country. Other female athletes have also been elected outstanding women.

In many countries of the southern hemisphere, individual sport development is hampered by the difficulty of securing equipment and adequate facilities. This is a particular problem in Nigeria and, to a lesser extent, in Brazil. In Taiwan there isn't much trouble in getting equipment. Schools supply the shoes, uniforms, birds, and rackets, but the players often prefer their own rackets. These may be imported or made in Taiwan, but in most cases, the players like to use foreign made rackets.

Brazil both manufactures and imports sport equipment. The current trend is toward the use of locally manufactured equipment, although there are many players who feel more comfortable in using an imported brand. Imported goods are more costly, however, and while the private soccer clubs can afford them, many individuals cannot. Brazil manufactures soccer balls, shoes, uniforms, and also whistles.

Facilities appropriate for competition also represent a big problem in Brazil. When there is a big competition, the indoor facilities are often insufficient, and the games must be held outside, making the weather an important aspect, too. Budget is of extreme importance and many competitive events cannot be held due to budget deficiencies. Another final aspect to be considered is the size of Brazil, which requires flying long distances to participate in many competitions.

Climate is another factor that is of utmost importance. In many countries all competitions must occur outside the rainy season because of the potential of storms and torrential rains; travel is sometimes impossible. Competitions are, also, often held in extreme heat, which greatly affects both the scheduling and the players. Some sports, like basketball, must be scheduled at midday, and playing on a cement court in such conditions is very debilitating.

Taiwan and Brazil both have well developed sports that operate somewhat independently of the government. In Taiwan, little league baseball is a good example. Little league teams are organized in each local area, and the team members are selected, according to age, from the local schools. The teams are supported by the local people and compete first locally, then regionally, and finally nationally. The team's coach is chosen from the school or from among former baseball players, depending on the committee of little league baseball, and the players are usually trained after classes or on the weekend.

Soccer and boxing are professional sports in Brazil. The private clubs sign million-dollar contracts with the soccer players for a period of time. The players also receive a bonus when the club wins a game, thus providing an incentive for victory among the players. Brazil has a few very good basketball players who are paid by the clubs they compete for. The tendency today is for sponsorship of athletes by Brazilian factories, in order to pay for the studies and support of these athletes.

Nigeria hosted the African Championship in soccer in 1980, and the Green Eagles emerged as champion for the first time ever. There was intense jubilation, and team members were given houses, cars, refrigerators, and official government recognition. They became heroes, household names, and it wasn't very long before they were seen endorsing products on television and in the print media. Government leaders took advantage of the situation to further their political fortunes, but also to build upon the national pride that was displayed.

To summarize we see that (a) governments pay for and promote sports to various degrees, particularly in the area of school sports competition; (b) financial limitations are a reality; and (c) governments use sports to promote feelings of nationalism and patriotism and also view it as a form of education, particularly through the folk festivals that often accompany sporting endeavors.

The panel concluded by concurring that sport has a major role to play in the North-South dialogue because of its universality; we all move, and in that there is unity. However, we must be willing to learn from others in the attitudes they display, the delight that is obvious, and the camaraderie that is present. Those things we can learn from others in the southern hemisphere, and we also have things to share—technique, technology, and perhaps a single-minded emphasis on excellence. Let's hope that we, as individuals, become aware of the differences and similarities and exercise our privilege to influence the dialogues that are taking place in sport.

Comparative Sport History: A Tale of Two Cities

Ralph C. Wilcox
Hofstra University

Picture if you will, an autumn afternoon in Boston, Massachusetts. A short way from the banks of the Charles River, 50,000 spectators are huddled together in Harvard Stadium. Kept warm by their H-emblazoned magenta sweaters and the waving of tribal banners, they cheer their college football team on to victory. Meanwhile, 3,500 miles eastward across the Atlantic divide and overlooking the River Avon, an old man and his dog stroll across the windswept expanse of Bristol University's playing field, pausing to observe the games of rugby and field hockey whose respective battlefields dictate his pathway. Here, few would understand the rationale behind paying the Harvard men for the privilege and luxury of representing their school; after all, the Bristol underclassmen were required to furnish a match fee for the dubious honor and frequent misery of such respite from study.

While the cities chosen in this study might equally have been Toronto, Melbourne, Paris, or other established urban centers, their selection is loosely based on a desire to investigate and better understand some of the similarities and differences encountered by sport in Great Britain and the United States of America. This paper offers a new attempt at comparing the significance of sport in each society and, through an historical component, seeks to explain some similarities and differences in the nations' contemporary sport programs.

The Role of Sport in Society

Although wishing to avoid vast expenditures of time and energy on definitional and operational interpretations of central terms used in this study, it is nonetheless essential that the nature and value of certain concepts be clarified. The intellectual efforts of scholars to come to grips with *sport*, while proving of great interest and import, have seldom provided utility for the historian. In recognizing a hierarchical differentiation between *informal*, *organized*, and *corporate* sport, the central theme will be taken as a generic term to encompass play, games, athletics, healthful exercise, physical education, man's concept of the body, and selected aspects of recreation and leisure.

Why one would wish to study the role of sport in past societies is a question too infrequently posed by students in the field. It is *not* enough to echo the established claim that sport represents a mirror as it reflects societal values, norms, and objectives. As such, sport is perceived as *a product of society* exhibiting the structure, framework, and ethics of the larger world in microcosm. A more important question that needs to be addressed is how can sport help us to better understand the structures and functions of past and present societies, or a part of them, for although sport may well have functioned to reinforce social order and stability, it also contributed to social change. This idea, broadly perceived as *society, a product of sport*, has received far too scant attention in comparison with the former. The fact that sport facilitated improved health in the city, modified the role of the church, increased employment opportunities in industry and transport, forged community and cultural integration and stability, provided a platform for democracy, and contributed to the emancipation of women, supports its significance as an agent of social change, particularly in Britain and America in the 19th century. However, not all changes brought about by sport were for the good; equally, sport provided the instrument to strengthen the bonds of social, cultural, racial, and sexual segregation.

The adoption of a comparative framework in this study affords greater structure and analysis in seeking to better understand the relationship of sport and society in the two nations. In considering the utilization of comparative study in sport history, one is immediately faced by a dichotomous model. On the one hand, such study may suggest a comparison of the past events (or series of events) of two or more *comparable* social or cultural groups. Exemplified in Arnold J. Toynbee's landmark *Study of Civilisations* and, more recently, John Keegan's *The Face of Battle*, this approach is clearly viewed as a *comparison between*. Alternatively, comparative history may be perceived as an analysis of two or more *comparable* events (or series of events) in the history of one social group, which many historians consider to represent a contemporary view of history; in essence, it is a *comparison within*. Offering the breadth of cross-national comparison and the depth of historical analysis, both approaches are utilized in this study, with greater weight being afforded the former. Reaching beyond descriptive reports, it would appear that the potential for sociocultural interpretation of the past far outreaches that of isolated, traditional historical and comparative approaches. Precipitating new questions, such a framework might only add to greater international understanding and self-evaluation, for as Nicholas Hans (1959, p. 309) so precisely put it more than 20 years ago:

> The historical approach tries to investigate the past causes of individual and group variations among religious or national communities. The differences of denominational attitudes, of national aspirations or of so called 'national character' go deep into the past and sometimes subconsciously determine the present. Only historical investigation can bring them to the surface, illuminate their potency in the cultural lives of nations and make Comparative Education really educative.

The Impact of Sport on Bristol and Boston 1870-1900

This paper is concerned with the evolution of sport in Britain and America during the years 1870 to 1900, that period during which modern, characteristic, national programs emerged. To most of a growing majority of urban residents, the 19th century city represented an inhospitable environment characterized by poverty, unsanitary conditions, and a sense of alienation. With each contributing to the others, civic leaders were faced with an ever-complicating problem of urban deterioration. Largely precipitated out of the Industrial Revolution, the city was seldom prepared to cope with the multiplying numbers of immigrants from its rural hinterland and other regions, who daily entered its gates. Yet the years 1870 to 1900 were to witness an unparalleled attempt at social melioration by municipal governments, middle-class philanthropists, and other reform agencies; beautifying crusades, civilizing missions, public health campaigns, and an ongoing search for community came to represent a combined effort at improving the city. The complexity of this trend should not be overlooked, as it was accompanied by an undercurrent of political change to the left, a more democratic distribution of wealth, and a change in the base of knowledge that was so crucial to the emergence of characteristic value systems.

The function of sport in this process has received all too little attention in the past. From its impact on the topography of the city through the rescue and reclamation of green belt "breathing spaces" to its role in filling the increasing number of leisure hours, sport found a prominent niche in the cause of social betterment. Further, the city was to have a marked impact on the nature of sport as it evolved from informal games in the agrarian world to the organized and corporate pursuits of the metropolis. To the historian, the city presents a manageable boundary in which the relationship of sport and urbanization might be investigated. Yet generalizations are to be avoided, for only after further study of sport in the city might commonalities be identified.

Situated on either side of the Atlantic Ocean, Boston's population of 250,000 in 1870 made it somewhat larger than Bristol's citizenry of 180,000. Yet it was the proportional increase in residents over the next 30 years that was to reflect the greatest demographic gulf between the two urban centers. Boston's population increased by 124% (the census for 1900 showed that 560,000 people were living in "the Hub"), while a modest increase of 80% gave the English city a population of 333,000. Both cities rested on a foundation of maritime trade, although each was to witness its preeminent status slipping to other more favored ports, notably Liverpool and New York.

Unlike its American counterpart, Bristol had grown out of the Middle Ages, with the city government early claimed by an aristocracy that had achieved its status by way of mercantile wealth rather than land ownership. Their faith and influence determined the future of Bristol's religious affiliation with Evangelists and Non-Conformists, setting the trend for theological thought and practice in the 19th century city. Boston was first settled during the early 17th century by Puritans. While their's remained the predominant mode of religious thought until the onset of the 19th century, the subsequent influx of immigrants from Ireland, and later Southern and Eastern Europe, led to a gradual erosion of orthodox, puritan values and a rise of Catholicism and Unitarianism.

The years 1870 to 1900 also witnessed a change in the governmental structure of each city. Once led by a wealthy, conservative elite, Bristol and Boston witnessed a gradual shift toward democracy by the end of the 19th century. This was evidenced by the rise to power of Yankee and Irish Democrats and Independent Mugwumps in Boston, and Liberals, Liberal-Unionists, and even some pioneering Socialists in Bristol. Yet the cities retained their image of "two nations in one" as their established aristocracies and emerging bourgeoisies remained on Beacon and Clifton hills closing their eyes to the dank, overcrowded pestilences of the North End and Easton below. While such socioeconomic polarization was manifested through education, politics, religion, and sport, neither city could claim to be a major industrial center, a factor that is frequently identified as the common denominator of social extremes. Indeed, their relative distance from the major sources of raw material meant that heavy industry was restricted to the urban periphery with the primary occupations becoming manufacturing and marketing.

Sport was not a new phenomenon to either city during the 19th century. Despite puritanical restraints, coupled with the absence of leisure hours and facilities, plentiful evidence remains for the practice of informal and organized sport by early Bristolians and Bostonians. Frequently determined by wealth, whereby the aristocracy might typically partake of bathing, lawn bowling, quoits, cricket, and field sports on their private estates, the Common and Downs (street and inn) became the centers of physical pursuits for the populace. Sometimes described as "trespass sports," cockfighting, bullbaiting, dogfighting, and ratting were popular among the working class and were practiced behind closed doors, safe from the church's critical view. Holy days and festivals provided the foremost opportunities for outdoor pursuits, and horseraces, pedestrian, and prizefighting meets were attended by a growing number of spectators. Yet the potential wealth of such pursuits was not to be realized, and their organization remained unstructured until the cities, faced by a deepening urban crisis, sought a solution for the betterment of their environment.

The Influence of Religion on Sport

The emergence of a social gospel in both cities during the 19th century promised a divergence from the traditional pattern of spiritual development. Partially out of a genuine concern for the deteriorating state of urban life, and partly in search of a larger congregation, missionary societies had early been established in Bristol and Boston. Supported by the platform of the Broad Church and the preaching of Christian Socialists, the role of the church was extended. Providing a meeting place for the working class together with organizing picnics, excursions, and sport events,

Bristol's Non-Conformist and Boston's Unitarian churches found particular favor among the urban populace. But the relationship between religion and sport in the 19th century city was to serve up a series of paradoxical situations as remnants of orthodox puritan thought led to the appearance of a Sabbatarian lobby, which was active in both Boston and Bristol. With its leaders scorning those who disregarded the belief that the Sabbath should be a day of rest, Blue Laws were relaxed and eventually repealed because of their nondemocratic nature; Sunday became a day of play by the turn of the century. Further, the increased leisure time and affluence of the laborer had early created a social problem of intemperance, as the public house and saloon became the major attraction of the working man. In seeking to offer alternatives, the Bristol Temperance Society (founded in 1836) established coffee houses and guilds, utilizing indoor games (e.g., skittles and billiards) and gymnasiums to attract members. While the Massachusetts Temperance Society (1833) faced a similar battle, it was the Young Men's Christian Association that came to the fore in offering an alternative to the degradation and corruption of the saloon.

Founded in London in 1841, the YMCA offers perhaps the best example of the social gospel at work in Boston and Bristol. Blending body, mind, and spirit, the Boston YMCA (1851) predates its Bristol counterpart (1853), which grew out of a bible reading class started in 1848. The Boston YMCA came to be a significant social force in the city, claiming a membership of 1,000 in 1854, whereas the Bristol YMCA did not register 1,000 members until the turn of the century. The physical program of the two Associations offers an interesting contrast, for while the Boston YMCA built its first "hall of health" in 1865, Bristol's Association was not able to boast a gymnasium until 1879; then, it fell short of the Boston facility in both dimensions and furnishings. Prompted by the work of Robert J. Roberts, it is not surprising that gymnastics formed the main thrust of the program in the wake of the Civil War. With limited interest in drill and gymnastics exhibited in the Bristol Association, the emphasis appears to have been on games-playing and character development. Forming its first cricket eleven in 1862, representative teams soon followed in football, field hockey, swimming, cross-country, and cycling. The end of the century brought a new innovation in both cities, as a return to the biocentric ethic led to the organization of summer camps for the boys of the Boston YMCA and those of the St. Agnes (Clifton College) Mission in Bristol. Supported by the efforts of nonchurch affiliated groups, including settlement houses in Boston and the boys' clubs in Bristol, the gospel of muscular Christianity was preached to middle- and working-class residents alike.

Political Attitudes Toward Sport

The City Councils of Boston and Bristol appeared more concerned with the visual realities facing them from day to day than the moral rectitude of their citizens. However, the contrast between the perceived responsibilities of the cities' leaders presents one of the more interesting observations of this study. While the Conservative government of Bristol was content to preserve the social order in the city at the expense of reform and change, the election of Josiah Quincy as Mayor of Boston in 1823 set an important precedent in establishing a municipal obligation and responsibility for the care of the city's residents. In this light, it is not surprising that, while Bristol's interest in sport was limited to an indirect concern for public health prompted by philanthropic Liberals, the Boston City Council instituted the City Regatta as early as 1854.

Public health represented a primary concern of the civic leaders of both cities throughout the 19th century. As ports, Bristol and Boston were gateways to exotic disease, which, when added to the already mounting list of endemic ailments, created an urban malaise of frightening proportions. Yet, through a process of legislative and reform measures, more salubrious surroundings emerged by 1870. With migration to the city continuing, and scientific advances guaranteeing a lower mortality rate, the population expanded, crowding into the already congested inner city. At the same time, the "lungs of the city" were being swallowed up by urbanization, leading to a changing priority in public health from the provision of fresh water and sewers to the search for open-air spaces.

The Boston Common and the Bristol Downs had long been the most popular playgrounds of each city. However, with increasing urbanization, access to these open spaces was restricted, and the dangerous and unsanitary world of the street became the baseball diamond and the football pitch for the urban child. Aware of the need for parks and playgrounds, the City Councils adopted contrasting philosophies. In Bristol the realization had come too late, and the Council, refusing to purchase land, decided to rely upon gifts. This was of little consequence to the middle classes, who could afford admission to the exclusive privacy of the Zoological Gardens in Clifton. Fortunately for the working-class citizens of Bristol, extensive lands were donated to the city; first the Downs, which had been purchased by the Society of Merchant Venturers, and then other munificent gifts of real estate, particularly during the last 2 decades of the 19th century. In fairness to the Bristol City Council, it should be noted that a motion was later passed to purchase a small package of land and to support the maintenance and improvement of existing parks.

In Boston, the city government played a much more active role in reclaiming and securing lands, particularly after approval of the Park Act in 1875. Culminating in the completion of Frederick L. Olmsted's "Emerald Necklace" in 1879, the role of providing parks and playgrounds in the city and surrounding townships was augmented with the establishment of the Metropolitan Park Commission (1892), the Massachusetts Emergency Hygiene Association (1884), and the Massachusetts Civic League (1897). In the provision of public bath houses, the situation appears to be reversed. While the 1846 Bath and Washhouses Act led to the construction of Bristol's first municipal bath at Broad Weir in 1850, it was 1860 before Boston opened the first public bath house in America, an event which was to spark the building of 14 more facilities by the end of the decade.

The Emergence of Team Sport

The provision of playgrounds and parks created a catalyst to the emergence of organized sport in the city. While pedestrianism and pugilism maintained their popularity (even if somewhat guarded), the transition to organized sport is most clearly witnessed through the appearance of team games in Bristol and Boston. Characterized by a greater structure, organization (through the establishment of leagues and governing bodies), and codification, such modernization eventually led to the advent of corporate sport colored by professionalism, spectatorism, the construction of private grounds and grandstands, the institution of admission fees, and the importation of nonlocal performers. Endeavoring to fulfill the needs of urbanization (and the pecuniary dreams of the owners), representative teams made their homes in the city, instilling a sense of civic pride in interested residents. Formed in 1870, the Gloucestershire County Cricket Club and the Boston Red Stockings (later the Boston Beaneaters) were testimony to this. The cricketers acquired three County Championship titles, and the baseball players 12 National League pennants by the end of the century.

Promoted by technological developments, particularly in communication and the mass production of cheap equipment, opportunity for mass participation in organized sport became a vague possibility. While district, cultural, industrial, and religious teams fostered group identity and occupied the leisure hours of residents, the middle-class stigma frequently accompanying team sports was no fallacy; participation presumed economic resources necessary for the purchase of equipment and clothing, club membership, and rental of grounds. Indeed, to working class Bristolians, static spectatorism suggested a lower financial outlay, a relief from the monotony of labor, a sense of community belonging, and an opportunity to win at a side bet. In Boston the motivation appeared to be a little different, although, with professional sports finding favor across all strata of society, the spectacle promised a greater opportunity for group interaction than in the English city.

For those finding little fascination with team sports, seaside resorts grew, which offered a type of corporate recreation to the citizens of Bristol and Boston. Providing something for everyone, railway and steamship companies carried the laboring classes to Weston-Super-Mare and Revere, and the more affluent to Clevedon and Nahant. Evidence suggests that Boston witnessed an earlier transition to corporate sport, as commercialism became more fully developed than in Bristol. With any replication of the English gentlemanly tradition and amateur ideal being whittled away by the belief that any man had the right to work in search of pecuniary success, corruption, exploitation, and excessive competition tended to characterize sport in late 19th century Boston. Yet it would be incorrect to assume that such traits were not to be found in Bristol sport.

Educational Involvement in Sport

The relationship of education and sport in Bristol and Boston offers an interesting contrast that would appear to be reflective of national trends. Both cities claimed a tradition in private education dating from the establishment of the Bristol Grammar School in 1532 and the Boston Public Latin School in 1635. On the other hand, the evolution of public education was reversed with the appearance of the Boston School Committee, which predated its Bristol counterpart by some 20 years.

Physical training had early been pioneered in Boston as Fowle, Follen, and Thayer, among others, promoted German gymnastics in their private facilities during the 1820s. After a 30-year lacuna, the Civil War prompted a revival of interest in ethnocentric programs. First, Winship and Lewis, and later Sargent and Posse (each supported by educational administrators), led the way in a gradual evolution from gymnastics to military drill and, eventually, a more humanistic style of Swedish calisthenics. While the trend was similar in the board schools of Bristol, the primary interest remained in physical programs that supported the egocentric ethic. Postelementary provision for physical education in both cities was poor, although The Bristol Evening Class and Recreation Society (1884 to 1895) did offer instruction for adults. However, the developments witnessed at Harvard, from the Hemenway gymnasium to programs at the Summer and Sargent Schools of Physical Training, and the first American degree in the field at the Lawrence Scientific School, supported the premier status of "the Hub" in physical education. By adding the contribution of the Normal School of Gymnastics and the city's hosting of landmark conferences toward the end of the 19th century, it is clear that the capitol of Massachusetts fully justified its claim to being the seedbed of American physical education.

Born in the English "public" schools, the moral ideology of muscular Christianity was nourished in a period characterized by immunity from international hostility and a notion changing from the asceticism of the classical, aristocratic, private institution to the relative liberalism of the new, bourgeois, philistine school. Witnessing an elevated status, the body was perceived as a means to develop such moral traits as manliness and courage. Followers of the supernal Headmaster, the pupils of private schools in both cities (for the Anglophile Brahmin soon established replicas of the English "public" school) spent their afternoons at the wicket or chasing the hare across the rural fringes of Boston and Bristol. Frequently fighting the forced discipline and constraints of drill and the physical monism of gymnastics, it was felt that the schoolboy would be adequately prepared for military service on the playing field.

As athleticism found favor at Clifton College, Bristol Grammar School, Bristol Cathedral School, St. Paul's School, Groton School, Phillip's Andover, Phillip's Exeter, and other private institutions, the uniqueness of each school was lost under a universal umbrella of games-playing. Opportunity existed for all to participate, whether in house matches or on the school teams. Each schoolboy was provided the chance to savor the meaning of patriotism which, it was hoped, would be manifested upon his leaving school. With "caps" and "colors" awarded to elite athletes, the ideals of character development were disseminated by means of a complex old boys' network and literature. Eventually the program of team sports was adopted by the public schools of both cities. The Interscholastic Football Union founded at Boston in 1888 (although this was primarily patronized by preparatory school), the Boston Interscholastic Athletic Association (1890), and the Bristol Schools' Rugby Union (1898), offered sorely needed structure and organization for their members. However, incidents of professionalism, violence, and obsessive play at the expense of study and the class distinction inherent in such programs led critics of athleticism to question the value of games in education and to predict the advent of commercialism in school and university athletics, particularly in Boston.

The universities of both cities followed the pattern of games-playing practiced at Oxford and Cambridge in England. The establishment of the Bristol Medical School in 1833 laid the foundation for the opening of a University College in 1876. It remained a private institution patronized by the middle class until 1889, and football, cricket, and field hockey were practiced by students and professors alike, in replication of the city's private schools. In Boston, the appearance of a tertiary level of education was witnessed as early as 1637 with the founding of Harvard College; this was further extended by the openings of Boston University (1839), Boston College (1863), Massachusetts Institute of Technology (1865), and other such institutions in the vicinity of "the Hub." Attended at the outset by the sons of Brahmins, the universities represented Boston society in microcosm. They reinforced its social values and order and in the process, reflected the transition from informal to organized and, eventually, corporate sport.

Promoted by both principles and professors, these American halls of academe came to be viewed as athletic clubs offering opportunities in the mold of the great English universities from the middle of the 19th century, but later rapidly developed their own characteristic model of athleticism to meet the needs of a changing society. Harvard became a leader in this movement. Forsaking cricket and mob football for baseball and American football during the 1870s, intercollegiate sport across the River Charles became increasingly serious with the ideals of muscular Christianity being forgotten in search of victory, prestige, and economic return. Prompting the faculty to grasp periodic control of athletics at the university, such pursuits, nevertheless, continued to assume all the characteristics of corporate sport: increased professionalism, spectatorism, violent outbursts, gate receipts, recruiting scandals, and even grade modification, as Harvard's athletic budget passed the $100,000 mark by the turn of the century. Opposed by those who pictured the eventual subordination of mind to body, the evolution from loose, informal games played on the Common at mid-century to the complex intercollegiate contest waged before a stadium filled with partisan spectators in 1900, appears to have been accelerated in an environment relatively divorced from the impact of external factors.

Effects of Sport on Socioeconomic Status

In contrast, the traditional social order of both cities, with regard to gender and socioeconomic class, realized slow and limited change over these years. The perception of the female body in 1870 was characterized by an image of delicacy and softness. Gradually, however, through a desire to end the monotony for workers' wives and the exploitation and declining health of females, reform measures were instituted to elevate the status of women in both nations. Although presented with an almost insurmountable barrier of tradition at the outset, sport played a significant role in the emancipation of women. As Bristol's girls' schools copied the games-playing traditions of the private boys' schools, and Beecher, Fowle, Lewis, Hemenway, and Sargent pioneered physical education programs for girls in Boston, the shackles of passive domesticity were cast aside. No longer did Ladies' Day mean a parade of the gentle sex uncomfortably attired in all its finery. Women, instead, discovered access to a variety of active pursuits, particularly tennis and cycling, which promised a new freedom, healthy activity, and social companionship.

Although the status of women in both cities realized significant melioration during the years 1870 to 1900, the socioeconomic structure remained more resistant to change. Unlike other centers that flourished through industrial prosperity, Bristol and Boston were built on a tradition of mercantile wealth. Personified by an aristocracy that reclined in the comforts of urban and suburban affluence, the societies of both cities reflected similar tastes and lifestyles. As economic change led to a migration of native agricultural laborers (and immigrants in Boston), society was marked off by a polarization of classes. Yet, the style of life accompanying urbanization and industrialization led to the emergence of a new bourgeois class intent on imitating their established socioeconomic superiors. While sport was being utilized to strengthen class identity and so maintain the social order, it also represented a significant force in the search for democracy.

Pursuing the field sports of their forefathers, conspicuous leisure became a mark of respectability among the upper strata of society. The fact that sport was perceived as nonproductive guaranteed a peculiar status to those involved. The Boston Brahmin and Bristol businessman were frequently found whiling away their days at the private club or racetrack. However, with the appearance of the working class at Beacon Park and Knowle racecourses, the settings lost their sense of respectability. This led to the relocation of the sports to other centers within reasonable proximity to Bristol and the formation of driving clubs by the followers of equestrianism in "the Hub," both in search of greater exclusivity.

In like manner, rowing clubs grew up in each city, primarily to serve as unifying forces for the wealthy. Evolving out of competition between wherrymen in the ports of Bristol and Boston, the rowing clubs' selection procedures and membership fees ensured that only the cream of society might be permitted to wear the club colors and fraternize with other patrons. With a Harvard boat club, formed in 1842, and the Union B.C., dating from 1851, the sport was established earlier in the American city than in Bristol. In that city, despite the formation of the Ariel B.C. in 1870 and others soon after, the tidal waters of the Avon were less conducive to the rise of rowing. In Boston, the annual city regatta promised interaction between all classes of society, overlooking economic barriers and facilitating democracy. Yet, in reaction to any such threat to their hegemony, the middle class typically withdrew to other vestiges of sport, such as yachting (which flourished after the formation of the Boston Y.C. in 1866 and offered an escape from the ills of industrial society) and the athletic club.

Initially intended for promoting the track and field programs of the private schools and universities, parent institutions were established at Boston in 1879 and at Bristol 3 years later. While the Bristol Athletic Club remained the primary sponsor of both track and field and cycling competitions throughout the remaining years of the 19th century, the Boston Association became a shrine to health and affluence, as its proudest claim was made in the wake of the first modern Olympic Games.

The ultimate in exclusive retreats remained the unexplored outdoors. Prompted by a revival of romantic thought, Bristol's wealthy citizens retreated to private estates, grandiloquent resorts, and the Continent. Meanwhile, proper Bostonians, who were unable to make the trip to the interior of New England, founded an American phenomenon, the country club. Here they established a select environment in which they might socialize and enjoy golf, tennis, shooting, hunting, and horse racing. Generally patronizing these and other bastions of male, Yankee sentiment, Brahmins chose to ignore team sports, participation that might eventually lead to a breakdown of traditional social boundaries within the city.

Organized sport had early been utilized by the working class of both cities as an instrument to social mobility. As long as man was geographically divided on the basis of economic means, group consciousness and eventual conflict was inevitable. To some observers, the playing field represented a socially acceptable environment in which the battle for democracy might be waged. Paralleled by social reform measures and an ongoing shift to the political left, trade unionism found less support in Boston than in Bristol, because the American belief in individualism tended to run counter to the ideals of combination. Yet in both cities, the pitiful conditions of working class life continued to mock advances in science and technology. Formerly restricted to unstructured meetings in the street and on the Common or Downs, the combined efforts of socio-religious, political, and commercial agencies led to a growing opportunity for the laborer to spend his newfound time and money in the cause of organized sport. Further promoted by employers' beliefs in recreation and eventual economic return, and legitimized by middle-class participation, the sporting interests of the working class readily extended beyond the billiard halls, ratpits, and gambling houses.

Recognizing a path to pecuniary success and overlooking the amateur gentleman ideal, the lower classes readily filled the role of professional athlete, becoming the focus of corporate sport. That role was spurned, however, by the middle class, which perceived working at play as non-respectable and opposed the idea of conspicuous leisure. For them, the traits of individualism, gamesmanship, and excessive competition manifested in professionalism ran counter to the gentlemanly ideals of team spirit, sportsmanship, and cooperation. Representing an extension of the popular 19th century pastime of labor baiting, discrimination against professionals was most clearly evident in Bristol. In the American city, the middle class appeared content to retreat to its social enclaves and accept the gradual erosion of traditional barriers, a process that was strengthened by the arrival of immigrants.

In contrast to the relative demographic homogeneity and stability of Bristol, the society of 19th-century Boston was to witness a radical transformation when that city's gateway to a traditionally white, Anglo-Saxon, Protestant stronghold was broached by a flood of mostly poor, European immigrants, arriving in two waves. The early denizens tended to share the cultural values of Bostonians, thus facilitating assimilation; the latter group, mostly of the Catholic and Jewish faiths and speaking in alien tongues, found life in their new homes less hospitable. Faced by opposition from the Know Nothing Movement, the American Protective League, and the Immigration Restriction League, the New Bostonian, who, ironically, represented the very foundation of the city's manufacturing economy, utilized sport increasingly both as a tool for group identity and mutual comfort, and as a means of assimilation to his adopted home. With generalizations made difficult, the clearest example of assimilation was shown by the English, whose values represented the basis of Brahmin society. Early attempts at clinging to cultural traditions by the Irish, however, were later forgotten as their assimilation to baseball, rowing, and pugilism, in particular, promised social elevation. The Scots and Germans, on the other hand, tended to be more wealthy, and discovered that the perpetuation of sporting traditions posed no threat to their acceptance into society. Moreover, the tartan-clad Bostonian was to witness his very own Caledonian Games adopted as the foundation of organized track and field in his new home. In essence, "the Hub" presented a pot into which the immigrants fell. The degree to which the city melted and welded them into stronger citizens was determined through the stance taken by civic leaders and the perceived need and desire of the New Bostonians to assimilate to their new surroundings. Perhaps the story is most clearly told by the appearance of immigrants and first generation Americans at the summit of Boston's sporting fraternity. No one provides better evidence of the significant contribution to sport in the American city than the "Boston Strong Boy," himself.

The international popularity of John L. Sullivan and W.G. Grace attested to the rising significance of sport in 19th century Boston and Bristol. Their lives reached beyond sporting achievements, telling a tale of two cities. In many respects, Bristol and Boston appeared linked by a cultural bridge spanning the Atlantic Ocean and reflecting a marked similarity in the role of sport in the city-building process, while underlying differences in structure and ideology were manifested in each city's asymmetrical evolution and characteristic sport pattern.

Summary

The process of urbanization was somewhat more advanced in Bristol by 1870, a time when Boston was recovering from the interruption of the Civil War. Nevertheless, sharing similar experiences with regard to economy, political trends, and religious affiliation, the primary concern of civic leaders during the next 30 years was with the improvement of public health and living conditions. Adopting a more active role than its British counterpart, the Boston City Council exemplified its commitment to civic uplift. Supported by physical education programs, which followed the ethnocentric ethic, the quest for a fitter, healthier, and stronger Bostonian was realized. In contrast, the pattern of physical education and games-playing in Bristol was based upon the belief in developing a citizen of upstanding moral character. Also representing the foundation of sport in Boston, the eventual triumph of Jacksonian democracy over the gentleman amateur ideal appears to have been the fundamental reason for the acceleration from organized to corporate sport in "the Hub," which reached extremes of commercialism unmatched in Bristol. As Boston's immigrants came to represent a significant force in effecting urban transition, Bristol's society remained relatively stable, and an established value system tempered the impact of change.

The two cities entered the 1870s facing similar problems wrought by urbanization and industrialization. Provided with comparable resources, sport was utilized in contrasting ways and for different purposes as the cities underwent ongoing improvement. Paralleled by a change in the complexity of sport, the earlier and more widespread appearance of an organized pattern in Bristol was overshadowed by the marked significance of corporate sport in Boston society by the turn of the century. Assuming a degree of comparability existed between the two cities in 1870, differences observed in the nature and function of sport up to the turn of the century might be considered indicative of national trends. Yet such conclusions require ongoing, cross-national investigation, for the findings of this study are unique, most accurately reflecting a tale of two cities.

Conclusions

A cyclical relationship between sport and human values is clearly borne out in this paper. While supporting the belief that sport reflected a more far-reaching value system in functioning to maintain social control, it also created a unique system of values that contributed to social control and change. In this way, sport must be seen as a useful, significant tool for examining and understanding the similarities and differences between societies. The utilization of sport as a means of communicating human values appears to be reflected at all levels of society. While the role of sport in the search for identity, improved health, and social control has been adequately investigated at the individual and institutional levels, this paper presents a model that, in considering both city and people, might be applied to other urban centers in search of greater understanding.

Although delimitation of this study has necessarily restricted generalizations, the findings suggest clear and fundamental differences in the relationship of national character and sport in the two cities. Born of the same womb, American life continued to be molded by England well after the Declaration of Independence until the trans-Atlantic bond began to founder under the weight of cultural and economic determinants. Many of the differences observed in the nature and function of contemporary sport in the two nations grew out of seeds sown during the late 19th century. Whether the product of ethnic diversity or capitalistic competition, sport in America changed to ensure a congruence with the national system of ultimate values.

In seeking to explain the more rapid evolution from organized to corporate sport in America, the author has identified a need for further study in the seemingly inexhaustible relationship of sport, ethnicity, and economy. Whether through similar urban comparisons set within the 19th century or more extensive investigation reaching beyond both the spatial and temporal boundaries of this study, such cross-national research can only strengthen and deepen understanding among nations.

References

Hans, N. (1953). The historical approach to comparative education. *International Review of Education, 5*(3), 299-307.

Wilcox, R.C. (1982). Toward a comparative sport history. In R. Day & P. Lindsay (Eds.), *Sport history research methodology* (pp. 129-139). Edmonton: University of Alberta Press.

Wilcox, R.C. (1982). *Sport in Bristol (U.K.) and Boston (U.S.A.): A cross-national comparison, 1870-1900.* Unpublished doctoral dissertation, University of Alberta.

A Comparison of Personal Beliefs Held by International Physical Educators, United States Leaders in Physical Education, and College Students Concerning Physical Education for College and University Students Who Are Not Studying to be Teachers/Coaches

Barry C. Pelton
University of Houston

According to Irwin Edman, "any man's world-view becomes more imaginative and liberated when he succeeds, if only for the time being, in seeing through the eyes of others." Sir Michael Sadler stated that the "practical value of studying in the right spirit and with scholarly accuracy the working of foreign systems of physical education is that it will result in our being better fitted to understand our own."

In presenting a world view of physical education, one sees a vast panorama revealing physical education and sport leaders looking outward to all continents to gain information and insights available from other countries' programs. Highly organized programs of physical education available to all students who are not training to be teachers of physical education or sports coaches are not common in many countries throughout the world. However, certain institutions or a particular school, such as a school of engineering, may require its students to take physical education, while the schools of law or economics at the same institution would not.

Ruth Abernathy (1970), stated that too little serious attention has been given to physical education for college men and women. This does not mean that careful planning has not gone into programs, that activities have not been thoughtfully studied, and that interests and choices of activities have not been thoroughly investigated. We still need, however, greater understanding of the meanings that college students, in general, assign to their physical education experience. Apparently, a great deal of the perceived value of physical education activities at the college level is dependent upon the type or the level of program in which the student is participating. It also would seem that students have varying views of college programs, depending on whether they participate, or whether they observe others participating. In any event, the personal bias is apparent.

What becomes more important to us in physical education is whether or not the personal bias of students is the governing factor in determining balance of program, or whether the personal bias of the instructional programs at the college level has a dual and difficult responsibility. These programs must be alert to the changing concerns of their student constituents, and they must be aware of developing trends in the theoretical base of their field. In other words, they must balance what is known and therefore appreciated by the students with what is becoming known as research strengthens the substantive base of the field.

Identifying, defining, and ranking the objectives of physical education has been an enduring effort of physical educators. Controversy can be expected, and confusion, particularly in the ranking process is unavoidable. What I find least easy to understand is that once this task is accomplished, it seems that the professional adjourns and fails to heed what had just been determined in terms of implementation. The physical educator's perception of the objectives of physical education at the college level is tempered by the concept held as to the nature of man and the value placed on certain knowledge and performance skills.

Historical Overview of the Objectives of Physical Education for Nonmajors at the College Level in the United States During the 1900s

Experts concluded, during this period, that general education in higher education recognized that a well integrated personality is not necessarily identical to another's personality, and asserted that in a democracy each individual has his unique worth. Even though a self-identity is inter-involved with others, each is a personal self-realization; thus the realization that the purposes of general education should be to produce a rich and vitalizing diversity, which leads, in turn, to the total unity of the student.

A synthesis of the purposes of general education in higher education highlighted the significance of the changing of human behavior. The desired changes seem to involve an acquisition of knowledge, social adjustments, and good mental and physical health.

There were very few accounts of the purposes of general college programs of physical education written between 1900 to 1950, possibly due to the changing emphasis in college curricula, the great depression of the 1930s, the influences of World Wars I and II, or a general lack of concern for this aspect of the physical education program. This review considers only the most pertinent of these early reports and concentrates on conference reports and the literature about college physical education programs from the 1950s to the present. It seems that the decade of the 1950s marked the first intense concern for the improvement of general college programs of physical education, although some earlier physical educators recognized the need for improvement. Hughes (1939) stated:

> The required physical education program is probably the least developed, yet one of the richest in opportunities to students in all higher education. There have been innumerable studies, researches, articles, and convention programs devoted to varsity and intramural athletics, swimming, dance, health instruction, and teacher training; but the service program has remained more or less the uninteresting, unexplored, unimproved, forgotten field. (p. 205)

Upon exploration of the literature in this area, this contention might still prove valid, as evidenced by the scarcity of available writings, research studies, general interest, and emphasis.

McCormick (1942) reported that about 85% of colleges and universities had a required program of physical education. He further implied that reports of the objectives of general college programs of physical education were limited due to the fact that physical educators had failed to produce written material specifically stating the objectives of those programs. McCormick cited the following as aims of the general college program of physical education:

- To orient the students in regard to the backgrounds, purposes and values of physical education, as well as certain departmental procedures, facilities, regulations, and services.
- To lend more meaning and significance to the emerging purposes of students by indicating the relationships of college physical education to other courses and practices of the curriculum, particularly to those related areas of health and physical recreation.
- To make students aware of the aims and objectives of physical education as these apply to each as an individual.
- To encourage each student to formulate a fact facing philosophy with regard to health, physical education and recreation in order that he will be aware of his individual needs to which physical education can contribute.
- To indicate to students, through individual and group guidance, how physical education can provide situations which will contribute to their needs and problems of life which fall within this division of education.

Another statement directly related to the objectives of general college programs of physical education was reported by Cobb (1943). These objectives placed emphasis on health, preparation for leisure, and character. In 1944, Lynn's research study concerning the major emphases in physical education during the history of the United States proposed certain objectives of physical education, but the study was not directly concerned with the general college program.

A report of the President's Commission on Higher Education (1947) credited physical education with making specific contributions to the general education program of higher education. These contributions or objectives were listed as follows:

- College men and women benefit from physical education in (a) the development of activity skills, (b) acquire more efficient physiological function, (c) more effective movement, and (d) improved human relationships.
- Activity skills provide opportunities to enjoy leisure time for living and for release from tension.
- Efficient physiological functioning enables the individual to participate more effectively and safely in the normal pursuits of everyday living.
- Physical education provides opportunities for (a) joy and satisfaction in movement, (b) the individual to develop an appreciation of the performance of others in all types of physical activity, (c) the individual to evaluate continuously, and redirect his efforts toward the realization of his maximum potentialities, (d) the continued development and improvement of democratic behavior, (e) the individual to develop an acceptable ethical code, (f) the individual to appreciate, understand, and accept individual and cultural differences, and (g) the individual to develop an awareness of the value of physical recreation in enrichment of personal and community life.

The literature of the decade, beginning with 1950, revealed a growing interest in the general college program of physical education. The changing social, political, and economic patterns of life, expansion in college enrollments, and increase in numbers and types of courses probably forced an evaluation of the educational programs in many institutions of higher learning in the United States. Reports of research studies related to general college programs of physical education appeared, and conferences specifically designed to study the problems and needs of this program were conducted.

According to Shea (1958) the need for an overall evaluation of educational practices and offerings contributed toward the focusing of attention on the further clarification of the nature and purposes of the general college program of physical education. In essence, this evaluation prompted the full realignment of these purposes with the broad aim of educating man liberally and broadly in an age of extreme diversification and specialization.

From 1950 to 1953, five studies appeared that dealt with certain aspects of the general college program of physical education. Wagner (1950) conducted a study for the purpose of determining the status of the required programs (general college programs) of physical education for men in colleges and universities of more than 5,000 students.

The organization and administration of physical education service programs (general college programs) in land-grant colleges and universities were explored by Hendricks (1951). Weber and Weber (1952) studied the relationship of physical fitness to success in college work and to personality. This study is mentioned because the attainment of fitness is commonly mentioned as one of the objectives of the general college program, and Weber's subjects were taken from required college physical education classes. Phillips (1953) studied the physical education service program (general college programs) in the Liberal Arts and Teachers' Colleges in New York, and Shepard conducted a study dealing with education for democracy through physical education. None of the preceding five studies represented a direct and comprehensive attempt to arrive at a conceptual framework of the purposes of general college programs of physical education.

In 1954, important recognition of the general college program of physical education was given by the College Physical Education Association and two additional organizations, the National Association for Physical Education for College Women and the American Association for Health, Physical Education, and Recreation. These groups joined efforts to organize the first national conference (1954) on physical education for college men and women.

Preconference planning identified four large areas upon which the conference was to center its attention. These areas were (1) philosophy and objectives, (2) administration, (3) program, and (4) evaluation. Abernathy firmly established this 1954 conference as the first of its kind in her opening address when she said,

> . . . the first national conference on physical education for the general college student . . . although in 1885, with the first meeting of the Society for the Improvement of Physical Education, which had the majority of its membership from colleges, we find a precedent . . .

Abernathy further emphasized the challenge of a new era related to this program when she proposed that the conference should attempt to answer three questions: Where are we (the profession)? What are we (the profession) all about? Where should we (the profession) go in physical education for the general college student?

Additional concepts revealed in her opening address dealt with the unique challenge that faced college physical education in 1954. She asserted that the hope for peace, the imperative need for men to think clearly, and the renewed proposals for shortening the workweek in industry and agriculture all contributed to a resounding "move-to-action" to physical education.

She proposed that college programs of physical education might include in their objectives the goal of supplying men and women with an understanding of the meaning of leisure. The need for the comprehension of how proper use of leisure time contributes toward a growing and enriched society, the need for the acquisition of improved skills, both general and specific, as requisites for security, and the need for an opportunity to enjoy physical activity were mentioned as worthy goals. The acceptance of self in movement and the appreciations preceding the seeking of breadth in recreational choices with active participation as their goals were mentioned as objectives. Lastly, Abernathy proposed that the satisfaction of working and playing with others and the relaxation from tension that enhances one's ability to think clearly were desirable objectives of general college programs of physical education.

Following this conference, there were a number of reports of surveys and research studies related to four of the aspects of the general college program of physical education; namely, philosophy and objectives, administration, program, and evaluation. The data revealed by reports from Buie (1956), Casady (1959), Cordts (1959), Fornia (1957), Harris (1951), Hunsicker (1954), Kenney (1955), Polonsky (1958), Spears (1956), and Turner (1957) serve as evidence that the concerns for the status of the college program of physical education had reached a high level in the decade of the 1950s.

By 1960, all areas of education were being carefully examined by educators. An ever-increasing urgency for the solidifying of the objectives of the general college program of physical education became apparent. Some reasons for this urgency apparently were (a) heightened mobility of our time or world mobility, not simply in the United States; (b) an increase in students eligible for college education; (c) competition for available funds and facilities; (d) competition for student time; (e) over-crowded curricula; (f) an increase in knowledge related to the known needs and interests of college students; and (g) demands for the reexamination of the goals of higher education.

Despite these forces, a review of the reports of research studies in physical education revealed scant attention to the general college program. In 1961, physical educators were still striving to arrive at central purposes upon which they might agree and base the general college program, as well as means by which the program might be interpreted to the public at large. Abernathy (1961), in a report to the National Conference on the Interpretation of Physical Education, stated the objectives of physical education for the general college student to be

- an opportunity for regular and needed exercise;
- an opportunity to improve skill;
- an opportunity to meet others;
- an opportunity to be a member of a class sufficiently small for individual identification; and
- an opportunity to improve health, fitness and a sense of well-being. (p. 33)

The Joint Committee on Physical Education for College Men and Women (1962), representing the same three associations which sponsored the 1954 conference, met again. The central purposes formulated for the forthcoming 1962 conference were to

- re-examine objectives, content and methods;
- revise standards; and

- improve programs so that college students may realize greater benefits from their physical education experiences.

Objectives of physical education for college men and women formulated by the 1962 conferees were (a) promotion of physical development; (b) improvement of neuromuscular skills; (c) acquisition of knowledge, understandings, and attitudes; and (d) growth in social competence and emotional stability (p. 25). In further attempts to clarify, establish, and interpret the objectives of the general college program of physical education, many individual collegiate institutions worked closely with this 1962 national committee to supplement the committee's efforts to improve this area of physical education.

In a booklet published by The Ohio State University's Department of Physical Education (1960), objectives that seem to represent current reports of physical education goals of individual colleges and universities are listed. It was proposed in this booklet that physical education at the college level should provide

- an opportunity for further development of the qualities comprising the biological aspects of fitness.
- an opportunity for the development of social competence and psychological points of view which attend participation with others in satisfying activities.
- an opportunity to learn the skills of individually chosen recreational activities which have life long use.
- an enrichment of creative aptitudes of the students through participation in the cultural media provided by dance as an art form.
- an adequate knowledge of the historical development, rules, courtesies, customs, strategies, and techniques of recreational sports.
- an appreciation of the role which recreation sports play in the modern world. (p. 2)

Pelton (1966) in a study of 29 countries entailing a questionnaire, revealed these purposes held by International leaders in Physical Education.

- To attain and maintain high-level physical fitness
- To acquire satisfactory skill in recreational activities
- To assure a healthy balance between mental and physical activity
- To aid in the proper social development among and between sexes
- To acquire the proper attitude of the need for continued participation throughout life and to understand the relationship of physical education to the total education process
- To detect and train gifted students for competitive athletics (Olympics)
- To obtain fitness for military service

In another study Pelton (1966) surveyed selected college physical educators and selected academic Vice-Presidents in the United States to determine differences in their beliefs concerning physical education for the general college student. However, each master concept (there were 10) had four subconcepts clarifying the master concept. Thus the data were not used in this comparison.

Oxendine (1978) prepared a status report on this program for the National Association for Sport and Physical Education. The researched topics included the availability of facilities, requirements, sex composition of classes, trends in courses taught, faculty, and grading. It is of interest to note that the perceived objectives were not researched.

Loucks (1979) did a comparative study of research by Rosentsweig (1969) and Tillman (1976) and American physical educators, and the analysis of these are noted in Tables 1 and 2.

The recent research conducted on this topic in the United States was completed by Everett and Soudan (1981) (see Tables 3 and 4). They state in their introduction, "It is current educational philosophy that objectives will be accomplished more successfully if they are determined on the basis of needs and interests as expressed by students themselves." The Everett-Soudan study researched college students at Florida State University. The Pelton study surveyed directors of physical education in their respective countries and representatives or officers in one of the international organizations of physical education and sport. Of the 101 questionnaires mailed 72 were returned. The rating of each of the 24 objectives is reported in Table 5. No further comparisons were made due to the fact that Everett-Soudan did not report beyond those listed in the previous tables.

Table 1 Comparison of Ranked Objectives of Physical Education

Objective	1967 to 1968 study[a]	Ranking 1975 graduate curriculum class[b]	1979 study physical education seniors[c]
Organic vigor	1	7	5
Neuromuscular skills	2	5 (tie)	1
Leisure time activities	3	4	6
Self-realization	4	1	3
Emotional stability	5	3	4
Democratic values	6	8	10
Mental development	7	2	2
Social competency	8	5 (tie)	7
Spiritual and moral strength	9	10	9
Cultural appreciation	10	9	8

[a]Rosentswieg study; [b]Tillman study; [c]Loucks study.

Table 2 Ranking of Objectives of Physical Education by Sex (Loucks Study)

Objective	Ranking	
	Males	Females
Neuromuscular skills	1	1
Mental development	2	2
Self-realization	3	3
Organic vigor	4	7
Emotional stability	5	4
Leisure time activities	6	5
Social competency	7	6
Cultural appreciation	8	9
Spiritual and moral values	9	8
Democratic values	10	10

Table 3 Comparison of the Conclusions of the Everett-Soudan Study With the Pelton Study

College students (Everett-Soudan)	International physical educators (Pelton)
• Keeping in good health and physical condition	• Keeping good health and physical condition
• Getting regular exercise	• Developing adequate organic vigor for performance of daily activities with skill and ease
• Having fun	• Getting regular exercise
• Improving self-confidence	• Developing self-realization

Conclusions

Based on the results of the findings of this investigation and within the limitations of the comparative method employed, these conclusions are offered.

• The objective (developing adequate organic vigor for performance of daily activities with skill and ease) reported as most important was the same for college students as for international leaders. This objective

Table 4   Objectives Expressed as Lowest in Importance

College students (Everett-Soudan)	International physical educators (Pelton)
• Achieving success	• Providing vocational leadership
• Developing leadership	• Developing leadership
• Developing skill in various sports	• Achieving success
• Understanding the mechanical principles of movement and the effects of exercise on the human body	• Keeping weight controlled
	• Understanding the mechanical principles of movement and the effects of exercise on the human body
• Providing vocational preparation	

Table 5   Survey to Determine the Personal Beliefs Held by International Physical Educators Concerning the Objectives of Physical Education for Students Not Training to be Athletic Coaches or Teachers of Physical Education

Item	Very important	Important	Somewhat important	Not important
1. Developing adequate organic vigor for performance of daily activities with skill and ease	52.2	31.3	12.5	
2. Having fun	27.1	50.0	16.7	
3. Making new friends	8.3	41.7	31.3	8.3
4. Getting regular exercise	52.1	29.2	10.4	
5. Understanding with other people	14.6	41.7	29.2	2.1
6. Improving self-confidence	31.3	29.2	20.8	6.3
7. Preventing, detecting, and correcting physical defects	20.8	35.4	20.8	6.3
8. Developing the habits of spending a portion of time in enjoyable physical activity	47.9	31.1	16.7	
9. Keeping good health and physical condition	56.3	31.3	10.4	2.1
10. Achieving success	8.3	35.4	39.6	12.5
11. Having ability to move freely and with control	20.8	50.0	22.9	4.2

(Cont.)

Table 5 (Cont.)

Item	Very important	Important	Somewhat important	Not important
12. Providing vocational preparation	6.3	22.9	39.6	31.3
13. Understanding the mechanical principles of movement and the effects of exercise on the human body	20.8	35.4	29.2	12.5
14. Developing positive mental qualities	20.8	52.1	20.1	8.3
15. Developing skill in various sports	16.7	45.8	25.0	8.3
16. Learning activities which could be continued outside of school	37.5	25.0	14.6	4.2
17. Developing sociability and social cooperation	33.3	33.3	27.1	4.2
18. Developing emotional stability	14.6	39.6	27.1	6.3
19. Developing self-realization	31.3	47.9	10.4	2.1
20. Keeping weight controlled	14.6	35.4	37.5	8.3
21. Developing sportsmanship	22.9	43.8	33.3	4.2
22. Developing and maintaining sound and proper physical functioning	31.3	41.7	16.7	2.1
23. Developing leadership	14.6	27.1	43.8	10.4
24. Maintaining an optimal level of physiological efficiency	29.2	50.0	14.6	6.3

is also comparable to the number one objective stated in Rosentsweig's and Louck's studies. Tillman's data revealed this objective to be number seven.

- Getting regular exercise was the number two objective expressed in college student preferences and number three for international leaders.
- There was no agreement as to the number two and four preference of international leaders when compared with college students.
- Of the objectives expressed as of lowest importance, none were listed for exact comparison. It is interesting to note that keeping weight controlled, listed third in least importance by international leaders, did not appear in the list by college students. In contrast, developing skills in

various sports was listed second in least importance by college students and did not appear in the international leaders list.
- There has been a noticeable interest in obtaining specific data on the values, needs, and interests of a variety of populations when planning programs of physical education, exercise, and dance for the student who is not planning to be a teacher of physical education or a coach.

In a closing philosophic comment, however, this analysis, in an historic sense, confirms the contention of many physical educators that the relative importance of the prevailing philosophy for a given program is tempered by the demands of the present. No doubt, as each physical educator reviews the findings of this study, he or she will recognize certain beliefs and practices similar to his or her own and those of his or her country. In the words of Rueben B. Frost, ''The opportunities are boundless . . . their commitment is clear . . . action has already begun . . . I have for our profession . . . a vision of greatness.''

International leaders in sport and physical education have a special opportunity. Regardless of race, religion, political ideology, or professional philosophy, they can come together to exchange ideas on how mankind can best utilize physical activity in the pursuit of optimum physical and mental development. The commitment to greater world understanding through health, physical education, recreation, and sports competition is a worthy goal shared by many. Action to bring about this understanding is underway, and the energy necessary to realize this goal must come from sport and physical education leaders who share this vision of greatness for their profession. We are living in the midst of a period requiring great readjustment. One of these adjustments may be to learn once more to hold beliefs.

References

Abernathy, R. (1970). *New curriculum perspectives* (p. XI). Dubuque, IA: William C. Brown.

American Association for Health, Physical Education and Recreation (1954, October 4, 5, 6). Physical education for college men and women. *Washington conference report* (pp. 40, 89). Washington, DC: Author.

American Association for Health, Physical Education and Recreation (1963). Professional report from the Joint Committee on Physical Education for College Men and Women. *Journal of Health, Physical Education and Recreation, XXXIV.*

Buie, G.E. (1956). *An evaluation of the women's non-major physical education program in selected American colleges and universities.* Unpublished doctoral dissertation, University of Wisconsin, Madison.

Casady, R.D. (1959). *Effect of lectures presented in required program of physical education.* Unpublished doctoral dissertation, State University of Iowa, Ames.

Cobb, L.S. (1943). A study of the functions of physical education in higher education. *Contributions to education* (No. 876, pp. 49-101). New York: Bureau of Publications, Teachers College, Columbia University.

Cordts, H.J. (1959). *Status of the physical education required or instructional program for men and women in the four-year colleges and universities of the United States.* Unpublished doctoral dissertation, Syracuse University, NY.

Everett, P.W., & Soudan, S.A. (1981, May). Physical education objectives expressed as needs by Florida State University students. *Journal of Physical Education and Recreation.* Reston, VA: AAHPERD.

Fornia, D.L. (1957). *Coeducational physical education in institutions of higher learning.* Unpublished doctoral dissertation, University of Southern California, Los Angeles.

Harris, W.H. (1951). *A study of the physical education programs for men at state institutions of higher learning in Arizona.* Unpublished doctoral dissertation, University of Kentucky, Lexington.

Hendricks, E.T. (1951). *The organization and administrative operation of physical education service programs in land-grant colleges and universities.* Unpublished doctoral dissertation, University of Missouri, St. Louis.

Hughes, L.H. (1939). The administration of health, physical education and recreation for men in colleges and universities. *College contributions to education* (No. 541). New York: Bureau of Publications, Teachers College, Columbia University.

Hunsicker, P.A. (1954). A survey of the service physical education programs in American colleges and universities. *57th Annual Proceedings of the College Physical Education Association,* pp. 29-31.

Kretchmar, R.R. (1949). *The development of coeducation in college physical education.* Unpublished doctoral dissertation, Teachers College, Columbia University, NY.

Loucks, H.D. (1979, September). New professionals reorder objectives. *Journal of Physical Education and Recreation.* Reston, VA: AAHPERD.

Lynn, M. (1944). *Major emphases of physical education in the United States.* Unpublished doctoral dissertation, University of Pittsburgh, PA.

McCormick, H.J. (1942). *Enriching the physical education service program in colleges and universities.* New York: Teachers College, Columbia University.

Ohio State University Department of Physical Education. (1960, November). *The contributions of health, education and physical education to the general education of students at the Ohio State University.* Columbus, OH: Author.

Oxendine, J.B. (1961, October 2). *Survey of the status and trends of required physical education programs in colleges and and universities of the United States* (p. 9). Washington, DC: American Association for Health, Physical Education and Recreation.

Oxendine, J.B. (1978, January). The general instruction program in physical education at four-year colleges and universities: 1977. *Journal of Physical Education and Recreation.* Reston, VA: AAHPERD.

Pelton, B.C. (1966). *A critical analysis of current concepts underlying general physical education programs in higher education.* Unpublished doctoral dissertation, University of Southern California, Los Angeles.

Pelton, B.C. (1968). International programs of physical education for college youth. *Gymnasium* (p. 11). Stuttgart, West Germany: ICHPER.

Phillips, B.M. (1953). *An evaluation of the physical education service programs in the liberal arts and teachers' colleges of New York state.* Unpublished doctoral dissertation, New York University, New York.

Polonsky, D.L. (1958). *An evaluation of selected physical education activities for college men: A comparative analysis of physical education activities to determine their educational potentials.* Unpublished doctoral dissertation, New York University, New York.

President's Commission on Higher Education (1947). Establishing goals. *Higher education for American democracy* (Vol. I). Washington, DC: U.S. Government Printing Office.

Rosentswieg, J. (1969, December). A ranking of the objectives of physical education. *Research Quarterly,* **40,** 783-787.

Shea, E.J. (1958, December). The status and role of physical education as a college and university requirement. *Journal of Health, Physical Education and Recreation,* **XXIX,** 31, 64.

Spears, B.M. (1956). *Philosophical bases for physical education experiences consistent with the goals of general education for women.* Unpublished doctoral dissertation, New York University, New York.

Tillman, K. (1976, May). Value shifts by physical educators. *The Reporter.* New Jersey: AHPER.

Turner, M.J. (1957). *An evaluation of the physical education program for its educative potential for democratic leadership development in college women.* Unpublished doctoral dissertation, Pennsylvania State University, State College.

Wagner, E.P. (1950). *Present status of required programs of physical education for men in colleges and universities enrolling more than 5,000.* Unpublished doctoral dissertation, State University of Iowa, Ames.

Weber, R., & Weber, J. (1952). *A study of the relationship of physical fitness to success in school and to personality.* Unpublished doctoral dissertation, State University of Iowa, Ames.

Special Physical Education and Sport in Mexico City

Georgina Grijalua Enciso
Department of Sport and Recreation for Special Populations,
Mexico City

It is the intention of this paper to describe to you the physical education and sport program for special populations (atipicos) that has only recently emerged in my country, Mexico. Although limited sports opportunity has existed since 1935 within the Mexican school system, it has only been since 1975 that extracurricular programs for the handicapped have been initiated and placed under the direction of the Department of Sport and Recreation for the Handicapped (atipicos) within the Mexican governmental system (i.e., as part of the state government offices illustrated in Figure 1).

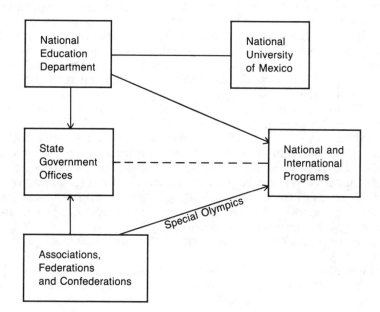

Figure 1 Relationships among physical education and sport programs in Mexico.

It is interesting to note that the growth of our interest in special populations seems to parallel the Public Law 94-142, Education for All Handicapped Children Act of 1975, within the United States. Our experience in Mexico, however, has been markedly different concerning the support and follow through of our programs compared to most of the programs in the United States. Nevertheless, the historical significance of our programs is beginning to impact on our entire country.

Our first classes with mentally retarded persons began in October, 1978, and were modeled after the "Play to Grow" and "From Beginners to Champions" of the Kennedy Foundation. They were based on both the Declaration established at the First Sports Congress of Mexico City that "All persons should have access to sport" and the commitment of our government to improve the lifestyle and quality of life of all residents of Mexico. The program as outlined is modest in nature, but beginning to gain full cooperation of the total Mexican governmental system. In 1978 we began with the mentally retarded, 1979 the motor handicapped, 1980 the visually handicapped, and 1981 the hearing impaired. In 1982 we completed our planned cycle with the inclusion of the emotionally disturbed. Our support and program have grown, but still we are only scratching the surface of what is needed.

Our programs, at present, are restricted to extracurricular school activity. Most of our participants register voluntarily for three, 2-hour classes per week, which are divided into recreational, cultural, athletic, and sport activities. Our sessions are conducted in parks, gardens, sports centers, community gymnasiums, and playgrounds; these facilities and their administration are a most pressing problem.

Teachers and volunteer workers are another problem. Our programs, like those conducted in the Washington, D.C., area, rely on volunteers; and parents, siblings, and friends of the participants are encouraged to actively participate. Seminars and training sessions are provided for the workers, and constant supervision by our staff is also maintained. Medical permissions and tests are used to screen and place our participants into classes of 12 to 25 participants, dividing into small clusters for maximum effectiveness. But there is no doubt that trained physical educators are missing. Adapted physical education instruction is lacking in colleges and universities, and most of our teachers have received their training in special 30-hour training courses or outside institutions in another country. Our staff of physical educators, social workers, special educators, and psychologists is just now beginning to provide a full-service program to meet the needs of the participants, their families, and our obligation to society. We are now providing some support services with private institutions, educational schools, and universities, and we will be able to improve the types and extent of human and financial assistance programs in the future.

Comparatively speaking, we are always seeking assistance and expertise to improve our delivery system of special physical education and sport. Educational programs including curriculum development, evaluation of methods, and participant progress are planned for future emphasis. Short- and long-range planning concerning the special needs, skill sequencing, teaching strategies, clinics, tutorial programs, and the like continue to be developed and coordinated by our agency with support from various phases of the government and community.

This seminar has offered me and the governmental department that I represent an opportunity to engage in meaningful and productive discussions concerning the building of future programs in special physical education and sport, and to share our program's structure, goals, and efforts in order to sensitize the rest of the world to the needs of the special populations of the globe.

Sport and the Hooligan

David Webb
Edgehill College of Higher Education

This paper is intended to be a descriptive analysis of dysfunction and sport. It is the intent of the author to leave the reader the comparisons of the various dysfunctions of sport in his or her own particular country and specific sport situation.

Most readers will be aware of the violence that often accompanies top-class football matches in the United Kingdom (UK). It is a sad reflection on the present state of affairs that hooliganism is no longer considered to be particularly newsworthy (Carroll, 1980). The reports in newspapers are now confined to the more serious incidents involving large numbers of people, and this paper will draw extensively on these reports. Lesser forms of hooliganism, however, have now become such an accepted part of the British soccer scene that they are no longer considered newsworthy. With the increase in international competition, this same violence has spread to other footballing nations where sport and turmoil seem synonymous. Over the past few years spectator hooliganism has caused both bans and fines to be imposed on British football clubs by the European Football Union.

A major problem to be faced when discussing football hooliganism concerns the definition of terms. Hooliganism is not a criminal offense in itself, but it is a term that has come to have a blanket meaning covering a variety of actions, some of which are criminal, while others are merely frightening or of nuisance value (Carroll, 1980). In this paper I shall follow the trend established by other writers in the field, and use the term to reflect behavior that ranges from excessive fanaticism and general rowdyism to acts of criminal violence against persons and malicious damage to property.

In the first part of the paper I shall attempt to paint a picture of the problem as it exists for those who have only a nodding acquaintance with the game of soccer in the U.K. I shall offer a description of both the violence and the football hooligan and go on to examine some of the arguments proposed to account for violence in sport. In doing so I shall seek to establish why this behavior in its worst form is associated with the UK in general, and with soccer in particular. While it may be argued that some discussion of possible solutions would be fruitful, the nature of the problem itself, which I believe is fundamental to society, and the pressures of time set it beyond the scope of this paper.

The Nature of the Problem

It is perhaps newspaper reports of incidents that paint the most complete picture of violence at soccer matches. The first, from which I shall quote, concerns a report of a London 'derby' game between Arsenal and West Ham written under the headline "May Day mayhem to fuel UEFA's fears," UEFA being the governing body of the sport in Europe. It is interesting to note that this four column article devotes only 10% of its space to a report of the actual soccer action. The rest is concerned with the behavior of the fans of both teams. It begins:

> The ultimate sanction of a ban on British clubs from European competition moved a step closer after the battle of Highbury on Saturday. Although this latest outbreak of hooliganism, which ended in one death and thirty arrests, was reserved for a domestic occasion, it will surely not have escaped UEFA's notice, coming only 24 hours after their disciplining of Aston Villa. A number of UEFA officials are understood to be disenchanted with Britain's chronic inability to prevent the transportation of violence to the continent and feel that the present punishments clearly do not fit the crime. After the mayhem in north London, which climaxed with an Arsenal supporter being stabbed to death after the match, any European observer must be tempted to ask: how can continental clubs control the lunatic fringe if British clubs cannot do so? (*Guardian*, 1982, May 3)

Two points emerge from these opening paragraphs. First, there is the question of punishment for offenders. Of course, the hooligans, themselves, are brought before the courts to undergo the due processes of law when they can be apprehended. However, there are so many that it is impossible to isolate all the offenders. Therefore, the football authorities, themselves, have generally taken action against the clubs whose fans have caused trouble. There is reference in the article to the heavy fine imposed on Aston Villa, later to become European champions, as a result of a disturbance in the semifinal round of the competition. Second, there is the question of what the clubs can do about it. The article continues,

> Yet it is difficult to see how Arsenal, a highly organized club with a good record of efficient crowd segregation, could have avoided Saturday's terrace violence. The main body of West Ham's support had gathered in the appropriate pen at the Clock End, but the remainder, wearing no colors and therefore unidentifiable to the police, had infiltrated a corner of the North Bank, the bastion of Arsenal's young support. This infiltration, on the evidence of later events, was clearly pre-planned. There were skirmishes in this area before the teams appeared, but nothing to suggest the eruption a split second before the kick-off. It was then that West Ham's anonymous supporters surged as one towards the middle of the North Bank. In the fighting that followed an orange smoke bomb exploded, obscuring the police's view and forcing hundreds of frightened supporters to take refuge on the pitch behind the goal. The referee, John Hunting, had no option but to stop the match—which he did after only 90 seconds—and take the teams off the pitch. There they remained for 11 minutes as the fighting raged. After order was restored

hundreds of Arsenal supporters were shepherded down the cinder track to the home section of the Clock End. Many of the invading West Ham fans meanwhile were herded into a strongly segregated section of the North Bank. Play and comparative peace was resumed, although there were further ter-race skirmishes towards the end. (*Guradian*, 1982, May 3)

The sense of helplessness among football clubs is emphasized by the com-ments of the managers of both teams.

The match itself, won comfortably by Arsenal, was inevitably an anti-climax. Afterwards a sense of frustration and helplessness—quite apart from the at-mosphere of violence—pervaded all quarters. Terry Neill, Arsenal's manager, spoke for everyone when he said: "I don't know where we go from here. It's frightening." Neill was visibly upset. "I don't think the press exaggerate as far as hooliganism is concerned. If it doesn't stop there'll be no game," he said, before asking the rhetorical question: "What sort of parents produce mindless morons like that?" He and his club now await the referee's report to the league, but Neill is adamant that Arsenal could have done nothing more to prevent the violence. John Lyall, West Ham's manager, restricted his views to the professional standpoint. "We (manager and players) feel terribly frus-trated about it. We're just as frustrated as everybody else. There's no rhyme or reason for it," he said. The depressing postmortem ended with both managers roundly praising the referee and police who will, of course, present their own report of the afternoon. (*Guardian*, 1982, May 3)

One more description of match violence will suffice to present the problems facing the game of football in the U.K. It concerns another En-glish First Division League game between West Bromwich Albion and Leeds United.

West Midlands police last night mounted a baton charge against rioting Leeds United fans who tried to stop the vital relegation match in which their team lost 2-0 to West Bromwich Albion. The officer who ordered the charge by 100 policemen, Superintendent John Mellor, said afterwards: "Police officers were in danger of being killed, so there was no other way than to give them what they were giving us. If we had had 2000 policemen they would still have tried to come over the fence." The police had had prior information that Leeds supporters would attempt to have the game . . . stopped if their team were losing near the end. Sure enough, with Leeds 2-0 down, a scoreline which could put them in the Second Division, some of their 4000 fans started to wreck the metal fence penning them in. The fans had the fence down just as the final whistle blew. Three mounted policemen charged onto the pitch to stop the fans invading. Then the police moved in with their batons. Su-perintendent Mellor said: "I have never seen anything like it. The terrible thing about this is the people who get injured are young police officers. We were all showered with coins and cans. There were only a hundred of us against all of them. It was pretty frightening. They were like a regimented army. (*Guardian*, 1982, May 19)

This particular incident shows the power fans try to have in determining the outcome of important matches. It is suggested that Leeds fans invad-ed the pitch because their team was losing a vital game, and such a loss would almost certainly cause them to be relegated to Division Two next season. While this may account for this particular incident to some extent, it does not offer fundamental reasons for crowd violence.

Who are Hooligans?

Who are these football hooligans? Some of them are indistinguishable from all the other supporters who stand on the terraces every Saturday afternoon watching football matches. Indeed, in another report of the same West Bromwich Albion/Leeds United match, the police chief suggested that some who invaded the pitch were in their 30s and 40s with young children in tow. This is not the usual picture of the tearaway teenage football hooligan. However, the general picture painted of the football hooligan is similar to that in a Spanish newspaper during the World Cup competition.

> The caption in the local morning newspaper read: ''An English fan shows he has enjoyed the game.'' This particular sporting ambassador was lying flat on his back in a Bilbao street, clad only in a flag and Union Jack underpants, swilling down the remnants of a bottle of local wine. . . . On TV, they (the Spaniards) have been shown skinheads with red, white, and blue hair, a supporter with ''Notts Forest'' tattooed on the inside of his lips, another sporting a tattooed dotted line around his neck, accompanied by the words ''cut here,'' and one with a chain running between studs in his ear and nose. (*Guardian*, 1982, June 20)

There are, of course, other more erudite, though less graphic, studies of hooligans and their activities, which go some way towards explaining their behavior. One of the most illuminating is that carried out by Marsh (1978). He examined the soccer subculture and, in particular, the subculture of the ''ends.'' Spectators at a soccer match usually have their own territory, and the area behind the goals (the ends) are usually occupied by the younger fans. Much of his study is, therefore, based upon the importance of territories, social groupings, social roles, the solidarity of sets of fans, and intensified social groupings within those sets of fans.

The study was based on Oxford United Football Club, not one of the major clubs of British soccer, and so emphasizes the widespread nature of hooliganism, which is not limited to the top teams who attract large crowds week after week. In his examination of the ends he identified five distinct social groups.

1. Novices. These are the younger fans who, as it were, are serving an apprenticeship;
2. Rowdies. This is the largest group, mainly teenagers, who wear the usual 'aggro' clothes of jeans, shortened or rolled up to show a pair of boots (a major weapon in any fight), and braces;
3. Townies. These are older fans, not sporting 'aggro' outfits, who are a kind of graduate of the fans' career structure;

4. A fourth group. This was formed by those on the delinquent fringe, a kind of halfway group between Rowdies and Townies;
5. A fifth group. This was a group of other fans who remained at a distance from the Rowdies group.

The members of the Rowdies conformed most closely to the traditional image of the football hooligan, and Marsh went on to identify distinct social roles within their group.

- Chant leaders, whose leadership was restricted to chanting;
- Aggro leaders, who were the hard cases when it came to potential violence, and whose leadership was not restricted;
- Nutters, who were even harder cases, and whose behavior was seen as outrageous, even by other Rowdies;
- Hooligans, who did know how far to go, and whose manner was generally funny;
- Organizers; who organized trips, petitions, and so forth.

There was much evidence to suggest that the fans know their positions in the various social groupings and keep to them, and that the social roles and groupings provide a career structure for them. Indeed, there was also strong evidence that the groups have their own rules for action, which are generally followed.

In my opinion, Marsh does little to explain the underlying causes of hooliganism in his study; but he does show that hooligans, far from being different from normal people as is often suggested, do in fact have a social structure within their groups that is little different from that to be found in other more respectable groups.

Explanations for Hooligan Behavior

It is to the explanations, as they exist, for this kind of behavior that I now turn the reader's attention. These fall into two broad categories: those based within sport, itself, and those within society at large.

Sport as a Factor Causing Hooliganism

While I believe that they are contributing factors, rather than the underlying causes, many popular commentators have argued that aspects of sport, itself, are the major factors causing hooliganism. The main force of their arguments goes something like this: violence among spectators is caused by the example set by the players on the field of play and by the boring nature of many of the games; boredom among spectators causes them to seek more excitement in hooligan behavior.

The kind of violence referred to on the field of play is well known in the physical contact sports. It is seen in the knee in the back of the rugby player after he is tackled; the over-the-ball tackle in soccer, which can cause serious injury; off-the-ball incidents; and the retaliatory punches, which are thrown in almost every sport. It should be pointed out, however, that this kind of violence is not confined to the physical contact sports. It has spread to that most gentlemanly of games, cricket. Wickets are kicked over by dissatisfied batsmen, batsmen are surreptitiously elbowed by fielders in mid-wicket and verbally provoked (commonly called sledging) by close fielders in order to destroy their concentration, and umpires are shouldered by displeased bowlers and fielders. A few years ago there was the widely reported incident of the famous Australian bowler, Denis Lillee's, kicking of the Pakistan captain, Majid Khan, who immediately began to retaliate by wielding his bat at the Australian.

Some acts by the players are less obviously violent, but equally provocative to the crowd. The dissent that meets almost every decision made by the referee in a soccer match often results in his being jostled and sometimes even kicked. Dissent in cricket is no longer uncommon, especially the dumb show when a batsmen refuses to look at the umpire after an appeal has been made. When he does finally accept that he has been given out after the umpire has repeated his decision, the umpire must suffer the glare of the player for a long time. Acts such as this can only serve to provoke similar unruly behavior in the crowd.

The reasons given for such player behavior are usually financial. Tatz (1981), in an article in the *Weekend Australian Magazine*, sums up the situation well, drawing his example from tennis.

> Where is tennis—even tough competitive tennis—amid those mindless TV Grand Prix tournaments, the ones in which an inevitable Gerulaitis plays an inevitable Vilas who loses to an inevitable McEnroe for the inevitable 45,000 dollar seventh prize or 40,000 dollar eighth? Or where someone called Jaeger wins thirty grand for fourth place in a four-woman championship in yet another Virginia Shlurps event?

This state of affairs can be contrasted with Jack Nicklaus' reported response when asked to play an 18 hole, match-play game of golf with Johnny Miller, then the rising star of golf, with the winner taking $1 million and the loser $500,000: "It would not be in the best interests of the game." Tatz goes on to talk about the 'mechanized human condition,' which leads to a belief that what the public wants is "sex, violence, thrills, spills, pain, war, nationalism, flags, noise, blare, fanfare, booze, fags, colors and lights: as spectacle which the pimps sell their patron sponsors all in the name of service to the game (and an honest capitalist quid or two)." He further suggests that

> professional sport has become sterile, profane, "unholy" because it lacks the spontaneity so needed for a play element to survive in organic society . . . Sadly . . . the players have imbibed and accepted the swill that poses as a game, a sport, spectacle, or even entertainment. They have become victims of the razzamatazz, the garbage, the rhetoric they have helped to create unwittingly at first perhaps. They are the victim contributors to the evocation and glorification of public yobbism—for money.

However, money may not be the sole cause of poor behavior on the field of play. It appears that the position of sport in the scale of human values has changed during the past few decades. Where does sport fit in the hierarchy of values that includes love, hatred, peace, and war? I think it was the Dutch philosopher, Johan Huizinga, who said that modern society has lost the important difference between play and seriousness. He spoke of the way in which play has made a "fatal shift towards seriousness."

An indication of the seriousness in which sport is held can be seen in the terms used to describe various sporting occasions and venues. Baistow (1982), in an article on newspaper coverage of the Falklands' invasion, speaks of the language of war, of bombs, missiles, and dogfights; a language that creates an excitement of its own and had been relegated to the sports pages since the last major military action:

> Those emotive red-blooded words that had been relegated to the sports pages after Kenya, Cyprus and Aden were recalled to the colors. "Hero," so long languishing as a label for forwards who fumbled home the winning goal in surrogate battles, was back at the front, all over the front. (*The Guardian*, 1982, May 10)

Significant, too, are the frequent sporting allusions to religion. I think it was Bill Shankley, the former manager of Liverpool Football Club, who first called football "the opium of the people." How often do we hear a football ground being called a shrine or Baseball's Hall of Fame described as a Mecca?

Perhaps wanting to win and caring about losing are being felt today more than ever before. It is certainly much more acceptable to express emotions on the field of play than it was a generation ago. Today's crowds demand excitement. It could be argued that the enjoyment of the crowd takes precedence over the enjoyment of playing, and most of the crowd's enjoyment appears to be derived from their team's winning. The will and the need to win create tensions in the players that make misbehavior more likely and more understandable. When it happens, however, we must not necessarily assume that only the money at stake is to blame. The emotions of the sportsmen, themselves, are an important factor in the apparent rise in poor behavior.

So much for factors within sport, itself. There is little to suggest that these are more than minor causes of hooliganism in sport. The underlying factors might more likely be found in wider society.

Societal Factors Causing Hooliganism

The relationship between sport and wider society is recognized even by some of the players, themselves, especially the more perceptive. Mike Brearley, then the English cricket captain, links England's performance against Australia in 1981 to the riots that took place on the streets of some English cities during that summer. England had performed badly in the early stages of the series. Brearley was recalled as captain, and England's fortunes changed. He writes of the letters he received at this time from the public.

> There were occasional hints of an awareness that the dramatic and precari-
> ous successes by the national team had some intangible effect on national
> morale. Unemployment was after all approaching three million; and urban
> riots reached a frightening level in the summer of 1981. . . . Perhaps it is too
> fantastical to surmise that so trivial a thing as cricket could have any impact
> on the explosive antagonisms within society, and yet the riots did subside.
> Possibly the royal wedding gave some sense of identity and romance to alien-
> ated sections of the community. And this fairytale event was flanked by two
> miraculous national successes. . . . It is not fanciful, certainly, to claim that
> these wins gave a lift, however fortuitous and irrelevant, to the lives of mil-
> lions. (1982)

Some writers suggest that hooliganism occurs because fans seek "male bonding" and have a propensity towards aggression (Marsh, 1975; SSRC, 1978; Tiger, 1969). It is also argued that the manifestation of the male bonding process is, for some, going to soccer matches, while aggression is evidenced within a framework of rituals such as chanting or the taking of ends (Carroll, 1980). This kind of activity is both symbolic and substitute warfare, an acceptable way of acting out aggressive tendencies. Sometimes, however, this behavior develops into hooliganism, which is unacceptable to the majority. Most of these writers are of the opinion that such aggression is inevitable but not innate, its arousal being determined by the culture.

Other writers have explained hooliganism by locating it in the context of changes in subcultures and changes in the sport itself (Clarke, 1978; Taylor, 1971). The usual starting point for such writers (who devote their attention almost exclusively to soccer) is the working-class roots of the game of soccer in the U.K. Incidentally, this is a false assumption. Football in its modern form was invented by the Victorian public schools as a means of character building (Andrew, 1982). Indeed, the FA Cup, the premier trophy of English soccer, was modeled on an interhouse competition at Harrow School when it was founded in 1871. However, it does remain true that many of the historical origins of soccer are within the working-class. Many churches and chapels believed that football could build the character of the working-classes as well as the public schoolboys. This year's European Cup holder, Aston Villa, was founded in 1874 by the Villa Cross Wesleyan Chapel. Everton was launched in 1878 by St. Domingo's Church Sunday School. One of its better known offshoots is now the Liverpool Football Club.

The main argument of these writers revolves around the structural changes that have occurred in soccer. The root of hooliganism is, they suggest, to be found in the changes that have taken place, causing the separation of the working-class from the club and the players to sever links with the subculture:

> Such changes as increasing professionalisation, commercialisation and inter-
> nationalism brought the abolition of maximum wages, greater mobility of play-

ers, huge transfer fees, sponsorship, increase in international competitions, greater television coverage, and more marked links with entertainment as an industry. (Carroll, 1980)

This argument can be taken a stage further by linking the phenomenon less directly to soccer and more closely to the social position of working-class youth (Clarke, 1978). The relationship between the young and adults has become one of greater freedom, resulting in a social and physical separation in the soccer ground so that control of the younger fans has been loosened.

This kind of study goes some way towards overcoming a major weakness concerned with current thinking about soccer hooliganism. It cannot be isolated from the rest of society, and should be seen as part of a more general malaise in what has been called an age of increasing violence.

Before starting to examine the problem from this wider perspective, it is also worth attempting to destroy one assumption that has done little to improve our understanding of sport and violence—that it is a relatively recent phenomenon. There is evidence to suggest that there has been a link between sport and violence for a long time. It is claimed that, even as early as the Middle Ages, football was synonymous with crowd violence (Andrew, 1982). So serious was the problem that the authorities tried to ban it both because of the violence and because it interfered with archery practice for the wars against the French. Philip Stubbes, the Elizabethan pamphleteer, wrote "I protest unto you it may be rather called a . . . bloody and murthering practise than a fellowly sporte or pastime" (quoted in Andrew, 1982).

During the Victorian and Edwardian periods, participation in football was the most ubiquitous cause of vandalism. Football, then, was an important aspect of street gang activities, providing a creative and physical outlet for tension and aggression. The game offered to young people the opportunity for group participation, the assertion of masculinity, and the creation of excitement (Humphries, 1981). Humphries speaks, too, of the resulting confrontation with police.

> But high-spirited participation in street football led gangs into bitter conflicts with the police who . . . enforced elaborate rules and regulations designed to prevent "dangerous play in the streets." (Humphries, 1981)

While recognizing that these regulations were necessary for law and order enforcement, Humphries does argue that there is evidence to suggest that the police were often brutal in their treatment of those who played street football as a result of the pressure applied by middle-class reformers, who wished to see the elimination of street activities. Then, just as now, some of the most serious problems arose when street gangs traveled to play their football in local parks. It was not uncommon for young people to be cautioned or arrested for exuberant activity. The following is the account of a witness remembering an occasion in the early years of the 20th century.

We used to go over and play football in the park. 'Course, coming back—the old trams was on the roads then—coming back the tram stopped and we was singing "Nellie Dean." And a copper got on the tram and I finished up in Bridewell, "disturbing the peace". . . . He catched hold of me, took me down to Bedminster police station and I was breaking me heart. I had to appear up Bridewell, and they fined me a shilling for disturbing the peace and I was singing "Nellie Dean." I shall never forget it. (Quoted in Humphries, 1981)

Understanding Hooliganism

The links between violence and sport are not new, then; and when they are viewed from an historical perspective, more light is shed on the problem. I argue, therefore, that there are three key elements necessary for an understanding of the phenomenon. The problem must be seen in the context of (a) wider society, (b) particularly the working-class in Britain, and (c) from an historical perspective.

The picture of working-class youth in Britain that generally emerges from studies is a catalog of ignorance, immorality, persistent rule-breaking, and opposition to authority, in spite of all the efforts of the state to rescue youth from the destructive effects of its culture and environment.

Focusing on the resultant violent behavior, of which I argue sporting violence is a part, mass culture critics tend to explain it in terms of a loss of community control and traditional authority, and by the development of depersonalized mass institutions and living conditions. Delinquency has, therefore, come to be associated with the lack of defensible space on housing estates and with the depersonalized conditions found at work.

The second major tradition in the history of the working-class is the deprivation theory. This concerns itself with a hereditary lack of potential for intellectual and emotional development among the working-classes. It is suggested that the biological and psychological conditions of working-class children and youth are genetically inferior to their middle-class counterparts. George Sims, writing in 1907, stated quite clearly the anxieties such a view caused.

The vital factor in the future of the British Empire is the child. . . . Thousands of the tortured children who suffer and survive will only do so with stunted bodies and enfeebled minds to become the physical, moral and mental wreckage which burdens the state and fills the lunatic asylums, the workhouses and the jails. Against the guilt of race suicide our men of science are everywhere preaching their sermons today. It is against the guilt of race murder that the cry of the children should ring through the land. (Sims, 1907)

This image of a feebleminded generation remains today in the "mindless morons" explanation of football violence. The most anxiety was aroused by those sections of working-class youth that most obviously flouted middle-class values and norms of behavior and most violently resisted authority.

If I were to accept either of these theories, which both for different reasons attribute to working-class cultures qualities of violence, brutality, and intolerance, it would invalidate what I believe to be the reason for violence in sport. In fact, it is acknowledged that the historical value of such theories is limited (Humphries, 1981). Violence in sport cannot, as I have said, be separated from wider society. What I propose is that football hooliganism is a form of working-class resistance to authority. It is the modern embodiment of a long historical tradition of protest in the U.K.

There has, in recent history, been a dramatic increase in state intervention that governs many aspects of family life, education, and work. I contend that the behavior of working-class youth, which I have highlighted in this paper, is a form of resistance to powerful attempts to inculcate conformist middle class modes of behavior through manipulation and control. This resistance takes the form of rule breaking, hooliganism, and violence, which has traditionally been viewed as working-class indiscipline or delinquency. Violence at soccer matches, for example, is the modern successor to a long line of activities, such as disaffection from school work, classroom disobedience, school strikes, larking about, social crime, street gang violence, rebellious sexual behavior, absenteeism, and acts of industrial sabotage. It cannot be treated in isolation from this tradition, which has been with us for a long time. It might be more appropriate, therefore, to stop talking about hooligans and begin to address problems of social reform in which the profession of physical education and sport can play a significant role.

References

Andrew, C. (1982, June 10). I am playing purely for my own pleasure, sir! *The Listener*, pp. 7-8.

Baistow, T. (1982, May 10). The Fleet Street warriors who turn from bingo to jingo in the battle of sagging sales. *The Guardian*.

Brearley, M. (1982). Phoenix from the ashes. Public disorders and sporting events. *Sports Council Joint Report*. London: Hodder and Stoughton.

Carroll, R. (1980). Football hooliganism in England. *International Review of Sport Sociology*, 2(15), 77-92.

Clarke, J. (1978). Football and working-class fans: Tradition and change. In R. Ingham et al. (Eds.), *Football hooliganism*. London: Inter Action.

The Guardian (1982, May 3, 19, 20).

Humphries, S. (1981). *Hooligans or rebels? An oral history of working-class childhood and youth 1889-1939*. Oxford: Blackwell.

Marsh, P. (1975, April 3). Understanding aggro. *New Society*.

Marsh, P. (1978). *The rules of disorder*. London: RKP.

Sims, G. (1907). *The black stain*. London: McMillan.

Sports Council Joint Report. (1978). Public disorders and sporting events. London: Author.

Tatz, C. (1981, February 21, 22). The cricket assassins. *The Weekend Australian.*

Taylor, I. (1971). Soccer consciousness and soccer hooliganism. In S. Cohen (Ed.), *Images of deviance.* Harmondsworth: Penguin.

Tiger, L. (1969). *Men in groups.* London: Nelson.

An Evaluation of the Contribution of Overseas Study Programs in the Education of Students

Joy Standeven
Brighton Polytechnic

Although overseas study is hardly an innovation in higher education, the amount of literature available is limited and is descriptive rather than evaluative. In common with many other British and overseas institutions, the Chelsea School of Human Movement, a department of Brighton Polytechnic, has promoted various overseas study programs. These include a 6 or 12 week exchange scheme with various North American and European institutions, and a one-year junior year program for Canadian and American students. This paper represents an attempt to evaluate these opportunities, and to develop a framework within which such study experiences may be conceptualized.

A change over in the curriculum of the Bachelor of Education degree provided the stimulus for undertaking this evaluation. While care had been exercised in the planning and administration of departmental overseas programs, no assessment of the value of such experiences had been attempted. Lack of evaluation is a weakness of study programs abroad that Pfinster (1971) alludes to in his paper. The intention exists within new departmental curricula proposals to retain the possibility of overseas study, but the precise nature and extent of such study and student eligibility to participate has not yet been fully defined. Since new policies and practices are about to be established within the department critical assessment of overseas study opportunities seemed appropriate.

This paper attempts to answer such questions as (a) what values accrue to the participant in overseas study programs, and what is considered their relative importance; (b) to what extent study abroad interrupts the cohesiveness of a college course, and whether such interruption is necessarily dysfunctional; (c) whether equivalence of academic standards needs to be seen in terms of course content; and (d) whether overseas study is a desirable alternative to be retained within a course, and what implications may be drawn for teaching.

Methods

The nature of this investigation sites it within the illuminative paradigm (Miller & Parlett, 1974).[1] Lacking any clearly defined goals, outcomes of the various overseas study programs with which the department is concerned have remained untested. This piece of research was designed to identify what ends are achieved, to promote discussion as to the appropriateness of such ends, and to provide a conceptualization as a basis for further research and planning.

The data used in this paper were collected by means of questionnaire and interview. The respondents represent all students, both British and overseas, engaged in the 1982 Exchange program and the 1981 to 1982 Junior Year Abroad course of the department; a sample of British students who participated in the Exchange program 1976 to 1981; a sample of overseas students who were either exchangees or participants in the Junior Year Abroad program 1976 to 1981; representative staff from all overseas institutions involved in these programs; and staff from the Eastbourne department of the Education Faculty and the Chelsea School of Human Movement, Brighton Polytechnic. A final response rate of 72% was achieved of the total 176 persons contacted.[2] Respondents were drawn from Australia, Holland, Israel and, primarily Canada, Great Britain, and the United States.

Three different questionnaires were used (a) one for participants in the 1982 programs; (b) one for those who had participated in overseas study prior to 1982; and (c) one for academic staff. Questionnaires allowed between 20 to 40% open-ended response, with some questions common to both staff and students permitting a comparison between their perceptions. A number of British and overseas students in the department who were interviewed contributed additional data.

Results

The results shown in Table 1 indicate that, in the total group, respondents were very equal in their distribution of opinion regarding the academically beneficial nature of overseas study. This masks the fact that British staff predominantly see it as reasonably beneficial, while their overseas counterparts are more equally divided, with almost 50% of them seeing it as very beneficial. British students consider it more beneficial than their teachers do, while overseas students are in total agreement with their teachers at the time of their study abroad. Distanced by at least one year, the experience is enhanced in their eyes, and overseas students show a marked change of view that upgrades the value of the experience when they have had opportunity to reflect on it.

Regarding the nature of the educational value of overseas study, the two predominant benefits were considered to be enrichment of the student's college course and improvement in the student's awareness and tolerance of cultural differences (Table 2). The enhancement that such

Table 1 Extent of Academic Benefit from Overseas Study

Respondents	Very beneficial	Percentage Reasonably beneficial	Not very beneficial
British staff	16	80	4
Overseas staff	46	46	8
British student			
At the time	51	46	3
On reflection	57	43	—
Overseas students			
At the time	46	46	8
On reflection	73	23	4
Total sample	48	49	3

Table 2 Nature of Benefit from Overseas Study

Benefit	Significant amount	Percentage Some	A little	Not at all
Enriching course	85	11	3	1
Contributing to study of physical education	56	34	7	3
Vocational relevance	36	31	25	8
Interdisciplinary	57	27	11	5
Tolerance of cultural differences	88	11	1	—
Understanding of own culture	65	24	8	3

experience gives to students' understanding of their own culture, the contribution that it makes to the study of physical education, and its value as a broadening interdisciplinary experience received substantial support. The value about which respondents were most divided (a third considered it to have little or no contribution to make) was its significance vocationally. Rank ordering of values revealed particular perceptions.

Consistently the most important value was rated as making students more aware and tolerant of cultural differences. British students alone rate this as secondary to enriching their college course. In ranking enrichment of the college course second, British staff demonstrated a measure of agreement with British students. Overseas students ranked this only third, and their staff ranked it one lower at fourth place. Staff, both British and overseas, believed students' understanding of their own culture was affected more than students found to be the case. British respondents ranked broadening interdisciplinary experience lower than overseas respondents. British students were alone in the relatively high ranking given to the direct contribution overseas experience makes to the study of their subject area in physical education. All respondents were agreed that vocational relevance was the least valued aspect of overseas study. In addition to the values listed, a large number of staff and students proposed that increased self-confidence was a value derived from overseas study.

Students considered that study abroad offered benefits that might not be regarded as "academic"; for example, opportunities to participate in non-curricula events, insight into different lifestyles, the establishment of new personal relationships, and travel. Staff response showed 84% of British staff and 100% of overseas staff considered that the "non-academic" aspects justified offering students' overseas study opportunities. A minority of British staff are represented by one who commented, "This aspect is important but not sufficient to *justify* offering it." The majority are characterized by comments such as, "I basically believe it is all academic, because I believe so strongly that some of our greatest learning comes in out-of-class settings" and "This seems crucial; if education is preparation for life at all, surely understanding the life of other cultures will tend away from jingoism." Twelve percent of the respondents questioned the use of the term "nonacademic," and in view of the different interpretations, the results may be considered dubious.

Immediately on return to their "home" institution, 29% of British students and 54% of overseas students perceived disadvantages in overseas study. Some experienced difficulty in adapting to different study expectations, some students perceived absence of particular pieces of work disadvantageous, but the majority commented on the inability of their home based peers to understand the newly broadened perspectives of their returning colleagues. Distanced from the experience, these percentages dropped by more than half, leaving 14% of British students and 22% of overseas students believing the disadvantages more long lasting. Staff views disagreed significantly with student views since 62% of British staff perceived disadvantages, though only 25% of these considered the disadvantages to be serious. On the other hand, 92% of overseas staff perceived no disadvantages. Reasons offered by British staff focused mainly on lack of cohesiveness to the home based course. Despite the interruption in their course, students generally do well, achieving high standards not only during their overseas study but in subsequent work at home. Students whose marks decline following their time abroad represent a small minority.

The length of overseas study varied from 3 to 42 weeks. Despite these marked differences 70% of both British and overseas students considered the length of their study program abroad "just right," while the 30% who found it too short were all students who participated in the half term/term exchange scheme (Table 3). The experience of overseas study was viewed by 40% of British students and 46% of overseas students as fitting in with their home based course; 37% and 27%, respectively, felt their period of study overseas was a little isolated in their total course, but less than 5% saw it as greatly isolated.

All students who took courses designed to help them understand the philosophy and practice of physical education in the country they visited saw their understanding enhanced by this. Without exception, those who did not take such a course believed it would have been helpful to do so. Courses regarded as most beneficial were primarily comparative, frequently including historical background, and proceeding to discussion of values and examination of curricula.

The maintenance of academic standards is a concern expressed by staff in connection with overseas study. The particular activities related to academic standards may vary, equivalence being expressed in terms of course content, intellectual skills, or a range of technical issues such as assessment practices, marks, and time allocations. The greatest consensus focused on course content, with more than 50% of the staff referring to similarity of subject matter, and approximately 10% to the development and use of intellectual skills. Twenty percent perceived equivalence in a quantitative sense, either as a time related concept or in respect to marks obtained. Staff made no reference to the nature of assessment; however, students commented on what they perceived as the greater intellectual demands of the essay assessment normally used in Britain compared with tests more frequently used in North America, in which many commented that they gained success through memorization and regurgitation. The majority of staff perceived equivalence as important, though only 14%

Table 3   Organization of Overseas Study

Category	Percentage	
	British students	Overseas students
Length of program		
Just right	70	70
Too short	30	30
Fit of program		
Fitted in	40	46
A little isolated	37	27
More isolated	20	23
Greatly isolated	3	4

saw it as essential and a further 11% as very important. Balancing this, 25% considered it not very important. Some commented that there was no such thing as equivalence (even within one culture), while others expressed the opinion that difference was a key value in overseas study. Students saw equivalence of work important only in order to fulfill institutional requirements.

The main behavior changes resulting from overseas study that were commented on by staff focused on three issues; namely, a perceived increase in motivational level described by one respondent as, "a more buoyant sense of participation," an enhanced perception of themselves (described in terms of maturity and self confidence), greater critical awareness, and a sharpened ability to think analytically. The latter two points were given equal prominence by staff who knew individual students well both before, and after, their studies abroad. In a few instances students' critical capabilities applied to their own courses were seen as a negative outcome because it led to some dissatisfaction, though some positive values were perceived in this too. A greater readiness to accept others' viewpoints was considered another outcome of study overseas. Students perceived changes in their own appreciation and understanding of cultural differences and in independence of action and judgment.

The students were in no doubt in their ratings of overseas study. Eighty percent considered it one of the most important experiences of their lives; 16% selected the second category of response, namely, "a great experience"; and 4% thought it "a good experience on the whole." British and overseas students were equally proportioned in their selection of categories of response. Comments typical of many were that, "it was one of the most exciting, enlightening and enriching things I've ever done;" and "I feel the opportunity to study overseas was the best experience of my college life." Twenty-two percent of all staff considered the retention of overseas study opportunities to be essential (9% of these were from Britain and 13% from overseas, which in view of their smaller number, represented 50% of the total overseas respondents). Forty-eight percent of staff felt retention very important (this included the bulk of the British staff), 26% rated it important, 2% not very important, and 2% failed to show a rating.

Discussion

From these findings it is possible to construct a model that will provide a tentative explanation of the perceived changes in behavior and the values attributed to the experience, to present a way of conceptualizing overseas study, and to point out implications as a guide to future planning.

According to Williams (1961) culture has to do with regular and persisting patterns and the doing of things in prescribed ways. To see alternatives is to engender questioning. Anthropological literature (Barth, 1969) argues that contact between ethnically different groups will heighten cultural differences and sharpen the definition of boundaries between people. Heterogeneity makes individuals and groups more, not less, conscious of differences. The findings indicate that awareness of cultural differences increased, as did tolerance for such differences. Overall, this was rated the most valued outcome of overseas study in which, for a period of time, the students develop the equivalent of ethnic identification. In questionnaire response and in interviews, students spoke of how being different attracted recognition both in and out of class, and thus changed their consciousness of themselves. Participating in a different cultural lifestyle promotes both awareness and understanding of others' differences and gives students a sense of responsibility as ambassadors of their home institution.

Herzberg (1976) believes that recognition, responsibility and the feeling of accomplishment act as "motivators" which give rise to feelings of satisfaction. Maslow's (1970) concept of self-actualization complements Herzberg's ideas on motivation and provides a way of understanding students' enhanced self-confidence and greater maturity. Specifically of interest in this study is the characteristic Maslow identified as self-actualizers' tendency to have values that are often in opposition to the mainstream of culture, in other words their tendency to nonconformity. It is postulated that being to some degree self-actualized contributes to the confidence students have to go against the tide, increasing their independence and their ability to formulate their own views.

Because differences can be said to exert a strain for explanation, the challenge of discrepant data "sets the stage for altering one's intellectual map." According to Goldsmid and Wilson (1980), "A questioning mind, is one that is conscious of differences." It can be seen that heightened consciousness of differences arising from the heterogeneity experienced during overseas study (the result of ethnic identification) and competing explanations offered abroad provide the stimulus to critical thinking. Benign disruption is a conceptualization offered by Goldsmid and Wilson that provides a way of explaining students' enhanced critical capacities following overseas study. They state, "Without differences there are no problems. Without problems there can be no answers. Without answers there is no learning. Differences—their discovery and explanation—are fundamental for critical thinking" (1980). Goldsmid and Wilson argue that by presenting either discrepant data about the social world or differing explanations for a single phenomenon, teachers can arrange "roadblocks," problems that students must solve if they are to go on their way. They further say, "it is only when the smooth, ongoing tenor of our lives is interrupted that thought and emotion emerge." A period of overseas study provides such an interruption and furnishes both the discrepant data and the competing explanations that encourage students to "think through to a new way of apprehending reality" (Goldsmid & Wilson, 1980).

Students abroad are forced to confront anomalous events, and it is suggested that their attempt to reconcile the problems they meet leads them to develop the skill of critical thinking. This suggests that lack of cohesiveness in a course, a point of concern to British staff in particular, may not necessarily be dysfunctional. However, failure by staff or peers to recognize students' new critical capacities may frustrate the realization of their potential abilities. This could imply a challenge to staff to make more extensive use of students' experiences on their return from overseas.

Comparatively speaking, this study is of interest for the remarkable similarity of students' views whatever their country of origin. When the findings are juxtaposed, significant differences are more perceptible in the way staff view the experience. In particular, British staff are concerned about cohesiveness in a course and equivalence of course content. Overseas staffs were more quantitatively focused towards equivalence in terms of time or marks. On the whole, British staff were less convinced of the value of the experience than their overseas counterparts. This may be due to the fact that the overseas respondents were organizers of overseas opportunities, from which their commitment may be assumed, while the British sample was more widely drawn across the department.

The rationale of the British curricula model is its integrated approach, hence the British concern with cohesiveness. This study suggests that the most appropriate consideration may be neither the substantive subject matter of course content that the British tend to focus on, nor the quantitative similarity that some overseas staff desire.

Teaching may be seen to have dual functions, the passing on of content or substantive subject matter, and the development of intellectual skills of enquiry and analytical thinking. The model presented here suggests that cultural differences, an interruption to the smooth cohesiveness of a course, and confrontation with anomalies need not be dysfunctional to academic development and achievement. It suggests, for example, that different course content need not impair or reflect a dysfunctional situation in overseas study that must be changed. Rather, what this suggests is a more positive view of heterogeneity. Specifically, it could be argued that stressing differences will create dissonance, exerting a strain that needs to be resolved. In so doing, students are not only stimulated into intellectual activity, their more buoyant sense of participation, but they also develop new ways of apprehending reality. It implies that overseas study might most appropriately be evaluated in terms of the development of critical thinking, and this could be the focus of concern for academic equivalence. One specific implication that may be suggested from this research is the need for teachers to contrive ways whereby *all* students, not only those who study overseas, may have their senses of differences sharpened. The model raises the question of what are appropriate 'roadblocks' for teachers to devise, and where in a course they need to occur. This may be more a matter of what is appropriate for each student when linked to their stage of intellectual development.

This perspective moves us away from a conceptualization of homogeneity and cohesiveness as constantly preferred states for a student within a course, and of learning as the accretion of selected bits of knowledge. It moves us, instead, towards a view that values heterogeneity and benign disruption for their power to induce students' intellectual activities, leading them to remake themselves with the potential for changing their environment.

Notes

1. The illuminative approach is increasingly recognized and outlined succinctly in Miller, C.M.L., & Parlett, M., *Up to the Mark*, London: Society for Research into Higher Education, Monograph 21, 1974. It can be characterized briefly as problem-centered, practitioner-oriented, cross-disciplinary, methodologically eclectic, and heuristically organized.
2. Final response rate of 72% was comprised as follows: staff of overseas institutions contacted, 100% ($n = 12$); staff of home based departments, 80% ($n = 36$); overseas students contacted, 60% ($n = 69$); and British students, 76% ($n = 65$). Total people responding equaled 182.

References

Barth, F. (1969). *Ethnic groups and boundaries*. Boston: Little, Brown & Co.

Goldsmid, C.A., & Wilson, E.K. (1980). *Passing on sociology*. Belmont, CA: Wadsworth.

Herzberg, F. (1976). *The motivation to work*. New York: Wiley.

Maslow, A.H. (1970). *Motivation and personality*. New York: Harper & Row.

Miller, C.M., & Parlett, M. (1974). *Up to the mark* (Monograph No. 21). London: Society for Research into Higher Education.

Perry, W.G. (1970). *Forms of intellectual and ethical development in college years: A scheme*. New York: Holt, Rinehart & Winston.

Pfinster, A.O. (1971, Fall). The evaluation of overseas study programs: Two case studies. *North Central Association Quarterly*, **XLVI**(2).

Wallace, A. (1970). *Culture and personality*. New York: Random House.

Williams, R. (1961). *The long revolution*. London: Chatto & Windus.

A Comparative Study of North American Subcultures

D. Margaret Toohey and Christine P. Swann
California State University, Long Beach

Pueblo is a name given to 19 different Indian tribes located in the Southwestern United States, primarily in Northern Arizona and New Mexico. The main characteristic of the Pueblo is their permanent village communities. The term "pueblo," in fact, is the Spanish word for small town. Because the Indians of this region first had contact with the "white-man" through the Spanish conquistadores and later the missionaries, many areas have been given Spanish names. While sharing many common beliefs and ceremonial rituals, these people come from three distinct language stocks; although a certain amount of cultural diffusion has taken place, the tribes still retain much of their own individuality.

This paper is concerned with a comparison of ritual sport and games among three "Pueblo" tribes, the Hopi and Tewa of Hano, who are located in Northern Arizona, and the Zuni located in New Mexico. It will attempt to show that sport and play have a viable significance to society even when taken out of the play context, and that sport is an important vehicle for cultural transmission among linguistically different groups. The sport and games analyzed will be Kachina racing, kick-ball, kick-stick, and shinny.

In Northern Arizona, east of the Grand Canyon and approximately 90 miles south of the Arizona-Utah border, lie the three mesas or plateaus known as the Hopi Reservation. The Hopi are the descendants of prehistoric cliff dwellers who live in a very dry, arid region and plant their corn in the washes that surround the mesas. Because of the harsh climatic conditions of this area, ceremonials for rain and fertility are important.

The Hopi reservation lies within the much larger Navajo reservation. The Navajo are not Pueblo Indians, and they come from a different language stock than the ones ascribed to Pueblo Indians. The Navajo live in the even drier area that surrounds the Hopi reservation. The Navajo were small herders and lived a nomadic lifestyle (Dennis, 1940). They survived the harsh region by living in small family units and moving about when pasture and water failed. In the past, the Navajo were not above raiding the Hopi corn fields. Because of increasing pressure from the

Navajo raids, the Hopi eventually moved to the third mesa, which was most easily defended.

According to Dennis (1940), mesas have been named in order of American exploration and contact; the easternmost is called first mesa, the middle is called second mesa, and finally, the westernmost is third mesa. On the first mesa is the village of Hano, in which lives a Tewa tribe whose members are linguistically different from the Hopi. Most of the Tewa tribes are located in New Mexico. One Tewan tribe, under pressure from the Spanish conquistadores, fled their New Mexican homeland and eventually settled at Hano on the first mesa of the Hopi reservation, where they remain today. Even though the Tewa of Hano speak a combination of Tewan and Hopi today, they, nevertheless, remain closely affiliated with their New Mexican relatives, sharing their clanage systems and religious beliefs.

To the east, near the Arizona-New Mexican border, lies the Zuni reservation. The Zuni are the most populous pueblo tribe, according to Sandro (1976). As one can see, these three tribes are situated within close proximity to one another, yet are linguistically separate. The Hopi are of a Uto-Aztecan language stock; the Tewa of Hano are of Tanoan language stock, the same as their New Mexican relatives; and the Zuni language is spoken only by the Zuni. All three tribes lie within the larger Navajo reservation.

Pueblo social organization revolves around the principle of clanship. Dennis (1940) states that clanship is responsible, not only for marriage choice and all forms of inherited property, but also chieftany and all ceremonial details. The clan to which one is born determines, to a large extent, the societies to which one may belong. The various clans are responsible for the different ceremonies. The ceremony chief is the chief of the clan in charge. Traditionally, he is the oldest son of the oldest sister in the lineage in charge. His mother, or the woman in charge of his home, is considered the clan mother.

Kivas are underground ceremonial and religious gathering places for men only. Membership to specific kiva is largely determined by clanship. Certain clans may belong to certain kivas, and membership can also be determined by societal membership. Once again, however, certain societal membership is open only to certain clans. Ceremonial racing is done by the members of the kivas participating in a particular ceremony. For most ceremonies the kiva serves as an assembly area.

Ceremonial Races

The Pueblos have two major types of ceremonial races: the relay race of the Tewa, and the kick-stick or kick-ball races of the Zuni and Hopi. These races are held each year in conjunction with the religious ceremonies for spring planting. The races are very systematic and are held over a period of ten days, one race each day. There are nine participating kivas. The first race is run by the members of the kiva in charge of ceremonial racing. The other kivas then take turns until, finally, all nine kivas have raced.

Since the region is very dry, ceremonies for rain are very important, and the kick-ball and kick-stick races are held in hopes of gaining favor with the Cloud Spirits. The races are mimetic magic in nature and purpose. They are held in a circuit of 3 to 4 miles, which runs along the dry arroyos. In the past, however, the circuit was 26 miles long, and the old men often joke about how soft the younger racers are. The racers imitate the rain, which they hope the Cloud Spirits will bring. The faster the course is run, the faster the rain will come down, and the faster the water will rush through the arroyos, and the faster the corn will grow. Value and emphasis are placed on swiftness, not on winning and losing. It is a great honor to be considered a swift runner.

Because the rain is so important to the area, Pueblo Indians continue to race to this day. Even though the Hopi, Tewa, and Zuni have taken to the automobile in place of the horse and blue jeans and T-shirts in place of traditional clothing, they continue their ceremonial racing each spring, as they have for centuries (Washburn, 1980).

Kick-Ball Racing

The first race to be examined is kick-ball, which is played by the Hopi. The equipment used are stone nodules. The stones are the most important symbol of kick-ball, for they represent the all important rain drops. It is how fast these stone nodules transverse the circuit, which surrounds the planting area, that mimics how fast the rain hopefully will fall.

The balls are made from piñon sap (a bush that grows in the desert) called sani, or sandstone. "The balls are approximately two inches in diameter and are squarish with the edges rounded off" (Titiev, 1972, p. 322). The balls are considered sacred objects and are prayed over prior to the race. Each kiva has its own balls, and these are usually kept by the chief of that particular kiva.

On the evening prior to the start of the next day's race, each kiva places its balls on the sacred altar located within the individual kiva. On the altar in front of the balls is a figurine of Tiiwa Boñtunsi, the mother of all the Kachina. The Kachina are the Pueblo Indian's gods, each of whom have a specific function. The balls are then prayed over and sacred pipes are smoked. Each kiva has its own sacred pipe. Starting with the chief of each kiva, the pipe is passed around until all the members of a particular kiva have had a smoke. Sacred meal is then sprinkled over the balls. Finally, the members leave their respective kiva, and the balls remain on the altar until the members return in the morning to start the race.

The chief of each kiva serves as the race announcer on the day his particular kiva is to race. He wears ox hooves, which are passed around to each of the kivas on its day to race. No meaning for the ox hooves was given. The racers are naked except for a breechcloth. No shoes are worn, and the balls are kicked barefoot.

The racers of each individual kiva are painted with the markings of that kiva, for example:

- Chief Kiva (the name of a particular kiva) members are decorated with a star or cross design in white clay across the face, on the breast, back and upper arm, front of thighs and calves.
- Wikwalobi kiva members wear a broad streak of yellow pigment across upper chest, leg from ankle to knee, band above knee, all of forearm and three finger marks on upper arm, same finger marks on each side of body, and band around waist. Blue-green pigment and two eagle tail feathers are worn by the chief of this particular kiva only.
- The members of Horn kiva are painted with white clay angular broad stripes or horizontal broad stripes surrounding body and limbs.
- Goat kiva members are painted with red ochre pigment over the entire body.
- Sichomovi kiva members are covered with valley sand and water over the whole body.
- The Hanoki (Tewa) kiva members are solidly covered by a yellow-brown pigment all over the face, limbs and body. (Stephen, 1936, p. 263)

These markings serve as uniforms and help the spectators identify the individual racers.

On the evening prior to the start of the races the kiva chief of Chief Kiva (name of kiva) announces to the chiefs of the other kivas that the races will begin in the morning. The kiva chiefs, in turn, announce that the individual members of their kivas are to assemble. This is analogous to professional sports players getting an announcement from their coach to assemble for spring training, or like the great tennis players from all over the world assembling in England for Wimbledon. The members assemble, and prayers are said, pipes smoked, and the balls are blessed.

At noon the next day, the men report to their kivas and receive a sacred meal of cornmeal gruel, wafer bread, parched corn kernels, and stewed peaches. The runners abstain from meat, salt, and sexual intercourse during the races. Around 1:00 p.m., the racers begin to strip down and start painting themselves in preparation for the 2:30 p.m. start (Parsons, 1939, p. 818).

On day one of the first race, the Chief Kiva is in charge. The chief of Chief Kiva and the lesser chiefs of Chief Kiva go into the valley toward the starting point. Each chief sprinkles meal on the sagebrush along the way and prays for strength. This responsibility is passed on to each kiva when it is its turn to be in charge of the race.

There are about 80 runners: 25 from Chief Kiva, 15 from Horn kiva, 15 from Half-way kiva, 8 from Goat kiva, and about 3 or 4 from the others. Each kiva group is lead by its kiva chief and as many runners as that kiva has balls. A representative from each kiva lines up behind a line drawn in the sand, and each kiva team lines up behind its leader. Each runner places a ball just in front of his right big toe. At the signal to start, he kicks the ball as high and as far as possible.

The balls are kicked in a lifting manner. The height they achieve mimics the clouds; their return to the ground, the rain drops; and the speed with which the circuit is covered, the good rain. The members of each kiva gather in clusters behind the balls that belong to their particular kiva. As the balls are advanced, the runners rush forward, trying to keep their kiva balls in the lead. They then kick again and continue after it until the circuit is covered. It is permissible to touch the ball with the hands in order to remove it from obstructions, such as cactus.

At a point about one hour's distance from the start, the kiva groups split up, each taking a different direction. The kiva chief or another member of each kiva takes along an extra ball for the group in case the first is lost. No time can be spent looking for a lost ball, and a backup is put into play immediately. The play of each kiva group is so smooth that it is hard to imagine the ball is being kicked. The feet of the runners are sore and the insteps red and swollen when the race is finished (Parsons, 1939, pp. 819-820).

It is important to remember that although kick-ball is considered a race, it is not a race in which the kiva groups actually compete against one another. There are no winners or losers as we know them. The emphasis is on the speed with which the kiva groups can cover the circuit. A fast race will assuredly impress the Cloud Spirits to bring a fast, hard rain. The sweat of the runners is, also, considered a good sign for rain, so warm days are preferred for the race.

While the race is run by the young, swift men in each participating kiva, there is plenty of activity going on among the spectators. Young boys often will chase after and run alongside the racers for short distances; and the women, who usually bring baskets of apple slices to eat like popcorn, will climb onto rooftops to gain a better view. Down in each kiva (remember, the kivas are underground), the men, who are either too old or too slow to run, will sometimes weave ceremonial belts, blankets, and dresses. After the race, the runners return to their families and a large festive dinner is eaten.

Various explanations are given for why the races are run, but the two major reasons are:

- It is good for the Hopi to run. Long ago when the Hopi had no sheep or horses or burros, they had to depend on fast running to survive. It is good for the Hopi to be swift as it will make the cloud spirits happy to send rain.
- All devout Hopi who run are relieved of all heaviness of heart, all sadness is dispelled, the flesh is made good and his health is renewed. (Parsons, 1939, pp. 820-821)

It is interesting to note that the Hopi were aware of both psychological and physiological benefits of running.

Kick-Stick Racing

Kick-stick racing is done by the Zuni. Although the symbolic purpose of the race is the same as kick-ball, there are some interesting variations. Kick-stick racing is done in two ways, by clan and by kiva. This is in contrast to the Hopi and Tewa of Hano who race by kiva.

On the afternoon prior to the race, the men will gather in the center of the village to place bets. Betting on the races is quite common among the Zuni, but is almost never done by the Hopi or Tewa of Hano. Bets are made with wearing apparel, such as blankets, belts, sashes, handkerchiefs and moccasins. Items are matched with similar items. For example, all bets made with blankets are matched together. The wagers are made, left in the center of the village, and collected by the winners after the race. Women's dresses are considered a very valuable bet (the Southwestern region of the United States is considered to be Atzlan, the legendary home of Quetzecotl, the main god of the Aztecs. The Aztecs often used women's dresses as a form of money).

The night before the race, the kick-sticks are prayed over in the kiva or clan house as the kick-balls are with the Hopi. The sticks are usually made of dried oakwood, have prayer feathers at one end, and are about 5 inches long. The purpose of the kick-stick is the same as the kick-ball, to impress the Cloud Spirits to bring good rain.

The Zuni, like the Hopi, wear only a breechcloth or small kilt. The Zuni also decorate themselves, but not as elaborately as the Hopi and Tewa of Hano. The hair of the runners is short, but the locks on top are tied together with string. Inside this cluster of hair is concealed an arrow point, which is a protective charm. The charm is needed, because black magic is practiced during the race. Cramps are said to be caused by black magic.

The race, itself, is done the same as the kick-ball race. The runners are barefoot and kick the sticks along the circuit in a sort of lifting manner. Emphasis is placed on height as well as distance. It is said the sticks are kicked as high as 20 to 25 feet in the air. Under no circumstances may hands touch the sticks once the race has begun. This is unlike the Hopi, who can touch the ball in order to remove it from obstructions. The sticks also may not be held between the toes when attempting to extricate them from crevices or brush.

The race is run in an anti-sunwise circuit, which is about seven or eight miles long and takes about one and one-half hours to complete. Like the Hopi, the older men like to brag that in the ancient days the race was much longer. Again, as with the Hopi, there are no true winners and losers. The emphasis is to mimic the rain they hope to bring. Stragglers from all teams fail to finish and are eventually picked up by horsemen.

The race finishes with a run around the area where the bets are later to be collected. The runners then return to their place of retreat (either kiva or clan house) where they are given an emetic to make them vomit (among many Pueblo Indians, vomiting is considered an important part of any ceremony because it is looked upon as a purification act). Everyone, including spectators, returns to where the bets are kept. The bets are then sprinkled with prayer meal (a blessing) and collected. They are sprinkled again when they are carried into the winners' home. Later that night, the winners are expected to give a big dinner.

The Game of Shinny

Shinny is one of the most widespread games played by the Indians of North America. Among the Tewa Indians, however, it is played ritualistically, and this is the only known instance in which it is played in conjunction with a ceremony. Shinny is played early in March, the day the Winter Chief gives the people over to the Sun Chief. On that day, the Tewa make their plants. This means that from every house, women bring a basket of seed to be blessed and leave it in the house of the Summer Chief. The Summer Chief blesses each basket and then stuffs the seeds into a buckskin ball. In the meantime, the War Captain collects the men and boys for the game. The game is played in an anti-sunwise circuit that goes all around town, and is usually played four times within the circuit. Only men and boys play; the women and girls watch. The women, however, grab the ball if it rolls near them and run into the house with it. They return outside in a few moments with bread and apple slices for some of the players.

The purpose of playing shinny is to insure crop fertility, and the game is played until the buckskin bursts, sprinkling the blessed seeds over the field. Emphasis is placed on the speed with which the ball is broken. The sooner the ball is broken, the better the crops and harvest will be. Balls that take a long time in breaking are understood as signs that a bad season and crop is imminent.

Sport as Part of Religious Dogma

Belief in Kachinas is common to all the Pueblo Indians. Kachinas are gods and spirits who are said to live on the peaks of the San Franciscan Mountains. There are many different kachinas, and different ones participate in different ceremonies. At many ceremonies men will dress up and impersonate the kachinas. During the various ceremonies, the kachinas who are known to be fast runners challenge the men of the village to race. The man who is chosen lines up with the kachina who has challenged him. At the word "go," the challenged is given a head start of several hundred yards. This is done, because the man impersonating the kachina is said to assume the kachina's supernatural powers. The race is about 2 or 3 miles long. If the kachina overtakes the man, the man is whipped with yucca or in some way is made fun of by the kachina. If the man wins, he is looked upon as a hero. As with all Pueblo Indians, swift runners are held in great esteem (Washburn, 1980).

There has been much discussion on the phenomenology of sport as a religious experience. However, these Indians use sport and sport activities not as a religious experience, but as an actual part of their religious dogma. In other words, the sport and game activities have been taken out of the play environment and have been used in an entirely different context. Betting, spectator behavior, and other activities commonly associated with the sporting or play experience are secondary to the religious function of ensuring rain and fertility. Those activities commonly associated as play, game, and sport can, and do, have value to society, even when taken out of the play context.

Although these three tribes are linguistically separate, and therefore not related, they enjoy a symbiotic relationship, borrowing from neighboring cultures and yet retaining some cultural variation. Finally, we have attempted to show that sport can be, and is, an important vehicle of cultural transmission and socialization.

References

Dennis, W. (1972). *The Hopi child*. New York: Arno Press & *The New York Times*.

Parsons, E.C. (1939). *Pueblo Indian religion*. Chicago: University of Chicago Press.

Sandro, J.S. (1976). *The Pueblo Indians*. San Francisco: The Indian Historian Press.

Stephen, A.M. (1936). Hopi journal. In E.C. Parsons (Ed.), *Columbia University Contributions to Anthropology*, **23**, 1-2.

Titiev, M. (1972). *The Hopi Indians of old Oraibi changes and continuity*. Ann Arbor: University of Michigan Press.

Washburn, D.K. (Ed.). (1980). *Hopi Kachina spirit of life*. Seattle: University of Washington Press.

Cheating in Sport: A Comparison of Attitudes Toward Cheating of Canadian and British Rugby Players

J. Graham Jones and John C. Pooley
Dalhousie University

"The desire to win is a necessary part of all competitive sport" (Kaelin, 1968, p. 17). However, this desire often leads to an obsession with winning, which manifests itself in the "win-at-all-cost" attitude. This, in turn, frequently results in deviant behavior on the part of players, coaches, owners, and officials. Deviation from the rules and norms in the sport setting is characterized by cheating, but an important factor that must be considered is that what constitutes deviance varies with different societies and subcultures. Consequently, attitudes toward cheating may also vary from culture to culture. It was the purpose of this study to investigate this variable and, more specifically, to examine whether the British playing members of Dalhousie University Rugby Club possessed a different attitude towards cheating in rugby than Canadian members.

It is important to realize that the manner in which a game is played may vary between cultures. "It follows that no behaviour is deviant in itself but only in so far as it violates the norms of some social system" (Cohen, 1968, p. 149). Thus, when one refers to deviant behavior, one must also specify the system of reference, as certain actions that may be viewed as acceptable in one culture may well be considered violations of rules and norms in another. Until recently, in European rugby, for example, "trampling" or stamping on an opponent in a ruck or maul was totally unacceptable both to players and officials, whereas in New Zealand it is viewed as a "normal" part of the game.

Cultural differences also exist in attitudes toward sport as a whole, and this may be illustrated by comparing and contrasting North American and British attitudes toward sport and their opinions on how it should be played. An examination of the importance each of these two cultures place on winning may provide some indicators of their propensities to deviance in sport.

Campbell (1968) aptly summed up the contrast in philosophies of sport between North America and Britain.

> Americans seem to have the idea that if you cannot do something well, you should not do it. In Britain we think that if something is worth doing, it is worth doing no matter how badly. (Hubbard, 1968, p. 43)

335

MacIntosh (1974) notes sharp contrasts in the sporting attitudes of the two nations. Sports clubs in Britain, he says, are organized so that varying degrees of skill and commitment can be accommodated, while in Canada those who are not good enough are often turned away and discouraged. MacIntosh also notes the absence of teaching professionals at the majority of sports clubs in Britain, which is another marked difference from the Canadian picture. The emphasis in Britain is on participation, to get as many enthusiasts playing as possible, and, perhaps most important of all, to enjoy the game. In Canada, however, according to MacIntosh, people have difficulty in accepting that "sport as play" is a different enterprise from "sport as work," and he feels that the viewing public is partly responsible for much of the deviance in sport: "(hockey) players will continue to fight and use illegal tactics as long as the public is anxious to be entertained by these antics" (p. 3). Another contributing factor may be that commercial sponsorship is now making itself felt in amateur as well as professional sport, making sport at the amateur level more competitive.

Meschery (1972) feels that by the time a North American boy reaches high school, he has been programed to believe that winning is everything. Sultzbach (1972), an American like Meschery, is equally critical of the situation and believes that North Americans stress the learning of skills at the expense of absorbing simple, genuine enthusiasm. Americans are taught at an early age to savor competition and to strive to win at all times. "The friendly game seems . . . to be a phoney game" (Van Dusen, 1974, p. 67). Thus, Vince Lombardi's statement that "winning isn't everything, but wanting to win is" (McKuen, 1971, p. 16) appears to represent a general North American attitude towards sport.

Darwin's (1940) view of the British attitude towards sport is "to set the game above the prize" (p. 13), implying that the British ideal is to enjoy the game and to place emphasis on the means rather than the end. Abraham's (1948) view of sport at the Olympic level is a reflection of the British attitude towards sport.

> First and foremost we must really get away from the point of view regarding only the winners of Olympic events as those who are worthy of praise. It is this very narrow point of view which is so strong and so unfair. (p. 14)

Although the views of Darwin and Abrahams may at first sight appear outdated, it is fair to assume that they still reflect the general British attitude towards sport today.

It is clear, therefore, that the sporting attitudes of the two cultures discussed differ to some extent. On the one hand, the North American attitude seems to be that winning is the most important aspect of sport; while, on the other hand, the British philosophy is to emphasize that sport is recreation, sport is for all, and it is of less consequence who wins. Of course, these attitudes may not truly represent the actual attitudes, as those discussed seem to lie at the two extremes of a continuum. The actual attitudes of the two cultures may not be so extreme and may, therefore, lie at points on the continuum, which would mean that the difference between attitudes is not as great as suggested.

Thus, it appears that North Americans possess a greater urge to win than Britons. Lüschen (1971) has hypothesized a strong relationship between "will to win" and cheating. As a team's will to win increases and approaches the "win-at-all-cost" attitude, so will its propensity to cheat be increased. Taking into account the views presented in this discussion, and in view of the proposed relationship between "will to win" and cheating, it is hypothesized that Canadian sportsmen have a greater propensity to cheat than their British counterparts; and, more specifically, that Canadian playing members of Dalhousie University Rugby Club will be more willing to cheat than British playing members.

Review of Literature

Cheating in Sport

Eitzen and Sage (1978) define cheating as "a violation of the rules to gain an unfair advantage on an opponent" (p. 94). McIntosh (1979) regards cheating as "breaking the rules to avoid the penalties" (p. 182), while Eitzen (1979) offers a more comprehensive definition in stating that cheating is synonymous with behavior that (a) violates the rules of the game, (b) offends the universal values of sportsmanship and fair play, and (c) illegitimately brings harm to persons or property.

Each game has its own set of rules by which participants must abide. In addition, many games, particularly rugby, also have an unwritten code of ethics that embodies the sportsmanlike behavior expected of the participants (Sherry, 1980). Cheating may, therefore, be regarded as violating not only the laws of a game but also the values and morals of that game. Thus, kicking or throwing the ball away after the play has been stopped, because wasting time is viewed as a violation of both the rules and the values of the game of rugby.

Several attempts have been made to classify cheating into certain types. Lüschen (1971) classified deviance in sport as either "open cheating" or "secret cheating." Examples of open cheating in rugby include deliberately tripping or "late-kicking" an opponent. In secret cheating, often only the cheater knows, according to Lüschen, and it rarely alters the course of the game. Examples include taking additive drugs before a game and using illegal equipment. Eitzen (1979) identified two forms of cheating. First, "institutionalized cheating" refers to those illegal acts that, for the most part, are accepted as part of the game (e.g., wasting time), and which are rarely discouraged and receive a minimum penalty. Second, "deviant cheating" is deviance that is not accepted and is subject to stern punishment (e.g., accepting a bribe).

Empirical evidence suggests that cheating is a widespread occurrence, not only among players, but also coaches, club administrators, and officials. The evidence also indicates that cheating may occur more often in highly competitive situations than in circumstances in which emphasis is placed on enjoyment of the game. Promoli (1976), for example, compared the attitudes toward the cheating of a university basketball team and a local recreational team. The survey revealed that 70% of the recreational team voted against cheating, while 72% of the varsity team voted in favor of it. Promoli's results indicated a greater unwillingness on the part of the recreational team to indulge in cheating and a greater tendency to respect the spirit of the rules.

In the same study, coaches were also found guilty of deviant practices. Promoli's results revealed that 60% of the recreational team and 86% of the varsity side indicated that their coaches encouraged rule breaking. In addition, 80% of the local players indicated that their coaches placed most value upon the idealistic benefits available through playing, while 86% of the varsity team felt their coaches valued winning the most.

As for the administrators, it was found by the National Association of Basketball Coaches that "one of every eight major colleges (in the U.S.) made illegal offers to prospects" (Denlinger and Shapiro, 1975, p. 42), while judges and officials are also guilty of cheating in some cases. The gymnastic judge from Switzerland at the 1976 Olympic Games commented "judges are collaborating with each other and deciding not only on scores but also on the distribution of medals" (McIntosh, 1979, p. 185).

Thus, it is clear that cheating is a widespread occurrence in sport today. Rugby is no exception, as cheating has infiltrated into the ranks of rugby players.

The Subculture of Rugby

"Rugby is not merely a sport, but a social event of ceremonial and ritual import: it is an amically proclaimed lifestyle whose practitioners form a recognizable subculture" (Sheard and Dunning, 1973, p. 7). Rugby football is a rugged, physical sport with each match characterized by hard hitting, aggressive play, which is embodied within an atmosphere of formality and protocol. Decorum is preserved on the field with strict rules governing the players' actions, while the code of ethics in force during the game includes clean, hard action (Sherry, 1980).

The game of rugby originally developed in the public schools of England in the mid-19th century and later spread to the universities of Oxford and Cambridge. In the early years, rugby was very much a middle and upper class game, and it is only in recent times that the lower classes have gained access to its ranks, although the administration of the game is still in the hands of the upper classes (Sheard and Dunning, 1973). In Canada, although it is one of the oldest games, it is only recently that the game has rapidly grown in popularity. "A game that spawned American and Canadian football, it is achieving a new popularity within the greater sport community of Canada" (Howe, 1972, p. 466).

Although rugby is a popular game in both the British and Canadian cultures, it has always had its critics on the question of violence, and such is the case today. Reason and James (1979) feel that the game of rugby today is in a dilemma:

> The world of rugby finds itself confronted by changes as profound and as perplexing as those taking place in society itself. The very amateurism on which the game was founded . . . is being eroded in an increasingly materialistic society. . . . The incidence of violence in the game appears to be increasing, which again, is a mirror of society. (p. 274)

Reason and James state that the game of rugby is developing and expanding at an astonishing rate throughout the world and that the values inherent in the game mirror the values of the culture in which it is played. In the case of North America, they feel that rugby may be exploited by the increased professionalism, which has produced "a very selective gladiatorial type of infra structure" (p. 280), especially in the United States. They foresee the most serious threat to rugby in North America as the possibility that the criteria applied to professional sport will begin to be applied to rugby, which would be in direct opposition to the view of rugby as an afternoon's enjoyment. They regard the British attitude towards rugby as "liking to win but not minding to lose" (p. 281), and that where the game is underwritten with money, the spirit of the game will suffer.

Williams (1976) admits that for many rugby coaches and players, winning becomes the "be-all and end-all." He is very much against this attitude and feels that the aim should not only be to play positive, effective rugby, but to do so within the laws of the game. Williams' philosophy is that a game of rugby should incorporate as much physical contact as is allowed within the rules of the game, but that "no player should ever be subjected to risks which are outside the laws of the game" (p. 23).

Thus, it is clear that the "win-at-all-cost" attitude may be just as rife in rugby as it is in other sports. Despite its stringent rules and code of ethics, rugby still has to contend with problems of deviance. The evidence discussed suggests that the attitudes toward rugby in Britain and North America certainly differ, with the game assuming a more "professional" and competitive structure in North America.

Method

The populations under investigation in this study were Canadian and British rugby players. The subjects were chosen from the playing members of Dalhousie University Rugby Club, but, due to the small number of British members ($N = 3$), it was necessary to use a stratified "grab" sample. Thus, the sample comprised three British players and three Canadian players ($N = 6$), whose rugby and educational backgrounds are outlined here.

Subject B1 was a 31-year-old postgraduate from Cardiff, Wales. He was in the second year of a master's degree program and had lived in Canada for approximately 19 months. He had played organized rugby for 20 years for club sides and at various educational institutions, including a grammar school in Cardiff, Cardiff College of Education, Carnegie College of Education (Leeds, England), and two seasons at Dalhousie. He had also represented Nova Scotia and the previous year had captained and coached the university team.

Subject B2 was a 25-year-old from Brighton, England. He was in the third year of his doctoral program and had lived in Canada for approximately 2 1/2 years. He had played organized rugby for 7 years (mainly as a second team player), including one season at Dalhousie during which he played mostly for the second team but did progress to the First XV on one or two occasions. His rugby experience in Britain was gained mainly at a grammar school in Brighton and at Aberystwyth University in Wales.

Subject B3 was a 25-year-old postgraduate from Manchester, England. He was in the first year of his doctoral program and had lived in Canada for approximately 10 months. He had played organized rugby for 12 years, including three seasons at Aberystwyth University in Wales and one season at Dalhousie, and he also played at a private school in Manchester, England, for approximately 6 years. In addition, he played for the Nova Scotia provincial side.

Subject C1 was a 24-year-old Canadian from Ottawa, Ontario. He was in the fourth year of an undergraduate degree program. He had played rugby for 8 years for a high school in Ottawa, for club sides in Ontario, at Carlton University, Ottawa, and for one season at Dalhousie. He had also played for the Nova Scotia provincial team. In addition, he had recently visited Britain on a rugby tour, playing in Scotland and London.

Subject C2 was a 23-year-old Canadian from Calgary, Alberta, who was in the first year of his undergraduate degree program. He had lived in Canada for 15 years, having spent the first 8 years of his life in the United States. He did not play rugby until he attended Queen's University in Ontario 3 years ago, and he had played one season for Dalhousie.

Subject C3 was a 24-year-old Canadian from Halifax, Nova Scotia, who was in the third year of an undergraduate degree program. He had played rugby for 4 years, including one season in Scotland where he attended a state secondary school. He had also played for Halifax Rugby Club and for 3 seasons at Dalhousie.

The instrument[1] used in the collection of the data was an interview with each of the six subjects. The questions posed in the interview were mostly open-ended and were designed to acquire information concerning the subject's rugby and educational background, to examine his attitude towards cheating, and to focus on comparisons between cheating in Britain and in Canada.

A pilot study was conducted prior to the collection of the data. The proposed interview was administered to two rugby players, a South African who played for Dalhousie and a Canadian who played for Halifax Rugby Club. The aim was to test the validity of the interview schedule, and the pilot study subjects were asked to express their opinions of the interview and to suggest changes and additional questions. The interview schedule was subsequently modified in preparation for the collection of the data.

The interviews were administered to the six subjects between February 27 and March 4, 1981. The subjects were located and agreed to participate in the interviews, which took place at Dalplex. The subjects were interviewed privately; their responses were recorded on a tape recorder. Each interview lasted approximately 25 minutes. The data were treated descriptively.

Results

All subjects classed winning as "fairly important" with the exception of Subject B2, who placed little or no importance on winning. The general view of losing was that it was followed by short-lived disappointment, depending on the importance of the game; this view was characterized by C3's statement that "it's nice to win but it doesn't bother me to lose," and B2's feeling that "as long as I'm involved, that's the main thing."

Each subject's definition of cheating was essentially the same, that is, knowingly breaking the rules. However, B1 suggested that this was not a sufficient definition. "When you play rugby, you do not play to the rules of the game but to the rules as the referee interprets them. If the referee lets you get away with something which is normally outside the rules, then I don't necessarily think that is cheating."

Two of the British subjects (B2 and B3) indicated that they had never intentionally cheated in rugby. Three others (B1, C2, and C3) stated that they occasionally cheated, while C1 admitted that he frequently cheated. However, none of the players interviewed had been encouraged to cheat in high school or by any of the coaches for whom they had played.

The subjects all believed that there were differences between the way the game is played by Canadians as compared to Britons. The Britons suggested that the spirit of the game was different in Canada, because rugby was organized on a very competitive league basis, whereas in Britain it was organized on a more "friendly" basis. The British felt that Canadian players were less disciplined, lost their tempers more easily, and abused the referee more. Above all, they viewed winning as all important to the Canadians. The Canadian subjects indicated that Britains were more skillful and had a greater knowledge of the game, while Canadians were more physical and were strongly influenced by American football.

All the British subjects expressed the opinion that Canadian players cheated more than their British counterparts, while the Canadian subjects indicated that British players cheated more. In addition, it was the general consensus of opinion that cheating by Britons is more subtle and that Canadian cheating is much more blatant. Reasons given for this were that Britons were much more experienced both at rugby and cheating: "Britons cheat more efficiently because of their greater experience" (B1).

As for the influence of the officiating on cheating in rugby, all subjects agreed that a player is more likely to "get away" with cheating with a Canadian than a British referee. This was attributed to lack of knowledge of the rules ("they don't know half the rules" [B1]), to their inexperience (Canadian referees miss a lot and lost control of the game [C2]), and the greater leniency of the part of the Canadian referees.

The responses to the four specific situations in a rugby game differed between the two cultures. The British respondents stated that they would not obstruct a man to prevent him from scoring a try or throw the ball away in order to waste time, but that they would continue running in the remaining two situations until the referee stopped play. C1 admitted that he would cheat on all four occasions, while C2 and C3 said they would

Table 1 Responses to Questions on Four Specific Situations in a Rugby Game

Subject	Question Number			
	1	2	3	4
B1	(a)	(a)	(b)	(b)
B2	(a)	(a)	(b)	(b)
B3	(a)	(a)	(b)	(b)
C1	(b)	(b)	(b)	(b)
C2	(b)	(a)	(b)	(b)
C3	(b)	(a)	(b)	(b)

Note. Questions 1 to 4 were as follows:
1. Imagine that your team is leading an important cup game by two points with one minute of play remaining. The opposing team is attacking and their winger only has you to beat to score a try. He chips the ball over your head and into the "in-goal." Do you:
   (a) allow him to run around you and hope that one of your own team reaches the ball first?
   (b) stand in his way and obstruct him?
2. In the same circumstances, play is stopped while you have the ball in your hands and a penalty is awarded to the opposition. Do you:
   (a) put the ball down and retreat ten meters?
   (b) throw or kick the ball away in order to waste time?
3. You are running down the wing with the ball in your hands. Your foot touches sideline (which is "out of play"), and you know it. Do you:
   (a) stop?
   (b) carry on running, hoping that the linesman didn't see it?
4. You receive a "forward pass" five meters from the oppositions try line. Do you:
   (a) stop?
   (b) score the try and hope the referee didn't see it?

cheat in three of the four situations, declining to throw the ball away in order to waste time (see Table 1 for full details).

There was general agreement that cheating by Britons was more subtle and cheating by Canadian players more blatant, probably due to the Britons' greater knowledge of the game and their greater experience. Cheating was seen to be influenced by the poor standard of officiating by Canadian referees and the view that "there are less opportunities to cheat in Britain" (B2). The differences in the way the game was played were attributed to the more competitive league structure inherent in Canadian rugby compared with the game organized on a more "friendly" basis in Britain. Canadians felt that Britons cheated more, while Britons believed that Canadians cheated more. In response to the four specific situations, the Canadian players revealed that they would be willing to cheat in more cases ($n = 10$) than the British players ($n = 6$).

Discussion

It appears that the most striking difference in cheating in rugby between the two cultures is in the forms and types. Britons seem to be more subtle and "sneakier" (C3) in their cheating, while Canadian rugby players appear to commit more blatant and open forms of cheating. This was largely due to the greater experience and knowledge of the game on the part of the Britons. They presumably knew what they could get away with and what they could do without the referee's seeing.

Of course, cheating in rugby is greatly influenced by the standard of officiating. Canadian referees, particularly in Nova Scotia, were often inexperienced and were not sufficiently acquainted with the laws to be able to enforce them efficiently. The subjects indicated that Canadian referees tended to be more lenient than their British counterparts and often lost control of the game. Thus, players could "get away" with considerably more malpractices than they could in Britain, where the referees were more experienced and had a better grasp of the rules, so that "there are less opportunities to cheat in Britain" (B2).

All the respondents suggested that cheating by Canadian rugby players was more obvious than cheating by Britons. The Canadian subjects, however, still felt that British players cheated more but that "they don't get caught" (C2), suggesting once again that experience was a vital factor in the question of deviance in rugby. The responses given to the four specific rugby situations are a further indication of the differences in the forms of cheating committed by Canadian and British rugby players. The pattern that emerged was that the British players would not openly cheat by obstructing a player or blatantly wasting time; but they would commit what Lüschen (1971) defines as "secret cheating" by carrying on running after they had gone out of bounds or a "forward pass" had occurred, hoping that they would not be detected. The Canadians revealed that they would be willing to commit both types of cheating. The Britons admitted that they would cheat in 6 out of the 12 situations, while the Canadians revealed that they would carry out the deviant response in

10 out of the 12 situations. Thus, based on those responses, it seemed that Canadian rugby players were more willing to cheat than British players.

Another point that emerged from this study was that players play to the rules as the referee interprets them. If a referee let them get away with an act that deviates from the laws, they would not necessarily consider it as cheating, although another referee might regard that act as a deviant one. Thus, there was the question of a more specific definition of cheating. Is cheating defined as practices that deviate from the laws of the game as they are written down, or does it involve acts that contravene the laws as interpreted by individual referees?

In conclusion, the evidence suggests that the major differences between cheating by Canadian and British rugby players was to be found in the forms and types of cheating. In addition, the hypothesis that Canadian members of Dalhousie University Rugby Club were more willing to cheat than British members was supported.

Note

1. Details for the interview instrument may be obtained by contacting the author.

References

Abrahams, J. (Ed.). (1948). *The sports book*. London: MacDonald.

Cohen, A.K. (1968). Deviant behaviour. In D.I. Sills (Ed.), *International Encyclopedia of the Social Sciences, Vol. 4* (pp. 148-154). New York: Macmillan and Free Press.

Darwin, B. (1940). *British sport and games*. London: Longmans, Greens, and Company.

Denlinger, K.G., & Shapiro, L. (1975). *Athletes for sale: An investigation into America's greatest sports scandal—athletic recruiting*. New York: Thomas Crowdell.

Eitzen, D.S. (1979). *Sport in contemporary society: An anthology*. New York: St. Martin's Press.

Eitzen, D.S., & Sage, G.H. (1978). *Sociology of American sport*. Dubuque, IA: William C. Brown.

Howe, B.L. (1972). Aggressive responses of rugby players. In I.D. Williams & L.M. Wankel (Eds.), *Proceedings of the Fourth Canadian Psycho-Motor Learning and Sport Psychology Symposium* (pp. 466-472). Ottawa: Fitness and Amateur Sport Directorate.

Hubbard, A.W. (1968, May). Some thoughts on motivation in sport. *Quest* (Monograph 10).

Kaelin, E.F. (May, 1968). The well-played game: Notes toward and aesthetics of sport. *Quest* (Monograph 10, pp. 16-28).

Lüschen, G. (1971, December 9). Cheating in sport. Paper presented at the Sport and Deviancy Symposium, Brockport, State University of New York.

MacIntosh, D. (1974, September). Reflections of sport in England. *Journal of the Canadian Association for Health, Physical Education and Recreation*, **40** (Suppl. Issue), 1-5.

McIntosh, P. (1979). *Fair play: Ethics in sport and education*. London: Heinemann.

McKuen, R. (Ed.). (1971). *The will to win*. New York: Random House.

Meschery, T. (1972). There is a disease in sports now. *Sports Illustrated*, **37**, pp. 14, 18-21.

Promoli, F. (1976). *Cheating in sport: A comparison of two basketball teams*. Unpublished paper, Dalhousie University.

Reason, J., & James, C. (1979). *The world of rugby: A history of rugby union football*. London: British Broadcasting Company.

Sheard, K.G., & Dunning, E.G. (1973). The rugby football club as a type of 'male preserve': Some sociological notes. *International Review of Sport Sociology*, pp. 3-4, 5-24.

Sherry, J.F., Jr. (1978). Verbal aggression in rugby ritual. In H.B. Schwartzman (Ed.), *Play and culture* (pp. 139-149). New York: Leisure Press.

Sultzbach, M.C. (1972). *Winning: A comparison and contrast of philosophies and attitudes between England and North America*. Unpublished paper, Dalhousie University.

Van Dusen, G. (1974, September). It's not whether you win or lose, it's how you play the game. *Journal of the Canadian Association for Health, Physical Education and Recreation*, **40** (Suppl. Issue), 67-68.

Williams, R. (1976). *Skillful rugby*. London: Souvenir Press.

The Roles of Physical Education and Games in Canadian Private Schools and English Public Schools: A Comparative Analysis

Tim Chandler
Stanford University

This paper, a review of the similarities and differences between the educational roles of physical education and games in the Canadian private schools and the English public schools, is divided into three major parts. The first is descriptive and is a discussion of the historical association between the two sets of schools. The notion of cultural borrowing is highlighted, and the contradictions in recent writings about the relationship between the two sets of schools, which led to the desire for clarification attempted by this preliminary study, are discussed.

The second section offers further description of the results of the study, highlighting the aims and perceived outcomes of programs in the two sets of schools. Interpretations of the results are drawn and are juxtaposed for comparison.

Finally, adopting the technique of "reflective thinking" recommended by Toohey (1979) when conducting topical and area studies, "intensive" comparisons (Mangan, 1981) and conclusions are drawn. Then, using the framework of cultural borrowing, an attempt is made to predict the future of physical education and games in these schools.

Background

The school motto, "Mens Sana in Corpore Sano" is proudly emblazoned on the noticeboard at the entrance to the driveway of one of the Canadian private schools. Another has an honors board simply entitled "Sportsmanship" with the names of prize winners elegantly displayed. One might have expected to find such emblems in the English public schools of the 19th century (Mangan, 1981) rather than in Canadian private schools in the latter part of the 20th century. However, as Howell and Howell (1979) have observed, cultural borrowing has long been part of comparative physical education; and, the English games tradition and system of games has been an important example of cultural borrowing in the Canadian private schools (Mutimer, 1980).

The English-speaking Canadian private schools were modeled on the English public schools[1] (Gossage, 1977). An important feature of this influence was the emphasis placed on games and sports as an integral part of the educational program of these new establishments (Metcalfe, 1970, 1974; Molloy, 1969; Watson, 1970, 1973). In Upper Canada particularly, private schools were founded as Canadian equivalents of Eton (Gossage, 1977; Mutimer, 1980). Their clientele were, in large part, the children of English officers and administrators serving in Canada. The journey back and forth to England was both long and treacherous. Thus, it was easier to bring English schools and schoolmasters to Canada, than to send children back to England, thousands of miles from home and immediate family (Mutimer, 1980). For example, Upper Canada College was founded almost entirely with staff from England (Gossage, 1977). However, as the English influence in Canada declined with the departure of the garrison forces and colonial administrators, it was the constant stream of schoolmasters from England that continued as the main link between the Canadian private schools and the English public schools. They, more than any other group, enabled cultural borrowing to continue. The numbers of British schoolmasters have declined in all of the schools; nevertheless, in 1980 the percentage of teachers familiar with the English public schools either as students or staff was still in some schools as high as 20%.

In a recent survey of private educational institutions around the world, conducted by Podmore (1977), it was stated that the private schools of English-speaking Canada approximated more closely the United Kingdom private (public) schools than the private schools of any other country. This study apparently confirmed the continuation of the link. However, with regard to physical education and games, Gossage (1977), in a national study of the Canadian private schools, suggested that there had been a move away from the traditional role of games as means of moral and social education and that more emphasis was being placed on "lifetime" activities and on sports "for their own sake." Yet two English public school headmasters, Silk (1974) and Emms (1976) reaffirmed the educative roles and values of games and physical education in the English public schools. They were still advocating the social and moral values of "the playing fields of Eton." This preliminary study was an attempt to clarify this apparent contradiction. Were the roles of physical education and games in the two sets of schools no longer similar? Had cultural borrowing from the English public schools by the Canadian private schools declined in this area of school life? Were they no longer comparable institutions in their educational use of games?

Method

The specific questions to which this study was addressed were:

• What were the two sets of schools trying to achieve through (a) physical education[3] and (b) games?[4]

- Were these aims being achieved?
- Were there inter- and intranational differences in the games and physical education programs offered by the two sets of schools?

Canadian private schools, selected to reflect the geographical distribution of private schools whose headmasters were members of the Canadian Headmasters' Association, and five English public schools, selected to reflect the geographical distribution of Headmasters' Conference schools, were sampled. Severe financial limitations and time constraints made these minimal sample sizes necessary. The biggest effect of this limitation was that there were large variations in student numbers among schools. Faculty suggested that this was an important factor influencing the games and physical education programs offered by their schools. This problem was unavoidable, but must be considered as a significant limitation of the study. Student numbers varied between 120 and 700 pupils in predominantly male, largely residential schools.

Data were collected between April 20 and August 20, 1980 in the form of interview and questionnaire responses from Headmasters, physical educators, staff, students, and alumni. The questionnaire and interview questions were based (with permission) on Kane's Schools' Council Project (1974) and were adapted to include student and alumni responses. Kane's questionnaire was developed from an extensive review of both British and North American literature on physical education, and was, therefore, adopted as an appropriate tool for this study. Furthermore, it had been specifically adapted for use in the English public schools.

Data were organized into frequency of response categories based on the "constant comparative method" outlined by Glaser and Strauss (1971). This process was performed for each group and for each question. Frequency of response tables were thereby constructed, enabling comparisons to be drawn both between and among groups. Summaries of the findings are shown in Tables 1-4. Response rates were 82% among faculty (n = 132), but only 45% from students and alumni (n = 174).

Results and Discussion

Physical Education in Canada and England

Students and alumni in Canada perceived that they had learned "very little" from their physical education programs (Table 1). The discrepancy between the aims and perceived outcomes was more pronounced here than in any other set of data. Furthermore, the lack of similarity among physical educators as to the aims of their physical education programs based on Kane's Nine Categories (Kendall's $W = 0.147$) was very pronounced. Many of the physical educators presented no clear rationale for their programs. There was a lack of publicized, organized curricula and programs of study. In only one school was an up to date scheme of work available for perusal. In a number of the schools, physical education was included in the curriculum to satisfy provincial government

Table 1 Summary of Aims and Perceived Outcomes for Physical Education in Canada

Aims	Perceived outcomes
Headmasters	
• A chance to be physically active during academic part of the day • Mixed ability class learning • To experience health education	• Skill learning • Variety of physical activity experience
Physical educators	
• Knowledge and development of fitness • Skill learning and development • Development of cooperation, team work, and discipline • Introduction to lifetime activities and activity patterns	• Improved skill levels • General development and increased self-knowledge • A concern for fitness • A love of activity and games • An introduction to lifetime sports • An understanding of group cooperation
Students and alumni	
• Health and fitness • Break from academic work • Skill-learning medium • Opportunity for mixed ability, cooperative learning • Part of a broad education	• "Very little" • Skills of certain games • Value of teamwork and interaction with others • Training and fitness methods

requirements that applied to public schools. Physical education was often referred to as a "time-filler" by students and alumni. The major content elements of the programs were, in order of frequency of inclusion: games, swimming, track and field, and gymnastics. Health and fitness classes (times per week) were included in all of the schools' physical education programs as follows:

Average: 65 mins per grade per week
Range: 32 to 100 mins
Grades: 8 to 12

Physical education programs in England were intended to fulfill a limited role in the total educational programs of the English public schools. Generally, programs were organized to introduce students to a wide range of activities; to promote organic development and awareness of physical fitness and health; and to encourage students to strive for optimal development in a sport or activity of their choice as a "lifetime" enterprise. Students and alumni appeared to have accepted these as perceived outcomes (Table 2).

Generally, programs appeared to be well organized and included similar content elements to those in the Canadian schools. Games were again the most frequently used medium, but in England, gymnastics and swimming were more common than track and field. The dovetailing of physical education and games' programs was a feature in these schools and was suggestive of an overarching educational plan. Meeting times per week were as follows:

Average: 50 mins
Range: 40 to 75 mins
Grades: 8 to 10 (optional PE in one school at Grade 11)

The English schools programs appeared to have been carefully devised to dovetail with the dominant games' programs. Physical education fulfilled the role of basic skills instruction, although it was also used to help the less able student find an athletic endeavor at which he could achieve.

Table 2 Summary of Aims and Perceived Outcomes for Physical Education in England

Aims	Perceived outcomes
Headmasters	
• Health and fitness • Skill development • Experience broad range of activities	No response
Physical educators	
• Development of motor skills • Organic development • Introduction to lifetime activities • Encourage self-realization	• Development of basic skills • Encourage participation • Understanding of health and fitness
Students and alumni	
• Knowledge of basic skills • Training and fitness methods • Introduction to a variety of activities	• Knowledge of some skill activities • Understanding of basic skills for games programs • Opportunity to try new sports • Awareness of health and fitness

In general, the Canadian programs were less well organized. Health education was stressed more than in the English schools, and was becoming an increasingly important element of the programs. However, despite the proposed role of physical education programs as being complementary to the games' programs in the Canadian schools, more often they duplicated the games' programs.

Responses from Canadian students and alumni suggested that their physical education experiences had been less valuable than those of the English alumni. To have learned "very little" from their physical education experiences suggests that these programs were not proving to be successful.

It should be noted, however, that in both sets of schools, physical education programs were overshadowed by games' programs which "took on" far greater importance in the minds of both faculty and students. To this extent the English games' tradition continued its hold over the total athletic programs offered by both sets of schools.

Games in Canada and England

The major feature of responses concerning the role of games in the Canadian private schools was the homogeneity of these responses from the groups questioned, both in terms of aims and perceived outcomes (Table 3). For faculty, four major elements emerged: (a) social cooperation and teamwork, (b) fitness and health development, (c) development of school spirit and corporate pride, and (d) the promotion of healthy competition.

Students and alumni perceived that they had learned (a) social cooperation and teamwork; (b) skills and physical development; a sense of self-worth; (c) leadership and responsibility; and (d) the enjoyment of participation, cooperation, and competition—encouraging them to continue in the future. The degree of similarity between these two lists suggested that, although there was not complete congruence between aims and perceived outcomes, the aims of the games' programs were, in large measure, being achieved.

Time was a vital factor in the difference of effectiveness of games and physical education programs. Nevertheless, as important was the fact that all members of staff, as part of their contract, were involved in the coaching of games. It was an integral part of school life for both faculty and students alike. All took part and took an interest in games in the same way that all took part in academic work. Students spent nearly as much time playing games each week as they spent on any single academic subject.

Average compulsory time: 180 mins per week (range: 120 to 220 mins)
Average possible time: 560 mins per week (range: 120 to 1,200 mins)

The one factor that clearly differentiated the English from the Canadian schools was the emphasis in the former on fun and enjoyment. Faculty saw this as an important aim of games in their schools, and students and

Table 3   Summary of Aims and Perceived Outcomes for Games in Canada

Aims	Perceived outcomes
Headmasters	
• Health and fitness development • Team games to encourage cooperation, sportsmanship, and leadership	• Social and emotional factors: precious memories, friend-ships, camaraderie, cooperative experiences, and self-confidence • Physical factors: a habit for exercise, awareness of fitness, knowledge of skills
Physical educators	
• Social cooperation through teamwork • Promotion of discipline, leadership, sportsmanship • Competition to promote 1 & 2 • To promote fitness and health through participation • The pursuit of excellence • Promotion of school and • community spirit	• Social and emotional effects: e.g., character-building, self-discipline, and interpersonal skills • A liking for sport • Interest in and understand-ing of health and fitness • Precious memories • Knowledge of and skill in games
Staff	
• Health and fitness • To encourage team spirit, citizenship, corporate pride • 'Mens sana in corpore sano' • Fun and enjoyment	• Cooperation and a sense of team effort • Sense of accomplishment and self-satisfaction • Sense of 'fair play' and sportsmanship • Knowledge and appreciation of health and fitness • Camaraderie and friendships • Better knowledge of self
Students and alumni	
• Promotion of activity for physical and mental health • Educating for a well-rounded personality • To keep students out of mischief • Opportunity to savor games experiences • To learn sportsmanship and develop discipline • The promotion of school spirit	• Understanding of teamwork, cooperation, and sports-manship • Skill development, both physical and social • Sense of self-worth • Leadership, responsibility, and cooperation • Importance of enjoyment gained from participation

alumni perceived it as an important outcome of their participation. Students and alumni stressed social, emotional, and moral factors as outcomes and were less concerned with the physical fitness aspects of participation than their Canadian counterparts (Table 4).

Faculty members felt that lifetime involvement in sport was an outcome of their games' programs. Alumni ("Old Boys") clubs were a very common feature of these schools' games-playing traditions. Graduating students were encouraged to join rugby, cricket, field hockey, squash, fives, rackets, and tennis clubs. Alumni groups competed regularly against students from their own and other schools, as well as against each other.

Table 4 Summary of Aims and Perceived Outcomes for Games in England

Aims	Perceived outcomes
Headmasters	
• 'Mens Sana in Corpore Sano' • Enjoyment • Development of character by subjecting body and mind to stress	• Creates enjoyment through excitement • Develops discipline through competition • Develops skills and fitness • Develops loyalties and understanding
Physical educators	
• Enjoyment • Social and moral values • Basis for lifetime activity	• Desire for lifetime involvement in sports and games • Social and emotional growth • Memories
Staff	
• Group cooperation: playing for a team • Enjoyment, fun • Physical health and fitness for life • Sportsmanship, fair play	• Sense of accomplishment and satisfaction for students • Better knowledge of self and own abilities • Ability to cooperate • Basis for lifetime participation
Students and alumni	
• Health and fitness • Education of the whole person • Promotion of house and school spirit • Enjoyment	• Teamwork and cooperation • Sportsmanship and fair play • Friendships • Enjoyment • Physical health and fitness

(There were even sponsored alumni competitions, e.g., The "Cricketer" Cup.) This was a large part of the games' tradition and bore witness to the "lifetime" aspects of these games' programs. Despite this, both physical educators and staff felt that even more could have been done to encourage students to continue participating in games in their postschool years. Gossage's (1977) comments about an increasing emphasis on "lifetime" sports seemed only to parallel efforts in the English schools.

> Average compulsory time: 180 mins per week (range: 120 to 220 mins)
> Average possible time: 560 mins per week (range: 120 to 1,200 mins)

Homogeneity of aims and perceived outcomes was the major feature of the responses concerning games in both sets of schools. This was particularly true at the intramural level, and it indicated that games were still an accepted part of the broad educational programs of these "elite institutions" (Weinberg, 1968). Games had been "tried and tested" as educational tools over many years in these schools, and their educational value was still upheld. They were one element in the total program of these strongly tradition-oriented schools; the other major elements being the classroom and the chapel.

In the English schools, games were seen to carry similar "powers" at both the intramural and interschool level. They were strongly believed to help instill honor, courage, good sportsmanship, and the benefits of "mens sana in corpore sano." This was also true of the Canadian schools at the intramural level, where, as one headmaster stated, "one learns a great deal in terms of self-sacrifice, loyalty, learning to work and cooperate with others, and submerging the self." That some authors perceive sports as building characters and not character (Tutko & Bruns, 1976) does not appear to have influenced the views held concerning the value of games and sports in these two sets of schools.

The games' programs at the interscholastic level in the Canadian private schools had become important as part of the "sales pitch" of these schools in attracting students away from each other and more importantly from the public schools. Offering interscholastic athletic competition to as many as 60% of a school at one time is unheard of in the Canadian public schools. As one headmaster quipped, "they couldn't find a bench big enough." Interscholastic sport was seen in the Canadian schools as being a means of attracting or even recruiting students.

Summary and Conclusions

The role of physical education in the Canadian private schools was less well defined than in the English public schools. Physical education (as opposed to physical training) was a relatively new addition to the curriculum on both sides of the Atlantic; but the dovetailing of the programs in the English schools around the longstanding and traditional games' programs appeared to have afforded it better acceptance. Physical educators in England had been forced to develop programs that "fitted in" with the overall educational programs of their schools. This had not been without some hostility; a senior member of staff at one of the English public schools felt that physical education was only good for "keeping boys' bowels open!"

Additionally, Canadian private school physical education curricula had been borrowed from the public school system. Teachers had been trained to teach in public schools, and very few of them had had experience in private schools before accepting employment in such establishments. In England, by comparison, over 50% of the physical educators were themselves products of the public school system (Public Schools Yearbook, 1980) and were therefore more "acceptable" to academic faculty. They understood the system and its games' emphasis more fully than their Canadian counterparts.

In a small percentage of the English public schools, the physical educationist has been viewed as a professional athlete. He has been classed with the cricket, squash, rackets, and tennis professionals also employed by these schools. There have been no qualified physical education teachers in this small proportion of the English public schools because, as Silk (1974) said, "the threat of this American professionalism of winning at all costs is in the air." The amateur ethic was being staunchly upheld in these English schools. The Canadian schools were less fearful of this "professional" influence. Physical education was used as a means of duplicating and reinforcing the skills learned on the games fields, often with the specific intention of increasing "time-on-task" to improve performances in interscholastic competition. Interscholastic sport was a high profile activity, and headmasters were cognizant of the fact that it was "an excellent medium for the advancement of a school's public image."

However, these public images had, in some cases, become a little tarnished. One headmaster suggested that, "the unhappy use of illegal means is becoming more and more common," and that "cracks have begun to appear in the 'amateur' edifice" and its accompanying doctrine of sportsmanship and fair play.

The Ontario Independent (private) schools Headmasters' Association had found it necessary to issue a "Code of Sportsmanship" to each student in its member schools as a result of behavioral misdemeanors both on and off the field during interschool competition. It should be noted that the instigator and architect of the Code was an Ontario private school headmaster, who had been a student, faculty member, and headmaster in English public schools. For this headmaster, the Canadian private schools were losing sight of the philosophy best summarized in a favorite saying of one of his predecessors. This was inscribed on a plaque in his school's new sports hall, and read

If you win, say nothing,
If you lose, say less.

In contrast to this need for a written Code, an English public school headmaster (Beer, 1978) recently re-echoed a colleague's comments (Silk, 1974) in an address to the English Public Schools Physical Education Conference, with regard to the role of games in these schools. He was keen that the "unwritten code" of sportsmanship and fair play should continue and he concurred that:

> The hold of simple athletic success over the heart of a small boy does not relax its time-honored and friendly grip. Courage, skill, hard work, restraint, unselfishness and a competitive instinct are some of the most important things we are trying to instill. (Silk, 1974, p. 24)

Silk (1974) has further suggested that the influence of willing and knowledgeable staff on student and alumni attitudes towards games was vital. He said:

> Many continue to play games after leaving school. Such recall, with gratitude, the dependence upon an enthusiastic young master, (and) the delight of the rare days when everything went right, and even the clowns played like princes. (p. 24)

In England, staff expect and desire to help with coaching; in Canada they are under contract to do so. In Ontario there is a written sportsmanship code; in England such a code is unwritten.

Such changes as the new Canadian immigration policies regarding United Kingdom nationals, and the recent "handing back of the Constitution" are emblematic of a continuing decline in "cultural borrowing" from England. Such changes may be mirrored by a further decline in the influence of the English public schools on the Canadian private schools. It seems unlikely that these Canadian "enclaves" of English traditionalism will continue to use games as they have in the past, particularly without the help of "enthusiastic young masters" from England to encourage this. If cultural borrowing is to continue in the future, it seems likely that the United States rather than England will be the primary source for Canada, and thus, indirectly, these institutions.

Both Molloy (1969) and Watson (1970) suggested that the type of games played in these Canadian schools between 1850 to 1930 changed from being the traditional games of rugby and cricket, to football and baseball, and yet the rationale behind the playing of games remained the same throughout this period. By 1980, there had been a rebirth of interest in rugby, staunch continuation of cricket, and a phenomenal growth in soccer. Yet it appeared that, particularly in Ontario, at the interschool level, a more professionalized approach was developing.

The future of the games tradition in the Canadian private schools is thus uncertain. That plaque in the sports hall may eventually become a monument to a bygone age on both sides of the Atlantic if the "air of professionalism" continues. However, for now, hanging on the wall of a brand new $500,000 facility, it may but symbolize the last vestige of the idealistic youth of the English games' tradition in the Canadian private schools.

Acknowledgments

The author wishes to extend his thanks to Dr. J.C. Pooley for his help in the execution of this study, and to Jerry Brodkey for his editorial help in the preparation of the manuscript.

Notes

1. These schools are private, fee-charging institutions whose headmasters are members of the Headmasters' Conference (H.M.C.).
2. Physical Education is defined as compulsory physical activity, timetabled during the academic part of the day—as English, science or languages might be scheduled.
3. Games are defined as those physical activities organized by staff, outside of academic time.

References

Beer, I. (1978, March). *Physical education—the role of games*. Paper presented at the Public Schools Physical Education Conference, Worksop College.

Bennett, B.L., Howell, M.L., & Simri, U. (1975). *Comparative physical education and sport*. Philadelphia: Lea & Febiger.

Bogdan, R.C., & Biklen, S.K. (1982). *Qualitative research for education: An introduction to theory and methods*. Boston: Allyn and Bacon.

Emms, D.A. (1976, October). Wondrous vital powers. *Conference, 13*(3), 10-13.

Gathorne-Hardy, J. (1977). *The public schools phenomenon*. London: Hodder & Stoughton.

Glaser, B.G., & Strauss, A.L. (1971). *The discovery of grounded theory: Strategies for qualitative research*. Chicago: Aldrine-Atherton.

Gossage, C. (1977). *A question of privilege*. Toronto: Peter Martin.

Howell, M.L., & Howell, R. (1979). Comparative physical education and sport: The area defined. In R. Howell, M.L. Howell, D.P. Toohey, & D.M. Toohey (Eds.), *Methodology in comparative physical education and sport* (pp. 1-15). Champaign, IL: Stipes.

Howell, R. (1975, Spring). The sociocultural area. *Sport Sociology Bulletin, 4*(1).

Kane, J.E. (1974). *Physical education in secondary schools*. London: Schools Council/Macmillan.

Mangan, J.A. (1981). *Athleticism in the Victorian and Edwardian public school.* Cambridge: University Press.

McIntosh, P.C. (1979). *Fair play: Ethics in sport and education.* London: Heingmann.

Metcalfe, A. (1970, September/October). Physical education in Ontario during the 19th century. *Canadian Association for Health, Physical Education and Recreation Journal,* **37**(1), 29-33.

Metcalfe, A. (1974, May). Some background influences on 19th century Canadian sport and physical education. *Canadian Journal of History of Sport and Physical Education,* **5**(1), 62-73.

Molloy, B.J. (1969, April). *Games—England's great gift to the world.* Unpublished master's thesis, University of Victoria.

Murphy, I.I. (no date). *The impact of the school games tradition on the attitudes of the boys towards games.* Unpublished paper, University of Leeds.

Mutimer, B.T. (1980, December). . . . .And some have greatness thrust upon them. *Canadian Journal of History of Sport and Physical Education,* **XI**(2), 45-55.

Newman, P.C. (1975). *The Canadian establishment.* Toronto: McClelland and Stewarts.

Podmore, C. (1977, December). Private schools—an international comparison. *Canadian and International Education,* **6**(2), 8-33.

Porter, J. (1966). *The vertical mosaic.* Toronto: University Press.

Silk, D.R. (1974, June). Clowns and princes. *Conference,* **11**(2), 19-24.

Tutko, T., & Bruns, W. (1976). *Winning is everything and other American myths.* New York: Macmillan.

Watson, G.G. (1970). *Sports and games in Ontario private schools, 1830-1930.* Unpublished master's thesis, University of Alberta.

Watson, G.G. (1973, September/October). The founding and major features of the sports and games in the Little Big Four Canadian private schools. *Canadian Association for Health, Physical Education and Recreation Journal,* **40**(1), 28-37.

Weinberg, I. (1968). Some methodological and field problems of social research in elite secondary schools. *Sociology of Education,* **41**, 141-155.